The Four Freedoms

Under Siege

Other Titles of Interest from Potomac Books

Secrecy Wars: National Security, Privacy, and the Public's Right to Know—Philip H. Melanson

The Mythology of American Politics: A Critical Response to Fundamental Questions—John T. Bookman

Who's Watching the Spies? Establishing Intelligence Service Accountability—Hans Born, Loch K. Johnson, and Ian Leigh

The Four Freedoms
Under Siege

The Clear and Present Danger from Our National Security State

Marcus Raskin and Robert Spero

Foreword by Barbara Ehrenreich

Potomac Books, Inc.
Washington, D.C.

Library of Congress Cataloging-in-Publication Data

Raskin, Marcus G.
  The four freedoms under siege : the clear and present danger from our national security state / Marcus Raskin and Robert Spero ; foreword by Barbara Ehrenreich.
    p. cm.
  Includes bibliographical references and index.
  ISBN 978-1-59797-217-8 (pbk. : alk. paper)
  1. Civil rights—United States. 2. National security—United States. I. Spero, Robert. II. Title.
  JC599.U5R27 2008
  323.4'90973—dc22
                                        2008036899

Potomac Books, Inc.
22841 Quicksilver Drive
Dulles, Virginia 20166

First Edition

10   9   8   7   6   5   4   3   2   1

To the family-nation Raskin: Erika Raskin Littlewood, Keith Littlewood, Jamie Raskin, Sarah Bloom Raskin, Noah Raskin, Eden Raskin, Heather Maurer, and my grandchildren: Emily, Jason, Zach, Maggie, Hannah, Tommy, Tabitha, Mariah, Bo, and Daisy. They all live the unwritten fifth freedom: the freedom to think and love. To my enormously gifted and beautiful wife, Lynn Raskin, who listened and loved in circumstances that I never made easy.

———————

For my parents, Lillian and Harvey Spero, who in the time of their lives both feared and fought the yoke of authoritarianism. And for the woman they lovingly called their daughter from the start, my wife, Jan Nathenson Spero, and for our grandchildren, Sam, Lauren, Sarah, and Henry, with the hope that their generation will take back the freedoms that should be their birthright.

The Four Freedoms

In the future days which we seek to make secure, we look forward to a world founded upon four essential human freedoms.

The first is freedom of speech and expression—everywhere in the world.

The second is freedom of every person to worship God in his own way—everywhere in the world.

The third is freedom from want, which, translated into world terms, means economic understandings which will secure to every nation a healthy peacetime life for its inhabitants—everywhere in the world.

The fourth is freedom from fear, which, translated into world terms, means a world-wide reduction of armaments to such a point and in such a thorough fashion that no nation will be in a position to commit an act of physical aggression against any neighbor—anywhere in the world.

—Franklin Delano Roosevelt,
Annual Message to Congress,
January 6, 1941

Contents

Acknowledgments   xi

Foreword by Barbara Ehrenreich   xiii

The Clear and Present Danger to Our Freedoms
from Our National Security State   xvii

Part One: Freedom of Speech

1: The U.S.A. Patriot Act Vs. the U.S. Constitution   3

2: September 11: A Golden Opportunity for Bush II
Conservatives   33

3: Lessons about Terrorism the Government Never Learns   43

4: When Is Danger Clear and Present?   53

5: Can the Homeland Ever Be Secure?   65

6: The Right to Vote, the Right to Have It Count   75

7: Do You Already Live in an Authoritarian State?   87

8: Escape from Authoritarianism   107

Part Two: Freedom to Worship

9: Our Religious Sea Change   127

10: Holier Than Thou   143

11: Religious War Without End: The Church Crosses
the State Line   149

12: How Silent Must Prayer Be?   161

13: Faith, Science, and Rationality   165

Part Three: Freedom from Want

14: The Business of Hunger   175

15: FDR's Economic Bill of Rights   189

16: The Haves and the Have-Nots   195

17: The National Health   203

18: Who Decides Who Gets Freedom from Want?   215

Part Four: Freedom from Fear

19: The United States Goes to War for Power, Peace,
and Profit. Subverts Constitutional Government.
And Makes Americans Fearful.   225

20: Can You Sign a Separate Peace?   261

Afterword: Lifting the Siege of the Four Freedoms:
What Needs to Be Undone   273

Last Words: Ahead of History: Marcus Raskin and the
Institute for Policy Studies   289

Notes   299

Index   337

About the Authors   357

Acknowledgments

The authors wish to thank Hilary Claggett, our esteemed editor at Praeger, who saw this project through its various iterations and was in our corner at every point. Needless to say, all errors are ours. We are grateful to Jennifer Boeree, electronic book editor at Scribe, for her valuable assistance—and understanding—on a complex project and to Stephanie Roulias, our copyeditor at Scribe, for her incisive questions and superb editing.

Special thanks to our gifted assistant and emissary on the project, Diana Alonzo, whose level-headed and "can do" attitude kept us on an even keel. Special thanks as well to Dorian Lipscombe, Scott Williams, Robin Weiss Castro, and Shaundra Cunningham, and Farrah Hassan.

MARCUS RASKIN

I wish to especially thank John Cavanagh, Phyllis Bennis, and Sarah Anderson of the Institute for Policy Studies. They are great public scholars who bring to their work passion, disinterested judgment, and intellectual integrity, qualities that are models for younger public scholars. The Institute's public scholars are engaged in the difficult task of analyzing our present situation in an historical context and suggest alternatives that they offer as the beginning, not the end, of a dialogue of reconstruction. Each of these public scholars are part of a unique community of public scholars that will serve well the future of humanity and the acquisition of knowledge: Robert Alvarez, Steve Cobble, Karen Dolan, Netfa Freeman, Martha Honey, Saul Landau, Nadia Martinez, Joia Nuri, Miriam Pemberton, Daniela Ponce, Saif Rahman, Elizabeth Schulman, Emily Schwartz Greco, Emira Woods, Daphne Wysham, and Joy Zarembka. And my thanks to Norman Birnbaum for his encyclopedic knowledge of European and American history.

At George Washington University, special thanks to Steve Trachtenberg, Don Lehman, Joseph Cordes, Bob Stoker, Hal Wolman,

Kathy Newcomer, and Professor Dick Katz, who have devoted themselves to building a great university.

Thanks also to Peter Kovler whose commitment to the spirit of the New
Deal made possible the Franklin D. Roosevelt Memorial Monument in
Washington, now shared by hundreds of thousands of people a year.
Further thanks are owed to the Trustees of the Institute for Policy Studies.

ROBERT SPERO

This book, like all my projects, began and ended with my wife, Professor
Jan Spero. This amazing woman's generosity, effervescence, and infinite
capacity to love belies a tough editorial judgment that caused me to
rethink many parts of the book I had thought were settled. Of her numerous talents, one not generally known to others is her patience with my
work habits. Why her patience continues, year after year, is a mystery to
me, but a blessing I am fortunate to have.

To our children, spread out, alas, across the country, who often seem
curiously unrelated to each other, yet at the same time are clearly joined
at the hip by our family's sensitivity, values, and love: Professor Joshua
Spero (master political scientist, political realist about the workings of
governments) and Reverend Ellen Rowse Spero in Massachusetts; Jeremy
Spero (Rocky Mountain legal eagle, keeper of our family's deeds) and
Lainie Spero in Colorado; and Jessica Spero (who compellingly steps to
the music of a different drummer in the practice of ancient Oriental medicine and life in the twenty-first century) in Oregon. Words are insufficient
to thank you for your support and love.

And to the Washington Speros, Dick and Irene, and to dear friends in
New York City and Long Island, the Berkshires, and California: my
thanks for your friendship during this unprecedented time of changing
waters in America and throughout the world.

Foreword

The Four Freedoms Under Siege is one of those rare books that helps illuminate the entire political landscape—an important task at a time when it's often hard to discern the underlying difference between liberals and conservatives. As I write this, for example, the Republicans, and to a somewhat lesser extent, the Democrats, are scrapping internally over Iraq and immigration. Some Democrats want an immediate withdrawal from Iraq; others are willing to "stay the course," wherever that course may lead. Some Republicans want to make illegal immigration a felony (although how we will manage to incarcerate approximately eleven million more people has not been made clear.) Others want an unlimited international supply of six-dollar-an-hour maids, busboys, and leaf rakers.

But the most confusing blurring of political differences has to do with the size of government. Traditionally, or at least according to time-honored cliché, liberals stood for "big government," and conservatives stood against it. Ronald Reagan's men wanted to "kill the beast" of government (not noticing how much Jimmy Carter's budget cuts had already starved it), and Newt Gingrich's gang eventually forced Bill Clinton to declare the "era of big government" over. It was Clinton—not Reagan or George H. W. Bush (Bush I)—who shrunk welfare into a program of limited wage supplementation for severely underpaid single mothers.

So how are we to understand the fact that it is under George W. Bush (Bush II)—surely the most right-wing president ever—that government has swollen to a condition of morbid obesity? Clinton left the federal government with a budget surplus. We now face an enormous *deficit*, and it's not all accounted for by Bush's lavish tax cuts for the wealthy. Government, especially the federal government, is piling on the pounds as we speak.

What's expanded, of course, is not the "nanny state" that Newt Gingrich once mocked. Welfare as we knew it is gone; Medicaid is under steady assault; we have no guaranteed access to health care; student loans

and grants are facing massive cuts. The only "nannyish" or compassionate move the Bush administration has made is toward partial Medicare
coverage of prescription drugs, and that program is still stumbling to get
to its feet.

As Marcus Raskin and Robert Spero make abundantly clear in the pages
that follow, the part of government that's been swelling nonstop is the part
that, generally speaking, deals with violence or, to put it in more conventional terms, "national security." It was Raskin who first coined the phrase
"National Security State" four decades ago, when the United States was
fighting the cold war. Since September 11, the military has ballooned back
to its cold war size; one recent estimate of the total cost of the Iraq War is
two trillion dollars. We now have not only the CIA, the FBI, and the
Pentagon but also the Department of Homeland Security, a director of
National Intelligence, and a National Counterterrorism Center, along with
many more budget-devouring agencies that Raskin and Spero document.

As the Right has long claimed, government agencies tend to suffer from
a bureaucratic imperative to expand and, as this book from the Left
shows, our national security agencies are no exception. They jostle for tax
dollars, fight turf wars, even spy on each other. As we now know from the
Valerie Plame Wilson spy-outing case, they may go so far as to try to discredit each other. Bush, as it turns out, authorized the leak not only to
discredit Ms. Wilson's husband but also because he was mad at the CIA
for refusing to produce the Iraq-related "intelligence" he wanted.

The proposition that our bloated national-security apparatus has made
us more secure is open to debate, if not to outright derision. The
Transportation Security Administration (TSA) makes us take off our shoes
but doesn't bother to check the cargo in the hold. Our ports are leaky; our
public health system—which we're depending on in case of biological
attack—is a shambles. As for the war and all the attendant detentions,
"renderings," and tortures: they've not only fanned Islamist terrorism
worldwide but also have earned us worldwide hatred and contempt.
Once a beacon of democracy, America has come to be perceived as a
predatory outlaw state.

So, thanks to Reagan, Clinton, and Bush II, we now have a government
with vastly expanded military and surveillance functions and sadly atro-
phied helping functions. Imagine—for an awkward zoological analogy—
a lioness with grossly enlarged claws and teeth but no mammary glands.
If you're a working class kid, like former Iraq heroine Jessica Lynch, the
government will probably not fund your college education, but it will welcome you into its military. The same could be said for First Persian Gulf
War–veteran Timothy McVeigh, who returned from the war to a six-dollar-
an-hour job as a security guard, educated only in the use of explosives.

We saw how dysfunctional the government has become when Katrina
struck New Orleans: there was no food for the people trapped in the convention center, but there were plenty of soldiers to keep them from getting

out and feeding themselves in the supermarkets. Yes, this was about racism, and the fact that the government's fear of black "looters" over-ruled the most basic humanitarian considerations. But the appalling response to Katrina sent a message to citizens of all colors: in its eagerness to make us "secure" from foreign threats, the government has forgotten how to save our lives.

It is not, then, a debate over the sheer size of government that sepa-rates liberals from conservatives. The real issue is the *function* of govern-ment: what do we want it to do? Raskin and Spero's response will come as a surprise to anyone who has accepted the clichés that frame what passes for political discourse today: they anchor their argument in the notion of *freedom*.

Traditionally, freedom, at least for markets, has been the catchword of the Right. Conservatives routinely oppose "big government" in the name of freedom. Whenever, for example, you mention the need for uni-versal health insurance, someone is bound to say, "But we don't want big government running our health care," as if we have any more freedom under the Republic of Aetna or some other giant corporate bureaucracy. There's another problem with the line of thought that big government equals lack of freedom: without government, what's to protect us from big capitalism—employers, for example, who want to default on pen-sions, dump toxins, or keep the factory doors locked?

And if freedom is the issue at stake, what should really make the Right writhe is the preternatural growth of state "security" and surveillance functions. Decades ago, conservatives argued against Medicare as a step toward socialism and hence, in their view, totalitarianism. So far, Medicare hasn't enslaved anyone, but the fabled "knock on the door" is more likely to come now than at any time since the 1920s. It won't be a social worker worried about your children's welfare. It'll be some govern-ment functionary who suspects you of ingesting banned substances or corresponding with Osama bin Laden.

Raskin and Spero's great contribution is to snatch the banner of free-dom back from the Right. They propose that the true function of govern-ment is to guarantee freedom—not to corporations and other bureaucratic entities—but to individual citizens. It was, after all, a liberal Democratic president, Franklin D. Roosevelt, who first enunciated the Four Freedoms that became a central goal for the United Nations: freedom of speech, free-dom to worship, freedom from want, and freedom from fear. Though hardly a perfect exemplar of his own principles—FDR presided over a racially segregated nation and the interment of Japanese Americans dur-ing the Second World War—he framed a vision of governance that still inspires people around the world.

Today, as Raskin and Spero grimly remind us, each of FDR's Four Freedoms is under attack. The burgeoning National Security State under-mines freedom of speech while offering no true freedom from fear. The

Christian Right menaces freedom of worship and promotes its vision of a theocratic state. As for freedom from want: decades of cuts in social programs have signaled the government's total abandonment of this central liberal goal. But liberals—Raskin and Spero included—have spoken "truth to power" many times before. With this book they do so again, and boldly frame the struggles that lie ahead.

—*Barbara Ehrenreich*

The Clear and Present Danger to Our Freedoms from Our National Security State

FDR'S VISION CHALLENGES THE TWENTY-FIRST CENTURY

With the specter of another world war looming in the background, Franklin Delano Roosevelt proclaimed the Four Freedoms in his Annual Message to Congress (the "State of the Union" message), January 6, 1941. America—which had just seen its freedoms jeopardized by the Great Depression—found them on the line again.

Eleven months before the Japanese attacked Pearl Harbor, FDR told the Congress, "I find it, unhappily, necessary to report that the future and the safety of our country and our democracy are overwhelmingly involved in events far beyond our borders."[1] As Judge Samuel Rosenman, special counsel to the president, recounts, FDR was nevertheless concerned with human rights in a bleak world:

> We were sitting in the president's study one night grouped around his desk as usual—Harry [Hopkins], Bob [Robert E. Sherwood] and I. The President held the original of the third draft [of the message] in his hand.
>
> The President announced...that he had an idea for a peroration. We waited as he leaned far back in his swivel chair with his gaze on the ceiling. It was a long pause—so long that it began to become uncomfortable. Then he leaned forward in his chair and said, "Dorothy [Dorothy Brady, his secretary], take a law." And he dictated the following:
>
> > We must look forward to a world based on four essential human freedoms. The first is freedom of speech and expression—everywhere in the world. The second is freedom of every person to worship God in his own way—everywhere in the world. The third is freedom from want—which, translated into world terms, means economic understandings which will secure to every nation everywhere a healthy peacetime life for its inhabitants. The fourth is freedom

from fear—which translated into international terms, means a worldwide reduction of armaments to such a point and in such a thorough
fashion that no nation anywhere will be in a position to commit an act
of physical aggression against any neighbor.

Although he had mentioned these freedoms in a press conference on July 5,
1940, as an offhand answer to a question about his long-range peace objectives, the words seemed now to roll off his tongue as though he had
rehearsed them many times to himself. A comparison with the final speech
will show that his dictation was changed by only a word here and there, so
perfect had been the formation in his own mind of the thought and phrases.[2]

The Four Freedoms were an attempt to codify a stage of freedom that
would distinguish the United States from the totalitarian powers, but they
also became the basis of FDR's Economic Bill of Rights in 1944–45 and the
foundation of the United Nations' Universal Declaration of Human
Rights. It was a moment, but perhaps more than a moment, that the
United States propounded a legal principle that leaders were to be held
personally accountable for aggressive war; no leaders—not America's nor
anyone else's—could hide under the cover of state sovereignty.

In the gathering storm, America—by example—became the beacon of
freedom to the world.[3]

No one can deny FDR's gifts as a master rhetorician. Such a fact did not
mean, however, that he could or would make a bad case into a better one.
What a master rhetorician is able to do in a democratic society is to perform as a coach, goading and challenging, as well as providing a model
through exemplary action, words, and deeds. FDR, living in a broken
body with spirit and grace, was a continuous reminder that pain could be
endured and, to some extent, overcome. Thus the speaking activity is
merely one feature of the democratic rhetorician's tool kit as he or she
encounters external problems of a profound nature and internal fears that
each generation suffers through and more or less shares with each other,
such as death, grief, and loneliness.

As FDR addressed Congress, war raged in "distant" Europe (and Asia
and Africa) and nations quaked before the boldness and strength of Nazi
Germany and the demonic rhetorical gifts of Adolf Hitler, whose project
was the violent destruction and "purification" of humanity through genocide among the conquered peoples: his gift to the German people. FDR
believed that the United States would have to act for the West as European
nations collapsed under the weight of the Nazi hammer. So in his State of
the Union message to Congress that January, he announced what he
thought could not be separated in that period of history: war and freedom.

However, FDR skirted making commitments to a war that in fact
Congress and the American people were not prepared to carry out. He

was not prepared to send American troops into war and had no interest in doing so without a declaration of war. The Axis Powers—Nazi Germany, fascist Italy, and imperial Japan—had not directly attacked the United States at that point, and given that strong pacifist feature in the American people and Congress, aggressive or preemptive war was not an option. But he saw other possibilities that seemed to fit in terms of the coherence, purpose, and mood of an America still reeling from the effects of economic depression. And he believed that these policies stayed inside the four corners of the Constitution and the politics (or the art) of the possible. FDR also knew that he would have to give Republicans who agreed with his foreign policies political cover. They would support him ("politics stops at the water's edge," was a popular expression of the bipartisanship that some wanted in those days), but the Republicans would not lead.

This was the backdrop for the Four Freedoms FDR presented to Congress and the country at the conclusion of his war message (now called the Four Freedoms Speech). There is little question that wars and killing must have a rationale in the modern state. But why the Four Freedoms? What did they personify, and why were they successful as an exercise in political mobilization and rhetoric? And would the Four Freedoms have mattered had the political context not been a war that presented stark alternatives for losers and winners?

Wars of a certain magnitude are exercises in breaking the spirit of an enemy. But for others they capture what the poorer classes are "fighting for," willingly accepting a status for which no immediate gain seems apparent. The Four Freedoms tapped into the long-term aspirations of the nation. The conditions fostered the idea that war could be a noble enterprise and that it would serve as the basis of securing a national project and a national identity for the common good.

Such rhetoric and action did not work well for future presidents; indeed, it resulted in a series of disasters and near disasters for the United States and the American people. George W. Bush tried to preach that democracy was on the march abroad, but he was just the latest—though among the more dangerous—usurper of democracy at home who, overwhelmed by dreams of glory, sees himself as the world's liberator or conqueror. Was FDR's rhetoric that much better than their rhetoric of sacrifice to prosecute their wars? Were the times so different, or had war lost its heroic privileged status?

In fact, the presidents after FDR had few skills as orators. John F. Kennedy used the cadence of a Roman orator offering the bone of sacrifice. Both George H. W. Bush (Bush I) and George W. Bush (Bush II) approached the English language as if it were their second language. Dwight D. Eisenhower, the cleverest among them, wanted to be defeated by syntax in order to maintain ambiguity and therefore freedom of action. Jimmy Carter was a scold. On his side, Harry S. Truman had a war—both manufactured and real—that carried him through his first full term. But as his speeches are analyzed, it is clear that he attempted to adopt the phraseology of the Four Freedoms speech but lacked the capacity to implement those freedoms in the face of a conservative Congress. Instead, it was the warrior part of FDR's State of the Union message that was adapted and used for defining American politics and consciousness. Together they used "threats," manufactured and real, to change the nature of American society into the National Security State (albeit a society whose liberties were expanded by the struggles of popular movements such as the civil rights movement) even as the state used the rhetoric of freedom to sustain an empire—anywhere in the world.

The twenty-first century is another time for a spin of the wheel of fortune. Can the Four Freedoms still serve as a foundational guide to everyday life and policy? This seems possible because, remarkably, the Four Freedoms—newly defined and applied—can help us make sense of our aspirations. The freedoms tell us not what to believe, but what needs to be done. They tell us about our material and spiritual needs and desires as humans. They tell us about the importance of communication because we are social beings in almost every moment of our lives. The Four Freedoms can guide us to confront the means of war, its inevitable results in the lives of the broken and broken-spirited, and its negative effects on individual freedoms. They can demystify the character of capitalism, which has turned self-interest into selfish interest and economic efficiency into the destruction of human values and the inefficient use of material goods as a result of a warped profit system. The Four Freedoms serve as a useful means to test out and then inscribe into the meaning of democracy how change—even radical change—can be made for a free and peaceful society, knowing that eventually international laws, modern communications, and people's movements will redefine sovereignty.

RED STATE OR BLUE STATE, YOU LIVE IN THE NATIONAL SECURITY STATE

The term "National Security State" was coined by Marcus Raskin in his testimony before a congressional committee in 1967 to characterize the nation America became at the end of the Second World War, one that would go on to know little peace even when it was not technically at war.

All these years later, the chosen few (more often than not Republicans, conservatives, the Right—designations which have been virtually interchangeable since the Right captured the House in 1994 and Bush II and Dick Cheney captured the White House and the ideology of the Right) still feast on the power and wealth generated by the National Security State, while the rest of the country simply accepts this state as the way of life without realizing its strangling effects on the freedom Raskin warned about:

The National Security State by its nature is expansionist for it deals with the continuous creation of activities in all aspects of public life and has become the single most important function of millions of federal workers, unions, police agencies, defense corporations, universities, and scientists.

The National Security State's link to military technology, nationalism, limited wars for interest and institutions such as universities uses the ideological music of the republic and the democracy as it continues its expansion abroad and transformation of American life into a garrison and launching pad for nuclear war.

It was taken for granted [by elected and nonelected officials] that as a super-power the United States will be continuously involved in conflict and there-fore needs a large standing armed force for conflicts as well as covert operations, to protect its policies and weaponry, and for an advanced mili-tary technology, namely missiles and nuclear weapons, to be brandished in negotiation.[4]

In the twenty-first century, the United States has entered a far more dan-gerous state. The National Security State has expanded beyond its con-ventional definition; it now engulfs the entire society. Often, the National Security State goes on behind the cover of everything and anything called "national security." In almost all cases, *it circumvents freedom of speech.*
Since September 11, citizens now face the following:

- Decreased liberties
- Increased jailing of people on secret charges for weeks, months, or indefinitely
- Increased military controls over our borders
- Threat of military tribunals
- Eavesdropping on heretofore privileged lawyer-client conversations
- Runaway defense budgets
- Growing dependence on the military to act as restraints on themselves and civilians enamored of war who work for the military (demonstrated by, for example, the torture of Iraqi prisoners both by U.S. troops and civilian contractors)[5]
- Increased restraints keeping legitimate protestors away from elected officials in the public space
- Technology like surveillance used to constrain and create feelings of personal insecurity, although people come to believe that they are actually protected through technology

Added to this grim list is the development of sophisticated, impersonal technologies that could become the tools for compulsory registration for a national identity card. Even such resolute conservatives as former *New York Times* columnist William Safire fear this government encroachment on individual liberties. Safire writes: "Nothing can compare to forcing every person in the United States—under penalty of law—to carry what the totalitarians used to call 'papers.'"[6]

Will Your Papers Be in Order?

A national identity card, probably imprinted on a computer chip, could contain a digital copy of a citizen's life: thumbprint and other distinguishing physical marks, driver's license and driving record, health history, credit history, financial records, and Social Security Number.

A national identity card will be more than an inconvenience. It will lead to a whole new category of crimes and, ironically, perhaps less identity than meets the eye, but it will give citizens a false sense of security nevertheless.

Many technical difficulties could occur with a national ID card, besides political ones. For example, several problematic questions arise: Who will control them? Who will have access to the printouts (the Internal Revenue Service?) and how reliable will they be? What if a person's driver's license (a de facto ID card) is fake, as many are? What if the birth certificate is not authentic? What if the Social Security Number is forged? What if you change addresses, or the machines that verify your identity break down, or you refuse to incriminate yourself? What if you state something on the card that is not true? What if you don't carry your card at all times? It is absolutely conceivable that any such offenses will be considered a misdemeanor or a felony. In 2004, the FBI mismatched a copy of the digital fingerprints of an American lawyer in Oregon, a Muslim convert, and jailed him for two weeks in connection with the deadly Madrid railroad bombing that year. But the lawyer had never been to Spain. Eventually, the FBI apologized.[7] But what if they decide in future cases of mistaken identity to hold other innocent ID cardholders incommunicado from lawyers and families?

Of course, for years the Social Security Card has also functioned as a de facto identity card for things having nothing to do with Social Security— bank and credit card records, health records, college records, and more kinds of identification that we now take for granted.

But a government-issued identity card could go much further. It could easily morph into an internal passport, which, unlike some foreign nations, we have never had in the United States. (However, in the nineteenth century and for much of the twentieth century, a form of ID card was frequently used to keep the poor and minorities out of certain U.S. towns and neighborhoods in cities. This was accomplished by racial profiling and the application of vagrancy laws.) You might have to produce your internal passport if authorities want to check on why you are traveling from, say,

Illinois to California or New York to Washington. It is interesting to note that an Ohio company "has embedded silicon chips in two of its employees—the first known case in which US workers have been 'tagged' electronically as a way of identifying them." The corporation is seeking contracts from government security agencies and police.[8]

Polls have shown that the majority of Americans are willing to give up some freedom for security; carrying a national ID card would be a small price to pay to be protected from terrorists. What adherents of the ID card are talking about is extending social control in the society, particularly over the middle class and part of the working class, through legal coercion with criminal penalties attached and the imprinting of new social customs. And that does not take into consideration social control—through both legal and illegal means—of the poor for the purpose of creating the class of the excluded and ultimately the hunted. In a democracy, this is a dangerous business, resulting in authoritarianism. During the Second World War, at least half a million Americans were on an FBI "watch and index" list. They were thought of as dangerous left-wing radicals who were to be picked up and moved to internment camps. With all that the government has sanctioned over the past decades, who can confidently predict that it can't happen here again?

This is not to say that there should be no protection from terrorists—or for that matter protection from the terrorism of our own state apparatus and that of other nations.

The question is what the nature of this protection is to be. Such a question leads to the distinction that Bush II has made between civil liberties and security. *The distinction is a mistake because it says that civil liberty is less important than security.* Bush II, his accomplices, and his followers—and those who may follow them—are saying that civil liberties and security are *not* equal. They are saying that in times of war—forget that they invented the war—you must give up some of your liberties, though they won't tell you how many liberties you will have to surrender.

Much disingenuousness and foolishness have arisen from our leaders regarding the question of civil liberties and nuclear weapons. We have assumed that our weapons of mass destruction, especially nuclear weapons, will keep us secure and relieve our fear. The reality is that military force and ill-advised foreign policies create fear. In turn, fear results in more so-called security, which leads to fewer liberties, which in turn leads to more fear, more security, and even fewer liberties. The cycle leads back to speech that freedom is supposed to protect.

Without Free Speech, the Other Freedoms Are in Doubt

Freedom of speech is a basic constitutional right under the First Amendment and is perhaps the central right for both protecting against government and for the making of government. It must contain within itself the continuing dialogue of freedom in relation to new circumstances.

There are two important ways to consider freedom of speech, and both contain paradoxes that can be confusing, even dangerous, in everyday life. The first is a view that so-called absolutists are inclined to take: free speech in all areas of thought must be preserved and protected irrespective of content. Most people are inclined to accept this doctrine, but it has its price. For example, hate speech, which often is more than offensive to the well being of the national community, is protected. (In *Brandenburg v. Ohio*, the Supreme Court made clear a powerful standard that protects free speech.)[9]

The second way to view freedom of speech is as part of the ongoing debate that seeks to link information and knowledge so that together they will be used intelligently by the public and government in the deliberations and actions of government and citizenry. Again there is a paradox because free speech is a scary concept to institutions and nations: those in power fear that free speech, if used too widely, will get out of hand and lead to revolutionary thoughts or something other than what passes for conventional wisdom. And free speech, because it touches on the interests of special interest groups, causes them to have to rethink what they are doing, say, in health care or the environment; special interest groups don't like doing that, and they will resist.

Freedom of speech can also produce fear: a person can be penalized for telling the truth to fellow citizens where grave harm, often in the form of outright lying, is being done, as numerous government and corporate whistleblowers know. It follows that when lies can be confronted, free speech and the body politic is strengthened—but by no means is it guaranteed to prevail over government and corporate lies. Thus it is a constant fight to attain or maintain free speech because it is a right that only has political and social meaning if it is *exercised*. Paradoxically, free speech can lead to unfree speech and constricted freedoms. In war, for example, the first casualty is free speech and the right to exercise it fully in the face of those who say, "Shut up and salute! Otherwise, you are an enemy!" This seems to have been the intention of anyone disagreeing with Bush II conservatives.

In *The Four Freedoms Under Siege*, Freedom of Speech will be used to explore the content of many issues that impinge on free speech, although citizens may not necessarily think that these are free speech issues. For example, we may think that freedom of speech is no longer a concern in the "Information Age" because technology has fulfilled this first of Roosevelt's freedoms. The paradox is that so much of the information that bombards us around the clock is propaganda and advertising puffery. A curious consequence is that freedom of speech protects advertising, but its wings have been clipped with regard to what we need to know as a free people. As a result, we are increasingly perplexed and constricted by inhibitions of thought and expression at precisely the moment we need to learn a great deal more about state secrets that are really coverups, security laws like the Patriot Act that really promote insecurity, and war without end.

Thus a prediction made years ago has become a reality: "Where free speech became a threat to the pyramidal structure, to those at the top of the structure who made deals with each other and brokered huge interests within the National Security State, then free speech would be eliminated, curtailed, or flooded by other information until people had no choice but to tune out."[10]

The clock is ticking fast for American society. As a society, we must work to understand ourselves further, and we must be clear about where we want to go. On the one hand, our society believes in its own capacities; on the other hand, it has a flawed Constitutional structure written for a slave society. We have—as will be shown—huge, seemingly insurmountable economic and social problems, yet many of them can be resolved with thought and goodwill if we are not afraid of each other and the outside world—and if we protect freedom of speech to examine ourselves and the "forbidden."

Few Americans, whether in red states or blue, think these are optimistic times in the United States. When we are frank with ourselves, we know that living in the National Security State subjects us to inequity, greed, fear, and surveillance ratcheted to new heights (or new lows). The repressive U.S.A. Patriot Act was enacted in 2001, and in 2006 it was cemented into law and our psyches by the same leaders and most of the same lawmakers as the U.S.A. Patriot Improvement and Reauthorization Act. Like the French Bourbons, our leaders and lawmakers never learn and never forget.

To say that nothing much comes from pessimism is to state the obvious. But while America is surely mired in a deep emotional depression, all is not lost—yet.

One way of looking at our condition is to say that the greatness of America, as it relates to other nations, is in its adolescence. For the adolescent, everything is open. There are endless possibilities. Ambiguities can be lived with or resolved, and we don't feel exhausted. It is a common belief of Americans that such possibilities define who we are, the "we" being the striving middle class that seeks a higher, more secure status and a different place from where it is. Some call this the search for excellence; others call it the search for the intangible American dream. But attached to it is an important caveat: inherent in striving is the possibility of failure, of feeling unfulfilled, insecure, marginalized, and damned.

Nevertheless, for the outside world, one of the shining achievements of American society is the porous nature of the class structure and the appearance and the reality in many, many cases of social mobility. Americans have the capacity to start at Place "A" and, through upward social movement, end up at Place "B." This is different from Europe, where social class matters far more than in the United States. Yet western European nations have been better able to ensure fundamental amenities and individual security to its citizens in their public space, which is missing in the United States.

There are options if we want to acknowledge them. Reconstructing a clear alternative agenda that deals with inequity, inequality, and discrimination and the idea of rationality with an indispensable dose of justice to balance the injustices of laws such as the Patriot Act would be the pragmatic and, at the same time, the truly compassionate answer to conservatives.

We don't need the attitude of triumphalism because what is so great about America is possibility. F. Scott Fitzgerald's notion that there are no second acts in American lives finally needs to be rejected. There is always a second act for individuals and for the society as whole. And if it is a longer play, one can even go to a fourth or fifth or sixth act. There should always be a sense of optimism and possibility. In such a case we can be a society that is yearning and striving, and our country can be an extraordinary place worthy of study and emulation if—and it is a big if—we are clear on who our models are.

What better models than FDR's Four Freedoms—to which he might have added a fifth, freedom of the mind, were he alive today—to challenge their diametric opposite, the clear and present danger of the National Security State?

———————

There is a logical sequence to our present danger that begins with a dream world of imperial power, which necessitates a new kind of secretive state that is reorganized to empower and support it. It requires changing and adding bureaucracies, new definitions of laws, and new types of civil servants. And, of course, it requires the capacity and will to wage war permanently and establish economic supremacy around the world. When citizens might object to this National Security State or fear it as a result of events that threaten them, laws will be passed ostensibly to make the people more secure, which in fact make them more submissive. The prime example in our time is the Patriot Act, whose implications have begun to close down free speech and a free society in the name of defense, security, and patriotism. Such laws require enforcement by a Big Brother government, however bumbling. Because of the magnitude of the Patriot Act in this sadly logical sequence, we must shine a bright light on the physiology and anatomy of the Act and its implications because, like any sequence short of all-out nuclear war (surely not out of the question in *this* state), this sequence can be interrupted once the citizens discover it and understand it for what it is.

Part One

Freedom of Speech

In the future days which we seek to make secure, we look forward to a world founded upon four essential human freedoms.

The first is freedom of speech and expression—everywhere in the world.

—Franklin Delano Roosevelt, January 6, 1941

Chapter 1

The U.S.A. Patriot Act Vs. the U.S. Constitution

THE BUSH II VERSION OF THE ALIEN AND SEDITION ACT

Six days after the September 11 attack, the new administration of George W. Bush "produced" legislation titled "Uniting and Strengthening America by Providing Appropriate Tools Required to Intercept and Obstruct Terrorism Act." It was the "Patriot Act," for short. The legislation was 342 pages long.

Although the Patriot Act altered at least fifteen federal statutes—radically in some cases—the ultra-Rightist Christian fundamentalist attorney general, John Ashcroft—who believed that the United States was "called to defend freedom that is not the grant of any government or document but is our endowment from God"[1]—demanded that Congress pass the bill by the end of that week.

But Senator Robert Byrd, a Democrat and a constitutional authority, cautioned that the Patriot Act would allow the executive branch to usurp the power of Congress, eroding the constitutional system of checks and balances. Ignoring Byrd's counsel, Congress—reeling from an anthrax scare that, at one point, evacuated the Capitol—was quick to turn over its critical faculties to an administration more confused than itself because the government, as it had for so long, relied on force and war as its panacea.

Forty-five days after September 11, Congress passed the Patriot Act by a nearly unanimous vote with little debate or testimony from expert, outside witnesses. (Besides, what member of Congress would stand in the way of a president with a 90 percent approval rating, who had quickly designated certain people as terrorists?) There was good reason to be fearful of an administration that intended to rule through fear, deception, secrecy, and division.

Under concerns for national security, Bush II and his advisors constantly pressed the courts and Congress for a restrictive reading of the Constitution, and legislation such as the Freedom of Information Act. (There was an early warning of this maneuver in 1974, as the National

Security Archives and Freedom Forum have shown. Two aides of President Gerald Ford named Cheney and Rumsfeld—pushed by a Justice Department lawyer named Antonin Scalia—persuaded him to veto amendments to the Freedom of Information Act, arguing that it was unconstitutional for the law or the courts to force release of any information the president wanted to withhold. Congress overrode Ford's veto.) The Bush II tactic, as Professor Anna Nelson pointed out, was not to amend; they said they were merely "clarifying"—with the following stark results:

- The Patriot Act not only violated many long-established civil liberties—it allowed the government to search and seize personal records without a warrant and without showing probable cause—but also made it a crime to tell anyone, including one's family and lawyer.

- Ashcroft imposed sanctions that had implications far beyond anything attempted by any attorney general since the days of Alexander Mitchell Palmer, Woodrow Wilson's attorney general, as they became part of the newly approved American legal standard. The standard included secret mass detentions of people the government deemed enemy combatants and eavesdropping on conversations between prisoners and their lawyers in violation of the Sixth Amendment (the right of a criminal defendant "to have the assistance of counsel for his defense"), the Fifth Amendment ("no person shall...be deprived of life, liberty or property, without due process of law"), and the Fourth Amendment (the right of citizens to be free of "unreasonable searches and seizures"), to say nothing of violating the First Amendment's right to free speech. But as we have learned, the passage of the Patriot Act was a sideshow compared to what the Bush II administration undertook under claims of executive power.

The sentiment in the Patriot Act is not new in America, nor is it the first time the actions of the federal government have gone to the very core of what and how the United States would conduct itself in moments of crisis. A fair reading of American history is that the nation is almost always in crisis and any particular event or series of events can be used as pretexts to cut back civil liberties.

Why does this happen?

There are a number of reasons. The first is the fear that those who practice civil liberties in times of war are unpatriotic; indeed, they may even be branded as traitors. (Congress has had a penchant for passing legislation that is intended to "protect" the citizenry from internal enemies.) This argument set in motion the Alien and Sedition Acts in 1798, which can be traced to concerns the Federalist Party had regarding the French Revolution and the friendship that some of the Anti-Federalists like Thomas Jefferson had for the ideals of that revolution. In the 1798 legislation, there was, of course, a practical side that outweighed the ideological: the issue of commerce so necessary to the fledgling Atlantic states. While it is true that John Adams and the Federalist Party were not friends to democracy—they in fact feared the results of democracy on the character of the American state and on the power and authority of the "better" people to govern—the immediate need for Adams and his group was to protect commerce with Great Britain. To this end they signed the Jay Treaty with the British that ended poaching on American ships and the British practice of holding American sailors captive. But soon thereafter, the French, who had been at war with the British, saw the American attempts at high-level diplomacy as nothing more than high-level duplicity. This caused the French to treat American ships on the high seas as pirates. This turn of events was quite different from the days when Lafayette fought in the American Revolution and Americans had affection for France.

By the end of the eighteenth century, the Federalists, frightened about the loss of their power, the changes in the racial and ethnic composition of the United States, and the possibility that Republicans would set in motion a series of fundamental changes if its adherents had their way, passed the Alien Act. The act gave extraordinary power to the executive branch to get rid of any noncitizen thought to be dangerous to the United States. In political terms, the act translated into an attempt by the Federalist Party to purge alien elements that might side with the Anti-Federalists. The implication was clear: immigration was to be controlled.

The Sedition Act was meant as the twin to the Alien Act and politically it seemed more far reaching. Under the Sedition Act, people could not criticize the government whether by word of mouth or in publication. This was intended by its champions to squelch debate, dissent, and any popular interest in revolutionary fervor. Its consequence was intended to lay the basis for a one-party state familiar to totalitarian governments in the twentieth century.

Taken together, the Alien and Sedition Acts were little more than an attempt to use the fight with the French as a political tool to get rid of the Anti-Federalist party in one swoop. The executive branch started its purge by closing several newspapers and bringing charges of sedition against Congressman Matthew Lyon from Vermont, who in fact went to prison and was expelled from Congress. (There were some parallels between Lyon and Victor Berger of Milwaukee, who was duly elected but not seated in Congress after the First World War because he was a Socialist, therefore considered a criminal, and out of the political mainstream.) It is understandable that the Federalists would try. Adams won his presidency by three electoral votes, and since he did not trust the people, his answer was to silence them. He was judged badly. Indeed, by 1840, members of Congress demurred at the Sedition Act, attacking Adams for this usurpation of political authority.

Besides the accusation of the usurpation of political authority, there was another troubling matter. James Madison held that the Sedition Act was unconstitutional because it did not consider that dissent and free speech were necessary to find the best answers to public problems. Furthermore, according to the American Constitution, leaders were responsible to the people and they could not shut off discussion. One could infer from this that the pretext of war and invasion could not be a bar to dissent and free speech.

Another objection to the Sedition Act resonates today. The question was raised of whether security is a competing principle to freedom or whether security is contained in freedom. In the future, this issue may be more concrete than abstract if the United States—as a result of permanent war around the globe that it engenders or participates in—makes a battlefield of its own soil.

Even those who have a certain amount of power or nerve to act as citizens are at risk for being considered to have dangerous thoughts. Thus, during the First World War, handing pamphlets to soldiers or throwing antiwar leaflets at them that in effect said, "You're fools to fight, this is not your battle, this is the battle of a worldwide conspiracy of the capitalists and exploiters," was deemed seditious. After the war, the Wilson government saw the victorious Bolsheviks in Russia as people whose ideology reached the United States and it had to be removed, if not destroyed, whatever ideological form it took. Attorney General Mitchell Palmer had ten thousand immigrants suspected of being communists and anarchists taken to the boundary of the United States in trucks and cattle cars and "deposited" over the border into Mexico.[2]

Similarly, in 1942, the FDR administration interned more than one hundred thousand Americans of Japanese ancestry or Japanese living in the United States who had never shown disloyalty toward America. More than 70 percent were citizens. They were forced to vacate their homes and businesses and relocate to camps in the United States for fear that they would be a Fifth Column. The "camps" were surrounded by barbed wire and patrolled by armed guards. As is invariably the case when people are thrown off their properties, someone else takes it over, leaving the Japanese landless when they were released four years later.

In the 1950s, McCarthyism and its precursors—a different strand of the same fear virus that led to FDR's Japanese internment—also led to surveillance, wiretaps, spying on citizens, and prison terms. Joseph R. McCarthy, an obscure Republican senator from Wisconsin, became a national figure by effectively charging—with ripe theatrics but no proof—that communists had infiltrated the government and influenced U.S. foreign policy. But he and his right-wing congressional supporters overreached when they criticized the army (denouncing one general as "unfit" to wear his uniform), seeking to show how its general staff were either naïve or secret traitors. These and other attacks resulted in a bureaucratic and industrial reign of terror that was also felt in the major media, particularly in television, radio, and Hollywood. By the late 1950s and early 1960s, there was a backlash against McCarthyism. But the reality was that every step of the way the building blocks for authoritarian control remained through legislation and the use of technology for social and political control.[3]

Thus the roots of the Patriot Act are in the Alien and Sedition Acts and other events of American history to the present. Just as other presidents and legislators throughout American history have sought authoritarian control against the citizenry, using fear as their instruments, so it is at the beginning of the twenty-first century.

WITH LIBERTY AND JUSTICE FOR SOME

Perhaps John Ashcroft believed that in his role as attorney general he had been chosen to do God's work. If so, the work seemed to include laying the groundwork for the Right's agenda with the Patriot Act.

Some fundamentalist Rightists saw September 11 as payback to American society for its evil ways, but the new Bush administration interpreted the attack as an opportunity for it to recast American criminal and national security law into a power grab for the authority of the state against the individual and the accused. Ashcroft demanded that Congress immediately pass the complex Patriot Act comprising many provisions they had rejected over the years. He admonished the Senate Judiciary Committee: "To those who scare peace loving people with phantoms of lost liberty, my message is this: Your tactics only aid terrorists, for they erode our national unity and diminish our resolve. They give ammunition to America's enemies, and pause to America's friends. They encourage people of good will to remain silent in the face of evil."[4]

The Patriot Act was ostensibly aimed at terrorists and anyone else the government claimed was aiding their cause, but in the weeks following its passage the new law began to chill the very freedoms the American military expedition to Afghanistan was said to be fighting for as we attempted to defeat the Taliban and kill Osama bin Laden and his al-Qaeda base. It looked like no contest. After all, the Afghanistan government was hardly a government and the United States had high-tech firepower and had gathered much information and intelligence about the Taliban and other groups because they had been American allies in the Afghan struggle against the Soviet Union in 1979. U.S. forces are still lodged in Afghanistan in 2006, as are the resurgent Taliban, as is Osama, and the bombings of military and civilian targets continues. After years of war and occupation, everyday life for the civilian population continues to deteriorate.

But the main event for the Bush II administration was always Iraq. Few beyond Bush's inner circle knew that planning for what would prove to be the twenty-first century American quagmire began in earnest soon after he took office. Paul O'Neill, Bush II's first secretary of treasury, was privy to the president's cabinet meeting in 2001, in which waging war with Afghanistan, and especially Iraq, was a clear objective from the start. George W. Bush sees the war on terrorism as "a religious war," an unnamed relative said. "His view of this is that they are trying to kill the Christians. And we the Christians will strike back with more force and more ferocity than they will ever know."[5]

In the case of both Afghanistan and Iraq, international rules of war were set aside in favor of brute force and destruction. The Iraq War was to be the vehicle to remake the Middle East, according to abstract notions that had little or nothing to do with the realities of life and beliefs in the Middle East but everything to do with Bush II's personal mission. While scholars talk of "national interest," which determines what leaders do, leaders in fact judge issues according to personal conflict and competition with presumed antagonists.

The Iraq War also was an intensely familial matter for Bush II, who wanted to trump his father's First Persian Gulf War a decade earlier, which left Saddam Hussein in place. A not unimportant incentive was that Bush II wanted to avenge the assassination attempt on his father's life that Saddam allegedly sought to engineer during a Bush I trip to Kuwait.

There were less emotional reasons that could be found for invading Iraq, such as the protection of Israel, the desire to build bases in the Middle East, and the protection of oil supplies. But such ideas came with the territory of normal imperial ambition. What was truly *new* was that some conservatives believed that the American people were growing soft, but victory in Iraq would finally rid us of the Vietnam Syndrome. (The Reagan administration had similarly hoped to cover this "stain" on the nation's character by supporting Rightist death squads in El Salvador who served as our proxy army. Counter-terrorism experts from the CIA and the Pentagon employed their skills a decade later in Iraq.)[6]

But the Bush II administration needed more. It needed to rid the country of those aspects of civil liberties and rights that stood in the way of the state. How ironic that a president who came to power in 2001 calling for limited government in fact shredded civil liberties using war as his instrument and the Patriot Act as the hari-kari knife on the American population, which was gulled into believing that Saddam possessed weapons of mass destruction.

A further irony is that in January, 2005, Bush's aides quietly acknowledged what UN weapons inspectors had said before the Iraq invasion and American inspectors concluded nearly two years into the occupation: there were no weapons of mass destruction in Iraq, nor had there been any since the early1990s. But the WMD myth persisted. In the summer of 2006, 50 percent of Americans still thought that Saddam had possessed such weapons when the United States invaded Iraq.[7] They did not seem overly concerned that hundreds of millions of their dollars had been allotted by Congress to look for the nonexistent WMDs, that there had been no public accounting of how the money was spent, or that the Pentagon refused to declassify the information. Such is the power of propaganda and self-deception in public life in America. But there are times when the actions of careless leaders—or lack of actions—cause them to implode in full view of even the most nearsighted. By the end of 2005, public opinion about the war and the credibility of the United States had shifted radically. But as so often happens, the public is left with many of the same dangerous problems unsolved.

It is not ironic but instead *expected* that wars in the name of freedom increase the likelihood of domestic repression through the law. Thus the Patriot Act almost instantly crept into the lives of every American. Then and now, many have simply resigned themselves to the law without understanding its shadowy ramifications for them and their families, friends, neighbors, and fellow citizens. Make no mistake: the Patriot Act is a powerful legal and political instrument intended to deprive people of their right of dissent and therefore their free speech, privacy, association; in the process, it also limits travel. Furthermore, it seriously alters the checks and balances of the Constitution by giving the executive branch unprecedented power, while taking power from the Congress and the judiciary. Stealing power from the people would be more accurate.

Unless the most obnoxious sections of the law are repealed, it will continue to be a legal tool to repress American citizens long after Bush II leaves office, even if a Democrat replaces him. After all, initially, the Patriot Act was passed with the support of every Democratic senator save for Russ Feingold of Wisconsin. So, except for the Progressives in the House of Representatives, one should not put too much faith in Democrats to suddenly become the guardians of civil liberties.

MAJOR PROVISIONS OF THE PATRIOT ACT (WHAT IT MEANS TO YOUR FREEDOM WHEN THE "BENIGN" LANGUAGE IS DECODED)

Increased Penalties

Criminal sentences for acts of terrorism or for harboring or financing terrorists or terrorist organizations are increased. Committing an act of terrorism against a mass transit system also becomes a federal crime.[8]

The problem with the language used in the Patriot Act is that the word "terrorist" or "terrorism" as a legal conception is shaky. There are at least half a dozen different definitions in the law for "terrorist" or "terrorism." When Timothy McVeigh, born and bred in the United States, blew up the federal building in Oklahoma City in 1995, it was a criminal act punishable by the death penalty. It was not necessary to refer to McVeigh as a terrorist unrelated to Islam. The zealots who wreaked havoc on the United States on September 11 could have been categorized as criminals or soldiers. But the latter category requires prisoner of war rights under the international law of war, which the United States was unwilling to grant the thousands it eventually "housed" as enemy combatants at our naval base in Guantanamo and secret CIA detention facilities in Iraq and other locations off U.S. soil.

Making a distinction between a terrorist and a zealot may seem like splitting hairs, but it leads to the question of how we are to treat others in the permanent war on terrorism and therefore how our troops will be treated if taken prisoner. (See Chapter 3 for a wider discussion of terrorists and zealots.)

THE SUPREME COURT TRIES TO HOLD BUSH II TO CONSTITUTIONAL LAW

The Pentagon's policies toward Afghan prisoners at Guantanamo and the revelations of torture and humiliation of Iraqis by American soldiers in Abu Ghraib prison near Baghdad were very brutal and reminiscent of the French in Algeria during that war and even the Nazi regime.

"Detainees" at Guantanamo attempted suicide; three hung themselves in June 2006. But this should not have surprised anyone since Bush II and Rumsfeld publicly disdained the Geneva Conventions (even though the United States was a signatory), stretching the powers of the president and destroying the intentions of the Constitution's founders and the Constitution itself on the grounds of urgency and necessity. In fact, six months earlier, after Bush signed the Defense Appropriations Bill—which included the McCain Amendment prohibiting "cruel, inhuman, or degrading treatment or punishment of persons under custody or control of the United States government"—Bush quietly issued a "signing statement" that in effect said he could interpret the new law, as he had, with restrictive signing statements on the Patriot Act, negating any limits to his power. He claimed that he could waive the explicit restriction of laws that touched on national security and internal security that Congress placed on the executive branch.[9] Thus Bush did not surrender his position that if he would use torture if he thought it was in the national interest. After all, administration lawyers, including Gonzales and Ashcroft—the legal enablers in blatant executive usurpation and disregard of settled law—told him that he was not bound by either an international treaty prohibiting torture or by a federal antitorture law because he had the authority as commander in chief to approve any technique needed to protect the nation's security.[10] (Apparently, these "techniques" were administered by improperly trained military police and others who had no training in so-called interrogation procedures. Too many were sanctified in their belief that war meant there were no limits to what they could do in the name of patriotism and a self-serving brand of sadistic certitude. It should not be forgotten that the young men and women torturers are also scarred for life. Nor that the demoralized American forces took anyone into the army, including skin-heads and avowed racists spoiling to return to civilian life after a cleans-ing race war. Such is one result of this war.)

The Supreme Court's majority understood what was at stake legally and socially. So on June 29, 2006, the Court abruptly changed Bush's authority on torture with a surprise ruling in *Hamdan v. Rumsfeld*.[11] By a five-to-three vote the Court rejected the president's plan to try terror detainees by secret military commissions.

That the Bush administration made an embarrassing zigzag twelve days later, allowing that detainees at Guantanamo and other prisoners in U.S. custody were entitled to protection under Common Article 3 of the Geneva Convention (though the White House press secretary insisted all detainees had been treated humanely), does not alter the fact that the *Hamdan* case laid down two important rules vital to the maintenance and, yes, the survival of freedom in moments that produce security laws that add to imprudence, irrationality, and demonstrative error in policies.

One rule upholds the decision taken in the historic Youngstown Steel Seizure case, in which the Supreme Court made clear that President Truman could not act outside specific congressional authority in seizing the steel mills, even during wartime.

A second rule following Justice Jackson's precept in the Youngstown Steel Seizure case is that executive authority on its own initiative is a far weaker prerogative and one that steps out of bounds when it in fact moves beyond what Congress has granted through law. It is why President Franklin D. Roosevelt, even in a time of extreme circumstances, concluded that his powers to make war against Japan were broad but not *unlimited*, thus requiring a congressional declaration of war against Japan after Pearl Harbor. It is why FDR waited for Germany to declare war on the United States a few days after Pearl Harbor. These are matters that are more than legalistic niceties, for they take into account the very meaning of a free society and the restraint that a president might exercise.

A nation such as the United States should never be understood with regard to national security as one that is unified in opinion and action, except in the most dire of circumstances. Mass mobilization and intimida-tion of the media or ordinary citizens by a leader and an auxiliary of a national or local police that swears allegiance to that leader without inter-est in the law is a recipe for authoritarianism, or worse. In the United States, as in other states, emergency laws are passed or executive orders given that are not predicated on the whim of a leader. Even in that case, it must be unambiguous that emergency laws and executive orders cannot be extended into months, years, or generations. That is to say, there must be a quick return to the protection of the rule of law as it relates to justice and civil liberties for all living under the flag of the United States. That includes aliens or citizens, combatants, detainees, or whatever category some lawyer may concoct to defend authoritarianism. Furthermore, there must be the recognition of differences and pluralism among the people as quickly as possible. This is not to deny that there exists a structure of laws that Americans accept as necessary for the formation and perpetuation of a free and inclusive society and the deepening of democracy. It is the development of that sensibility and consciousness within the society that defines a free people. This consciousness comes from struggle, then is protected by law, and, indeed, aids people further in perpetuating, deepening, and expanding their rights and their collective humanity. This we have seen in many successful cases, for example, in rights of citizens to live where they choose, irrespective of racially inspired housing covenants, or in the desegregation of public facilities from swimming pools to buses to schools.

But where a nation transforms itself into a unitary state mediating opinion and actions through the executive, the state and executive take upon themselves the power to define the unity of the nation and of the government without reference to the civil society. In those cases, the state's leader takes on the authoritarian form of government. In authoritarian governments, differing opinions and laws can be turned into so much used tissue at the whim of the executive, who operates out of misperception, single-minded mission, grandiosity, misplaced zeal, or willful manipulation of the various sectors of government that otherwise might have a disinterested view of information and intelligence: committed citizens, journalists, and scholars. Presidents who see themselves as commanders, above any law, choose secret means for decision making instead of an open democratic process. They fear contradiction because they do not trust the institutions of the nation or the citizenry, nor do they believe that the divided judgments of their own government are able to withstand public scrutiny. They prefer to act on their own "inherent" authority, an authority that executives come to believe is innate once they take office.[12]

Some federal courts have sought to limit the power of the executive, which used the threat of international terrorism to buttress its argument for breaching international law, laws of detention, and laws limiting its authority. The ruling in the *Hamdan* case was an attempt to put a brake on such power. As Justice Breyer put it in his concurring opinion, "Judicial insistence upon [consultation with Congress] does not weaken our Nation's ability to deal with danger. To the contrary, that insistence strengthens the Nation's ability to determine—through democratic means—how best to do so. The Constitution places its faith in those democratic means. Our Court today simply does the same."

During the Bush II period we see several important political realities that touch upon the Supreme Court and the *Hamdan* case. The first is that the Supreme Court, for all intents and purposes, *chose* Bush II as president of the United States by one vote in 2000. It did so by overturning settled law with regard to equal protection. It did so by saying that it would only do so in *Bush v. Gore*, in which the Court acted for what they thought was conservative stability.

Second, the conservative-minded Supreme Court made clear in *Hamdan* that it did not give President George W. Bush an open path to authoritarianism. It was Justice Stevens, a Republican chosen by President Gerald Ford, who stated that the Republican Bush II had overstepped his constitutional bounds.

But one should not be fooled into thinking that authoritarianism (some call it fascism) has suddenly vanished from the land as a result of this Court's five-to-three decision. There are other authoritarian options; consider, for example, the following:

- Congress can (and the 109th Congress did) rewrite legislation, including narrowing *habeas corpus*, for terrorist suspects in military tribunals that could override Supreme Court muster, and the prisoners—and the American people—would be back to where they were before *Hamdan*. (In the *Hamdan* ruling, the Court noted that Common Article 3 of the Geneva Conventions "obviously tolerates a great degree of flexibility in trying individuals captured during armed conflict," although standards as outlined in the U.S. Uniform Code of Military Justice still apply.)

- Mr. Hamdan and other prisoners could still be tried by regular sanctioned court martial.

- Bush could choose not to try the Guantanamo prisoners, letting them wither in prison until this phase of the war without end concludes or he leaves office. But since the United States has been a warrior nation throughout its history (see especially Chapter 19), citizens hoping for a more just solution (while not ignoring threats of more terrorist attacks on America) may not fare much better under succeeding presidents from either political party or under a pliant Congress, regardless of which party controls the two houses.

- With the death or resignation of one justice, the composition of the Supreme Court that gave us Hamdan could shift overnight and become "activist," with an ironclad conservative majority for a generation. (Justice Stevens, as of this writing, is eighty-seven years old. Unless the Senate rejects Bush II nationalist triumphalism, it is likely that his replacement will not be a Ford Republican in philosophical outlook.)

THE RIGHT'S ALARMING CONCEPTION OF AMERICA'S ROLE

President Bush II and Vice President Cheney (and conservatives in positions of influence throughout the political system, from the federal level down to the local) have no intention of backing down on their conception of America's international role, even if it means stating that the United States is now in a condition of permanent war. This war requires government intrusion that goes well beyond the domestic controls suggested during the cold war by Senator Joseph McCarthy, the Subversive Activities Control Board, and activist members of the military and national security establishment in charge of assessing and developing threat situations in the third world. Indeed, the Bush II White House has made it clear that nothing they have done or are doing is illegal; in fact, they say their actions are necessary to sustain the United States and American foreign and national security policy.

The Bush II administration has demonstrated that in the end it believes that America should be in conflict with the world, although from time to time they will shift their rhetoric or give the appearance of listening to other nations' needs and complaints. The triumphal nationalists accept the belief that they are both hated and feared. Their great insecurity is that they will look foolish, but they have assessed their fears carefully, knowing that their primary interest is in "staying the course," a phrase whose meaning is either elliptical or already defined by Bush II as permanent war for the sake of interests that grow out of being a triumphal superpower.

The Bush II administration hits upon two diametrically opposed views of the American reality. The first is that American wars are aberrant and civil liberties must be restored quickly after they are over, whether the wars have been cold wars or hot wars. Liberals think of wars as time bound. The First World War is an example where liberties were taken away but slowly restored. Similarly, during the Eisenhower era, the Supreme Court sought to end aspects of the National Security State made even more dangerous by McCarthyism, which undercut civil liberties and freedoms for dissenters, those caught in the vise of loyalty investigations, or the dispossessed who seemed to have no rights. By the end of the Vietnam War, attempts were made in Congress to control executive power and continuous war making, especially where the war appeared to be unsuccessful.

The Republican Party, once known for its isolationism and prudent stance with regard to American military intervention, and even imperialism, did an about-face in 2000. It became the Republican Party under Bush II, Cheney, Rumsfeld, and former Democrats who discovered that the United States was in a third world war and that the civil society, as well as the courts, Congress, and the press, had better "get with the program" or shut up. This point of view is based on the belief that the United States is hated around the world, especially in the third world. Further, their view is that the United States must be feared, and making it so requires strong military and economic imperial measures abroad. This leads to continuous military engagement, which means that the American people must harden up and define patriotism as passivity or, in the worst case, hound those within the country who disagree. It also means using the armed forces for undefined missions, risking the breakup of families within the United States, and creating another generation of young soldiers permanently scarred by war.

The second view is found in the Supreme Court's *Hamdan* decision. Justice Stevens made it clear that the United States, as a matter of treaty obligation, must accept the Geneva Conventions against torture and provide minimum standards for those detained or imprisoned by the United States. One would think that this makes good sense in terms of policy, self-defense, and international law. But here again we see another Bush II agenda that could easily be carried into future presidential actions. While the United States pressed hard for the 1949 Geneva Convention, it now finds itself in a different position—or so the advocates of the Bush II triumphal position believe (except for tactical purposes):

- International law is a fiction and it is time to replace it with American imperial law, which will be written in Washington by American law professors and government officials who see their chance to write a new code that replaces uncomfortable elements of international law that are based on international agreement, harmony of pragmatic reason, and the logic of symmetrical justice. That is, the Bush II administration wants to do away with the idea that what is good for one state is good for all, and what is required of one may be required of all.

- American imperial law is constructed by the most powerful nation in the world. In this reading of imperial law, power defines law and justice as formulated in Washington.

American imperial law has virtually no support among other nations and little support in the United States itself; it flies in the face of policies absolutely necessary for the well-being of the United States. All this should cause any prudent American political leader to pause before pursuing authoritarianism or imperialism, but it has done nothing to slow Bush II, Cheney, and their people.

Some in the Democratic Party hope that they can recapture the "glory" days of the early cold war. But we may discount that reading of American history as hagiographic; it does not pay adequate attention to the astonishing costs of the cold war to the United States. To return to the glory days of Truman and Acheson, for example, takes no account of the profoundly different problems now facing the United States and the world.

We should recognize that the Four Freedoms are not freedoms defined by authoritarian cabals in Washington as freedoms to act against the world. The Four Freedoms are not a recipe for continuous war against other nations, just as they are not a handbook for those FDR called "economic royalists"[13] to retain economic, social, and political power over and against those within the United States and the world who favor rules of law and justice. They surely do not include the evisceration of human rights, which are devastated by permanent war. Nor do they mean stepping on the wretched as they seek well-being in the American nation or stepping on other nations as they seek well-being in the framework of those covenants and foundational documents that do not count war, exploitation, and human misery as a good. It is not any single nation's mission to eradicate these evils without the support of the world; the United States, in its attempt to do so, is undertaking exactly the means of exploitation and oppression it claims to oppose. Clothing it in the language of God, human rights, justice, democracy, or other sweet-sounding words results only in misery and vengeful feelings in future generations.

That the Supreme Court in *Hamdan* understands these arguments and reaches out to the Geneva Convention and other ideas about humane treatment and international law is a significant but small crack of the door. This crack needs to be further opened politically and legally, beginning with meetings, conferences, and public discussions. Otherwise, others will seek to close down free speech or over time barter away the Stevens decision, and that will be another nail in the casket of freedom.

Committing an act of terrorism against a mass transit system is now a federal crime, but mass transit in the United States is vulnerable because of structural negligence. The system suffers from a gross lack of funds, according to a report of the American Society of Civil Engineers, which claims funding would have to double to maintain the level of operating capacity it has in 1998.

A further problem with the mass transit provision of the Patriot Act is the question of how indiscriminately the authorities define the law for terrorist acts. Is it an act of terrorism if you paste a message on a subway window—or anywhere else—saying "U.S. Out of Iraq" or is it a temporary spoiling of the subway's appearance? Is handing out pamphlets in the street calling the president and his coterie "blood-thirsty murderers" an act of terrorism? In the war without end, context will probably abridge free speech under an antiterrorism law. The Supreme Court would reach back to the *Schenck* case in order to interrupt free expression (see Chapter 4).

Bioterrorism

It becomes illegal for people or groups to possess substances that can be used as biological or chemical weapons for any purpose besides a "peaceful" one.[14]

The bioterrorism provision is an extraordinary case of hypocrisy since the Bush II administration pulled out of an international treaty against biological and chemical warfare. Also, the American relationship to the use of biological and chemical weapons is quite ambiguous. After all, for testing purposes, the United States used such weapons for a long time on its own armed forces and civilian populations. How this qualifies as a "peaceful" purpose is unclear. Furthermore, the United States did not complain about the use of such weapons by Saddam Hussein on his own people in the 1980s. People do not like being reminded, but the United States interceded for Saddam in those days—quietly, of course—at the UN on his use of the dreadful weapons.

Stating that the use of biological or chemical weapons is illegal is language unsupported by our resolve since September 11. Four years later, the Department of Homeland Security created fifteen scenarios of terrorist attacks that could devastate parts of the United States in terms of human life and economic impact.[15] Nine of the scenarios concerned biological and chemical attacks such as the spread of anthrax by aerosol and the release of nerve agents in cities. Such hypothetical scenarios have been discussed openly for years as disasters waiting to happen, but if precautions against these attacks—or medical antidotes for vast civilian populations if attacks should occur—have been taken by the federal government, the public is in the dark about them. In fact, neither the federal government nor state and local governments have realistic evacuation plans for large cities in case of such attacks. Look at the hapless evacuations of New Orleans and Galveston, Texas, before the Gulf Coast hurricanes of 2005.

Detention

> The attorney general or the commissioner of immigration may certify an immigrant as being under suspicion of involvement in terrorism. Those individuals may then be held for up to seven days for questioning, after which they must be released if they are not charged with violations of the criminal or immigration codes.[16]

There is a trick to the detention provision. The government can change the category of the person by finding some illegal act, such as an expired visa or driver's license, which would keep the person in a state of detention usually without bail. This system of prosecution was not invented by Attorney General Ashcroft. It is a standard operating procedure of prosecutors, but the difference here is a remarkable one. The defendant might never come to trial as cunning prosecutors seek to find new charges (if they need any) of an insubstantial nature like driving without a seat belt or running a red light.

Professor Peter Raven-Hansen of the George Washington University Law School has correctly noted that the intention of the Bush II administration was to circumvent the usual guarantees found in American law in which the burden to prove guilt beyond a reasonable doubt is placed on the government. Instead, using the word "terrorism" as a legal and political club, Bush made clear that his government can and should use preventive detention against anyone it deems necessary to hold in detention.

Such a radical departure from the Constitution and accepted rules of law now makes it possible to hold aliens, residents, and citizens alike for an unlimited time for whatever reasons and for whatever putative crimes or possible information the government claims it needs. Here, the government can act as the military, the CIA, Justice Department, FBI, Coast Guard, Homeland Security, or any official body.

In fact, Georgetown law professor David Cole recounts,

> There were over 5,000 people detained since September 11th in anti-terrorism initiatives undertaken by the Justice Department. And of those 5,000, only three were charged with any crime related to terrorism. And of those three, only one was convicted, and not actually of engaging in terrorist activity or even planning terrorist activity, but of conspiring to support some unidentified terrorist act in the unidentified future. So you got 5,000 people locked up on pretexts who had nothing to do with terrorism.

The Justice Department under Ashcroft rejected "any concerns about human rights, about civil liberties, about fairness as simply aiding the enemy. As not even appropriate to be on the table," Cole said."[17]

Further fallout has resulted from the abuse of the Constitution:

Rendition. Detainees may include suspected terrorists often kidnapped by CIA operatives in neutral countries and transferred to secret bases and prisons in other countries such as Egypt that are known for aggressive interrogation and torture.[18] The process, called "rendition," is mentioned in the Patriot Act. While it goes back to Clinton's presidency—and was widely used by the United States during the Vietnam War and more recently in El Salvador—it certainly has occurred more frequently after September 11. What happens to these detainees is left to the imaginations of the prisoner's families.

Right to a Lawyer? Not surprisingly, there have been cases where the government listened in to discussions between lawyer and client, which effectively ends the confidentiality privilege. Unless this practice is ended by congressional statutes, it will spread beyond the immigration category.

The right to a lawyer is relatively new in our country, dating back only to 1962 when it was established by *Gideon v. Wainwright.*[19] The Bush II administration, however, had other ideas. Anthony Lewis has argued the following:

> In a war against terrorism, any process that the president says is essential to the war is due process. Government lawyers argue that in wartime, courts must defer to the president's judgment.... About the time the Gideon case was decided, we began to hear about the imperial presidency. The terrorist

attacks of Sept. 11, 2001, and now the war on Iraq have renewed that concept in even more extreme form. Bush had little trouble with a supine Congress. He wants the Constitution, too, as our judges enforce it, to yield to the supremacy of the president."[20]

Here, Bush was like other presidents.

So illegal immigrants are at risk today, but who knows what political case might be made against innocent citizens tomorrow, landmark cases like *Gideon* notwithstanding? Americans need to be vigilant, for the government constantly tests the limits of what it can do by holding citizens incommunicado without benefit of counsel.

Some believe that the Supreme Court remedied this problem with its enemy combatant ruling in 2004, when it decided that "a state of war is not a blank check for the President." The case seemed to affirm that the indefinite detention of U.S. citizens (the petitioner, Yaser Esam Hamdi, was an American citizen) designated as enemy combatants both in the United States and at Guantanamo must be given the ability to challenge their detention before a judge or other neutral decision-maker."[21] Whether this unexceptional statement covers the detainees given over to other nations is dubious. The Bush II administration fought it tooth and nail. Furthermore, the Court let the government determine the definition of decision-maker. In fact, the decision-making process seemed to exclude open hearings.

Government Loopholes. Even in cases where decisions appear to be almost unanimous, the Supreme Court leaves loopholes for the government. In the detainee cases, it is true that the Supreme Court under Rehnquist essentially told Bush: You can't do what you are doing. However, if you set up procedures for what you are doing that pass the *minimum smell test*, you can. For example, what seemed to be a broad decision in 1954 ending public school segregation actually was narrowed by the phrase "deliberate speed." Harry Truman's lawyers lost the Youngstown Steel Seizure case during the Korean War because they did not show Congress's approval of the seizure action through its laws. The Supreme Court tried to put limits on executive power when it came to seizing private property but human rights did not have that high a priority, as the Connecticut eminent domain decision demonstrated in 2005.[22]

Obviously, the values of the decisions will also depend on the trajectory of the idea of war without end. If the courts and society see the continuation of the war on terrorism or future preemptive wars of the United States as wars without end, the courts will not be able to do much, nor will they want to if a president has the cover of war to justify any sort of action he or she might take.

Lost in Translation: Individual Freedom. In order to make the Patriot Act work administratively, the government, as a repressive instrument, needs to become more centralized and expand, becoming less efficient. Furthermore, the government needs to employ thousands of new agents and train them, set up language schools, and hire speakers in the six-hundred-plus languages extant around the world. But years after September 11, the government still has difficulty finding people who can speak and translate crucial languages like Arabic, Farsi (spoken in Iran), Chinese and other Asian languages, and Pashtu (spoken in Pakistan and Afghanistan). This did not stop the army from dismissing nine linguists between 2001 and 2002 because they were gay. Six were specializing in Arabic, two were studying Korean, one was studying Mandarin Chinese.[23] The National Security Agency (NSA), once so secretive it barely acknowledged its existence, alone collects two million pieces of information around the world per *hour*. The organization claims they spot check for meaningful information. But the NSA, with its thirty-eight thousand employees, as well as the CIA, has a shocking shortage of translators and interpreters. The problem also applies to the CIA and FBI: as of 2005, FBI linguists had a backlog of some eighty-three hundred hours of material that has not been translated, including "information that could be critical to terrorism investigations."[24] Translating such information, much of it "chatter," is a huge problem in terms of U.S. security—if the information means anything. If it does, odds are that it is ambiguous and contradictory and does not tell the government how to act. Indeed, it may be an inducement to government agencies to use questionable means such as false arrests to "get at the truth."

Roving Wiretaps

Law enforcement officials may obtain from the special intelligence court the authority for roving wiretaps on a person suspected of involvement in terrorism so that any telephone used by that person may be monitored. Previously, officials needed separate authorizations for each phone used by the person.[25]

Purpose of Investigations

National security investigators are able to obtain from a special intelligence court the authority to wiretap suspects in terrorism cases if they assert that foreign intelligence operations are a significant purpose of the investigation. Previously, foreign intelligence had to be the only purpose of the investigation to win such authorization.[26]

These provisions of the Patriot Act deal with wiretapping. Both are linked to a special secret appellate court eerily named United States Foreign Intelligence Surveillance Court of Review, or the FISA court, which takes its name from the Foreign Intelligence Surveillance Act of 1978.

Imaginative federal investigators will be in a position to "barter" information they receive under writs that FISA grants. The information is bartered with local authorities that seek it for drug and other criminal cases. The tendency to violate the rights of defendants in national security criminal cases is great because the defendant will be excluded from access to information gathered by a secret agency.

One should not lay all of the blame for the roving wiretap provision on Bush II because Democrats wanted such a right for years as a means of catching drug dealers that move from place to place, getting rid of their cell phones as they travel. In the give-and-take of the legislative process, Republicans gave Democrats the roving cell phone inclusion. A historian will find that much in the Patriot Act was surrendered for the Democrats' idea. But the issue of drugs goes way beyond roving cell phone operators. It goes to the banks that launder drug money and to the CIA's use of assets—such as spies and informers—which, of course, the U.S. government does not acknowledge.

The reality of closed sessions in a secret court is profoundly dangerous for Americans because it means that the government, if it is able to get such a court to go along with it, can try suspects in secret chambers in a high-security room in the Justice Department. The right to closed sessions divides FISA from the rest of the federal judiciary; the former gets secret information and the latter has no access to it.

What really goes on in its own court system is not the only thing the public is in the dark about. According to the American Civil Liberties Union (ACLU), the government—usually the FBI—can now tap the phone of any citizens suspected of being terrorists; intercept their mail; spy on them while they are on the Internet; illegally spy on political, anti-war, environmental, and faith-based groups (often through the use of the Joint Terrorism Task Forces and local police) in order to build a file on activists; and build an electronic dossier on every citizen—suspects as well as ordinary folks totally uninvolved politically but who might have the "wrong" last name or facial characteristics.[27] In 2004, a U.S. Court of Appeals ruled that companies providing e-mail services can read and copy a customer's e-mail and use the information any way they want. There is certainly nothing to prevent them from feeding that information to the government.

Since Ashcroft's term, tens of thousands in America are again on a security index of people to be watched or picked up by the Justice Department and its immigration roughriders.[28] Although such a list did not start with Bush II, it reached frightening new heights during his administration. The reality is reminiscent of the loyalty oaths and purges of the 1950s that broke tens of thousand of people and scared millions of others into silence. Starchy New Englanders and upper-class communist sympathizers were not immune. They, like many today, suffered loss of jobs, surveillance, prison, and congressional investigation. Keep in mind that during the Second World War, some five hundred thousand people were on a watch list to be arrested or detained by the government.[29]

Search Warrants

Federal officials are allowed to obtain nationwide search warrants for terrorism investigations.[30]

The importance of this provision revolves around the word "nationwide" for two reasons. On a bureaucratic level, the assumption is that the feds have enough information but no capacity to *coordinate* what they have. This has been corrected supposedly with an intelligence czar whose responsibilty is assuring that coordination occurs. But as with the NSA, there is nothing to suggest that the government being flooded with more information will increase your personal freedom and your feelings of security, which is ostensibly the central purpose of the government's war on terrorism. Moreover—and this is crucial—there is no reason to believe that nationwide search warrants against immigrants, which are a form of roundups, will cause *anyone* to feel more secure.

On the other hand, roundups do have an *in terrorem* ("in fear") effect. Roundups have two characteristics. They show the citizen that the government is doing "something" in their behalf, but they are also a form of state terror. Roundups can backfire unless the government is prepared to control as much of a person's life as possible, including his or her thoughts. The name for this in some countries is *totalitarian government*.

Probably no single activity will turn many Americans against this aspect of the Patriot Act than a situation where a large number of people are picked up in the Latin American or Arab communities or other closely knit communities. If the press and media remain somewhat free and there is a broad-based civil liberties movement—if the public is sufficiently aroused—it may be that roundups and detention will fail.

In a multiethnic, multicultural society such as ours, patriotism takes on a different meaning when specific communities find they are being attacked. While it is true that first generation Americans are more likely to accept the dominant mores and definition of patriotism, this has yet to be really tested in the post-September 11 context. In such an environment, searches without warrants are part of the package of being an American and any putative violation is grist for those in power whose focus is not terrorism as much as it is their own bureaucratic interests and ideological bias.

The "Insidious" Section 215

The ACLU (among other organizations and First Amendment scholars and lawyers) believes Section 215 of the Patriot Act violates free speech rights protected by the First Amendment. Their argument has great weight. Those subpoenaed under this Section are under a gag order. They are prohibited from telling anyone that the FBI has demanded information even if the information is not tied to a particular suspect and poses no risk to national security.

Section 215 also violates privacy and due process rights guaranteed by the Fourth Amendment. It allows the government to search and seize personal records and belongings from the homes of ordinary people living in the United States, including U.S. citizens and residents, without a warrant and without showing probable cause. (Under the equally insidious Section 505, the government can issue "National Security Letters" to average Americans, compelling them to turn over private records that include with whom they live and have lived, what they search for and read on the Web, and such financial records as what they make, spend, and invest. The NSL was created in the 1970s to counter espionage and terrorism, but the FBI now issues over thirty thousand NSLs a year, a hundred-fold annual increase since the Patriot Act restrictions on its use.)

Section 215 does not require the government to provide an individual with notice that his or her records or belongings have been seized; you may never know that your privacy has been invaded or why. The government can seize:

- Your medical records, including psychiatric records.

- Your computers, discs, photocopier, files, books, letters, journals.

- A list of people who have visited a particular Web site.

- Membership lists from advocacy organizations like Greenpeace, the ACLU, and even the right-leaning Federalist Society, unlikely as it would be.

- A list of worshipers at a particular church, mosque, temple, or synagogue.

- A list of subscribers to particular magazines and newspapers.

- A list of people who have borrowed a particular book from a public library, including reference requests from patrons, books they check out, and computer stations they use for the Internet.

Some librarians simply avoided Section 215 by shredding data before the FBI made such a request; some stopped keeping records on who borrows what books. The Justice Department claims it never used its counterterrorism powers to search library or bookstore records. Ashcroft charged librarians with "baseless hysteria." Yet two nationwide surveys conducted at the University of Illinois after September 11 found that more than two hundred out of fifteen hundred libraries surveyed had turned over information to law enforcement officials.[31] The Justice Department subsequently said that the number of libraries subpoenaed is "classified information."[32] Even a very limited amendment to cut off funds for FBI searches of bookstores and libraries, cosponsored by 145 members of both parties, was narrowly defeated—the vote was tied—in 2004 under heavy White House pressure.[33]

Control over what is read, and who reads what may seem like a small concern in a period that is burdened with war, disease, and poverty. But book banning and surveillance through what is read is a strong indication that a nation is not free; rather, it uses "security" as a means of public and private control by assuring that what is read and thought about is within the scope of the state police apparatus. Surveillance through books is hardly surprising since reading is essential in the exercise of intelligence and the pursuit of knowledge. Dictators and authoritarians know that liberty must be controlled. The search for terrorists is an excellent rationalization for power over writers and readers.

Patriot Act "II" Sneaks In

Bush II hoped to walk through this profound political action—which very much resembled the door to Joe McCarthy's "Church of Internal Security"—with a scheme for Patriot Act II, when he addressed the FBI Academy in 2003: "For the sake of the American people, Congress should change the law and give law enforcement officials the same tools they have to fight terror that they have to fight other crime."[34]

These "tools" would further expand the government's wiretapping authority, give it unprecedented power to seize documents and force testimony without a court order, subpoena private medical, financial, and other records, and allow for collection of DNA samples of citizens.[35]

The Patriot Act II would also make it a crime to tell someone if you are subpoenaed—the "someone" apparently could include a family member or a lawyer. If you do not comply, the government could imprison you as well as the person you told. This is the classic meaning of "guilt by association," so popular in the 1950s. But there is a more deceptive feature. The purpose of Patriot II is to isolate the accused, while exempting the government from public scrutiny and accountability in a Kafkaesque manner.

This was too much for many on both the Right and the Left, and the Patriot Act II as such was never taken up by Congress. *Or so it seemed.* To avoid debate, Ashcroft quietly broke the Patriot Act II into small pieces and began sneaking what he could get away with into appropriations bills. For example, on December 13, 2005—a Saturday, an otherwise quiet news day—while most Americans were glued to their television sets watching the capture of Saddam Hussein by U.S. troops (the same pictures—his hole-in-the-ground hiding place, checking his head lice—shown over and over), Bush II signed a law giving the FBI unprecedented powers to obtain personal information from a financial institution without a court order. The law also expanded the definition of financial institution to include stockbrokers, car dealerships, casinos, credit card companies, insurance agencies, jewelers, airlines, the U.S. Post Office, and any other business "whose cash transactions have a high degree of useful-ness in criminal, tax, or regulatory matters."[36]

The task for civil liberties advocates was made vastly more complicated when Congress overwhelmingly passed the Intelligence Reform and Terrorist Prevention Act of 2004, the largest reorganization of government intelligence since the National Security Act of 1947 created the CIA and the Departments of Defense and Air Force. In fact, the Intelligence Bill rewarded the Bush II administration with "weapons" that they had hoped the Patriot Act II would give them: more electronic surveillance and detention powers, thousands of new federal agents to patrol American borders, and the likelihood of a national driver's license lead-ing to a national ID system.

The Patriot Act and FISA Court: Fig Leaf of Legality for Bush II

The wrangling over the Patriot Act in Congress and with President Bush II in 2005 and 2006 revolved around the question of whether the execu-tive branch was mandated to get a court order from the FISA court to undertake virtually all manner of intrusion under the guise of suspected terrorism, whether inside or outside the United States, or between people who associate with terrorists.

The position taken by moderates was that the 1978 law mandated that the executive branch needed a court order to proceed with intelligence work. But this is kind of a game; the court operated as a virtual rubber stamp, demanding at most that the papers be "in order" technically. Within a generation, the FISA court turned down no more than a handful of requests while legitimating thousands of other requests. It should be noted that this fig leaf of legality that involves a court comprising judges who are sworn to secrecy and who are committed to definitions of national security that invariably favor the executive branch (including the military, police, and intelligence agencies) now passes for the *protection* of civil and individual liberties. It does so because a request is blessed by the FISA court which can allow the executive branch to act first and then within a few days receive permission for their actions. Rather than accept the idea that Congress has the authority and power to declare war and regulate the army and navy under the Constitution, Bush II saw such reg-ulation as *intruding* on his idea of "inherent" powers. (In a surprising com-promise, Bush II agreed that his administration would take some cases to the FISA court when, at his discretion, he decided it was necessary.)

But the bottom line is that the executive branch was not satisfied with the fig leaf of the FISA court. They were committed to the exercise of *naked power*, over which they wanted absolute control.

The Bush II administration made clear that any control exercised over the government vis-a-vis spying is to be regulated and articulated by the pres-ident alone according to the theory that anything less is an infringement of the absolute power of the president as commander and chief to defend the United States. The administration wants to be able to decide —*on its own say-so*—either for moral or immoral reasons, or on a whim—who is to be fingered as a terrorist or associate to be dealt with, whether by surveillance or rendition (including torture), and whether to make or expand war. Such power would include the use of nuclear weapons.

Because of the Patriot Act (and its reauthorization in 2006 that made minor adjustments to a few provisions)[37] and the FISA court, we are left depending on secret evidence in a secret court without knowing the crime or who the target is. The scenario is consistent with the idea of laws that have symbolic or ritual meaning but are actually feel-good, rubber-stamp functions that help citizens deceive themselves into the idea that they are governed by rules of law.

The political reality, though, is that a president like George W. Bush will use national security to argue that he need not go to a court for approval, however meaningless and symbolic the role of the court is as an instrument to inhibit the executive branch over national security matters. Thus there are two immediate, intersecting realities. One is the use of laws and courts as a ritual means of checks and balances toward the executive branch (which it will virtually never do in security cases and when the United States is at war, a condition the United States finds itself in the first years of the twenty-first century and almost certainly beyond). Second, the executive branch has no time for symbolic technicalities and will brush them aside anytime it feels like doing so.

The citizen, therefore, is walking on a razor's edge where he or she is counted on to be passive and accepting of any direction leadership takes. This will be the reality as long as depleting constitutional law, governance, and freedom of anything but symbolic meaning continues.

Sharing Intelligence and Criminal Information

Intelligence officials and criminal justice officials are allowed to share information on investigations.[38]

With the passage of the Intelligence Act in 2004, a new purpose and rationale seemed to have been put into this provision. A new layer of intelligence was created. The new director took over the daily briefing of the president from the CIA, disbanding the CIA Center on Arms Control and Nonproliferation in favor of a nonproliferation center that reports to the new director, thereby downgrading the CIA and its director. It's likely that the director of National Intelligence will be no more able to coordinate government-wide activities among all the independent agencies in order to present rational understanding of events than former CIA directors were. Indeed, the problem is much worse as a result of greatly increased collection capacities. But the decision of Congress and the executive branch to accept a new bureaucratic structure intended to increase internal coordination of intelligence-gathering agencies is an example of an idea that conceptually sounds plausible—coordinating fifteen intelligence agencies, including the CIA, as an early warning against terrorist and possible terrorist activity—but in reality merely adds to the nightmare of state oppression. (As if there were not sufficient sharing, the Patriot Act Improvement and Reauthorization Act of 2006 included a provision to create a new position in the Justice Department, the assistant attorney general for National Security. The new position, said a Justice Department fact sheet in March 2006, would "allow the Justice Department to bring together its national security, counterterrorism, counterintelligence, and foreign intelligence surveillance operations under a single authority."

For government organizations, there are three important determinants of power in Washington during the rein of the National Security State. The first is access, which is usually achieved through money, although it can also occur for the one seeking access through moral persuasion or having an independent interest base. For example, well-connected Republican lobbyist Jack Abramoff used money to obtain access while presenting himself as an Orthodox-observant Jew. The second is through information, which may have the short life one might find in Internet chat rooms. The third is shooing away potential trespassers from your turf. Government agencies—or rather the entrenched bureaucrats who operate them—focus on the second and third determinants. Part of the job of government agencies such as the CIA, FBI, and NSA is expansion and infighting.

There is nothing in the Intelligence Act that will give the public greater access to governmental actions and policies. *Any* access is more to the point since for half a century, tens of thousands of people in the CIA and NSA have operated by their *own* closed rules with annual budgets into the billions. (The total annual intelligence budget is forty-four billion dollars.)[39] Even more dangerous intelligence agencies operate by developing for themselves a tradition that claims service to the state as its highest function and then operates out of the sight of citizens and elected representatives. (Congress will pass a feel-good authorization to establish a commission to declassify documents, but will not pass a one-hundred-thousand-dollar *total* appropriations budget for it!)

Bush II's creation of a director of National Intelligence—the so-called czar of the "intelligence community," a cabinet-level position—will prove a futile exercise because it will not take away from the Defense Department part of their intelligence function. The first czar selected by Bush, longtime diplomat John Negroponte, was controversial. When he was ambassador to Honduras in the 1980s, "the CIA station and the embassy were accused of turning a blind eye to torture and other abuses by the Hondurans, and of shading reports of the situation for political or ideological reasons."[40] The Pentagon, with support from Congress, will replace what might be lost to the intelligence czar with its own new agency. Similarly, the CIA and FBI will find ways of expanding their activities that will duplicate much of what the new intelligence organization under the president is supposed to do.

President Nixon sought to override the CIA by setting up an intelligence unit in the White House—the so-called "plumbers"—independent of both the CIA and the FBI. A White House advisor concocted what was called the Huston Plan.[41] It was intended to justify break-ins, surveillance, and other pollution of civil liberties through the prosecutorial process and the judicial system. The idea was rejected because FBI Director J. Edgar Hoover, of all people, believed it was "un-American" to trample on people's liberties. Now this intelligence plan in its most objectionable form has finally found its way into law under the rubric of greater coordination and efficiency. Indeed, the line between surveillance and criminal process has disappeared just as the line that assigned the FBI to domestic matters and the CIA to foreign "jurisdiction" has been erased. This is now thought of as a quaint fiction just as international law is thought of as "quaint" under Bush II. (To be charitable to Bush II, he merely followed more "liberal" presidents such as Nixon, Kennedy, and Clinton.)

The organizational structure of the new intelligence agency follows the pyramidal structure of the Defense Department, and we may expect the intelligence czar to try to expand his office by poaching on Defense and other agencies, who will respond by constructing parallel structures. Indeed, the fight organizationally will be between parallel structures claiming jurisdictional responsibilities over people, funding, and issues. In most cases, the CIA, FBI, and the Departments of Defense, State, and Treasury will not surrender pieces of their bureaucracy and jurisdiction either to the director of National Intelligence or the new guys on the block, the Department of Homeland Security. In other words, the director of National Intelligence and the other departments and agencies will have no choice but to be in a constant turf war. To believe that more intelligence and wisdom will result, that greater and more astute assessments will come forward, and that the intelligence czar will or should override political judgments is extremely naïve.

It is more important for purposes of analysis not to be ground down by the Intelligence Act; it is important to comprehend how it becomes part of the anatomical skeleton of the increasingly expanding National Security State. With the Department of Homeland Security, expanding Defense Department, local police functions, and crippling of courts' independence, another nail is driven into freedom and civil liberties. (Note: Michael Chertoff, who succeeded Tom Ridge as secretary of Homeland Security, was a primary author of the Patriot Act, including the "no bond" detention policy, when he headed the criminal division of the Justice Department under Ashcroft. Moreover, Chertoff was "a zealous proponent of the arrest of more than a thousand people, mostly Muslims, after

September 11—a roundup that resulted in widespread mistreatment of detainees but not a single terrorism-related charge.")[42]

There is a rule that hard cases make bad law. The result of September 11 and the willingness to test the limits of executive power by the Bush II administration proves the truth of this platitude.

Monitoring of Computers

Officials are allowed to subpoena the addresses and times of e-mail messages sent by terrorism suspects. E-mail communications are now equal to those made by telephone, for which the authorities can use a subpoena to obtain records of numbers called and the duration of calls.[43]

The question is who becomes a "suspect"? During the cold war, a communist suspect was anyone who had Russian or revolutionary books in his house. Even scholars who received foreign language books, articles, and other communications became suspects. Organizational leaders, as was the case at that time with the ACLU, became informers.[44] And those who spoke out or worked with groups on civil rights and peace issues were automatically suspect. The definition of a suspect is a wholly subjective judgment based on what? Information perhaps, hunches and prejudice no doubt; but it is always based on fear of freedom.

The chances of sending and receiving fake messages that entrap a terrorism suspect is greatly increased by the "monitors," including the director of National Intelligence, the CIA, and the FBI. However, the FBI has a real problem. In the wake of September 11, it spent one hundred and seventy million dollars to upgrade its antiquated computer system to include Internet surveillance technology designed to read e-mails and other online communications of suspected criminals, terrorists, and spies. But as Maureen Dowd wrote, the bureau's computers could not even accomplish "such difficult tasks as simultaneously searching for 'aviation' and 'schools.'"[45] The system was junked. The Bush II government turned to "private" enterprise to carry their water. In 2006, FBI Director Robert Mueller and Attorney General Gonzales asked the Internet companies America Online, Microsoft, Google, Verizon, and Comcast to retain records on the Web-surfing activities of their customers. These vast databases could be subpoenaed through existing law. This would further nullify the Fourth Amendment. Thus there is an open-ended character to the monitoring: it can go on for years, long after any FBI director or intelligence director or president has left the scene.

Money Laundering

The Treasury Department is able to require banks to make much greater efforts to determine the sources of large overseas private banking accounts. The Treasury is also able to impose sanctions on nations that refuse to provide information on depositors to American investigators.[46]

Shell Banks

American banks are barred from doing business with offshore shell banks, which have no connection to any regulated banking industry.[47]

These provisions of the Patriot Act focus on banking. Each can be enforced against *anyone* the government decides is an enemy of the United States—including people from the Middle East, people of color, those of Muslim faith, and so on. Courts may inhibit the state, but it will not be easy. However, if the government or Congress really bears down on individuals or institutions, the same provisions could also effect business relations that banks *in* the United States have with banks abroad that may launder money or invest in dubious enterprises. In either case, the law grants an open checkbook to prosecutors and is very tough to fight unless you happen to own an offshore bank that is used to skirt the banking rules of the United States.

Another of the ironies of the Patriot Act is that it undercuts the ideology of globalization as put forward by American corporations and politicians by prohibiting the enforcement of the free flow of goods and services internationally.

Questions About the Patriot Act Washington Never Asks

Will any of the Patriot Act's features really stop an attack on American society or a series of attacks by those who are enraged or disaffected? It is likely that the potential for such attacks now goes with the territory of being a superpower that refuses to rethink its own imperial policies.

Bush II's advisors—and those who will follow them—must know that if there is war without borders, or they *say* there is a war without borders, the only solution is that America frame and dictate terms for other nations that must bend to its sovereign will. In other words, Bush II authoritarians demand a strong state at home in terms of the military, curtailment of civil liberties, and a fading of the Bill of Rights into desuetude, as lawyers say. There are two other questions perhaps more important than the question of U.S. safety. As Americans forfeit more and more of their civil liberties, will they be bludgeoned into silence by a conflict between laws as odious as the segregation laws were? Has American democracy come this long way only to be stopped by the lingering ideology of Bush II, his administration, and future followers?

The truth is that sometimes it is the few—the dominated—who step over their own personal fears to take risks that put them in jeopardy, but whose actions extend freedom and say to the powerful: "Don't you cross this line!" "Enough of your lies!"

They claim that dignity and decency must inform our lives and therefore the lives of our institutions. They find in these institutions people who agree with them and support their claims. Together, the insider and the outsider work for positive change. In American history the people who have acted this way are numerous but unknown. It is one of the sad things about the way history is written that it does not take into account the numerous unsung heroes. The Internet, though, may help to close this gap.

In the final analysis, it is a citizen with others who writes his or her own script. Modern thought and practice have made it abundantly clear that each of us is framed by the choices of others and by institutions, which we must either confront or accept. Much of the outcome will depend on how passive Americans remain. This is why we need to act either for or against institutional structures and constraints that might be trampling on the future or on the graves of those who did so much to develop the freedom, and, yes, the security we have.[48] It is not elliptical or ironic to say that our liberty *is* our security. The Patriot Act and its allied laws are prime examples of what individuals must confront to ensure free speech and peaceful democracy, shed of imperial illusions, for their own sense of self—and self-protection.

Chapter 2

September 11: A Golden Opportunity for Bush II Conservatives

WAR WITHOUT END GIVES BUSH HIS WISH LIST

In politics, traumatic events are often used as a pretext to radically shift the focus of the nation. Pearl Harbor silenced the antiwar and isolationist forces in American politics—an objective devoutly wished for by the interventionists. September 11 gave the Bush II administration the excuse to put into place the agenda they really wanted before that infamous day but did not know how to handle in terms of public relations.

Before September 11, there still was a cloud over George W. Bush, a man with no foreign policy experience and limited domestic policy experience as a Texas governor. He did not complete his second term in this office, which seasoned Texas politicians see as largely symbolic. Bush II was not even really elected to the presidency: he did not get the popular vote, he was literally selected by the Supreme Court, and he was considered by much of the media and the academic community as an illegitimate leader. He was blessed, though, with a passive electorate and a Democratic Party diminished in purpose by the presidency of Bill Clinton, who was impeached and tried (though not convicted) in the months leading up to the 2000 election. Democrats, fearing a constitutional crisis, withdrew from the field of battle. In everyday life, this meant plutocracy and militarism punctuated by religious fervor as the American practice and ideal, as well as new modes of repression, developed through surveillance technology that profiles individuals.

When Bush took power, he took it very quickly because he understood—or his mentors understood—that unless he did, he would be on even thinner ice than he was at that moment. Machiavelli understood the notion of acting on cruelty quickly. FDR understood that in a tripartite government there was never much of a honeymoon. Bush I also understood this. So the Bush II advisors (some from Bush I, others from Reagan and Nixon, as well as the corporate patrons of conservative think tanks such as Richard Mellon Scaife, John M. Olin, Lynde and Harry Bradley, and Joseph Coors)[1] acted quickly. Their rule of politics was to charm adversaries, who were flabby on alternative policies, and move quickly to right-wing positions that would shock Democrats by their boldness. Not forty-eight hours after September 11, congressional Republicans tried to exploit the attack to pass a cut in the capital gains tax. An internal White House document that surfaced in 2002 revealed that Bush's reelection strategy would make the war on terrorism and domestic security his big issues. Incidentally, four years later, while gearing up for the congressional elections—despite the media blitz of Bush's war and his failure to privatize Social Security as a means of generating the doctrine of individualism and generating a bonanza for Wall Street and corporate investors—Republicans sought to make virtue out of vulnerability by doggedly making "national security" and spying on Americans their big issue. For Bush conservatives, it was a class issue: taking care of the richest people in America first.

There was and is every reason to be cynical about the conservative Right agenda, but the record of history goes beyond the 2002 campaign document. It is just a fact that there are ways in which leaders and their bureaucracies—both conservative and much less conservative—create the idea within people's minds that there are real dangers.

So September 11 and the subsequent wars in Afghanistan and Iraq gave the Bush II administration some of the items on their wish list that was drawn up by Rightists in 1992, though Ronald Reagan was its godfather.[2]

Such Rightists have no interest in traditional conservatives. "History has called us into action, here at home and internationally," Bush II said. "We've been given a chance to lead, and we're going to seize the moment in this country."[3] Bush's tough-guy stance is why the Right continues to talk about war without end because if the nation is always at war there is always a clear and present danger—even if leaders don't actually, immediately go to war against obvious enemies. In policy terms, this equals talking tough so that one *might* go to war. Forget the present. Forget the Iraq fiasco. Maybe next time it will be with Iran. Maybe next time it will be with North Korea or Syria or Hezbollah or maybe even with the Hamas in Palestine. There is no end to the possibilities if you are serious about the idea of war. Nothing is unthinkable. The idea of war without end is part of a future statement that is internalized into American habits so that it seems to define what the country is about. Of course, the idea of war without end is also a way—or so the Bush II administration has believed—to bring about massive changes within the United States.

To back up their war talk, when Bush II, Vice President Dick Cheney, and Secretary of Defense Donald Rumsfeld took power in 2000, they set out to "modernize" the military. To do this, they provided it with a more mobile army and increased firepower against a world with no comparable firepower that was not apt to get it unless they bought it from the United States, the number one conventional arms dealer in the world, controlling nearly half the market. America has been called the world's candy store for guns. "Anything you need to run a small guerrilla army, you can buy here in America," a gunrunner told *60 Minutes*. "You just have to have a credit card and a clear record."[4] U.S. arms sales to foreign nations totaled $177.5 billion between 1992 and 2003.[5]

Interestingly, the initial Bush defense budgets were not as much, or so it appeared, as what Al Gore intended in the case he won in 2000. Bush II quickly changed that after September 11. By 2006, military spending was a half-trillion dollars a year,[6] about 50 percent of the federal discretionary budget. As taxpayers began to feel it in their pocketbooks and see evidence of it in decreasing municipal and health care services and education, the military demanded countless billions more as it became clear that the Iraq War and other military needs were interminable, necessitating frequent multibillion-dollar infusions of supplemental budgets that are not part of the regular budget.

SUSPENSION OF CIVIL LIBERTIES WITHOUT END

War without end of the Bush II type has several new elements not seen since the founding of the country.

First, to the extent the president's people can get away with it, a moderate to severe suspension of civil liberties has occurred. Past presidents— John Adams, Thomas Jefferson, Abraham Lincoln, Woodrow Wilson, Franklin D. Roosevelt, Richard Nixon, and Ronald Reagan—suspended various civil liberties in times of war, but when the particular war was over, civil liberties were restored. But if the flames of war are fanned without end, then civil liberties can be suspended without end.

A second element of war without end is a new balancing act between unilateralism and multilateralism. The Bush people struck out on their own when it suited their agenda, and when that strategy backfired, they retreated a little, seeking allies to bail them out.

Third, much less attention is paid to questions of balance of power, which could have had the effect of keeping U.S. leaders in check from making bad judgments. Before going to war in Afghanistan in 2001, the Joint Chiefs of Staff were very cautious about intervention. They feared the Vietnam quagmire: being caught in a losing battle with the American public if the war took too long, revealing American moral flaws, and showing poor postmilitary planning while exposing the United States to defeat and an indefensible number of casualties. Such fears were realized soon after the Iraq occupation, even though the outcome was entirely predictable before the military dropped a single bomb.

The fourth new element of Bush II's war without end is that the United States attempted to rewrite or replace international law with American-framed imperial law that would exclude it from international punishment. Loosely stated, it is comparable to the way some want to exempt local police from punishment. The most notorious example was the United States' flouting of the Geneva Conventions, which long ago established international humanitarian standards for war including protecting prisoners of war from torture. In a 2002 draft memo to Bush, Alberto Gonzales—at the time White House Counsel—judged Geneva "obsolete" and "quaint," claiming that U.S. torture laws "do not apply to the president's detention and interrogation of enemy combatants."[7] This gave a green light to the torture and sexual humiliation of prisoners at American-run prisons in Abu Ghraib and Guantanamo. (Gonzales was promoted by Bush that year to replace Ashcroft as attorney general, but most of Ashcroft's programs remain on the books.)

Domestically, although Bush was simply carrying out a not-very-saintly tradition, the government would legitimate whatever it did through law and "inherent" executive power beyond constitutional constraints or through what might be called "para-law." Para-law can be described as directives created by the executive branch and national security bureaucracies that rely on custom, may be secret, and are usually outside of congressional accountability and public scrutiny. Para-law gives the appearance of deliberation, but its real purpose is to justify power, whatever the executive branch's purpose or intention. Thus, as a result of the Supreme Court decision in the *Hamdan* case, Bush II sought to give the *appearance* of accepting the Geneva Conventions. Such a method of governing ensures that the citizenry are supportive and compliant.

Fifth, the United States will seek the partial or full occupation of areas of the world where oil and other resources could be denied to us or where the prices could fluctuate severely, adversely affecting U.S. stability. Since oil comprises a quarter of U.S. imports, it follows that if nations deny us "our" oil, they will be considered a threat.

AS ALWAYS, DEMOCRATS ARE SHOCKED, SHOCKED

Some Republicans were sincere about a number of policies when they ran for office in 2000. Nothing was said about undercutting civil liberties per se, but they always aimed to pack the federal judiciary with extremely conservative judges who intended to destroy the last vestiges of the New Deal's economic policy decisions and the Warren Court's decisions favoring individual civil liberties and group rights such as class actions against corporations. That is what they did and continue to do in many cases. Before 2000, most Republicans, to maintain their coalition, supported antiabortion policies, the public display of the Ten Commandments, and prayer in the public schools. This program was integral to a 1950s-style states' rights agenda that implicitly favored resegregation. On the other hand, when it served the conservative purpose, Congress, with Bush's approval, passed a "midnight" law granting the parents of Terri Schiavo—a Florida woman who had existed in a persistent vegetative state for fifteen years—the right to sue in federal court to force the resumption of her life support. Republicans still continued to favor executions despite declining public support for the death penalty—except in Illinois, where a Republican governor, George Ryan, led the way against execution because of no DNA evidence. The death penalty continued to disturb the courts. In an action that stunned conservatives and liberals, but for different reasons, the Supreme Court struck down the death penalty for juveniles under the age of eighteen in 2005, stating that their decision was required by the Eighth Amendment's prohibition of cruel and unusual punishment and because the Court wanted to end U.S. international isolation. "It is fair to say," wrote Republican Justice Anthony Kennedy, invoking the United Nations' Convention on the Rights of the Child, "that the United States now stands alone in a world that has turned its face against the juvenile death penalty.... The opinion of the world community, while not controlling our outcome, does provide respected and significant confirmation for our own conclusions."[8]

Long before the Bush II people came into power, conservatives were prepared to get out of various longstanding treaties, or not sign certain treaties, or weaken or not carry out treaties, or generally sabotage any treaty or agreement they did not like—in defiance of the Constitution, which makes any treaty ratified by the Senate "the supreme law of the land." However, the Constitution is silent on how the United States can renounce a treaty or whether such renouncements are the province of the executive branch or Congress. Thus, when Bush II came to power, he deliberately muddied the waters on which treaties his administration would renounce and which treaties they would pretend to adopt. The result created great instability in the international legal and diplomatic system. Renouncing treaties was an important link in the chain of replacing settled international law with American imperial law. This has been the conservative Rightist project all along. Conservatives said in effect: "We want the freedom to do what we want, and furthermore we don't believe in treaties—they are worthless pieces of paper." One scholar counted up some twenty-seven actions in which the United States postponed or withdrew from treaty obligations, even those we first initiated like the International Criminal Court. Some analysts contend that in reality the United States follows a treaty even after we pull out of it, but this is an unconvincing argument. A partial list of "ex-treaties" highlights the disregard conservatives have for the rest of the world—and for the freedom at home the treaties helped protect:[9]

- The Nuclear Nonproliferation Treaty

- The Comprehensive Nuclear Test Ban Treaty

- The Anti-Ballistic Missile Treaty, which among other dangers banned space-based missile defenses; renunciation triggered a possible nuclear war in the skies

- The Biological Weapons Convention (which was thirty years old)
- The Chemical Weapons Convention
- The International Criminal Court, which eight-nine other nations have joined
- The Fissile Material Cutoff Treaty

Other instances of the Bush II administration's reluctance or refusal to participate in treaties include the following:

- The Bush II administration only gave tepid support to the Nunn-Lugar Act, which was designed to dispose of Russian nuclear weapons and weapons-grade material so it would not fall into the wrong hands by theft or sale. Former Senator Sam Nunn said, "If one of the great cities of the world goes up in smoke, and you look back on [bureaucratic hurdles], it will make our retroactive rear-view mirror look at September 11th [seem] like a waltz."[10]

- The United States did not sign a treaty against torture because it would have had to report and aggregate all police violations at all levels of the government.

Besides such instances, Bush II refused to sign the Kyoto Protocol, an international agreement to stem global warming. It went into effect in 2005 after one hundred and twenty nations—nearly all of them industrialized—ratified it. Clinton signed the Kyoto Protocol in 1998 after a decade of research from respected scientists demonstrated that gas emissions trapped in the atmosphere attributable to human activities—the "greenhouse effect"—were putting the earth's climate at risk, adversely affecting the air and the oceans.[11] Kyoto's goal was to reduce the greenhouse effect by just 5.2 percent by 2012. Some scientists, though, believe the earth needs "20 times Kyoto" to rescue the environment.[12] Although the United States is responsible for a quarter of the world's gas emissions, Bush II said signing Kyoto "would have wrecked our economy."[13]

The refusal flew in the face of dramatic environmental results achieved by Portland, Oregon, released in 2005—about the time Bush failed to support the Kyoto Protocol. Since 1993, Portland and surrounding Multnomah County dramatically reduced greenhouse gas emissions to below the level of 1990—down 13 percent per capita—while bringing huge benefits, including less tax money spent on energy, which helped local businesses win contracts worldwide.[14]

In 2002 and 2003, the White House removed data on the risks of global warming from public reports of the Environmental Protection Agency (EPA).[15] In 2005, the New York Times reported that in 2002 and 2003, Philip Cooney, chief of staff for the White House Council on Environmental

Quality, "removed or adjusted descriptions of climate research that government scientists and their supervisors, including some senior Bush administration officials had already approved."[16] Cooney was not a scientist, but he was an expert at playing down the effects of greenhouse gas. As a lobbyist at the American Petroleum Institute, where he headed the climate program, he led the oil industry's fight against limits on gas emissions. Two days after the *Times* article, Cooney resigned from the White House and went to work for Exxon Mobil.

THE BUSH FEAR FACTOR

Another thing that changed for the worse after September 11 was the welling up of fear among the populace and Bush II's determination to capitalize—as columnist Helena Cobban put it—on the "'terrorist threat' in order to keep Americans in a state of fearfulness."[17] It was as simple as that. And as dangerous as that.

FDR's warning to America about fear took on ominous inverted meanings during Bush II. His administration played on American insecurity and vulnerability for the purpose of increasing White House command authority in the National Security State and decreasing the role of civil liberties in American society. For Bush II and Cheney, there was not only a threat from abroad but also a new threat from within. That threat included those people deemed unpatriotic because they questioned the policies of the administration or came from the wrong parts of the world, judging by their dress or look.

Alexis de Tocqueville's *The Old Regime and the French Revolution*, written in 1856, can be applied to the situation today: the revolution occurs, but who then comes into power? The answer is the bureaucracy, who have readied their various plans and will push them forward any way they can. This was a major reason Bush II and his Republican predecessors were committed to breaking the civil service—"privatizing" it—for fear that New Deal–type plans hidden in the desks of bureaucrats would reemerge if Bush II and his successors were interrupted from their grand project.

Older and younger conservatives—there is little difference between them except some of the younger ones are more to the right—have a very clearly articulated view of what this world should be: the United States is triumphant, always victorious. They say, "We set the terms of reference. We can use nuclear weapons if and when we want. We can mobilize a population here at home for that purpose. We are rich and our definition of capitalism is different from other countries' brands of capitalism in that we insist that it can be used to dominate other cultures." Such elements comprise the framework of the Right's agenda—an imperial oligarchic agenda with the Christian Right acting as the wedge for popular support. But the Right is hardly alone in this view. In the grand sweep of American foreign and national security since the Second World War, the framework of U.S. policy is that we expect all nations to follow our lead, whether or not they are in an alliance with us.

CONSERVATIVE VS. CONSERVATIVE

For all the seeming power of the conservative machine, it is overrated by both liberals and conservatives—and by the media. There has been and is a split in conservative ranks.

Conservatives are caught in all kinds of contradictions, which are managed through coalitions around slogans. There are conservative factions that are not in agreement in what they believe and what they will act on. This does not mean that they eschew working together when it means obtaining power. Of course, there are certain agreed-upon premises. For one, voting should be restricted and maybe, if no one is watching, the "wrong" people should be prevented from voting, like blacks in the 2000 Florida elections and the 2004 Ohio elections.

Some Rightists like Newt Gingrich speak as if they are populists trying to get elected. This is nonsense. Rightist Libertarians in places like the Cato Institute often have the kind of faith in the so-called free market that others reserve for belief in God. They claim to want virtually no government at all as a means to assure personal liberty. They say: "We care about property; we accept the corporation. The obvious contradiction is the dependence of the defense corporations on government for their profitability.

Some conservatives such as Bush II and Cheney—before they occupied the White House—favored states' rights. But more moderate conservatives are not as enthusiastic. The radical intervention into the Schiavo case by the conservative Congress and president was a political miscalculation that accentuated the split between "social" conservatives and "process" conservatives. Christopher Shays, a moderate Republican congressman, said, "My party is demonstrating that they are for states' rights unless they don't like what the states are doing."[18]

There are conservatives who are isolationist and oppose interventions whether they are called humanitarian or triumphal. A sharp philosophical disagreement within the editorial board of the *National Interest*—the leading conservative magazine—over U.S. occupation in Iraq caused "10 well-known board members, including...Midge Decter, Samuel P. Huntington, and Francis Fukuyama," to resign in 2005.[19] Another part of the conservative movement is unabashedly nationalist and imperialist. They favor interventions domestically and internationally. They are more prone to want to squelch freedom of speech and introduce more surveillance. They are certainly not afraid of imprisoning thousands and supporting anti-immigration policies.

Regarding the conservative split on the immigrant question, xenophobic instincts govern. As it was throughout the twentieth century, immigration is still an important aspect of electoral politics. Industrialists once wanted immigrants from eastern Europe as cheap labor; labor unions were strongly opposed because it would create a large pool of unorganized workers. Now the scenario has been reversed. Since American corporations can go abroad for cheap labor, immigration has been seen as undercutting the moral fabric of the nation, adding to welfare rolls. Labor unions in desperate need of relevance and membership now accept immigration, hoping the "new Americans" will support social welfare legislation even as they continue their strong Christian fundamentalist beliefs.

There are antiabortion conservatives based largely in the Southwest and South who relate to faith-based politics. They believe: "We have to be religious; this is a religious country as we've been taught by Billy Graham." They are committed to the righteousness of their causes and are willing to be at war (like bombing abortion clinics) for their pro-life beliefs. Christian fundamentalists believe in their grassroots power, and they have pushed aside conservative nonbelievers.

None of these issues, however, reflect a basic conservative split, that is, one that would have caused the Rightist leaders to split apart from the more moderate wing. Ideology in politics—sometimes—is strong, as are personal principles. But they are not as strong as the drive for power and retention of power and one's seat at its seductive table.

So here is this disparate group of conservatives seemingly marching under a single banner. But the question is: what is the conservative project beyond finding a way to rid the nation of the social reforms that were made over the last three generations? Remember, it is the Right that felt put upon by those who wished for a new covenant of inclusiveness, of improvement in the status of the many people denied a public voice. Indeed, in fairness to their position, inclusiveness changes institutions and conservative assumptions, which, conservatives like to claim, are the basis of a well-ordered society where "everyone knows his place."

But such a belief in the social structure of nonenvy and pyramidalism is hard to sustain in a democratic society based on aspiration and market capitalism. Nonetheless, an underlying fact of American life is that there is a working class, and polls suggest that they are not split over the economic purposes that FDR claimed for the New Deal. However, Americans do rely on stability and the guarantee of a future with a pension sufficient to live at an adequate level. Just as capitalists had expectations in terms of profit, so workers had their own expectations, regardless of their politics. They expected their pensions as a result of work done throughout their lives, not as a gift but as a contract. Since the New Deal, workers, like the middle class of small businessmen, believed that they would be protected by capitalism and hard work. For the foreseeable future, it is likely that millions of people will be sorely disappointed—and worse. The bonds of affection that existed between millions of people seemed to speak to a new definition of the social contract, politics, and democracy. One of the most important elements of the civil rights movement was its nonviolent characteristics that started from the idea of affection between people as the basis of politics. When what the Declaration of Independence calls the "bonds of affection" are broken, the results can be catastrophic, leading to war. It should be noted that the women's movement has not only been a struggle for rights but the repair of affection between people. These movements were sustained through free speech accompanied by collective action. This notion of affection was at the heart of the social contract, dependent, as all contracts are, on trust. But such a direction faces another force of history: the old politics of fear, controlled war, resource hogging, and irremediable inequalities.

Bush II might not have been able to hold his coalition together had he not acted with the "aura" of command when he became president in January 2001. But for all of Bush's strutting, September 11 saved his coalition and got most citizens behind him, at least for a period of time. For the Rightist leaders, the despicable horror of New York and Washington was an organizing political principle—the basis for reorganizing the state, even the society, behind a selected president.

Whether Rightist leaders from the Bush II era and others who may follow are clever enough to keep this conservative movement together is up in the air after the disasters, natural and manmade, that took place at the beginning of Bush II's second term: from Hurricane Katrina to corruption involving his advisers and some members of Congress and their staffs.

All administrations have their scandals; sometimes they pass and are hardly remembered in history. Bush II and the conservative Rightists' direction shows that the perpetrators do not know they have done wrongly by conventional standards of public morality and responsibility. Indeed, they seem to be rewarded for their efforts and antediluvian stance. By flying the flag of patriotic war, they and prudent imperialists of both political parties thought they found an organizing principle for mass mobilization and citizenship that FDR found in the Second World War. Then it was Nazis. Now they seek to make it terrorists and their tactics.

Chapter 3

Lessons about Terrorism the Government Never Learns

WAS SEPTEMBER 11 REALLY A BOLT OUT OF THE BLUE?

Why was al-Qaeda's attack on the Twin Towers at the World Trade Center and the Pentagon a shock to Americans—and seemingly to our government? Why was it a surprise that its promoter was Osama bin Laden? Just eight years earlier, in 1993, there were indications that Osama's al-Qaeda, or one of its growing associated groups, bombed one of the Twin Towers (killing six, injuring over one thousand, and causing extensive damage)[1] and attacked U.S. forces in Mogadishu. In 1996, al-Qaeda very likely bombed the U.S. Air Force barracks in Saudi Arabia, killing nineteen servicemen. In 1998, al-Qaeda bombed American embassies in Kenya and Tanzania. In 2000, it crippled and nearly sank the USS Cole in Yemen.[2]

Before September 11, the United States accepted these casualties as the cost of being an empire. In fact, officials in the Bush II government were very much aware of the likelihood of an attack on the United States:

- January 25, 2001, five days after George W. Bush was sworn in as president, counterterrorism chief Richard Clarke, a holdover from the Clinton administration, wrote in a memo to Condoleezza Rice, who was then national security advisor: "We *urgently* need a Principals level review of the al Quida [*sic*] network."[3]

- August 6, 2001, during a month-long vacation at his Crawford, Texas, ranch, Bush received a CIA report titled "Bin Laden Determined to Attack Inside the United States."[4]

- September 4, 2001, a Principals meeting was held for the first time since Clarke's urgent January 25 memo.[5]

Later, Rice would say, "I don't think anybody could have predicted that these people would take an airplane and slam it into the World Trade Center...that they would try to use an airplane as a missile."[6] History will determine why Bush and his advisors sat on their hands.

What was shocking was that al-Qaeda used American planes—that Americans died for their purpose. After a lifetime of being filled with stories of our invulnerability as a superpower, despite the threat of nuclear attack—nuclear bombs in the form of missiles and, in so-called modern times, nuclear bombs in suitcases—Americans never thought anything like this could occur on their soil by a supposedly technically challenged guerrilla group.

The reason for the belief in invulnerability is that historically the United States has had a "forward defense perimeter." This means there have been at least seven hundred U.S. bases—including secret bases—in some one hundred and thirty countries stretching from Greenland to South Africa, from Japan through Europe to the Middle East. These have been buttressed by an armada of thirteen naval task forces, all so that we could fight wars elsewhere.[7]

Before September 11, not many could imagine that we would fight a war on American soil anymore; wasn't that taken care of by destroying the American Indians and by the Southern rebellion? So in order to fight wars continuously all over the world—and not in the United States—it was necessary to have an imperial thrust that would not only sustain American sovereignty but also inhibit that of other nations. One of the effects of this was an increase of the number of police-type activities that the United States undertakes to protect its borders, which it does by going into other countries, thereby extending our borders and strategic reach.

The facts of September 11 and the negligence of the Bush II administration should not be minimized, but if Americans really want to learn from the attack—and there are critical lessons to be learned—we need to move beyond emotionalism, even grief, and get at the root of what caused September 11 and other kinds of attacks we have put ourselves in a position to attract.

LESSONS ABOUT WAR—AND PERHAPS ABOUT PEACE

Lesson 1: The Price of Triumphalism

After the initial shock and despair, there was the fear in many parts of the country—mostly from liberals and moderates—that the attacks would lead to the ultimate National Security State in which elections, so far as they touched on war and peace issues, would be beside the point. The fear came from the fact that leaders of both major political parties—including, for example, Democrats like Senator Joseph Lieberman—would put the nation on a permanent war footing. The fear had been borne out after the 2000 elections and reinforced by the 2004 elections.

Both Democrats and Republicans believe in American triumphalism. Democrats believe in "prudent imperialism" and Republicans believe in "nationalist triumphalism." Both are bounded by the realities of budget costs. Neither party can or will find a way at this stage to dismantle the national security apparatus and escape superpower hubris. Democrats believe in a "bipartisan" foreign policy that is supposedly more nuanced than that of the Republicans. But these are slight distinctions. They do not solve the fundamental problem that is as important for this century as slavery was for the nineteenth century: how much freedom can the citizen expect in a National Security State that accepts, if not demands, permanent conflict, possibly permanent war, and the unaccountability of global corporations?

Lesson 2: The Price of Language

Since September 11, the country has seemed unaware of the language of deciding that certain people are "terrorists" and certain people are "zealots" and how to deal with each group. The distinction is not trivial because correct usage will tell the public and perhaps some lawmakers whether such people are to be dealt with in the context of law and international law or if our response is war against those who are assigned the status of terrorist by government and in turn by our follow-the-leader broadcast media.

A way to begin to understand the present American predicament is to acknowledge that there is a difference between a terrorist and a zealot and the shades of meaning cannot be glossed over by the Right or Left.

A zealot is prepared to die, prepared to end it all with a premeditated, self-inflicted bomb blast in a public space. Yet we continue to wonder why an Iraqi zealot or Palestinian zealot—any zealot—kills himself or herself blowing up a police station in Baghdad or a bus in Jerusalem. There are obvious answers. Iraqi insurgents and Palestinian insurgents know that the cost in "military benefits" (one zealot gives his or her life to kill scores of the "enemy," civilian or not) is far superior for them than it is for their adversaries (Americans, Israelis, UN forces), who depend on technology for mass killing. They know that "collateral damage" is a term of propaganda, not war as it is fought by both sides.

But the interesting thing about war is that when it is mobilized from the top down in the lofty offices of the White House and Defense Department, you expect the soldier to be prepared to die or to be grievously wounded. That is what soldiers are signed on to do. If we are rich and technologically oriented, we are going to give soldiers the equipment they need, soften up the enemy, and invent new techniques to lessen their chances of dying. But in the final analysis, a soldier signs on to accept death. (But not everybody does, apparently. In 2005, the army did not meet its recruiting goals. So bad had the administration's handling of the Iraq War become that parents feared that their children could be injured or killed for no good reason.)[8]

Zealots on principle are prepared to sacrifice themselves for religious reasons much in the way that the Temple in Jerusalem was destroyed among the ancient Jewish Zealots. In that case, the notion was: let's hold out for as long as possible, but we know that we are going to die in the end. Zealots may or may not be fanatics. Their concern is not immediate victory in this world but for Allah. (However, Nathan Hale, the great American secular patriot, said, "I only regret that I have but one life to give to my country." His life-size statue with this inscription stands near the entrance of the original headquarters building of the CIA. Terrorists, however, want to come back and fight another day. They are prepared to do this again and again, although in the final analysis they, too, are prepared to pay with their lives.)

Terrorists, however, want to come back and fight another day. They are prepared to do this again and again, although in the final analysis they, too, are prepared to pay with their lives.

In the United States, we should be very precise about what we mean by terrorists; the term has become a catchall around the world since the collapse of empires. In Sudan, for example, journalists are sometimes called terrorists; this presumably happens when they take the government to task. In China, dissenters are called terrorists. All the more reason to be careful that every movement for this, that, or the other reason is not identified as terrorism. Otherwise, there will be no distinction between insurgency, nonviolence, and terrorism. Such a reality will then play into the hands of reactionaries in the United States trying to freeze the world into their fundamentalist status quo.

As some are beginning to grasp, there is also "state" terrorism. But this term has different meanings to different groups. The U.S. attacks on Cuba over the last forty years are examples of state terrorism, whether they have been attempts to kill Castro, destroy Cuban agricultural crops, blow up various facilities, or limit American tourism. On the other hand, Bush II, with the support of a compliant media, sold the idea that Saddam Hussein's Iraq was a terrorist state even though the United States supported Saddam in his war with Iran in the 1980s. (Remember the photograph of Donald Rumsfeld, then special envoy of President Reagan, warmly shaking hands with Saddam in Baghdad in 1983?) The United States looked the other way when Saddam used internal terror as a means of preventing the dissolution of Iraq into warring religious and nonreligious groups.

Not since the Church Senate Committee hearings in 1975 has there been a congressional investigation into a subject American leaders want brought up: namely, American state terrorism.[9] The 9/11 Commission investigation in 2004 (which Bush initially opposed) did not come close to getting at the whole truth of the American purpose and its effects on the politics of the Middle East.[10] Like Latin America, the Middle East has been designated by American policymakers as a military and political opportunity for American, western European, and Russian (Soviet) geopoliticians. This may explain why Bush blithely repeated the fiction of the link of Iraq with al-Qaeda terrorists, despite all evidence to the contrary. By 2006, the media—finally—was less compliant. (Virtually none of the recommendations of the 9/11 Commission is even suggestive of how the war on terror is to be won. Nor is it clear what terrorism really is, how it relates to American foreign and national security policy, or how it can be stopped.)[11]

Whether state terrorists or insurgent terrorists simply manifest their incapacity to find suitable political outlets for their anger and frustration, they believe in change in the here and now. Certainly the Jewish terrorist gangs in the 1940s in Palestine, which was then controlled by Britain, thought they were fighting about freedom and oppression. And Yitzhak Shamir and Menachem Begin, who were terrorist leaders, each ended up being prime minister of democratic Israel. The same is true of other new states as well.

Lesson 3: The Anger over U.S. Foreign Policy

In virtually all discussions of terrorism, there are very few in Congress who want to investigate American foreign policy in order to ascertain what it is that so angers certain sectors of the world. Is it likely that there is more than crazed irrationality that motivates the terrorists?

One possible answer is that in stories of international intrigue, where wars are covert or small scale, it may be more productive to follow the money and the players who personally benefited because national security and personal profit and livelihood are invariably intertwined. Take the development of an oil pipeline from Turkmenistan through western Afghanistan and Pakistan to the Indian Ocean. It so happened that in 2003, a consultant to Unocal Corporation—which held substantial oil and gas contracts in that region—Zalmay Khalilzad, became U.S. ambassador to Afghanistan and, in 2005, ambassador to Iraq. (In January 1998, Khalizad, who was born in Afghanistan but had long been a Washington foreign policy insider, signed a letter to President Clinton from the Project for the New American Century stating that "American policy toward Iraq is not succeeding.... The only acceptable strategy is one that eliminates the possibility that Iraq will be able to use or threaten to use weapons of mass destruction. In the near term, this means a willingness to undertake military action as diplomacy is clearly failing. In the long term, it means removing Saddam Hussein and his regime from power. That now needs to become the aim of American foreign policy." Other signatories included future Iraq War architects Donald Rumsfeld, Paul Wolfowitz, Richard Perle, and William Kristol, editor of the influential right-wing *Weekly Standard*.)

Another answer is that just as Osama bin Laden, al-Qaeda, and many other groups in the Middle East wanted the United States out and were prepared to kill for that purpose, so the United States and various corporations were equally prepared to stay in the Middle East for political, economic, social, and religious reasons, using armed force, death squads, and rhetoric about democracy, freedom, and free markets. Osama bin Laden did Allah's work with the purpose of creating a theocracy through murder, and America's leaders and energy corporations say they did their work by protecting our way of life—that is, boundless oil consumption and wastefulness.

BUT DON'T LET TERRORISTS OFF THE HOOK

Present-day terrorists are criminals, and they should be held to account as criminals. However, they only can be held that way, completely legally, if the United States helps build up, rather than derail, the International Criminal Court and an international system that supports such a court and process.[12] But the United States opposes an international court on the grounds that we do not want to be held responsible under international law for *our* state terrorism.

That is to say, there is a great deal of cynicism around the meaning of terrorism, especially if the United States decides that it wants to feel or do certain things with impunity. The point is that there must be a rule of law across the board that makes sense for everybody in the world. The United States assumes that "collateral damage," because it is not intentional against innocent populations, cannot be thought of as terrorism. This argument falls of its own weight once casualty lists of noncombatants and their appalling numbers are examined.

If the United States really subscribed to an International Criminal Court, that might very limit aggressive war and insurgent attacks on civilizations. Indeed, the European Union has such a court—with growing legitimacy.

Leaders of large states in past negotiations have objected to an International Criminal Court on the grounds of sovereignty and the argument that nonelected judges (not dissimilar from our own nonelected federal judges) should not be able to decide the fate of millions of people. This concern is only partly valid since those who sit on the court will be vetted by the General Assembly and the Security Council. Cases are prosecuted only where the criminal offense is egregious and where the state in question refuses its responsibilities under international law. This is hardly a standard that nations, no matter how jealous of their sovereignty, should have trouble accepting. As nation-states stumble while finding their place in a nonimperialist, interdependent world, the question of the role of international agencies deserves serious attention. A solid case can be made in the legal sphere itself, where laws are increasingly "transnationalized" and national supreme courts (like our own) apply standards found in comparative law of other nations and international law.[13]

The answer also must be seen in something other than legal terms. U.S. governments through the years thought that they knew the answer; they thought the answer was through the hammer and anvil of war, accompanied by the American media's derisive and humiliating comments about Arabs, Muslims, and Palestinians. But punishing civilians and the wretched with economic sanctions, or finally waging war on them, does not work. What needs to be done—call it the last resort or the pragmatic first—however offensive it may be initially, is to adopt and follow the standards of international human rights that demand that *no one* be left out of public discourse. Since violence in the twenty-first century only breeds more violence and worse forms of it, continuous discourse (including through the Internet), serious sustained diplomacy (as opposed to bullying threats), and new rules of what is really old-fashioned common sense and common behavior are the only ways to control violence. The starting point should be through UN resolutions and the various economic and political covenants.

But there has been little public discourse around these questions, especially since the rise of Bush II. Many problems, however, were created by past administrations, as Senator J. William Fulbright proved. Fulbright, a former chairman of the Senate Foreign Relations Committee during the Vietnam War, exposed the roots of American official actions toward the rest of the world. Students of Fulbright exposed American arrogance to the rest of the world.[14] Since Bush II's vow to hunt down every last terrorist was mathematically absurd, other things must be seriously examined.

First, terrorism, whether waged by rich or poor, also has to be seen as a mode of communication. The terrorist is saying: "I am here and don't think that I am not here. Now pay attention!" Americans *do* pay attention to terrorism. But contrary to the views of leaders like Bush II, this is not the kind of attention that will change the relationship of the United States to the world in a positive way. And if one believes that such justice is for "girlie-men" (as Governor Arnold Schwarzenegger so elegantly put it), that will still not change the relationship of the United States to the world in a pragmatic way either.

Second, what is in our policy—the West's economic-social-political policy—that is causing this sort of extraordinary fearlessness amongst the insurgents, the dispossessed, and the humiliated? Throughout the West and parts of the Middle East, there is a sense of futility that grips large numbers of people who feel robbed of their identity and dignity. They believe that there is nothing to be gained from secular values of capitalism and socialism. Many have no interest in democracy. Yet many of the poor believe that they are trapped with no possibility of bettering themselves economically. It is in this context that the hereafter seems desirable to so many. Leaders of al-Qaeda, Hezbollah, and Hamas were quick to seize the moment and build schools and health clinics for the poor. And while the leaders were doing that, they preached the importance of heroism and self-sacrifice. So this kind of sentiment grows, and it has very much been growing since the assassination of Anwar Sadat, president of

Egypt, in 1981. These attitudes become a very important element in dealing with the whole diplomatic question.

Except through back channels in the CIA, the moral position of the United States neither recognizes nor negotiates with gangs, thugs, or terrorists. Nevertheless, we simply must deal with people who have different points of view, who have no real home or no so-called state sovereignty to protect them, and who have lived through certain injustices and want those injustices to stop. Negotiating may not stop these injustices totally, but it would tend to change the atmosphere and relationship between hostile parties.

Third, there is the assumption of unfounded arrogance that, somehow, America knows the answers to everybody's problems and an American president has the right—backed up by America's military and economic power—to insist on these answers for the world. So having decided the question of the United States as the unchallenged superpower—quietly formalized as a defense doctrine inside the Pentagon and Bush I White House, by Secretary of Defense Dick Cheney and then undersecretary of Defense for Policy Paul Wolfowitz, it should not come as a surprise that the United States is the clear target. This is especially true when the wretched have real complaints about their condition and when others view our technologically advanced system as reinforcing cultural permissiveness and unabated militarism—much to the chagrin of fundamentalists everywhere, even though they are happy to use technology for their ends. (Ironically, the Christian Right's Pat Robertsons and Jerry Falwells of the world would find much to admire in bin Laden's religious dogmatism, although one doubts if they would adopt his views on polygamy.)

Fourth, for sanity's sake and for the sake of the next generation, we must come to grips with the fact that we live in the world as it is, not as a utopian—or Bush II conservative—might wish it to be.

SECURITY FOR YOU MAY NOT BE SECURITY FOR ME

When the word "security" is used, it raises the important question: whose security are we really talking about?

As a result of the September 11 attack directly on the United States, security is now defined much more broadly for American society: it trades individual space, civil liberties, and other kinds of free speech for what political leaders say is "security." It intends to encompass the entire society and all its aspects. However, prior to September 11, an argument could have—and should have—been made that national security in the way it was defined during the cold war was really the basis for American imperialism abroad but with a handful of expanded civil liberties thrown in.

The Supreme Court "energized" civil liberties, as conservatives claimed. It was the Warren Court that responded to the protection of voter rights and desegregation. The Warren Court carved out rights to privacy in a period when individuals were losing their personal space, exercise of freedom of thought, speech, association, and movements. By the late 1950s to the end of Nixon's presidency, it seemed as if the movements for social justice that included millions of people had their champions in the Supreme Court majority.[15]

The Bush II administration, which started out as supposedly a quasi-isolationist administration, turned itself into an administration that little interest in the point of view of other nations. The Bush task was to enhance U.S. security. Their new domestic mission asserted its legitimacy through war and social control parading as security and Bush II's definition of "civilization."

Suddenly, its mission was to assert its legitimacy through war and social control parading as security. This was mediated through the National Security State, which in fact has a very particular role to play internally now in the United States both in terms of social control and in terms of managing imperialism. Bush II made some diplomatic gestures to soften this stance in his second term, then turned around and selected conservative unilateralists Paul Wolfowitz, deputy secretary of Defense, to head the multilateralist World Bank, and John R. Bolton, undersecretary of State for Arms Control and International Security—who had derided the United Nations—to be his UN ambassador. Was Bush throwing a few bones to his conservative base or were these two more examples of a president who seemed to enjoy sticking a finger in the world's eye?

September 11 also heightened nationalism and brought out a sense of patriotism. People and institutions that rarely if ever flew the American flag before began flying it every day. Suddenly, "God Bless America" was sung at public events; it was even heard at public Christmas caroling. In the beginning, this was moving, perhaps necessary. Then, inadvertently, it began legitimizing Bush II's policies. It is interesting that after September 11, intellectuals like Michael Walzer—an editor of *Dissent* magazine, who certainly sees himself as part of the Left and whose stock in trade is distinguishing between just and unjust wars (in his mind the Israelis are fighting just wars)—signed a statement sponsored by the conservative, faith-based Institute for American Values, which was also signed by such Rightists as Francis Fukuyama (whose position changed radically by 2006), Samuel Huntington, and Michael Novak.

Another interesting feature of the post–September 11 period was that it gave the moribund North Atlantic Treaty Organization new purpose—but on American terms. The Bush II administration continued Bill Clinton's strategy of spearheading NATO's expansion into eastern Europe while changing it from a defensive and internal security alliance into something akin to the alliances for policing the poor that was so prevalent before the First World War.

These purposes of NATO are transformative. Those who have been arguing that there is a struggle between modernism and a particular kind of Middle-Ages Muslim civilization claim that the struggle will go on and that the so-called modern world—whether ideologically capitalist, socialist, or even authoritarian—will organize together against the Muslims in places like the Middle East, France, the Philippines, and Indonesia. In part, this is because the state structures in each of these countries—except for France—are very weak and can be attacked with impunity.

The American position as the sole superpower seemed unassailable before September 11. It was generally believed that "permission" had to be granted by the United States for any major policy a third world nation might want to initiate. To this end, the United States was prepared to use covert and overt means to get its way. Now the United States may find itself in a quid pro quo situation where it must give much more in order to remain the leader of the world. That is what has happened in terms of apparent deals cut with Pakistan, India, Russia, China, and others. These nations are saying, "if you want X, you will have to give up Y." Our military dominance does not necessarily mean that the weaker nations will automatically go along with us, as we've seen with France, Germany, Spain, and others before and during the Iraq War. Nor does it mean that winning a war guarantees a stable peace, as we have also seen time and again, Iraq being the latest agonizing example.

American policy makers are being presented with hard lessons. But with the Bush II people and conservatives of their mold, citizens must be concerned. It appears conservative minds are stuffed with clichés and visions of domination while their eyes are shielded from reality and their hearts hardened against suffering that they participated in or initiated. These men of action, who never served in combat, had certitude and were invariably prepared to take risks—with the lives of others.

Chapter 4

When Is Danger Clear and Present?

SOMETIMES, YOU CAN SHOUT, "FIRE!"

Would Justice Oliver Wendell Holmes Jr. have thought that freedom of speech gave George W. Bush the right to "shout" that Iraq was a "clear and present danger" to America?

The "clear and present danger" doctrine, one of the most famous legal doctrines in American history, was born out of *Schenck v. United States* in 1919. The question before the Supreme Court was whether the defendant, Charles Schenck, the general secretary of the Socialist Party of America, had a First-Amendment right to distribute pamphlets opposed to the draft during the First World War.

Holmes believed that the context of the words mattered. His concern was not whether free speech in a particular case was an absolute right (which he did not care much about), but whether Congress could be stopped from doing their job during wartime. The Court ruled unanimously that Charles Schenck did not have that right. In his classic opinion, Holmes wrote:

> We admit that in many places and in ordinary times the defendants in saying all that was said in the circular would have been within their constitutional rights. But the character of every act depends upon the circumstances in which it is done. The most stringent protection of free speech would not protect a man in *falsely shouting fire in a theatre and causing a panic* [italics added]. It does not even protect a man from an injunction against uttering words that may have all the effect of force. The question in every case is whether the words used are used in such circumstances and are of such a nature as to *create clear and present danger* [italics added] that they will bring about the substantive evils that Congress has a right to prevent. It is a question of proximity and degree. When a nation is at war many things that might be said in time of peace are such a hindrance to its effort that their utterance will not be endured so long as men fight and that no Court could regard them as protected by any constitutional right.[1]

Schenck was the Court's first important free-speech decision. Yet in *Abrams v. United States* that same year, Holmes *dissented* and made a pitch for free speech. Thus clear and present danger was not thought to be an absolutistic standard for free speech.

But it is *Schenck* that presidents have exploited ever since, as Bush did when the danger of Saddam Hussein to the United States either was unclear or patently false but in both cases seriously undermined the freedoms of Americans he was sworn to protect.

HOW THE QUEST FOR SECURITY LEADS TO INSECURITY

Clear and present danger really came into its own when the Soviets got their own nuclear weapons in 1949. Throughout the cold war there were various meanings of the word "threat." During John F. Kennedy's presidency, the Department of Defense came up with seventeen threats around the world it claimed the United States had to be fearful of. Those threats fell into several categories. One was nuclear war, specifically regarding the Soviet Union. Other threats had to do with revolutionary insurrectionists groups that would in one way or another change the status quo or the stability of the relationship with our national security apparatus. Another threat was the particular markets or access to raw materials—chiefly oil—being closed to the United States. So an American citizen could have looked at the Soviet Union and said: "It's a threat to the United States—and me—because the Soviets have nuclear weapons." But U.S. citizens have always been faced with notions of threats, subjectively perceived or self-created, which have been used as the basis for rationalizing power, violence, and expansion.

When facing what they believe are threats, a country will think about two things. One is protecting or expanding its own territory or its credibility, which is used as an instrument of fear. The second thing that a country may do is try to figure out what prudence is: how it can be prudent in terms of defending and extending its own interests, that is, defending what it already has while creating new interests in order to defend its old interests. For example, a military installation intended to defend a particular geographic area becomes an interest to be defended as well.

But prudence in politics has a way of tailing off into paranoia: one begins to see threats everywhere. One of the difficulties of international politics is that it adds to the paranoia level in the world because of a nation-state's fear that it may or could be attacked. Some common fears are that a state may want to expand and compete, or it may want to have economic relations with a particular place that others think they should not. For example, the United States is concerned about China's economic relations with Venezuela and Brazil.

Threats require officials concerned with national security and the national interest to ask disagreeable questions: How do you define "threat"? What really is a threat and how do you deal with it? How can you be sure that what you are doing is not causing a threat to yourself? Then those people begin to ask both geopolitical and psychological questions—how something occurs in a particular form (where, for example, one leader snubs another leader at a conference) and whether or not that particular form of threat can be broken, and if so, how. What is crucial here is not only diplomacy but also law; law defines what nation-states can or cannot do as well as what they could be doing together in terms of changing the framework—from the arms race to disarmament, from war to peace, from insurrection to some form of liberation, including liberating billions of people from starvation and disease. The threat analysis does not yield very much when examined in a problem-solving framework. Instead, the agenda must change to common international security and cooperation for what (if one really follows the Bible) obviously should be peaceful and humane ends. This idea can also be found in President Jimmy Carter's work. However, it is not the doctrine of the Democratic Party.

The more the United States follows policies of expansion, the more we follow policies of triumphalism, the more we believe we are omnipotent, the more presidents are aided by political flatterers and court journalists who play the role of sycophant, the more likely that we will set ourselves up for various kinds of threats, real and imagined, from different groups of people around the world and different nations.

With a belief in our omnipotence comes great insecurity. In part, it has to do with our boundless faith in technology, which only some people understand in this country. (How many know how the Internet works, or for that matter how a light bulb works when you turn on a light switch?) So when we say that this is a highly technological society, in one sense that is right, but for most people this causes its own insecurity. And if the entire society itself is dependent on a particular kind of technology that most people don't really quite understand, we are deceiving ourselves.

In a society that prides itself on political conservatism and revolution through technology, which is ever changing, there is a skewing of what we think we know. There's also an extraordinary amount of reliance on other Americans not to do harm to us, not to make mistakes, whether they are doctors or engineers or airline pilots or presidents of the United States. We are a society of specialists. We trust others who are specialists in things we don't understand. But that has made us more secure.

This was the stage on which George W. Bush made his entrance, the latest in a long line of ambitious actors with little experience but, as it turned out, good timing.

THE PARADE OF GOLEMS MARCHES ON

It did not require much lobbying from Dick Cheney, Donald Rumsfeld, and Paul Wolfowitz to push a president itching for a fight with Saddam into waging a multibillion-dollar war that would produce tens of thousands of deaths and maimed bodies on all sides. The Bush II adventure and the events that ensued from the original White House decisions required the recalibration of the military, intelligence, and diplomatic elites in the government.

In examining the Bush II "negotiating" within the military, certain features need to be emphasized. The military—as opposed to civilians in the military—had little interest in going to war. On the other hand, the Pentagon's Joint Chiefs of Staff knew that the Iraqi military was vastly downgraded as a result of the first Gulf War. Some in the military wanted to test the new "shock and awe" doctrine that assumed a weak enemy that would fold quickly. This strategy would *not* require large forces and was predicated on heavy aerial bombardment.

Virtually all of the intelligence experts from the CIA said that Iraq was no threat to the United States, nor was there any present indication of weapons of mass destruction or nuclear weapons. Since no sane general would have gone to war if it was truly believed that Iraq had nuclear weapons, it was necessary to bully the CIA into "cooking" its information, which it did under White House pressure.

Every step of the way, the Bush II administration engaged the world in a ruse that degraded the American people. That ruse, as General Wesley Clark put it, produced "an elective war" or, as the judgment at Nuremberg would have concluded, a preventive war: a war crime from its initiation to its debilitating present.

For the ruse to work, Bush II had to soften up the public for the invasion. It began with the palace court media. They gravely broadcast administration alerts like sirens, over and over, then the alert vanished into thin air, and no one ever said what the source of the alert was or why the color-coded alerts changed from day to day or if the alerts were real or what the citizen was supposed to do besides "be vigilant, report suspicious people and packages, and go about your normal life." This "friendly advice" from the government had unintended consequences for private and public relationships. Everyone had become a potential informer whose complaints sometimes reached beyond terrorism—some Americans turned in other Americans because they didn't like them or because they looked a certain way. The floodgates of venom and suspicion were officially opened. The doctrine of clear and present danger became the justification for Bush II's ideological mission and imperial adventures, as this chronology shows:

- September 24, 2001: Attorney General John Ashcroft tells the House Judiciary Committee, "Terrorism is a clear and present danger to Americans today."[2]

- October 26, 2001: Bush signs the Patriot Act, saying that the new law would "give intelligence and enforcement officials important new tools to fight a present danger."[3]

- July 23, 2002: "The Downing Street Memo" (the minutes of a prime minister's meeting in which the chief of British overseas intelligence reported his recent trip to Washington) claims that "Bush wanted to remove Saddam through military action, justified by the conjunction of terrorism and WMD. But the intelligence and facts were being fixed around policy" to justify Bush's determination to invade Iraq. "But the case was thin," the memo says. "Saddam was not threatening his neighbors, and his WMD capacity was less than that of Libya, North Korea or Iran." The documents remain secret until May 2005 when they are obtained by the *Sunday Times* of London.[4] That June, Bush meets with Prime Minister Tony Blair in the White House and denies assertions in the memo: "There's nothing farther from the truth, Mr. Bush said."[5]

- September 8, 2002: Trying to sell the trumped-up notion that Saddam was seeking to acquire nuclear weapons, Condoleezza Rice on Sunday talk shows warns that "we don't want the smoking gun to be a mushroom cloud."[6]

- September 12, 2002: In a speech at the United Nations, Bush says, "Saddam Hussein's regime is a grave and gathering danger."[7]

- October 7, 2002: In a speech in Cincinnati, Bush outlines the Iraq threat and uses the word "danger" nine times.[8]

- October 8, 2002: U.S. Ambassador J. Richard Blankenship says, "As President Bush so clearly said, Saddam Hussein represents a clear and present danger for not just the United States, but for the entire world."[9]

- January 28, 2003: Rejecting history and facts in his State of the Union address, Bush tells Congress and the American people, "The threat is new; America's duty is familiar.... With nuclear arms or a full arsenal of chemical and biological weapons, Saddam Hussein could resume his ambitions of conquest in the Middle East and create deadly havoc in that region. And this Congress and the American people must recognize another threat. Evidence from intelligence sources, secret communications, and statements by people now in custody reveal that Saddam Hussein aids and protects terrorists, including members of al-Qaeda. Secretly, and without fingerprints, he could provide one of his hidden weapons to terrorists, or help them develop their own."[10]

- February 5, 2003: Secretary of State Colin Powell tells the Security Council and millions watching on television, "The facts and Iraq's behavior show that Saddam Hussein and his regime are concealing their efforts to produce *more* [italics added] weapons of mass destruction." He "convinces many doubters, particularly among American Democrats and independents, that the Iraqi government was a clear and present danger to the rest of the world," writes the *International Herald Tribune*.[11]

- February 7, 2003: One month before the United States is set to invade Iraq, three State Department bureau chiefs send a secret memorandum to a superior warning of "serious planning gaps for post-conflict public security and humanitarian assistance." The officials say the military is reluctant "to take on 'policing' roles" in Iraq after the overthrow of Saddam Hussein. They warn that "a failure to address short-term public security and humanitarian assistance concerns could result in serious human rights abuses which would undermine an otherwise successful military campaign, and our reputation internationally."[12]

- February 14, 2003: Hans Blix, UN chief inspector for biological and chemical weapons, tells the Security Council he has found no evidence of weapons of mass destruction.[13]

- March 17, 2003: Two days before the invasion of Iraq, Bush tells the nation, "The danger is clear: using chemical, biological or, one day, nuclear weapons, obtained with the help of Iraq, the terrorists could fulfill their stated ambitions and kill thousands or hundreds of thousands of innocent people in our country, or any other.... Intelligence gathered by this and other governments leaves no doubt that the Iraq regime continues to possess and conceal some of the most lethal weapons ever devised." He gives Saddam forty-eight hours to leave Iraq.[14]

- March 17, 2003: Senator George Allen, a member of the Senate Foreign Relations Committee, in a prepared statement says: "Make no mistake, Saddam Hussein presents a clear and present danger to the United States."[15]

- March 19, 2003: Announcing the start of the Iraq War in a brief television address, Bush says: "At this hour American and coalition forces are in the early stages of military operations to disarm Iraq, to free its people and to defend the world from grave danger."[16]

- January 28, 2004: David Kay, leader of the Iraq Survey Group charged with finding weapons in Iraq, tells Congress that

Iraq did not have any large stockpiles of chemical or biological weapons by the time the war began.[17]

- May 26, 2004: Ashcroft says al-Qaeda intends to attack the United States. He displays pictures of seven people he says "pose a clear and present danger to America."[18]

To a new generation, these events may appear staged (and, of course, many were), but there has been an air of unreality to modern war for a very long time. Some reporters were chosen by the Pentagon to be "embedded" with U.S. forces during the Iraq invasion. It was a clever public relations tactic, as most reporters and their bosses knew. Predictably, real information was at a premium and much of what the public ended up seeing were reruns of bomb blasts, bomb craters, burning cars, and bursts of fighting filtered through the green-glow of night photography. The Committee to Protect Journalists reported that seventy-one journalists died in Iraq through June 2006, more than were killed in Vietnam, more than were killed in the Second World War.

One of the great lessons the federal government learned from the Vietnam War, which up to a point was graphically covered by the U.S. media, was that you have to discipline the media and be sure that it's pointed in the "right" direction. As Hitler's propaganda minister Joseph Goebbels knew, you have to control the news, sanitize it, be sure that the country's various classes are on board both in terms of the purpose of the national activity and of the perception of how you read particular events. In this the Bush people excelled. CNN's Christiane Amanpour verified that such a situation took place during the Iraq War when she told another cable network,

> I think the press was muzzled, and I think the press self-muzzled. I'm sorry to say, but certainly television and, perhaps, to a certain extent, my station was intimidated by the administration and its foot soldiers at Fox News. And it did, in fact, put a climate of fear and self-censorship, in my view, in terms of the kind of broadcast work we did.[19]

Early in the Iraq War, opponents believed that when American casualties reached eight hundred, public outrage would force Bush to pull out. Perhaps they counted on television pictures of dead American soldiers coming home night after night in flag-draped coffins to rouse the public's ire. But except for an enterprising photographer who sneaked pictures of coffins lined up as if in formation at the Dover Air Force Base mortuary, the Pentagon managed to keep nearly all other pictures of coffins out of public view. (Two years after the war began, Ted Koppel ran names and pictures of U.S. forces killed in Iraq on ABC's *Nightline* and was accused of being un-American, opportunistic, and spreading antiwar propaganda.) Not until April 2005 did the Pentagon, responding to lawsuits, release some photographs of coffins bearing American soldiers killed in Iraq. So unreal had Bush's war become that when the body count passed two thousand in 2005 and the number of wounded passed sixteen thousand, much of the public shook their heads—and went about their business. The American occupation went on, and the multiple insurgencies accelerated deadly roadside bombings. From the administration's point of view, the deaths probably did not seem unreasonable. But as the Iraq War entered its fourth year in 2006, over twenty-five hundred American troops had been killed (some twenty-four hundred since Bush's "Mission Accomplished" boast in 2003), and over nineteen thousand had been wounded—though some believe the "official" numbers were higher. And Iraqi civilians were engulfed in multiple civil wars.

Thus the TV viewer's life—really, everybody's life—is now edited and citizens are absolutely put in the position of being colonized without knowing it. Danger, even when clear, has been sloganized to death.

DANGERS NOT ALWAYS CLEAR, BUT ALWAYS PRESENT

There was and is a clear and present danger that exists regarding the United States' and other nations' nuclear weapons and how they are prepared to use them. This includes terrorism (the "nth country" problem of nuclear proliferation), though not for the reasons Bush II stated; nuclear weapons could also come from nonstate actors like bin Laden, if they could get them.

The problem of nonstate actors having nuclear weapons has been a fear of experts since the 1940s. The "nth country" problem has also been a great concern as nuclear technology and weapons spread. This problem gave impetus to Article 6 of the Nuclear Nonproliferation Treaty, which called for nuclear disarmament and general disarmament. The article was meant to be the tradeoff for nonnuclear states forswearing present and future nuclear programs. But Article 6 was *not* pursued by the nuclear signatories to the treaty. The United States paid no attention to it in its strategy and acquisition of weaponry.

In retrospect, those who believed and still believe that being a nuclear power is "costless" as a military strategy did not consider the deterrent cost, the long-term cost of despoiling the earth and atmosphere, or the cost of damaging the genetic pool of future generations.

There is a great deal of talk about a biochemical threat from terrorists and, while no one should minimize it, one must question how dangerous it really is compared to more pressing threats. For example, American society accepts the poisoning of our air and water by corporations, which is ongoing and could easily reach an epidemic stage. That too is an invasion of individual freedom.

Certainly, the poisoning of Americans as a result of radioactive waste remains a clear and present danger that not many talk about and most accept as a cost of living. There are some twelve million tons of radioactive waste piled on bare ground just seven hundred and fifty feet away from the Colorado River in Utah. That part of the river provides drinking water to twenty-five million people, most of them in California.[20] That number of people is very small, however, compared to the hundreds of thousands of metric tons of high-level radioactive waste left behind over the years from the production of U.S. nuclear weapons. This radioactive waste is stored in underground tanks at various Department of Energy sites. It is believed that at least a third of the aging tanks leak.

It is textbook national security strategy that nations protect their sovereignty, will resort to any weapon if their leaders think their national survival is at risk. If a nation is in a conventional battle and it appears it is losing, it will consider using a nuclear weapon. And nations will take the chance of poisoning their own people with nuclear testing and nuclear toxic waste as a means of protecting what they believe is their national interest, even when there is no war or threat. In the 1950s, when the government was testing nuclear weapons in New Mexico, prevailing winds blew radioactive fallout north toward Utah. The government tried to cover it up,[21] but a documentary made about journalist Paul Jacobs showed that people and animals were poisoned, eventually got cancer, and died.[22] (Jacobs probably contracted the cancer he died from while doing his research in Utah.)

Many clear and present dangers are not going to be successfully dealt with by enlarging the U.S. stockpile of weapons of mass destruction, but that is what the Pentagon does. According to Anthony H. Cordesman, the Pentagon generally underestimates future costs by as much as 50 percent. He points out that the Government Accountability Office found that "the cost escalation [as of March 2005] in the department's seventy largest procurement programs was $1.3 trillion.... A survey of 26 major systems showed a cost escalation of $42.7 billion in their Research, Development, Test, and Evaluation costs."[23]

Outsourcing goods and services once produced in the United States has been a clear and present economic danger for decades. So has globalization, a concept that is part hype and part reflection of the destruction of the welfare state and the political economy of expansion and greed organized to a very narrow definition of the "bottom line." Globalization has had surprisingly adverse effects on the American economy, turning the United States into a debtor nation, a status that accompanies its attitude of arrogant self-deception. China and South Korea, which hold hundreds of billions in U.S. Treasury bills, have propped up our economy for years but could pull the plug at any time. For example, the mere suggestion in the spring of 2005 that South Korea might diversify its currency holdings away from the U.S. dollar—later retracted—helped send U.S. stocks to their biggest one-day plunge since May 2003. America's major exports are now the dreams and violence of Hollywood plus military materials. Paradoxically, globalization also transformed the U.S. defense manufacturing system, making it in part dependent on foreign services and manufacturing skill.

Another clear danger is a worldwide pandemic that could break out while the United States prepares for its next war. Imagine a heightened AIDS pandemic spread by a regional war along with other diseases such as cholera and flu. (The influenza pandemic after the First World War killed tens of millions of people—more than the war itself!)

FROM SECOND STRIKE TO FIRST STRIKE—THEN WHERE?

There might be a lessening of clear and present danger if the United States is prepared to change its policies as to how to live in the world. But Bush II's policies greatly increased danger for American society because no limits have been placed on what the United States intends to do, as Bush's new *first*-strike (and first use), preemptive, and preventive war policy, announced at West Point in 2002, vividly demonstrated; in fact, it paved the way for the Iraq War.

The publicly stated military doctrine of the United States from the beginning of the cold war up until the West Point speech was *second* strike. (However, in its military planning and Nuclear Readiness System, the United States retained the first use of the nuclear weapons option as well as a preemptive nuclear war option. These two ideas governed American military strategy.) Second strike was to be invoked after the other side used its nuclear weapons first. Then the United States would respond, using different nuclear options including massive retaliation. There can be any number of variants of the effect of the first-strike doctrine, but one thing is clear: the number of dead and dying can very quickly escalate into the hundreds of millions. Of course, there will be no such thing as a noncombatant or neutral nation. Everyone, at least in neighboring areas, will feel the heat of such a tragedy. While these arguments may appear abstract, they are anything but. In a conservative White House and Congress, however, there will be little if anything in the formal structure to stop from undertaking wild fantasies.

Bush II simply reasserted the first-strike doctrine to the American public, its soldiers, and its national guard (who would make up nearly a third of the army in Iraq but whose training did not include violent and difficult occupation) without any discussion, although discussion would have been largely superfluous since most Democrats agreed with him. After all, under Harry S. Truman, the United States was the only country to use nuclear weapons in actual warfare—on Hiroshima and Nagasaki. And there was serious consideration by Lyndon B. Johnson to use nuclear bombs during the Vietnam War when we were losing. Under Richard Nixon, the nuclear threat was used to scare the Soviets in the Middle East during the 1973 Israeli-Arab War[24] and again during the Soviet intervention in Afghanistan in 1979 when Jimmy Carter was president.[25]

But the Bush II first-strike doctrine was different from such instances in the past. It says that it is not only OK for the United States to attack first any country that we say is a military threat, but also that it is our duty. Of course, Bush was very selective about who was a military threat and who was not. Apparently, North Korea, with its likely nuclear capability, was not a sufficient threat but Iraq, without a nuclear capability, was. Bush II, who once called North Korea's dictator Kim Jong-il a "pygmy," doubtless began to rethink his tough position in July 2006, when North Korea tested seven missiles capable of carrying nuclear warheads, including one missile with the potential to hit Alaska. (It should be noted that a few weeks before that, the United States conducted its most recent missile tests in the Pacific.) North Korea's missile tests failed, but it vowed to conduct more tests, which it said it had a legal right to do. This came on the heels of the Iranian government telling the United States that it had a legal right to develop its nuclear program, which could provide nuclear energy or weapons or both, whether the United States liked it or not. The United States did not like it, but what realistic answer did Bush II have? Bomb the nuclear energy sites of North Korea and Iran? He could use tactical nuclear weapons, as some conservative hard-liners advocated, but that was something the Pentagon's top brass was very wary of doing. The political fallout around the world would be as lethal as the nuclear fallout.

First use during the cold war was thought of as a nuclear strike against the Soviet Union's military forces in Europe. This could occur for any number of reasons. A first strike by the United States would have triggered a response from the Soviets, whose leaders would have sought to destroy the urban industrial land space of the United States. (Supposedly, the United States and the Russians are more civilized now because we no longer aim our nuclear missiles at each other. In fact, both sides can retarget each other in less than two minutes.) The frightening part of the scenario is that for all the political talk about reducing nuclear weapons, both countries still have some twenty-seven thousand nuclear missiles and bombs between them. If only a tiny fraction of this arsenal were ever used, it could bring both countries to their knees and render much of the planet uninhabitable.

First strike may be done with smaller or tactical nuclear weapons under battle conditions. Throughout the cold war, there were strategists tied to particular weapons systems that wanted to test nuclear weapons. Now their heirs have either intentionally or luckily hit upon a strategy to do so. One way to look at how the nuclear line has been erased from conventional weapons is to note the introduction into combat of tactical uranium-tipped, armor-piercing shells used in Bush I's First Persian Gulf War and Bush II's Iraq War rather than tactical nuclear weapons (which are still at the ready just in case). Bush II sought "bunker-busting" nuclear weapons as ordinary battlefield weapons. This idea eviscerates the Comprehensive Test Ban Treaty to the point where it has little meaning. Now the assumption is that the United States does not have to change its nuclear bomb acquisitions, but others must do so under a willful misreading of the Nuclear

Nonproliferation Treaty. (Even depleted uranium shells are dangerous. Using a Geiger counter during the Iraq invasion, a reporter measured radiation levels in several Baghdad neighborhoods of between one thousand and nearly two thousand times higher than normal background levels.)[26]

It must have been comforting to the Bush II administration that polls consistently showed so many Americans favored using our own weapons of mass destruction against Afghanistan and Iraq. But the thrill of armchair battle soon wears off. To maintain the public's interest in war without end, the government must have more targets to keep the danger present. Once the president of the United States says there is a war on, once the government is organized to go after different states around the world, you are at war. And if one says: "This is not a threat to the United States," the answer will come back: "No, no, that's not the answer because we are still at war and will always be at war and in conflict." (There is, for example, no peace treaty with North Korea.) This is a form of fear and insecurity that in effect states that everyone must be in lockstep with us, otherwise they are our enemies. As Bush II put this sentiment: "You are either with us or you are against us in the fight against terror."[27] Government is predicated on an enemy-other. It has to be sure that everybody is saluting to the war or wars that are occurring. A government must be sure that any sort of difference or dissent about "command decisions" can very easily be nominated as treason. To make the policy work, there must be a single voice in the country itself that finds its way through every part of the society.

It does not take long for this mentality to filter down through society. Early in the Iraq War, a schoolteacher in Vermont was fired for discussing various points of view about the war. His students supported the lesson. The teacher got into trouble, however, when a policeman from a neighboring town illegally broke into the school one night and photographed the "incriminating evidence"—the lesson—and made it into a public, patriotic issue.

Every citizen should fear that any citizen who does not accept Bush II's "official story" will be defined as a clear and present danger. That may also be true for future administrations; after all, that is how many administrations before him sought to define dissenters. (Over two years after the Iraq War began, Dick Cheney called its critics "dishonest and reprehensible.")[28] So those who say that the young should not fight or that the military should not fire their missiles will be branded as criminals against the state. They will also insist that there must be continued vigilance not only against present enemies but also against past and future enemies, even one's friends and neighbors.

This is the way we have come to define clear and present danger.

Chapter 5

Can the Homeland Ever Be Secure?

TERRORISTS AT THE GATES?

It has been calculated that several hundred thousand *correct* decisions would have to be made each day to keep terrorists and weapons out of the United States.

As a political matter, after September 11 Bush II needed to deflect criticism of his administration, which was sure to be made, that there had been multiple warnings of an impending attack. Thus, speaking to a joint session of Congress on September 20, 2001, he proposed the creation of a cabinet-level position reporting directly to him: the Office of Homeland Security. Bush left the office mainly to Tom Ridge, former governor of Pennsylvania, saying with a serious mien, "Together we will confront the threat of terrorism...and while we do so, we will not sacrifice the freedoms that make our land unique."[1] At Ridge's swearing-in, Bush said the new office would "strengthen and help protect our transportation systems, our food and water systems and our critical infrastructure by making them less vulnerable to attack."[2] Bush did not mention even more explosive targets like nuclear reactors (and the even more radioactive pools of spent nuclear materials they produce), oil refineries, pipelines, offshore drilling platforms, storage tanks, or chemical plants. There was one small matter: Ridge's new office lacked statutory authority and budgetary power to fulfill its supposed mission.

Bush II had put his foot in it, yet he continued to perpetrate the cruel hoax on the public with the result that to this day Americans are hardly more secure than they were on September 10, 2001. Arguably, as a nation we are less secure, with many more enemies and a war of attrition, and we spend huge amounts of money for dubious protection that would have been better spent on programs such as universal health care and well-stocked hospitals rather than on laws that erode individual freedoms.

In his second term, Bush II proposed a few immigration safeguards here and a little more money for border security there. Mostly, though, he paid lip service to homeland security (conquering Iraq and dismantling New Deal programs was the goal), appealing to Americans to be patient and alert and not "abandon" their "lifestyles."

But breathing down Bush II's neck was Senator Joseph Lieberman, the Democratic vice presidential candidate in 2000. One month after the terrorist attacks, Lieberman introduced legislation to create a *Department* of Homeland Security. Bush II initially opposed a new jumbo bureaucracy to fight terrorism: "The President believes the Office of Homeland Security, under Governor Ridge, is working extraordinarily well," said White House Press Secretary Ari Fleischer in March 2002.[3] Later in 2003, however, the president cobbled together a Department of Homeland Security from twenty-two existing federal agencies and departments, including some that had allowed the nineteen al-Qaeda men, many with expired visas, to slip into the United States undetected. The new department was the largest reorganization of the federal government since the creation of the Defense Department in 1947, the year the National Security State was born. It suddenly became the third-largest employer in the executive branch. So much for the conservative rant about the evils of big government.

Homeland Security had tens of thousands of employees scattered in offices all over Washington and an annual budget of some thirty-five billion dollars. Adding to the confusion—or incompetence—eighty-eight congressional committees and subcommittees had jurisdiction over formerly independent agencies like the Coast Guard, Immigration and Naturalization Service, the Secret Service, and the Federal Emergency Management Agency (FEMA). (A few years later, FEMA became notorious for its mishandling of Hurricane Katrina, which was breathtaking even by bureaucratic standards. It would come to include what one Republican senator called blatant fraud costing taxpayers two billion dollars. One major problem, critics said, was jamming FEMA into the new department rather than letting it continue to report directly to the president, as it had done successfully under Bill Clinton.)

Of course, some citizens were reassured that the new department was watching out for their security. At the time of the bill's passage, however, Republican Senator Robert F. Bennett of Utah opined on the Senate floor that it would take five years to rationalize the diverse elements into a single cabinet department. His estimate was conservative.

The Department of Homeland Security was very much up to speed, however, when it came to pork-barrel projects of members of Congress, with rural areas like the following getting a disproportionate share:

- A county in western Washington state spent $63,000 for HAZMAT (hazardous material) equipment, even though it had no HAZMAT team.[4]

- A North Carolina county paid $44,000 for a decontamination trailer with showers but expected to use it only if farmers were exposed to chemicals and pesticides used on their crops.[5]

- Christian County, Kentucky, received $36,800 for equipment that would be used to respond to chemical, biological, or radiological emergencies. The puzzled local emergency-services director said that the high-tech equipment did not suit the more routine needs of his small rural community.[6]

- The Steamship Authority in Massachusetts, which runs ferries to Martha's Vineyard, received $900,000. The local harbormaster said that he did not know what he was going to do with it, but "quite honestly, you don't turn down grant money."[7]

By the end of July 2006, Homeland Security had become such a mess of corruption, significant overcharges, wasteful spending, and mismanagement that even Congress took note of it. In the meantime, while vulnerable New York City and northern New Jersey begged for their fair share of the money, the Department of Homeland Security became a national laughingstock when the hapless Ridge recommended that Americans use plastic sheeting and duct tape to make an "internal room" in their homes that would be safe from a chemical or biological attack.

When Tom Ridge faded in 2005, he was replaced by a conservative U.S. Court of Appeals judge, Michael Chertoff, who had been on the bench since leaving the Justice Department in 1993. As the son of a rabbi, perhaps Chertoff was expected to apply hairsplitting reason of Talmudic discourse to governmental organizational problems, but in federal organization, difficult problems were not solved. Instead, new departments were manufactured to paper over the problem. This actually might have worked for the man Bush II wanted after Ridge, Bernard Kerik, a protégé of the former mayor of New York, Rudolph Giuliani. Kerik, who had been New York City Police Commissioner, was forced to withdraw from the federal appointment because of his habit of petty larceny. His replacement, Michael Chertoff, was also a protégé of Giuliani's and counsel to former Senator Alphonse d'Amato.

Did shuffling at the top really matter? Only politicians new to politics were surprised that the Department of Homeland Security was seen as a potential jurisdictional threat and that there was fighting in the form of turf wars, tensions, and disputes from the inside by the merged agencies who were not keen on sharing information with each other, let alone with other agencies. That the CIA, FBI, and the NSA were not really part of Homeland Security suggested that such a department was an exercise in appearances for the public, but with the hope that "coordination" between the turf warriors could be achieved. The deeper question is whether it mattered if they were all within one department, given that the political process had not decided in practical terms what the problem was beyond the word "terrorism." In other words, terrorism became a synonym for evil and the "Big, Bad Wolf." The task of Homeland Security was to guard American society against both.

TO BE ALIVE IS TO TAKE A RISK

The notion of risk that was deliberately muddied by the Bush II people after September 11 has to be put into perspective. Risk comes in many forms—all of which may create fear in one way or another—yet each has different consequences, as the following examples remind us.

Daily Risk. Human beings constantly take risks that cannot be guarded against without substantial changes in attitudes, regulation, and technology. Some forty thousand people are killed each year on our highways.[8] Nearly two hundred thousand people died as a result of medical errors in each of the years 2000, 2001, and 2002.[9] That is just the reality. The difference between what happened on September 11 and what happens every day is that we foolishly accept the latter as part of being an American.

Invented Risk. In the domestic political economy, an aware citizenry would ask, "Is the risk of terrorism the cost of living in the modern world?" For most, however, the question has become moot because of Bush II's quest to pump up American triumphalism anew. The Bush II–conservative story has been one of keeping people both pacified and immobilized through nationalist patriotism. Some will say that has a *1984* ring to it. It is more than a ring. People hear the government saying, "Our enemy this week is Oceania, our enemy next week is Terrorism; it's this or it's that, and we have to hunt down that enemy-other wherever he or she is." One "bad guy" is quickly replaced by another—a constant propaganda refrain used, for example, to describe the Iraqi insurgents.

The state sees this as a way of keeping mobilized for war or mobilized, as it were, without having to question the institutional underpinning of the state. If it believes its first responsibility is protecting its national sovereignty against what former CIA Director R. James Woolsey Jr. said are the snakes out there, then the state will see other nations or groups as snakes, not human beings. Then the state is going to have problems because other nations will see the United States as a snake and a threat.

Unaccountable Risk. The National Security State under Bush II took advantage of the fears of its citizens by turning the society inside out and extending itself inward.

For example, it is now very hard to get into the Capitol to keep an official appointment; it has become a virtual fortress because authorities are afraid a visitor might be carrying an explosive device or an envelope containing anthrax powder. But the problem of assessing threats is wildly difficult. There are thousands of threats every day on the government and other government buildings besides the Capitol. Similar numbers of threats are made every day on the president and federal and state officials. But that is a problem bureaucracies always face. The real question is, once you do know about the threat and the risk, what do you do about it? The authorities in charge of the Capitol have said, it's too difficult to figure it out, so what we're going to do is to examine everybody who comes into these buildings with the result that you can stand in line for forty minutes to get into the Capitol to keep an official appointment. That in turn throws the member of Congress off because he was expecting you at time X not time X plus 40. It is more than a mere personal inconvenience; in effect, it decreases the productivity of the society. (At the Metropolitan Museum of Art in New York, guards quickly examine handbags and briefcases. This raises the question of which is more valuable: a member of Congress or a Rembrandt?)

It is important to see how the risk issue plays out outside of Congress. For example, there has been double-talk about airport security since September 11. Passengers have to be at the airport hours before their flight to be "screened" for security purposes, but they seem willing to put up with the inconvenience if it makes them safer in the skies. Does it? Two things are clear: the security system has been captured by various national security contractors whose task is to sell fear by claiming that their products create security for the frightened, even as the U.S. government has cut some six thousand airport screeners since 2003.

At a certain point the government and the citizens also have to ask: How much time, energy, and lost income is going into the examination of each person? How do you examine every loaded marine container (some six million cargo containers a year—a number expected to quadruple by 2022) for nuclear devices on ships arriving in the United States at 361 different ports?[10] (In fact only about 5 percent of containers entering U.S. ports *are* inspected for nuclear devices or anything else.) How do you search every mile of railroad track for bombs twenty-four hours a day?

Most citizens intuitively know the answer, but it is hard nevertheless to grasp when the media is pacifying you and mobilizing you toward a warlike condition, which you accept, partly because there are so many other immediate everyday concerns such as paying the rent or mortgage and having enough food and medicine for the family. One of the great problems that we've had over the years is, as Robert J. Lifton says, a kind of "psychic numbing" that degrades our affections and damages our critical faculties.

Public Space Risk. There is another important aspect to the Capitol problem that is not talked about. The Capitol, like all federal and state buildings, is owned by the people and is, therefore, public space—the people's space. But how much of the public space does the public really own these days? That becomes a very important issue because if the public space is closed in or closed down, that means that free speech becomes less important for the freedom of the people. The public space is where access to others for the purpose of participation and deliberations occur. Where such space does not exist or is truncated, democracy is mythical because it lacks a social reality component.

The "securitarians" answer that it is all well and good that the Capitol is public space, but the government is doing the people's business and, therefore, it has to be secure for the people who work there. But what happens when some people believe that the government is not doing its business or when its actions lead to more Waco incidents or absurd preemptive wars? After all, tens of millions of Americans do not want to go to war over terrorism or zealotry—especially against the wretched—and they are unwilling, for political reasons, to overlook such likely terrorist conspirators inside Pakistan and Saudi Arabia that, for strategic reasons, our government is prepared to downplay for fear that the natural structures of these nations would collapse if the United States pressed its case too vociferously.

RISK MANAGEMENT FOR THE NEXT TERRORIST ATTACK

Bush II played on our fears by the traditional use of foreign policy as a means to build and mobilize patriotism around a set of rituals that reinforce the power of the leader. Of course, the greatest aid to Bush came from the work of the zealots on September 11, who justified his permanent war project. Here he was helped by the passivity of American citizens and a pliant and accommodating national media whose primary task is to "cover" what the White House claims it is doing to protect the citizens, like creating a Department of Homeland Security, and often ends up fanning the flames of fear and anxiety.

There is no running away from the dreaded question: what if there is another terrorist attack or a series of attacks on U.S. soil? There are three answers interrelated to some degree. The first answer is based on the imprint of September 11: Even those not directly affected by an attack will experience some shock and anger and the fear and anxiety that there is no place to hide in the United States. Giving up yet more individual freedom will not seem unreasonable if it *seems* to provide more security to stop the next attack.

The second answer is more complicated, yet more benign: Americans might begin to accept the attacks as they have accepted and internalized the attacks of our local American terrorists and zealots. The culprits, who were judged according to the criminal law, include Timothy McVeigh, who bombed the federal building in Oklahoma City; Ted Kaczynski, the "Unabomber"; the Columbine, Colorado, high school students who massacred classmates and a teacher before committing suicide; the Brookfield, Wisconsin, parishioner who killed seven fellow worshipers during a church service before killing himself; the teenager at the Red Lake, Minnesota, Indian reservation who shot and killed his grandfather and the grandfather's companion and then killed nine people and wounded seven at his high school before killing himself; the murderers of a federal judge in Atlanta and a judge's family in Chicago; and Eric Robert

Rudolph, who is serving a life sentence for bombing the 1996 Olympics in Atlanta and abortion clinics.

What no longer seems absurd is that foreign terrorists are not so different from our own domestic terrorists, murderers, and zealots. We learn to live with their destructive behavior as a society similar to the way we tolerate hurricanes, floods, epidemics, stock market bubbles, and free-market health care.

That said, there is absolutely no question that, especially after September 11, Americans must be protected on our own soil. But what is the nature of this protection going to be, and what are the consequences? Again, this depends on calculated and cumulative risk. It is not only a matter of assessing the false dichotomy between them, it is also our unwillingness to reexamine what we do in practice in the world versus what we tell ourselves at ritual events on Memorial Day, July Fourth, and September 11 anniversaries.

There was not so much an answer to this by the Bush administration as there was an official admission from Homeland Security Secretary Chertoff that the United States cannot protect its citizens from every terrorist attack. "I don't want to get up in public and say the sky is falling if it's not falling. I'm going to try to be very realistic and sensible and serious about the kinds of tradeoffs that we consider when we're making decisions about protecting ourselves," he said in the spring of 2005.[11]

In a speech that was in part sensible and in part based on a standard government defense posture, Chertoff said,

> Threats are important, but they should not be automatic instigators of action. A terrorist attack on the two-lane bridge down the street from my house is bad but has a relatively low consequence compared to an attack on the Golden Gate Bridge. At the other end of the spectrum, even a remote threat to detonate a nuclear bomb is a high-level priority because of the catastrophic effect. Each threat must be weighed, therefore, along with consequence and vulnerabilities...we must calibrate an approach to security that incorporates prevention and protection into our lives in a way that respects our liberty and our privacy, and fosters our prosperity. One large element will be giving people options: If people want the shorter line at the airport or expedited processing at our borders they can achieve it by *agreeing to provide some limited personal information that assures us of their good faith. That trade-off will be their choice* [italics added].[12]

The tradeoff for Chertoff was a de facto national identity card that "uses biometrics—fingerscans and digital photographs—to identify and cross-check foreigners wishing to enter the United States." An identity card like this is, of course, a serious infringement on civil liberties, but this may be academic: Homeland Security, the FBI, and the State Department cannot agree on whether all ten fingers or just two fingers should be used on a biometric device.[13] The practical result is that 99 percent of foreign visitors entering the United States do not have their fingerprints properly checked.

Therefore, Chertoff proposed adopting "a risk-based approach in both our operations and our philosophy. Wise judgment must guide our decision-making as we examine how we can best organize to prevent, respond to, and recover from an attack. This will entail assessing risks and deciding which ones require action from the coordinated levels of government. For that reason, the Department of Homeland Security is working with state, local, and private sector partners on a National Preparedness Plan to target resources where the risk is greatest"[14]—that is, to decide who lives and who dies.

Whether it is called risk management or risk assessment, the new Homeland Security strategy boils down to a familiar corporate strategy of doing business. Risks are gauged by assessing the cost for each risk. Corporations build this strategy into their way of doing business; in effect, they say: "We can go so far without having to really worry about a problem like a crash. So if over, say, a three or four year period, we lose one airliner, that is what we do—we lose one airliner and a few hundred people." It is less expensive to pay off survivors and the families of victims than to give the public the safest possible planes or more flight inspectors. (Airlines carry large insurance policies to protect them in most crashes.)[15]

Chertoff seemed to admit that, for all the technology at his fingertips, his words were mostly crowd-pleasing rhetoric: "As the President said just last week, our immediate strategy is to eliminate terrorist threats abroad, so we do not have to face them here at home."[16] In effect, that is the third answer to the question of another terrorist attack on U.S. soil.

EIGHT WAYS TO END THE STATUS QUO OF TERRORISM

The wars the United States has fought since 1945 are warning signs that its leaders have, in different degrees, surrendered reason and wisdom to force. Such leadership leads to a useless and ultimately self-destructive enterprise. The American covert armed military interventions in Latin America and Indochina are examples of failed actions that increased anger at the United States and the American people. It shows itself in the incapacity of a nation that finds itself unable to successfully respond militarily to nations and groups that have relatively little or no military power compared to the United States; the United States does not know how to confront popular movements and is stymied by asymmetric warfare, as in Iraq.

This being the case, what can American democracy, withering away from constant war, do for itself? To begin, advantage must be taken of its pillars, one of which is the exercise of free speech and reason. In this regard, the media has a critical role. As Justice Hugo L. Black said in *New York Times v. United States*:

Paramount among the responsibilities of a free press is the duty to prevent any part of the government from deceiving the people and sending them off to distant lands to die of foreign fevers and foreign shot and shell.[17]

Another important reason for a free press is that it is a defense against propaganda and the trivialization of speech. Propaganda masks ideas that set forth policies and programs beyond force. If our leaders stay with the present frame of reference and the notions of force that define the United States, the twenty-first century will be a tragic one for American democracy. If we are to avoid such a tragedy, a framework for debate and consideration is a necessity. These are some issues we should expect to consider *regularly* if we want a media system committed to free speech and deliberation:

1. We must determine how we as a free people should determine our national and international interests. Should we as a nation have "passionate attachments" to any nation?

2. We must accept that there is great instability of governing in the sheik systems of warlords and corrupt leaders that the United States has supported, especially where there are examples of alternative possibilities. The changes that will most likely occur will be from the inside of the various nation-states whose leaders up until recently have been in the back pocket of the United States. But as these nations erupt, moved by what they "hear" as the siren of democracy and freedom—or traditional fundamentalism—the United States will have to step aside and accept the result that emerges from the body politic of other nations. It will be disconcerting to some that freedom has a very different meaning and consequence, for example, to Shiite Muslims who, through election, may favor a theocratic state for a period of time.

3. We must support arms control and disarmament for all states in the Middle East and stop solving our balance of payments by selling arms.

4. We must not either support or be seen as supporting activities that destroy the Palestinians as a people entitled to their own land and government; nor should we appear to jeopardize Lebanon, Syria, or Iran.

5. We must make clear that the United States supports a pluralist society and the Universal Declaration of Human Rights even though pluralism, for a time, might increase class divisions. According to Ian Seiderman, legal adviser to the International Commission of Jurists, the United States under Bush II, "stands virtually alone in rejecting the validity of economic, social, and cultural rights. That posture was evident…at the United Nations Commission on Human Rights. The United States was again the sole dissenter in separate votes of 52 to 1 on resolutions on the right to food and the right to the highest attainable standard of physical and mental health."[18]

6. We must desist from participating in state terrorism, assuming that the United States is sheriff, judge, and enforcer of its imperial law internationally.

7. We must support the International Criminal Court, where international and domestic state and nonstate terrorists will be brought to justice, and the United States must be bound by international law.

8. We must give up dreams of American imperial law as the substitute for international world law. This will allow Americans to begin in earnest the tasks of the twenty-first century, namely, global disarmament and fighting environmental degradation, disease, poverty, hunger, and unaccountable economic corporations.

It seems to be in the DNA of conservatives to scorn the International Criminal Court. Contrast that with Franklin D. Roosevelt, who would have favored such a court judging from his commitment to the London Agreements setting up the Nuremberg trials, which could have been expanded to nonstate actors like Osama bin Laden. Indeed, at the end of the Second World War, there was a choice for the United States. Was it going to go toward a Nuremberg-type situation, which would mean that all government officials in the world, including the United States, would be held accountable for their actions—for crimes against humanity? Or was it going to move toward a situation like that of the cold war, in which questions around accountability would be lost?

What is extraordinary and hopeful is that the Nuremberg direction has not been lost; it is still there and it is fighting to be heard in terms of the International Criminal Court, in terms of the Augusto Pinochet case, where even Henry Kissinger is afraid to go to some countries, fearing he will be arrested. And Slobodan Milosevic and others are being tried in court for their state terrorism. (Milosevic would die in his prison cell in The Hague in March 2006, apparently from a heart attack, as his trial was winding up.) War crimes trials, when they apply equally to victor and vanquished, are an advantage in human history, as would be free elections that serve to assert legitimacy to the governing and decision-making process.

Chapter 6

The Right to Vote, the Right to Have It Count

AS FLORIDA GOES, SO GOES THE NATION

Where elections in a democracy are considered to be important by at least some people, the likelihood is that all means, short of armed insurrection, will be used to attain or hold onto power.

This is not to say that some will not believe in the structure of traditional institutions, as well as the independence of courts and Congress, and will accept truthfulness and trust as central ingredients of a society. Thus our constitutional government is predicated on the election and its means—up to a point—since legitimacy of means has changed as more people who were formerly outside of the election process, such as the poor, blacks, women, Hispanics, and Indians, may want to participate. Even if they refrain from exercising that right, they may want to know they at least have the right to make their thoughts and feelings count. There are others, of course, who believe that voting is a waste of time because it is irrelevant to them and their problems.

Thus a question of great concern in a democracy is, what means are to be used to "win" or "convince" another to maintain loyalty to, or at least acceptance of, that democracy? In religion, proof may be through the exemplary action of prophets, through revelation, through the analysis of texts, and through religious tradition. With the advent of scientific explanations of how things work, religion has sought to incorporate scientific beliefs. In these cases, the methods used by religion and science are linked to persuasion, rhetoric, rational discourse defined as logic, and the resolution of apparent contradictions. These are relativist methods based on proofs that are open to revision and change.

There is another side to religion and science—the politics of legitimacy. This is found in every human institution whether governed by popes or city mayors. In many instances, we find coercion, bribery, extortion, terror, and breaking of the bonds of trust between those who may disagree with one another and may turn to murder as the means of resolving disputes and questions of control.

The hope is that democratic electoral politics is predicated on rational persuasion rather than force, fraud, and callous manipulation. These activities are usually hidden behind a curtain that very few care to open.

But sometimes the curtain is opened for a moment and then, for those who care to see, the system is exposed. Whether any care to see and then act on the basis of what is palpably obvious is quite another question. Some, like the distinguished Court of Appeals Judge Richard A. Posner make the argument that, of course, the Supreme Court was wrong in its legal reasoning and its reporting of the "facts" in 2000 in Florida but was correct in the result because it reaffirmed "stability" of the system at a time of great uncertainty.[1] Posner concludes, better to have a wrong result than to wait for a more reasonable result no matter how long it might take. This view is defended by the kind of closure that the assertion of power brings to any situation in which the bold or successful thief is willing to use any means necessary to assert and hold power. In practice this meant that the curtain would remain closed from the realities of American politics even though more was known and shared about electoral skullduggery as a result of the communications systems.

On the other hand, Democrats in 2000 were also prepared to keep the curtain closed. Hiding from themselves the truth about American elections and their own unsavory part in the conspiracy of both major political parties, having refused until it was too late to call for a recount in all of the counties of Florida until a feckless attempt was made to ask for such a recount, the Democrats lost their legitimacy. They were caught in the net the Republicans provided for the Democrats seeking counts in particular counties and leaving intact an electoral system that was flawed beyond repair.

Long before election day 2000, George W. Bush and his advisors saw the importance of taking advantage of the inherent biases of the electoral system, especially in Florida where the Republicans, through Governor Jeb Bush, Bush II's younger brother, dominated the election machinery and the interpretation of election laws. Thus the attitude of Bush II and the Bush family consigliere James A. Baker III was that anything short of murder would be used to obtain the presidency.

The machinations in Florida in 2000 that gave the state to George W. Bush by 537 votes, and subsequently made him president, could have been foretold by watching *Key Largo*, a 1948 movie in which the gangster Johnny Rocco speaks these prophetic lines:

> Let me tell you about Florida politicians. I make them. I make them out of whole cloth, just like a tailor makes a suit. I get their name in the newspaper. I get them some publicity and get them on the ballot. Then after the election, we count the votes. And if they don't turn out right, we recount them. And recount them again. Until they do.

For thirty-seven days following election day, November 7, the winner in Florida appeared to be in doubt, but there was every indication that state Republican officials attempted to "ice" the election for Bush before the election and during the questionable recount:

- The months before the election: Governor Jeb Bush, with Florida's elected secretary of state Katherine Harris, George W. Bush's Florida campaign co-chair and a future member of Congress, ordered Florida election officials to remove some fifty-seven thousand citizens from voter rolls because, it was claimed, they were convicted felons and under Florida law were denied the right to vote. Most were black, 90 percent were Democrats. The original intent of the law was to exclude as many blacks as possible from voting. Local and state laws were used against blacks for a variety of "crimes" such as vagrancy. After the election was settled, it was "discovered" that some 20,000 were not felons after all.[2] Obviously, if even a fraction had voted, Democratic candidate Al Gore would have won Florida, the state's electoral votes, and the election.

- November 7: Thousands of legally registered blacks in Democratic districts brought their official voter registration cards to designated polling places, but the presence of an unusual number of police made them so anxious many did not vote, even though black voter registration in Florida was up four percent in 2000. Blacks who did vote had their ballots invalidated at a much higher rate than whites. In Gadsden County, with the highest percentage of black voters in the state, one in eight votes were not counted for various reasons. In neighboring Tallahassee, the capital, which has a white majority, almost every vote was counted.[3]

- November 8: The race was too close to call. A machine recount would be conducted. Charges of irregularities and vote fraud, real and rumor, flew around the state. Tens of thousands of disputed votes were at stake. "Hanging chads" and "pregnant chads" became grist for late-night television comedy.

- The lawyers invaded Florida: Gore's lawyers, though brilliant, came off as academic and long-winded, not unlike Gore. Bush's lawyers were headed by James Baker, who "dug in like a pit bull." Baker spoke to the press loudly and often, and his message was that Bush had won on November 7. Any further inspection would result only in "mischief." Privately, however, he knew that at the start he was on shaky political ground: "We're getting killed on 'count all the votes,' he told his team." His order to Republicans was to never appear to be behind at any stage of the vote count. The aura had to be created that Gore was the continuous losing challenger in the election and recount.[4]

- November 17: With Bush barely in the lead and "with the last of the absentee ballots ostensibly in, Harris announced that she would certify the election by the next morning. The Florida Supreme Court intervened this time, declaring she could not do that, and deciding, with a weekend to think about it, that the three target counties could take until Sunday, November 26, to finish counting—or, if Harris so deigned, until Monday, November 27.... The Bush campaign petitioned the United States Supreme Court to stop everything, citing two highly technical federal issues for it to consider."[5]

- December 1: The United States Supreme Court asked the Florida Supreme Court to clarify its position.

- December 8: The Florida Supreme Court ordered a statewide recount of some sixty-one thousand disputed ballots that voting machines had missed. The Republican's carefully planned election was unraveling. Bush's lead shrank to 154 votes. The Bush campaign asked the U.S. Supreme Court to halt the recount.

    Observers believed that the U.S. Supreme Court's conservative majority feared the voting would eventually go for Gore, who was ahead in the popular vote by half a million votes nationally. A clerk for Justice Sandra Day O'Connor reportedly told fellow clerks that she "was determined to overturn the Florida decision and was merely looking for grounds."[6] Justice Antonin Scalia found that "the counting of votes that are of questionable legality does...threaten irreparable harm to the petitioner [George W. Bush], and to the country, by casting a cloud upon what he claims to be the legitimacy of his election."[7] In an extraordinary conclusion based on backward reasoning and the inversion of the equal protection clause, the Court claimed with Scalia that to count all the votes would violate the rights of voters who had already voted, not those who were denied the right to vote as a result of racism, structured deficiencies, or egregious miscounting.[8]

- December 9: The high court halted the recount. John R. Bolton, summoned to Florida by Baker, his former State Department boss, burst into a Tallahassee library, where the count was still going on, and announced: "I'm with the Bush-Cheney team, and I'm here to stop the vote."[9]

- December 12, as midnight approached: The Supreme Court, in a "judicial coup d'état," reversed the Florida court five to four; the conservative justices had "selected" the forty-third president of the United States, George W. Bush.

In a melancholy dissent, Justice Stevens said: "Although we may never know with complete certainty the identity of the winner of this year's Presidential election, the identity of the loser is perfectly clear. It is the Nation's confidence in the judge as an impartial guardian of the rule of law."[10] A columnist for the *St. Petersburg Times* was more blunt: "This was a court unhinged from the law, operating in a purely political guise, bereft of legitimacy."[11]

No matter; Bush and his mentors moved quickly to recast the election as a mandate for the conservative agenda, which proved remarkably easy to do as dazed Democrats across the land became the new silent majority. (If the shoe had been on the other foot, it's a safe bet that conservatives would have pounded away about a "selected" president from day one to the next election.) Indeed, the conservative onslaught was nothing less than a counter-revolution, which took the form of dismantling the domestic political architecture of the New Deal that had been in place for more than three generations.

So just as Johnny Rocco had predicted, "after the election, we count the votes. And if they don't turn out right, we recount them. And recount them again. Until they do."

There was a coda to the 2000 campaign that would have pleased Mr. Rocco. In 2005, as George W. Bush began his second term by trying to dismantle Roosevelt's Social Security program, James A. Baker III was named cochair with former president Jimmy Carter of the Commission on Federal Election Reform. Said Baker, apparently with a straight face, "America's democracy is the backbone of our society, and only through fair elections can we guarantee that our system remains healthy."[12] But whom did the suddenly pious Baker mean by "our"? It certainly did not include the poor and blacks of the nation.

WHY IT'S NECESSARY TO REHASH THE 2000 ELECTION

The 2000 presidential election legitimated the illegitimate. It legitimated Bush. It legitimated policies that people do not want to have legitimated, like war without end, unprincipled tax cuts for the rich, and crippling deficits.

That election legitimated serious infringements on free speech, which include the right of reasoned thought without which the value of the vote is diminished in the first place; the right of expression outside of voting, whether artistic, literary, or in the schools, is diminished; and public participation in the economy is diminished.

It delegitimized whole sections of the landmark Voting Rights Act of 1965. Spurred on by the murder of voting-rights activists in Philadelphia, Mississippi, the unprovoked attack by state troopers on peaceful marchers in Selma, Alabama, and numerous other acts of violence and terrorism, Lyndon Johnson overcame Southern legislators to push for legislation that would break the grip of state disfranchisement.

The Voting Rights Act was meant to ensure that racial and language-minority citizens would have the same opportunity as other Americans to participate in the nation's political life, including equal access to polling places. Yet in the 2000 election, according to a Caltech-MIT study, four to six million votes nationwide were lost due to problems with ballots, equipment, or registration at the polling place.[13] An estimated one million of the lost votes were cast by blacks.

The 2004 race for president turned on a reverse polling situation. Nationally, President George W. Bush was three million votes ahead in the popular vote, but was in danger of losing Ohio's electoral votes, which constitutionally would have given the presidency to Senator John Kerry of Massachusetts. As in 2000, many voting inaccuracies immediately surfaced. Vote tampering of different kinds was claimed. Congressman John Conyers, senior Democrat on the House Judiciary Committee, called for an investigation by the Government Accounting Office of Congress.

It was noted that there "was a wide discrepancy between the availability of voting machines in heavily minority Democratic and urban areas compared to heavily Republican suburban and exurban areas." Witnesses claimed that voting machines had been removed from minority areas prior to election day, resulting in these areas having fewer voting machines than they'd had for elections in 2002. Other distressing features of the Ohio elections concerned vote challenges. Judge Susan Dlott also noted that racial disparity was inherent in challenges, citing that "only 14% of new voters in white areas would face challenges, while up to 97% of new voters in black areas would face them."[14]

Every four years Americans are reminded that voting is the responsibility of every eligible citizen. But increasingly for those who exercise the privilege, voting is an exercise in futility because whether your side wins or loses, the real result is that you are legitimating the system that makes the illegitimacy possible.

Elections are often obviously manipulated in the most basic sense through the media, through obscene amounts of financing by corporations and the rich—campaign finance reform has made only a dent in the operation—and ultimately at the polling booth by exclusion of voters.

This should not be laid on the conservatives alone. The two major political parties use elections to legitimate their version of power and to be sure that those who vote against the winner will accept the results of the election. In fact, the institutions of government financing are predicated on the exclusion of third parties—it has kept many extraordinary truth-tellers off the ballot, just as it has kept in place old voting equipment or put in place electronic touch screen voting machines (some made by companies friendly to top politicians), which malfunction, are potential prey for hackers who can change votes, and often have no paper backup to recount challenged votes. (The best kind of voting equipment may still be pen and pencil with paper. Canada and Sweden vote on paper ballots with little "spoiled" and without suspicious counts.)

When all of this is added up, several things become apparent. One, people who are in power tend to like the way elections are held. It is not that this is a conspiracy, it is who they are and what they are. It is what the American political system presently is. Two, September 11 emphasized that elections—so far as they touch war and peace issues—are beside the point because leaders of both parties have put the nation on a permanent war footing.

It was always assumed in the United States that voting was the best poll and most people went along with that assumption for a long time. Now it turns out that, according to opinion polls, if you ask people questions, they are to the left of their leadership and to the left of the way congressional members vote and the way things in the country are going. Yet the half of the country that votes in presidential elections gives the Right a thin majority.

How much of that majority is the result of structured electoral flaws in the system or conviction on the part of the party electorate? The answer cannot be easily determined since there would have to be a willingness to review the various strands of the electoral system, which includes the laws, economics, and media determinants, as well as clashing definitions of power, democracy, access, and exclusivity. There can only be one provisional conclusion: elections like the 2000 presidential election are shams and shameful, which is why it has become increasingly apparent that the half that does not vote is alienated. Paradoxically, the other half is accepting but often skeptical and cynical.

So in this sense, Florida, as Ohio was in 2004, is a metaphor that goes far beyond the selection of Bush II.

DO WE REALLY HAVE A DEMOCRACY?

There are two answers. The first, obviously, is no. The second answer, however, is burdened by more than two centuries of myth: the United States never was a true democracy.

Judge Posner, in saying that the Supreme Court was absolutely right to have stepped in for the 2000 election, is really saying that the United States surely is not a participatory democracy and the courts can step in when they want to. But the issue is not that we don't have a participatory democracy. We do not even have a *representative* democracy! Simply put, what we have in the United States is a formalist republic. A republic is simply not a democracy, no matter how often politicians and commentators crow about "this great democracy of ours."

Unlike a formalist republic, predicated on secrecy and the National Security State, a true working democracy would genuinely depend on the shared intelligence of the people to govern. That is, those in power, rather than following the latest polls (whose accuracy has often proved questionable) before making important decisions, would include the shared intelligence of the people they represent, who pay their salaries and part of their benefits and pensions. Americans should understand this precisely because it makes a difference in how we view and use our freedoms.

To understand the difference, we must go back to the founding of the country when there was, perhaps, the last serious discussion about the theory of the republic. The "new" United States was split into very different factions. According to Madison's "Federalist No. 10," the different factions would struggle with each other. These factions themselves would, therefore, allow the individual maximum capacity to survive against a government that might usurp power against the person. James Madison believed that if you could keep different groups at each other's throats, everything would be OK. The best government was a deadlocked government where competing passions stalemated each other. That was one view of how the federal government should operate or not operate.[15]

This was not Alexander Hamilton's idea. His position, from a capitalist point of view, was that to survive, the United States had to have a strong federal government. (In "Federalist No. 15," Hamilton asked, "Why has government been instituted at all? Because the passions of men will not conform to the dictates of reason and justice without constraint."[16] Not incidentally, Hamilton believed that a strong federal government would spur the manufacturing class.) The nation needed a political economy to be able to control credit, control money, develop roads, and so forth. Of course, in practical terms, the founding fathers who became president believed in a strong national government. President Jefferson, the states' rights advocate without parallel, orchestrated the Louisiana Purchase, which extended U.S. borders to Indian territories and to vast lands the French owned. He acted against his principles for reasons of security and made the purchase without any involvement of the states.

Our republican form of government today has hardly changed since Jefferson's day. It is as anachronistic as the British House of Lords. Constitutionally, we see it in the way that Rhode Island with a million people has two senators and California with thirty-four million people has two senators. Forget for the moment that some of the most liberal senators represent the smallest states or that the sparsely populated western states elect some of the most powerful conservative senators, there is something quite mad about this—and unjust—if we accept the idea of one person, one vote whether in the public or economic sphere.

We see the frustration of voters who know that they do not directly elect the president, but instead are forced to submit to a presidential electoral system. In other words, there is a disconnect between the people and this political nation. But in this political nation, which is dominated by the National Security State, the "government" is only able to operate in a legitimate way because it gives the appearance of having the support of the people.

This is the principle of authority and the essence of something that is not thought about in modern America: the ongoing colonization of its citizens, where white people and people of color alike are subjected, often from below the political radar screen, to more and more governmental authority, which was being put in place long before Bush II and September 11.[17]

While today's rich may not think so, every citizen in varying degrees is colonized in America—the poor, of course, certainly the middle class, and even the rich themselves. The Patriot Act is an example of this. Terrorists notwithstanding, what this means, whether you vote or not, is that the very few in America actually decide the country's foreign and domestic policies. They arrogate constitutional legitimacy that has only the most tenuous relevance to the actual operations of government and the wielding of power.

TIME TO STOP GENUFLECTING TO THE CONSTITUTION

There is nothing in the Constitution that declares that American citizens have an inherent right to vote and that our vote should count, at least as interpreted by the Rehnquist Court. But as Florida proved—and many other states in our history proved long before Florida—while voting is all very nice, the vote can be thrown out, cut down, or denied on trumped-up charges.[18]

We have developed a system of voting in the United States that guarantees flaws and guarantees that the votes of certain groups will not count or that unequal representations are accepted. Nevertheless, we have also put forward in our legislation ideas of what voting should be, and we don't hesitate to lay "proper electoral systems" on other societies—except, of course, where we want dictators and thugs to remain if we deem it in our national military and economic interest.

On the other hand, there is another line of authority that comes across through a series of legal cases. While the Warren Court championed an inalienable right to vote that defines democracy—including one person, one vote—the Rehnquist Court was not a proponent of this idea. Yet historically this country has witnessed terrible battles between those people who say, "You have the right to vote" versus those people who say, "You don't have the right to vote." The latter idea has a very long constitutional life:

- The Fifteenth Amendment giving black males the right to vote was added to the Constitution just after the Civil War, but poll taxes and literacy tests kept many poor, uneducated former slaves from voting in many states (but did not disen-franchise poor, uneducated whites) until 1966, when the Supreme Court ruled that poll taxes in state elections violated the equal protection clause of the Fourteenth Amendment.

- Women could not vote until 1920—and it required the ratifi-cation of the Nineteenth Amendment to give them that right.

- American Indians could not vote until 1924.

- Young men and women ages eighteen to twenty-one, who were eligible to be killed and maimed fighting the wars of the United States, could not vote until the Twenty-sixth Amend-ment was ratified in 1970, while many of them were fighting in Vietnam.

- Under various state laws, some 4.7 million ex-felons, one-third of whom are off parole and "free," are barred from vot-ing, though presumably they are not disenfranchised from paying taxes—if they can get a job.[19] Ex-felons cannot serve as teachers, firefighters, or often even barbers or plumbers, nor can they receive food stamps or live in public housing.

It is high time to resolve the many serious issues before the nation. The legal means of resolving them is to stop genuflecting to the Constitution as if it was God's covenant and proceed with its correction.

Before both liberals and strict conservative constructionists faint dead away from such treacherous talk, it is crucial to give a critical reading to this eighteenth-century document in light of present needs.

In the first place, what we know—what we should understand—is that the original Constitution, as intellectually stunning a guide as it was and is, for the most part was drafted by younger but mature men whose bril-liance cannot be doubted. But they did not have the benefit of the decades and the seasoning of a lived experience to bring about a democracy of inclusiveness.

Democracy was not the primary or even secondary interest of the founding fathers. A majority were simply interested in having the federal government absorb the debts owed to private individuals and the states for the Revolutionary War, though many were also concerned that dis-united colonies would fall prey to European "predators" and Indians.

Second, one of the great fears of the Constitution, as distinct from the Declaration of Independence, was that the Constitution for the most part was a means of holding back the people—not giving them more than was absolutely necessary, yet leaving the legal door open for democratic change should that change come from an aroused people.

Third, the Constitution was a document based on slavery.

Fourth, the Constitution was a document that changed and lasted over the years as a result of very profound political struggles that redefined the whole nature of who was a citizen and who wasn't. But when the Constitution was written, it was clearly based on a very constricted notion of who would be citizens. It was also based on a constricted notion about property. And there was a constricted notion about property rights—that is, power—which bled into the question of voting. For that matter, the Constitution also has not meant the right to housing, the right to education, the right to health, or the right to decency and dignity, even though these are rights that are talked about in international documents that the United States went along with rhetorically but pulled away from in practice.

This is not the eighteenth century, and although certain notions of freedom may be considered invariant, other notions, which were thought of as trivial, are not. (For example, while the founding fathers sometimes spoke of empire, it is another story entirely to spend several hundred years constructing one.) But there was in the Constitution room for future generations to maneuver: it had as its beginning "We the people of the United States" and had appended to it the Bill of Rights. That was something that the future generations hung onto. (It is interesting that the Constitution's General Welfare clause opens up a Pandora's box for conservatives and reactionaries but was crucial to the New Deal and is crucial to civil liberties advocates once they link economic rights to political rights.)

The point is that the Constitution can and should be changed when it is critical to do so. In the 1960s and 1970s, Democrats and liberals and populists were scared to death of changing the Constitution because they feared the people. It was the Republicans and conservatives who said: Let's have school prayer, let's not have abortion rights, let's teach creationism, or as advocates call it, "intelligent design."

Liberals and progressives should not be so frightened. They should put forward their own set of purposes, their own constitutional amendments, their own notion of what the Constitution in the twenty-first century should read like and be like—that is, in keeping with the common good. The question is: will there be a calamity—one of irreversible proportions—before then? That is why electoral reform is so important. It is the prologue to extensive changes in the Constitution.

Naturally, there will be those who say: "We can't, so let's make believe there are no inherent contradictions." Under certain circumstances this strategy might be admirable, because its purpose is to synthesize and coordinate opposites. This was the great skill of FDR. But lesser political people say: "Let's forget about our slave past and its present manifestations. Don't bring it up." Then your past never has to be looked at, your experiments never have to be thought about, your purposes never have to be thought about, and you have no humility as a society because you can always "put it behind you."

This is the same habit of mind that operated at the end of the cold war. A meeting of former senators that took place after the Berlin Wall collapsed illustrates the point. They were brought together to talk about releasing a statement regarding changes necessary in U.S. policy as a result of the Soviet demise. The nonpolitician in the group said that for good consequences in the future it was necessary to discuss the American role in the cold war because without that reevaluation there would be no changes in American foreign and national security policy. The senators rejected the idea, saying that it would be viewed as promoting a cause and not putting problems and past mistakes "behind us."

But if you don't examine your policies and what you did or who you are, then you don't know what to correct. You don't know why others— say, in the third world—react negatively, as they do. This degrades the democratic process, which must include transparency of government and openness about the past.

Under the present circumstances, the Constitution is unable to overcome such fundamental questions as Bush II's claims about war without end and his interpretation that as commander in chief of the armed forces he trumps the sole constitutional power of Congress to declare war and declares it himself, even though Congress is empowered with the regulation of the Army and the Navy. In his hands and in those of future presidents, the Constitution becomes nothing more than a piece of parchment in a display case to hide governmental behavior. The executive creep in terms of war-making power is an old story in American history. However, it was finally "codified" with the emergence of the National Security State.

The Constitution needs change. It needs an amendment naming the right to vote among the other rights named. Otherwise, elections will continue to be stolen with impunity, millions of votes will continue to be denied, the direction of the country will continue to be controlled by the undemocratic few, and the Armageddon many conservatives devoutly pray for may well come in the form of the most tragic mushroom cloud of all. Paradoxically, in order to protect the intentions of the founding writers of the Constitution in regard to the preservation of Congress' sole power to declare war, the Constitution will require an amendment in order to make it crystal clear that this power is in the hands of Congress.

Chapter 7

Do You Already Live In an Authoritarian State?

TYRANNY COMES IN MANY GUISES IN THE LAND OF THE FREE

Since America transformed itself into a national security state at the end of the Second World War, U.S. armed forces have fought more than one hundred overt and covert wars and interventions.

Most Americans do not really stop to think about the dominating military and police system in which they live, although the society has militarized itself through surveillance techniques, security systems, profiling, computer monitoring, police, and other state-sponsored authoritarian controls that were internalized in American life long before the terrorism of Timothy McVeigh and the September 11 gang in ways which were difficult to do a few generations ago. Thus there are now tens of thousands of surveillance cameras across the country (no one knows the exact count), many linked to government and police databases, snooping on citizens in public spaces from jammed Times Square to tiny Porterville, California, hoping to catch criminals or terrorists in the act. (Ask your elected representatives how many terrorists have been apprehended as a result of evidence from surveillance cameras.)

What the government's surveillance cameras *have* discovered is another way to take away the citizen's long-held right to anonymity. The surveillance system is based on hidden boundaries, which those with authority administer, control, and shift so that the surveilled may suddenly find themselves in the category of suspects or potential suspects.

Acceptance of authority, as it has played out again and again in our country and in others, is how you keep your head and get ahead. If you don't accept authority, that could be a problem. But there is also a problem with the unconditional acceptance of authority and legitimacy: citizens are hesitant, if not afraid, to tamper with established authority that appears to be legitimate and appropriate even though the government's action may be both unlawful and illegitimate. It is hardly a leap to conclude that free speech is inhibited for fear that "Big Brother" is listening. The chilling effect on free speech is obvious, and it is then that propaganda takes over.

THE AUTHORITARIANISM OF GOVERNMENT PROPAGANDA AND SECRET CONDUCT

Propaganda's primary purpose is to eliminate critical thought so that people will remain passive. Propaganda is also managed speech for a particular end and at a certain point, if it lasts long enough, everyone who makes propaganda may come to believe it. People who create advertising believe what they're saying about the product, just as politicians believe the political line they hand out because it seems to be their reason for being. This is what they do, this is what they believe, and it is then hardened into a reality that others internalize. There are, of course, politicians who believe in nothing but their own ambition. They are fixers and brokers. The question is whether or not the people at the very top still believe their propaganda because they have other information that is held in secret.

The people at the bottom see things through their own eyes; they see a different reality than the one that is presented to them. One gets a sense of this when people on the street are interviewed on local television about the state of the nation or the local culture. Most answer questions on the spot with intuition and clarity. Of course, they are not asked why they have little or no political and social power—nor do they suggest answers.

Bureaucracy is managed to function as an instrument of social control so that large numbers of people, particularly the poor, cannot function as discerning citizens exercising their judgment on the basis of the best information available, even when it is contradictory. Instead, we have the kinds of control that give the *appearance* that the society needs security, and that security means security from essential information.

The vital issue for citizens is that so much information that should be available to them and the media is classified as "secret" by the government when it is really not secret. This makes it difficult, if not impossible, to assess potential danger and whether the government has done enough to prevent it beyond, say, warning of a "possible" terrorist attack with simple-minded color codes. Bush II, like Reagan, Nixon, and Johnson, hid information and developed nonsecret but classified categories of information, which then could not be released to the public or to political opponents. This goes against a human being's natural inclination to communicate, whether it be about political matters, social relationships, or pleas for help.

Instead, citizens are "educated" through public relations, advertising, and continuous war propaganda, which are packaged as patriotism. In the United States, unlike some other countries, it is not necessary for the government to actually own the media: it can simply control it at no cost. Thought control is also practiced in public buildings—city halls, police stations, prisons, and schools. Without the support of a strong interest group, access to public space is beyond the grasp of most people; much of that space has become an adjunct to the police station and private security forces. So what does it mean that public buildings, in fact, turn out to be police fortresses that exclude the citizen from being there, from being engaged? Imagine what poor, single mothers must go through to get public assistance in public buildings even if they are organized. But also note the issue of political rights in the public space. This leads to the question of freedom of association. In authoritarian and totalitarian countries, more than three people meeting together is seen as a conspiracy, and the meeting could be broken up and the people jailed. In that sense, association is very important because it results in communication among people. But when the state bureaucracy or ruling clique sees that, they want to control association, which they will do through manufactured association, that is, through national organizational structures, which the state controls or operates through a system of spying. Or, the state will pass laws dictating that when more than a few people congregate they must have a permit.

In the United States, before the civil rights struggle, there were sedition statutes that said that no more than seven people could meet together. Those statutes have not been repealed, although in most states they are not enforced and just lie dormant because there is no turbulence to speak of in the society. But because of September 11, they could be used for a punitive purpose if necessary. In the 1960s, a federal statute was passed ostensibly to protect civil rights activists who were intimidated by state law. That is, state law would be preempted. The first person charged was the radical H. Rap Brown for a speech he made in Maryland. At this point, a permit is needed in the District of Columbia if more than a handful of people get together for political purposes.

Measures promoted by the state through *secret edict* have begun to seep into the American consciousness to the point at which we accept that what is happening to us does not really sound all that different from the totalitarian countries the United States says it is fighting to set free. No one, not even the citizen with a spotless record, is immune from being shadowed through the technology of profiling, surveillance, and biometrics.

Leading up to and into Bush II's second term, Americans suddenly realized how flagrant his administration's abuse of their civil liberties really was:

- Demonstrators were routinely photographed and videotaped by police and federal agents. Weeks before the 2004 Republican Convention in New York, the FBI knocked on doors across the country to interrogate people they identified as political "troublemakers."[1] Civil rights advocates said these interrogations had a chilling effect. The Justice Department said the impact was negligible and constitutional.

- On December 14, 2005, NBC News revealed that it had obtained a secret 400-page Defense Department document listing more than fifteen hundred "suspicious incidents" across the country over a ten-month period in 2004. One suspicious group was a Quaker Meeting House in Lake Worth, Florida.[2]

- On December 16, 2005, the *New York Times* revealed that "months after the Sept. 11 attacks, President Bush secretly authorized the National Security Agency to eavesdrop on Americans and others inside the United States to search for evidence of terrorist activity without the court-approved warrants ordinarily required for domestic spying, according to government officials.... 'This is really a sea change,' said a former senior official who specializes in national security law. 'It's almost a mainstay of this country that the N.S.A. only does foreign searches'.... Some officials familiar with the continuing operation questioned whether the surveillance has stretched, if not crossed, constitutional limits on legal searches."[3]

- On December 17, 2005, President Bush, in his weekly radio address, rather than apologize for the warrantless eavesdropping, came out swinging. He said: "I authorized the National Security Agency, consistent with U.S. law and the Constitution, to intercept the international communications of people with known links to al-Qaeda and related terrorist organizations."[4] Legal scholars and many in Congress, irrespective of political party, strongly disagreed.

- On December 20, 2005, it was revealed that after September 11, FBI counterterrorism agents had been conducting surveillance and other intelligence-gathering operations on groups active in causes such as the environment (Greenpeace), animal cruelty (People for the Ethical Treatment of Animals), and antipoverty efforts (Catholic Workers group).[5]

- On May 10, 2006, *USA Today* reported that the National Security Agency had been "secretly collecting phone call records of tens of millions of ordinary Americans, using data provided by AT&T, Verizon, and BellSouth.... The NSA program reaches into homes and businesses across the nation by amassing information about the calls of ordinary Americans— most of whom aren't suspected of any crime.... The agency's goal is 'to create a database of every call ever made' within the nation's borders," a source told the paper.[6]

- On June 23, 2006, the *New York Times* reported that "under a secret Bush administration program initiated weeks after the Sept. 11 attacks, counterterrorism officials have gained access to financial records from a vast international database and

examined banking transactions involving thousands of
Americans and others in the United States." The *Times'*
sources were current and former government and industry
officials, some of whom "expressed reservations about the
program, saying that what they viewed as an urgent, temporary measure had become permanent nearly five years later
without specific congressional approval or formal authorization." Following its by now dog-eared script, the administration quickly blamed the messenger. Cheney defended the
secret database as "absolutely essential," while lambasting
"some of the news media [who] take it upon themselves to
disclose vital national security programs." Bush II called the
disclosure "disgraceful." A Republican congressman labeled
it treasonous.[7]

Thus political speech is circumscribed by these institutional realities.
But the public should not delude itself; this feature of American life, with
the FBI leading the way, was well along before September 11.

The real question, however, is whether our "first responders," to justify
their existence, will be used to track American citizens in the homeland
and not just alleged terrorists, as well as members of civil rights and antiwar groups. It is not an overstatement to say that the cumulative effect of
shadowing has the consequence of making you feel less than who you
are. (You may even internalize the profile of yourself as a potential danger and an enemy. This is what the Stalinists specialized in doing to the
Russian people.)

In our society the process is not as intense or blatant, unless you happen to be an immigrant or a member of a minority group, but make no
mistake, it is still there for whites. You may watch your words. You may
think twice about whom you speak to. Anxiety grips every class of people caught in a Kafkaesque world of government that no longer feels quite
human. One feels politically and psychologically de-centered: Where is
the authority? Where am I in all of this? Where do I fit in this society?
What I feel and know firsthand is not the way it is "objectively" described
by the expert or bureaucratic journalist or government propagandist.
Today, I am a patriotic, taxpaying, law-abiding, god-fearing citizen.
Tomorrow, I may be labeled an enemy.

Bush II classified all kinds of information as secret in the name of "national
security" when much of it was for political reasons, ranging from starting
war under a false pretext to attempting to keep his papers as governor
secret in defiance of the Texas open records law. (The Security Oversight
Office, a government agency that reviews security classification programs,
says federal employees issued a record 15.6 million decisions to classify
information in 2004, a 10 percent increase from 2003.)[8] Bush did not have

a corner on the market in this regard; there is a long line of government officials past and present who are not so different from him in making it easier for the government to keep documents secret and thereby deprive citizens of the right of transparency and democratic sovereignty, the right to know how the government spends their money and why it is being spent on projects they don't want and not on other projects they need.

This is not the exclusive domain of the executive branch. Congress routinely tries to attach legislation to omnibus spending bills that makes it next to impossible to vote against them without scuttling the whole bill and possibly risking one's political reputation. Congressional committees hold numerous closed-door sessions on crucial debates over legislation that directly affects the public. New laws on intelligence, patriotism, and secret wars are minimally explained in secret hearings to co-opt the members.

There are fundamental reasons for the government's secrecy. If something is secret, it increases the power and status of those who happen to have that information, whether or not that information is "black box," that is, there is nothing in the box except words meant to obfuscate the reality of the government's behavior. Those people who have that particular classification have power, status, and authority.

Another reason for secrecy is that it can become a means of covering up illegality and immorality after the fact or even beforehand if you know something will cause trouble or possibly political embarrassment if made public. Leaders may then indulge in what might be called the "sadism of statesmen." Henry Kissinger falls into the sadistic category of those who wallow in the idea of secrecy. As secretary of state, Kissinger upbraided the American ambassador to Chile, telling him to stop lecturing that country's dictator, Augusto Pinochet, about human rights, while Pinochet had organized the disappearance and murder of thousands of Chileans.

A third reason for government secrecy can be illustrated with a story that is part history, part parable. After the Second World War, the Soviet Union was an exhausted nation with tens of millions dead and injured, fears that a new war initiated by the West could occur that would be aimed at the Soviets, and the belief that it could not afford unfriendly states on its borders. To answer those problems, the Soviets maintained a huge military establishment that did not come cheap—while making disarmament proposals. Soviet propagandists went on as if everything was fine. "You better watch out," they blustered to the West. "We can't show you our secrets," they would say, when what they were really saying was, "We can't show you our secrets because we are very weak."

Often in history, cruelty and sadism are signs of weakness. As a general rule, weak regimes and insecure leaders have a habit of imprisoning their people. (Stalin fashioned a brutal state in the Soviet Union by destroying the old Bolsheviks and turning dissent into a one-way trip to a gulag or worse.) A speechwriter for Khrushchev said that when foreign officials visited Soviet nuclear-bomb-making facilities, the guards faced outward, as if they were protecting the facilities, the scientists, and technologists against possible intruders. Once the visitors left, the guards did an about-face and saw the scientific workers as prisoners to be watched.

Fast-forward to the United States today, expand on scientific workers to include *all* citizens, add surveillance cameras to the police, FBI, and state authoritarian controls such as the Patriot Act, and it could be asked: how close are we to living a parallel story?

THE AUTHORITARIANISM OF NUCLEARISM AND WAR

When freedom of speech and the other freedoms are looked at in the broad sweep of the National Security State, it becomes clear that there are critical things over which the citizen has no authority. The military, that is, senior officers, is a good case in point. The military is predicated on the belief that it provides us with protection. But if, in effect, the military is offering you up as a hostage as a result of technology (using nuclear weapons and playing nuclear chicken could provoke a massive retaliation on U.S. targets), you have to ask: does the military really give you protection? And you have to ask why you have no control over whether millions of people live or die if the commander in chief of the military, the president, decides to order their deaths within a one-hour period using nuclear weapons.

Although Congress passed the War Powers Act in 1973 to brake the president from unilaterally deciding when to go to war, the act has so many loopholes in it that neither it nor any other U.S. law can really stop the president, if he believes the United States is threatened, from using conventional weapons or nuclear weapons for what he claims is the defense of the United States. This threat can be real or a fantasy. The latter was the premise of the 1997 movie *Wag the Dog*, a dark comedy about a Washington spin doctor who invents a war to deflect media attention from a White House scandal. Like much of art, the threat is reality-based. It is either a reflection or a warning. Furthermore, there is nothing that says that a president, before ordering the firing of weapons of mass destruction such as nuclear weapons, must seek counsel from Congress. It is one of the great tragedies and contradictions of Congress that its war-making powers are curtailed while its willingness to use force is unbounded. Thus a president could order, without legal consequences or much criticism from Congress, a first strike anywhere in the world. Paradoxically, to countermand such a presidential order, the United States would have to use its uniformed military.

Ironically, what power Congress has to declare war, and therefore to have its collective will exercised, has been subverted by its own hand with the passage of the War Powers Act, which gives the president a free hand in the exercise of war for sixty days and then for another thirty days if he simply informs Congress of the "need" to continue that war. Only then must the president come forward to ask for a declaration of war. This approaches the absurd since Congress has declared war just eleven times in U.S. history, beginning in 1812 against Great Britain. (The last time was in 1942 against Bulgaria, Hungary, and Rumania.) Like so much well-intentioned legislation, the War Powers Act was thought to be a reform favoring Congress' constitutional authority. But presidents have said that even this flaccid law is an invasion of *their* prerogatives!

This leads to the question of sovereignty. Sovereignty for nation-states is thought of by states as the way to define their existence since it means control and the power to control everything within their borders. Sovereignty as a concept paradoxically becomes utterly crucial to states that have weapons of mass destruction—that is to say, their use and preparation for use destroys the sovereignty of the person, supposedly the root of the democratic nation, even in powerful nations.

THE AUTHORITARIANISM OF PREMEDITATED BUDGET DEFICITS

When a government's risky economic schemes put the nation in debt to the rich and to other nations, economic insecurity sets in for citizens who are then left with no place to turn for relief but to the very government that put them in these financial straits through abysmal judgment.

Clinton supposedly left Bush II with a $237 billion budget surplus[9] that could have been used as a down payment to repair the nation's infrastructure. Bush squandered the surplus on huge tax cuts for the richest one percent of the country (at a projected cost to *all* Americans of $1.7 trillion over ten years, including higher interest payments),[10] war, and the Pentagon's budget. The Pentagon's spending, which had increased since 2001 by 35 percent to about $400 billion[11] (it grew to $437 billion by 2006), included unneeded equipment, redundant and useless weapons systems, duplication, hidden fat, waste, and inefficiency.

By the beginning of Bush's second term, the federal deficit had risen to historically high levels. As of July 2006, the estimated cost of the war on terror was three hundred billion dollars with no limits placed on spending by the Bush administration.[12] Yale economist William D. Nordhaus calculated that such costs as fighting, occupation, and reconstruction in Iraq, plus lost economic output in the United States, could run the bill up to $1.9 trillion.[13]

The nonpartisan Congressional Budget Office issued an unusual warning: "If Congressional Republicans and the administration get their wish and extend all the tax cuts now set to expire [in 2005], and if they pass a limited prescription drug benefit for Medicare [which the Bush people pushed through Congress by lying about the cost of the program and threatening to fire Medicare's chief actuary if he told Congress the truth about the real projected cost] and keep spending at its current level, the deficit by 2013 will have built up to $6.2 trillion.... Once the baby boomers begin retiring at the end of this decade, that course will lead either to drastically higher taxes, severe spending cuts or 'unsustainable levels of debt.'"[14] Some believe the troubled Medicare program will represent a fiscal problem of roughly twenty trillion dollars in the not-too-distant future.

The Republican Party of big business and fiscal responsibility became the party of big government, big business, and fiscal irresponsibility. Was it self-deception or a premeditated scheme going back to the Reagan model of "starving the beast": cutting taxes while spending hundreds of billions on the cold war, thus seeming to justify the necessity of "starving" those domestic programs that conservatives hated? Was it plain bad advice from conservative economists with overblown reputations? Or was it like the question that baseball manager Casey Stengel asked about his inept New York Mets: "Can't anybody here play this game?"[15]

Conservatives may not have played well, but it was no game to the likes of influential Grover Norquist, head of Americans for Tax Reform, who had the ear of many in Washington. One of the most receptive, apparently, was George W. Bush. When NPR's Terry Gross asked Norquist if he thought the United States "was in a tough spot, needing a lot of money, to rebuild those two countries [Iraq and Afghanistan] at the same time that we're cutting taxes," his answer verged on a form of communication known as Stengelese:

> When the government doesn't take as much of your money next year as it did last year, we have more money. The government has a lower tax rate, and depending on economic growth, may have more or less money, but we, the people, have more money. So it is a good thing for us to have lower taxes.[16]

"Kill the taxes and you kill the government" was Norquist's song,[17] but reports of big government's death under Bush II were exaggerated to say the least. Midway through his first term, a Brookings Institution study showed that the federal government employed, directly or through government contracts and grants, twelve million people, or a million more than it did under Clinton. And these additional million people were not working solely or even largely on the war on terrorism.[18]

To pay for war without end without raising taxes, Bush, the "compassionate conservative" of the 2000 presidential campaign, wanted to cut school lunch assistance, federal housing programs, nutrition for poor pregnant women, and programs to combat juvenile delinquency, student loans, environmental protection, and food stamps. Later in his presidency, Bush tried to cut funding from children's programs such as day care for the poor, Head Start, child abuse and child neglect, children's health insurance, and training for pediatricians at children's hospitals. (An increasing number of people were denied food stamps long before September 11 because of the way the bureaucracy is organized, which is to make it more and more difficult to get the stamps. On the other hand, the number of soup kitchens for poor people continues to grow even without natural disasters.)

Bush II also proposed cutting tens of billions dollars from the Departments of Education, Transportation, and even Homeland Security. He spoke often to veterans' organizations whose members inexplicably cheered the noncombat veteran who tried to cut their benefits, including combat pay, health care, and death benefits for survivors. (Was Bush concerned that an estimated five hundred thousand veterans are homeless at some time during the year?)[19]

"I earned capital in the campaign, political capital, and now I intend to spend it. It is my style,"[20] Bush said after his election to a second term. What he had in mind was spending the people's capital on plums for conservatives, such as privatization of Social Security. Various analysts estimated the cost of shifting to private accounts would be between one trillion and two trillion dollars. (Despite Bush's vigorous campaign to privatize Social Security, the public rejected the program, although conservatives will surely keep pushing for it.) The conservatives' fight against Social Security has been a consistent, long-term effort that began with their opposition to FDR's limited success in establishing Social Security as a pillar of American society.

Numbers, numbers, and more numbers, coming at the public without letup from the White House, government departments, the Congress, the Federal Reserve, the public, and private economic forecasters and without explaining how such sums related to alternatives and the material depletion of the society.

There is an old theory about government spending that was noted by social critic Paul Goodman: the more the number of zeros, the less people can figure out where the money is being spent and how it's being spent. For example, if you find out that there is a small-time cheat called a "Welfare Queen," as Reagan put it, or somebody who has stolen a hundred dollars or a few thousand dollars from the government till, that becomes news that people can understand. But the big money stuff, such as the budget for the Pentagon or for Homeland Security, is so overwhelming that it can't be easily comprehended.

THE AUTHORITARIANISM OF UNBRIDLED CORPORATE POWER

Authoritarianism in most corporate organizations remains the ruling ideology, not entirely dissimilar to feudal baronies. Unless you are a political person or a multimillionaire, you can only tilt at these huge institutional structures; it is nearly impossible to get beyond them. Yet they define what you can and cannot do, whom you represent in power, who represents you (whether or not you approve) as a "gun for hire," and sometimes whom you speak to.

In the corporate world, the bottom line is really a statement of authoritarianism. It is a statement of the demands that the corporate and government world make on workers to perform in a certain way. Workers are expected to internalize the purpose of the organization. They are expected to take commands and agree to act in a certain way. They are not really living a satisfying lived life so much as they are living a *used* life in which productivity and production are everything—and woe to workers who dare to claim free speech as a natural and constitutional right on work time.

In the National Security State, the defense baronies—the Lockheed Martins, McDonnell Douglas's, Hughes's (a division of General Motors), Halliburtons, Bechtels, Boeings, General Electrics, and many others, as well as their cronies on Capitol Hill—depend on war to sell their goods and services: planes, ships, equipment, and weapons systems, and the construction and reconstruction sites the military barony has helped to blow up. When the defense and military baronies link up, as they must in order to survive and thrive in the National Security State, they can control much of U.S. foreign policy. They also feast on military pork. For decades, members of Congress have voted for redundant weapons systems meant more for feathering the nest of defense contractors in their districts (and keeping jobs in those districts) than for fighting real and imagined enemies. Case in point: after canceling the notoriously dysfunctional C-130J Hercules military transport plane, Secretary Rumsfeld yielded to congressional pressure to keep the two-billion-dollar program going, although the Pentagon's top independent weapons tester found that it failed its initial evaluation and was "neither operationally effective nor operationally suitable."[21]

The defense baronies, like other corporate baronies, make a killing in more ways than one since over two-thirds of foreign-based multinational corporations—and only a slightly smaller number of U.S.-based multinational corporations—pay no or very low federal income tax.[22] But without war, the bottom line of the defense baronies might dramatically suffer. Profits may not meet Wall Street forecasts, traders may sell their stocks, corporate heads may roll, there may be unsolicited take-over bids. It may even be hard to stay in business.

As workers and managers know, to protect the bottom line, a corporate barony will do whatever is in its best interests regardless of the impact on its employees and their communities. The corporation will cut the pay and benefits of workers (but rarely those of top management), terminate jobs, move plants and offices to states with lower taxes or to countries where taxes barely exist, where workers' pay is a fraction of U.S. wages, and where unions are hard-pressed to organize (if they are not prohibited as they are at Wal-Mart). When the "friendly skies" of United Airlines went bankrupt because of its inability to compete in the fast-changing airline passenger market, United began terminating the ten-billion-dollar pension plans of employees and retirees in 2005. The government's Pension Guaranty Corporation assumed the responsibility of United's pensions, but it had its own troubles with a liability of sixty-two billion dollars in pension benefit payments in 2005.[23]

Why have the fortunes of the American worker sunk to the point at which 12.5 percent of wage and salaried workers belonged to unions in 2004 compared with 32.5 percent in 1953?[24] What has it meant for workers that their sense of union solidarity is utterly diminished, and what is the alternative for the kind of solidarity that was so important to the making of the New Deal?

To answer this question, other questions must be raised. Do you as a worker, employer, citizen, and taxpayer really want to have shared authority? Do you want to find a way, both through the group and individually, to be able to express your views? Do you want to have some sort of control over your destiny?

Most workers would say, "Yes, of course, we want to control our destiny. Isn't that our right as citizens, just as freedom of speech is our right?" But the *appearance* in this country is often quite different. Those in power say, "Look, we *give* you control over your destiny. You can go as *far* as you like—be upwardly mobile, a mover and shaker, and more." There is just enough truth to this belief that those who are not ambitious or aggressive soon internalize their own inferiority. Sadly, America is full of institutions, such as poor schools and prisons, that *actually* encourage the less ambitious and aggressive to say about themselves: "I didn't cut it, I wasn't able to compete, I couldn't meet the standards, so therefore I'm going to accept the position I'm in. And therefore I shouldn't have *any* authority at all because public matters are too complicated and my economic, political, and social rights can be—maybe should be—curtailed."

This attitude is reinforced by the aura of winning and competition. Football coach Vince Lombardi's line, "Winning isn't everything, it's the only thing," has almost been codified in our culture. What is so interesting about that statement is that America's extraordinary technological achievement stems much more from *cooperation* and *teamwork* than it does from *competition*.

Yet we live in a society that purports to love competition: Who is best at sports, who is best at war, who is the richest, the prettiest, the smartest? When the competitive attitude is taken into politics—and into corporate politics, which is virtually a carbon copy—where it is played as a winner-take-all sport, the issue is: who will have the ear of the winner? The most powerful, by virtue of their economic power or celebrity, although celebrity is transitory, always have the ear of the political winner. Indeed, they may have more than the politician's ear.

This rather pessimistic attitude was supposed to have been corrected for workers through unions. In the twentieth century, unions played a difficult role as they sought to help workers develop an attitude of solidarity that transcended competition. There is little sense of solidarity among workers today. During Roosevelt's New Deal, workers through their labor unions found that they had the power to successfully encourage legislation such as the Wagner Act (the National Labor Relations Act, 1935), which was intended to recognize the existence of an American working class committed to industrial democracy.[25]

In fact, exercising free speech was the alternative to the violent struggles between capital and labor. To the extent that free speech dominated, violence receded, and capital found itself having to relinquish some of its authority and power. Certain ideas flowed from this view, including freedom of speech at the workplace. There was to be citizenship in the workplace for the full flowering of personhood and individual dignity. With these ideas of citizenship, workers were to argue for their own interests, even share authority in the workplace while debating and implementing the common good beyond any immediate parochial interest. Such ideas were never far from the surface of liberal and radical thought, whether of Clarence Darrow, an attorney well-known for his labor interests, as well as for his celebrated cases such as the Scopes "monkey" trial; the socialism of Eugene V. Debs, defended by Darrow for his role in the 1894 Pullman strike;[26] or the political and philosophical arguments of others who championed industrial democracy.

Yet American workers today, unionized or not, continue to lose their rights in the workplace. If not for freedom of the press, it would be difficult to know what occurs inside a corporation, unless you were a worker in the corporation or a member of the worker's family. Ninety-three years after seamstresses at New York's Triangle Shirtwaist factory perished in a fire because doors did not open, the media is still digging out stories of employers locking employees in. In 1991, we learned that a fire at a chicken processing factory in North Carolina killed twenty-five workers and injured scores of others because the doors were locked from the outside to prevent employees from stealing chickens.[27] In 2004, it was reported that, for fifteen years, 10 percent of Wal-Mart stores locked in overnight workers to protect stores and employees from crime. It did not hurt that this also prevented Wal-Mart "associates" (Wal-Mart's PR name for its clerks and other workers) from stealing.[28] Not long ago, it was revealed that men working in a cast iron corporation had to urinate in their pants because they were not allowed a bathroom break.

There are thousands of labor abuses in the twenty-first century workplace, and companies still spend freely to dodge responsibility for obvious job-related injuries. They have been aided in this by Bush II, who signed legislation to repeal the Ergonomics Program adopted in late 2000 by the Occupational Safety and Health Administration (OSHA) because it was "an unduly burdensome and overly broad regulation." Furthermore, "the ergonomics rule would have cost both large and small employers billions of dollars and presented employers with overwhelming compliance challenges," Bush explained in a written statement.[29] Compassionate conservatism was a campaign ploy to steal workers' votes and their rights.

But union leadership and nonunionized white-collar workers bear a responsibility for their plight. Unions certainly have to deliver on wages and benefits. But they will also have to be more aggressive, working with the local community and regionally with other unions and communities. Unions will have to be the champions of local reconstruction that includes all the "shareholders" in a community affected by corporations. And they will have to work out the way in which those corporate entities are used for the common good. Above all, union leadership is going to have to put much greater emphasis on organizing and changing their mental habits in order to help professional workers. For example, some highly skilled doctors and engineers began organizing unions at the beginning of the twenty-first century as they saw their material and professional skills attacked by corporations, health maintenance organizations (HMOs), and even universities.

Union organizing is an enormous change for the white-collar class, which is predicated on the belief that the United States is built on the idea of individualism. Hence, it is difficult to get beyond all the preaching of individualism because people internalize the notion, "Well, if X has made it, I can or I should be able to make it." Consequently, they don't see themselves being involved with unions. The white-collar class was taught to believe that workers are *blue* collar. But increasingly, many middle- and lower-class white-collar workers wonder whether corporate entities as presently organized serve their common good or if they are really in the same boat as most blue-collar workers. The wages of white-collar workers are also down or stagnant while their cost of living keeps rising. And many white-collar workers are heavily in debt from years of buying into the American materialistic dream—the big house, the boat, the SUV. So one of the things that white-collar workers have to get beyond is that antiunion feeling. Where is the shame if sales people see themselves as workers struggling for wages and benefits as a group? Yet sales people have long felt that they are not like people on the assembly line.

In this regard, sales people are not so different from knowledge and information workers who somehow see themselves as existing independently, when in fact they are supported by an army of blue-collar workers, mostly women, usually poor, who spend their lives at machines. Everything is on the backs of those women, just as agriculture is on the backs of poor women around the world, where they toil for a few dollars a day if they are extremely fortunate. (In Haiti, it is closer to twenty-five cents a day!) The reality is that both here and around the world these workers are up against the wall. And when their eyesight weakens and their hands become less nimble, as they will in too short a time, they will be tossed aside so younger eyes and hands can produce for the corporation.

It is clear in today's digital age that *every* worker needs to have decent wages, health benefits, and good working conditions. Workers can either do that by struggling with corporations, which unions have to lead, or by obtaining these benefits through the society. Either way, workers in a democracy must have them.

The question is often asked, if employers don't give workers what is right and necessary to live decent lives, why don't the workers stage general strikes as workers do in European countries? In theory, it is not at all difficult. And a general strike, of course, is the thing that is most frightening to any system. In fact, there have been attempts at general strikes over the last forty-five years in the United States, but they have failed. One reason is that general strikes such as secondary boycotts are outlawed.

Secondary boycotts have usually been understood as attempts on the part of unions to hinder commerce and trade beyond a particular industry in which unions were not parties of direct financial interest. Secondary boycotts are exercises as free speech, which arguably could lead to negative consequences such as extreme violence. This possible consequence does not change the validity of the free-speech argument. Indeed, if the exercise of free speech can lead to negative consequences, so can symbolic speech such as picket lines where signs are carried or brochures handed out. This is why big business, which is dependent on the free speech of advertising, fears the free speech of workers since it may denigrate corporate property rights.

It also has become clear that conservatives used the U.S. Supreme Court as a means of claiming that Congress acted unconstitutionally when it sought to expand rights to individuals either under the general welfare clause, the Bill of Rights, the Commerce clause, or the Fourteenth Amendment. This was the gift of Rehnquist's constitutional position to the common good. Secondary boycotts are examples of support for those deprived of economic rights. Indeed, by their nature, they remain economic and do not result in overturning the political system. Associations may appear intimidating, especially in economic matters, whether for capital or labor, but they are not unconstitutional per se. Nevertheless, conservatives have historically fought the association of workers. As a result, tens of millions of American workers still check their freedoms at the factory or office door.

One of the reconstructions that must occur in order to repair this sorry situation is free speech at the workplace. The free speech issue has not raised its head in the workplace, as it did in automobile pioneer Henry Ford's day, because the people who are involved at mid- and higher-level management in corporations generally are the ones who earn their keep by talking and thinking and, in that way, they would not want to be denied the right of "ever irrelevant" political speech and discussions at their place of work. Speech is still controlled in a variety of ways. For example, when employees are fired, it is common practice for them to turn in their computers with their work on it to the corporation. The question is, does that work belong to the employee, who may have gathered information on his or her own, or to the employer? That boils down to the sometimes-murky question of property law, whether or not property is speech and vice versa. What is clear, however, is that free speech is deemed to be less important than property prerogatives. Similarly, the issue of political speech is less important than property rights, say, if people are demonstrating at Wal-Mart or other mall parking lots.

The question in a democracy may come down to the importance of adjusting and protecting voting rights.

THE AUTHORITARIANISM OF THE FALSE MAJORITY

The winning party in a presidential election actually represents a distinct minority of the nation, yet often acts (as most recently has Bush II) as if it had a *national mandate* for an ideologically driven agenda. Its task is often one of exclusivity: controlling the boundaries of citizenship—who's in, who's out—and the language for domination and exclusivity, which is meant to be internalized through education, the media, and institutions where speech is controlled, namely in the workplace. This begins to explain the importance of voting, especially for young people.

About 50 percent of Americans age eighteen and older did not vote in the 2004 presidential election—about the average percentage of nonvoters in recent elections. Thus in 2004 Bush II won 51 percent of the half that voted—but only about 25 percent of Americans of voting age. So while half the people do not exercise their right to vote, *everyone's* life is changed by the waging of preemptive war (the effects of which will last long past the term of the warring administration), the foisting of cultural values on hundreds of millions of people who strongly disagree with those values, the giving of lifetime appointments to right-wing judges, and the killing off of crucial environmentally sound programs from the Kyoto accords to meat inspection.

The fact remains that the dereliction of nonvoters further dilutes the checks and objections to authoritarian government and the National Security State. Conservatives voted in great numbers in 2000 and 2004. The irony is that nonvoters who were disillusioned with both the system and the radical agenda of the conservatives very likely were Democrats and liberals who could have stopped much of that agenda in its tracks. Their lack of interest suggests that they do not believe that the Democrats will implement a program that will benefit them. In fact, many of these Democrats may actually feel that they have no political party that encompasses a sufficient number of their views to make it worth their while to vote.

THE AUTHORITARIANISM OF ANTIENVIRONMENTALISM

The Republican Party of Theodore Roosevelt, who has been called America's first conservationist president, became the anticonservationist party under George W. Bush. Once Bush was given the presidency, he announced that he would "put public lands to work," which for his administration was code for looting of the public lands by oil and gas drilling companies and big timber interests, many of whom were friends, former associates, and big campaign contributors of the Bush family and Dick Cheney.

The Bush II propaganda machine created an image of him as a great admirer of Teddy Roosevelt, which was certainly true with regard to imperialism. But as the respected Wilderness Society has pointed out, he was TR's polar opposite on conservation questions:

> Roosevelt started the National Wildlife Refuge System; Bush wants to allow oil drilling in the most spectacular refuge. Roosevelt protected a number of the areas in our National Park System; Bush is fighting Park Service efforts to temper off-road vehicle traffic. Roosevelt greatly expanded the National Forest System; Bush is undermining protection of pristine portions of those forests. Roosevelt was the first to create national monuments by using the Antiquities Act; Bush is trying to weaken protection of the monuments created during the past five years.[30]

It followed that Bush would nominate Gale Norton, a protege of James Watt, Reagan's antienvironmentalist, antiregulatory secretary of interior, to be his interior secretary since the department controls one out of every five acres of land in the United States, a juicy prize indeed for drillers, miners, and timber companies.

Why anyone who voted to confirm Norton, including Democrats, should have expected anything different is puzzling since her resume was hardly a secret. According to the Natural Resources Defense Council, before becoming secretary, Norton consistently supported "takings" laws that would have the effect of rolling back decades of environmental protection while favoring pro-development policies that encourage environmental degradation, and pro-sprawl initiatives. As attorney general of Colorado, she "asserted that the Surface Mining Act and the Endangered Species Act are unconstitutional."[31] (In fact, the Bush administration began to undermine the law administratively and in courts in its first months in office.) With the omnipresent Grover Norquist, Norton founded the Council of Republicans for Environmental Advocacy, a group sponsored by mining, chemical, and chlorine industries.[32] (But the incestuous intertwining between Bush II administration officials and their powerful friends would catch up to people like Norquist. On June 25, 2006, the *Washington Post* reported that documents concerning the Abramoff fraud investigation showed how the lobbyist "secretly routed his clients' funds through tax-exempt organizations with the acquiescence of those in charge, including prominent conservative activist Grover Norquist.... Among the organizations used by Abramoff was [Grover] Norquist's Americans for Tax Reform.... A second group Norquist was involved with, the Council of Republicans for Environmental Advocacy, received about $500,000 in Abramoff client funds.")

Like other departments under Bush II, Interior doled out high-level jobs to lobbyists, attorneys, and spokespeople from the industries that they were supposed to oversee. The administration of Warren Harding, thought of as the signature corrupt administration of the twentieth century, was an example of good government compared to the Bush II administration.

J. Steven Griles, whose lobbying firm represented more than forty coal, oil, gas, and electric companies and trade associations, became Norton's deputy interior secretary with broad authority over national parks and national monuments,[33] and William G. Myers III, a lobbyist for grazing and mining interests was appointed Solicitor charged with the legal safeguarding of the federal government's vast park lands, wilderness, range land, and other natural resources.[34] (The Pentagon during the Bush administration was stocked with Secretaries, Under Secretaries, and Deputies who had worked for weapons suppliers. Old Washington hands had never seen anything like this civilian-to-military exchange.)

The Bush administration sought to circumvent three decades of national environmental-protection policy. They were tigers at obstructing the rights of opponents of their market-driven standards. At every turn, they tried to block environmental organizations from halting insatiable logging in western public lands by such Bush timber industry supporters as the American Forest and Paper Association. (In a full-page advertisement in the *New York Times*, environmental groups accused the association of waging a multimillion-dollar public relations campaign called the "Sustainable Forestry Initiative" to mask such destructive practices as large-scale clear-cutting of old growth and endangered forests.)[35] Environmentalists claimed that timber interests used fires that destroyed thousands of acres of forests in 2002 as a smokescreen to roll back forest protection rules—the Bush administration called it the "Healthy Forests Initiative"—even though the two largest fires in Colorado and Arizona that year were the result of arson.

Bush propagandists hoodwinked much of the public and many lawmakers to deflect criticism about their true intentions. They loathed the term "global warming" so they renamed it "climate change." The Teddy Roosevelt-sounding "conservationist" was substituted for "environmentalist." "Clear Skies" became a stealth term to disguise their antiregulatory agenda of easing the standards of airborne pollutants such as mercury emissions from aging coal-fired power plants. (The *Los Angeles Times* reported in 2004 that there was growing evidence that mercury had made its way into the aquatic food chain and was a serious threat. A National Research Council study in 2000 found that about sixty thousand children a year could suffer learning disabilities from exposure to mercury while in the womb because their mothers ate fish contaminated by the toxin.)[36]

This leads to what should logically be considered an absurd question, but with this brand of conservatism, it has become deadly serious: If you are not an environmentalist, what are you? Is it OK that someone else's drinking water is contaminated as long as your water isn't? Is toxic air OK as long as you don't have to breathe it? Are you unconcerned about dumping hazardous waste where someone else's children play?

Today's conservatives have lost their moorings; they have adopted the worst elements of modernism, which encourage the destruction of nature, whether it is public lands in the American West or the Amazon River basin in Brazil, and dropping out of modest environmental treaties.

Conservatives talk a great deal about preserving life, but it turns out that they don't conserve much of anything except big corporate interests—that is, selfish interests.

WHY DO WE PUT UP WITH AUTHORITARIANS?

The best source to go to in order to find out why Americans are shut out of the political process is the authoritarians themselves. If authoritarians would admit it, they would say—and it would not be a sarcastic commentary on the quality of the American electorate—"We don't want active citizens. We don't want the people's representatives who disagree with us in the public space making laws unencumbered by corruption, bribery, or coercion." Authoritarians also believe that citizens want to be told what to do and that they will accept hierarchy as a means of turning away from freedom.

But why are so many Americans willing to give up so much of their public and personal freedom with barely a whimper? Is it because they don't believe they really have freedom in everyday life? Is it because authoritarians are always prepared to give people entertainment instead of freedom? How can we explain Congress being tied up for months during Clinton's second term arguing over whether fellatio counted as sexual relations? For many social conservatives, sin is synonymous with freedom.

Another aspect of political authoritarianism is that it comes out of an ingrained masculine and militarist belief: authoritarianism gets the job done because people learn to take orders. Just as important, authoritarianism allows people to be inactive or submerge their own feelings to avoid tension. Authoritarianism in the political sense allows people to pursue their own interests—so long as those interests don't get in the way of political authority. In reality, what happens is that authoritarianism works very well with the way corporations have operated. The Catholic Church and other religious institutions operate on the basis of authoritarianism. Some religions give people hymns and rituals and even a place in heaven if they will just be quiet while they are here on Earth. Most corporations and the armed forces operate on a similar command system. Their experience is that efficiency and order work best.

Employees of bankrupt corporations seem to have internalized masculine-militarist authoritarianism so well that they are intimidated even when the corporations are bankrupted through no fault of the workers. Why else were employees of Enron and WorldCom—who lost their pensions and saw their 401(k) plans loaded with company stock reduced to virtual "101(k)" accounts—so docile in the face of the immoral actions of their superiors? If ever there were a time for those workers to exercise their freedom of speech to rant and rave, one would have thought that would have been it.

But freedom can be a very elusive idea. It must be understood in a context and relationship. Its genius is that it *creates* context and relationship. Freedom certainly does not mean the same thing to people in their everyday lives. Politically, the question becomes: Do you receive political freedom as an elective of the state and the corporation that guarantee those freedoms in a negative way by telling you what you can't do? Or are there certain natural rights and freedoms that are inherent? We know that free speech opens the door to true democracy—to access, participation, deliberation, and implementation—but does freedom of speech give you political rights of effective participation?

Professor Richard McKeon noted another form of freedom: the right to have the right answer and the right to have the wrong answer. In a political sense that also defines freedom. It does not define freedom in terms of economic questions. People who work in industrial plants under inhuman and dangerous conditions are treated as commodities when they are not organized collectively. They do not believe they have the luxury of the Bill of Rights. Is it because they are indifferent to the system? Or don't they have time to think about it because they are consumed with their families and jobs? Or do they have no use for the politicians they don't trust in the first place?

There is an answer, and it has a variety of meanings. There are those who take the position that politics is not everything, and therefore what they want from politics is to just come and go as they please and do their own work, whatever that work may be. The truth is that people want "someone else" to think for them. Whether it be political, economic, or medical issues, they want an expert or bureaus of experts and commentators to tell them what to think about matters that they don't want to take the time to think about or care about themselves. This is true even though most questions in public policy and politics require that citizens, more than anything else, use their own judgment.

Unfortunately, a passive attitude is also a statement about citizenship. It says that citizenship is not an important activity because it requires too much time and energy. So at this point, it is the people who really allow political authoritarianism to continue.

Chapter 8

Escape from Authoritarianism

A LIBERAL PROJECT CONSERVATIVES COULD LOVE

If the government suddenly restored your right to obtain the information necessary to live a truly democratic life, the yoke of authoritarianism would not be much lighter; you would still be confronted by the distinction between knowing about authoritarianism and *acting* on what you know. Even in dispirited times, there is a way to begin to throw off this yoke. It is called the Liberal Project. But give it whatever name you like, for the Liberal Project is actually a big tent for many diverse projects, large and small, that can make every aspect of modern living work.

At its heart, the Liberal Project is about the discovery and realization of needs, including the desires to pursue progress and happiness, which are there in all of us. The project is really the story of ideas, mutually shared intelligence, and action. It is about understanding the ways in which human beings are open to changing themselves and their social organizations. That is why conservatives, if they would think about it, would conclude they have no vested interest in poverty, racism, sexism, oligopoly, and capitalism as currently practiced, and they would find that they could benefit if not embrace the Liberal Project every bit as much as any radical liberal, moderate, or independent could embrace it.

The question for the Liberal Project is whether state power is necessary in order for projects to succeed or if it is enough to seed them in the culture outside of state power. It does not seem likely that the projects can go forward without paying attention to achieving state power and changing the character of the state, keeping in mind two stubborn facts that are not contradictory: government is needed to sustain the way people organize themselves, while at the same time it is the government that must be confronted and changed radically in order to deal with earth-shaking problems such as nuclear war, triumphal imperialism, destruction of the environment for corporate profit, and the type of globalism that is destructive of one third of the world, including parts of America. Such understandings and values, which are part of our current dilemma, are the basis of a politics that could allow the human race to endure.

Unpersuaded conservatives will say that these are liberal pie-in-the-sky ideas. But that only proves what many know: it is the conservatives who are the pessimists. After all, comparatively few men considered rape in wartime a crime until some women took it upon themselves to transform the thinking of men—conservatives as well as liberals—and helped pass a law making wartime rape as much of a crime as rape out of the battle zone. That in itself is an outstanding example of the Liberal Project because what has changed is that certain behaviors are thought to be beyond the pale. Such an idea begins a whole new process that goes even beyond the issue of rape in wartime. The national interest or international interest is no longer defined only by men and their warlike concerns. Interests must take into account and be defined by women equally with men. Laws are one step in the process of social change and new attitudes. Being appalled and revulsed by injustice is an important step in changing collective consciousness.

The Four Freedoms become crucial for such an understanding to guide women and men in their actions. Obviously, this process is hardly over. In fact, it is just beginning. Thus in every area of life there are those who have undertaken projects that by their nature serve as the seedbed for profound change, and those projects can and have occurred in every area of human endeavor.

Not many at the beginning of the twentieth century believed that we could rid ourselves of various diseases or see the end of domination as a legal right of whites over nonwhites. These problems may have appeared to be insurmountable back then, but they have been overcome through efforts that have been enormously successful, often to the chagrin of the Right. Technology and the information revolution, aided immeasurably by the ignorance and power-madness of leaders, makes this notion more than a dream; it could lead to international support for projects that by their nature force those in power to accept a changed reality in which people's interests, commitments, and loyalties are not necessarily geographically based. The problem, of course, is that new solutions to problems bring with them their own problems, which are sometimes relatively easy to solve but not always. Here, the powers of reason, will, passion, and good fortune go a long way.

Freedom of thought and free speech still guarantee what can be called "reasoned instability." This is the essence of democracy because it includes freedom in the political sense of choice, which is open, shared, and invariably conflict-laden in the context of cooperative rules. It is not really paradoxical to say that this kind of instability is truly necessary for freedom and reconstruction to succeed. That is the essence of the Liberal Project and the essence of a saner twenty-first century, as this cross section of projects (many originated by the Institute for Policy Studies) illustrates.

CITIZEN BUDGET JURIES

If we are to restore sanity to the country FDR liked to call these *United States*, we must again follow the money, beginning with *our* federal budget.

There is a way for the citizen to have a real voice about the federal budget process, a way to fight back against big-money special-interest groups and congressional pork projects. Following the jury system model, Citizen Budget Juries would be created throughout the country that would have a say in how tax money is spent, how much the federal government's departments should get from each tax dollar, how much departments such as Defense should *not* get for unnecessary and redundant weapons or, for that matter, waging preemptive war without a genuine national discussion.[1] Thus free speech becomes attached to practical problems of governing while creating ties among the participants, thereby strengthening democracy.

In Washington, they would say it is naïve to think that citizens "out of the loop" can know very much about the workings of government and politics. The cynicism is beside the point. Where there is citizen discourse and education, and where people are in a position to use their minds and hearts and deliberate toward reasonable solutions, much in the manner of our civil and criminal jury system, citizens will almost always make intelligent judgments in the right direction. Furthermore, there are antecedents for Citizen Budget Juries that are clearly constitutional. The citizen's role in maintaining and preserving the separation of powers is embedded in the Constitution: "The trial of all crimes, except in cases of impeachment, shall be by jury; and such trial shall be held in the State where the said crimes shall have been committed; but when not committed within any State, the trial shall be at such place or places as the Congress may by law have directed."[2] More important, Citizen Budget Juries are the manifestation of the Ninth Amendment, which grants participatory rights to individuals.

Citizen Budget Juries would begin their work with the federal budget because the budget is where the trouble begins in the United States and where a great deal of it could be fixed. The juries should also deliberate their states' budgets. And if they do not begin immediately at the federal and state level, then they should begin at the municipal level.

If this sounds like a debating society, that would be all to the good. New England town meetings have been great democratic vehicles for citizens' complaints and input. Citizens of Vermont pack numerous town meetings held by their Independent-Progressive Senator Bernie Sanders.

Citizen Budget Juries would open a new and different kind of dialogue between the citizenry. It has implications for all kinds of problems that stem from budget allocation: war, health care, education, Social Security, environment, the deficit—the list is practically endless because the problem is massive and growing worse by the day.

Citizen Budget Juries would be at least an important adjunct to Congress because there is no practical mechanism by which citizens can seriously cross-examine their government and its experts on major issues. The juries would provide the mechanism to dig into issues by cross-examining experts in a particular field, as was done by various groups and individuals in the environmental field in the 1970s and 1980s. For example, they examined the safety and efficacy of building new nuclear reactors by calling on experts to counter the claims of the nuclear power industry and its so-called federal regulatory agency. There is little doubt that these revelations influenced the banks that pulled the plug on building new reactors.

The Citizen Budget Juries would help to shut the door to the special-interest lobbyists and crony capitalists who are wired into the White House, Congress, and state houses as never before. With Bush II, lobbyists walked into previously closed-door congressional committee sessions and wrote legislation favorable to their clients. The nation's capital had become the corporate capital of America. (The number of registered lobbyists in Washington more than doubled from 2000 to 2005 to some thirty-five thousand. Starting salaries for the best-connected aides moving from Capitol Hill or the Bush administration to the big K Street lobby firms were about three hundred thousand dollars a year.)[3] In 2005, the moralist John Ashcroft started his own lobbying firm on K Street.[4]

Citizen Budget Juries would go a long way toward ending the practice of giving huge, no-bid contracts of the kind handed on a silver platter to Halliburton, the company Dick Cheney headed before becoming Bush II's vice president, to help rebuild Iraq after the damage that Cheney was instrumental in causing (and, critics say, overcharging the Pentagon in the bargain).

To be effective, Citizen Budget Juries should be official. Citizens would be picked at random from the jury rolls, as they are for civil, criminal, and grand juries. Results of their deliberations would be made public as they occur and would be disseminated through the media and the Internet. The findings would almost certainly have an affect on politicians. Over time, a "national citizen's budget" would be organized as the third alternative to the congressional or the president's budget. Every congressional district would have thirteen citizen juries of twenty-three people who would serve for two years—the length of a congressional term. They would hear testimony and analyze federal programs and their effect on their respective districts. The costs would be borne through the federal budget.

An easy way to implement the findings would be check-off boxes on your income tax return similar to the box on it now to give money to presidential election campaigns. Here you would designate what percentage of your taxes you want to give to each department—so much to education, so much to health, so much to defense, and so on, but up to a limited amount.

Of course, people will say it's crazy to have more juries when the envelope to report to the courthouse is already the summons everyone dreads and the duty everyone wants to avoid.

There are answers to that. First, the jury system is where democracy truly works because citizens have access to one another, they participate, they deliberate, their decisions are implemented, and they know that something they have done really counts. It is a way for people to be in the political space.

Second, in terms of political democracy, the jury system must be preserved as part of American life—an important part that is beginning to erode, as we are seeing with the secret Surveillance Court. The Citizen Budget Jury is a way to *ensure* the democratic system. It builds on transparency, assessment, and debate around collective needs and definitions of decency for everyone.

Third, citizen Budget Juries have a role to play in giving freedom of speech back to the people. There is no hiding the fact that in U.S. history, especially in Southern history, juries have not always been able to transcend racism and sexism. These juries were understood to be adjuncts to the office of prosecutors before any evidence was presented. Thus the entire system was corrupt because it was predicated on white supremacy, a feature of fascists. It was hardly a surprise that juries would not be able to transcend a rigged system of repression, given its cultural and economic roots in the South. But liberal lawyers successfully challenged the entire system of repression and restored the jury system to its role as a powerful democratic forum of citizen inclusion irrespective of race. This is another reason law projects in the 1960s were so important. They were able to use the law and cause judges to see the laws, especially the Bill of Rights, in ways that favored human rights over property rights and the power of the prosecutors.

Fourth, if the smoke and mirrors of the federal budget game are not challenged, the people will remain cut off from the process and will continue to feel defeated, and politicians like Bush II will continue to mislead the public and misallocate the public's funds. The current budget process is an antidemocratic and antieducational process because it does not begin from the principle of participation, understanding, and betterment for the largest number of people; there is no effective way to discuss and debate the political and ethical question of personal interests versus responsibility to others in the budget process. Presently, the budget is organized as a huge feeding trough that caters to the narrow, the parochial, and the personal with little sense of social responsibility manifested in choices.

Fifth, as journalist and political commentator Walter Lippmann argued, is it necessary to have elites interpret the government's statements to the people and the people's views to the government? The real issue is not expertise per se because expertise really is still dependent on judgment:

do you believe this set of statistics or that set of statistics? It is also based on credibility: do you believe what this person says or what that person says? So expertise is in a sense authority: Do you really believe that authority? Do you believe in peer review or is that system nothing more than an "old boy" network? If you can get behind that authority—and Citizen Budget Juries will provide a way to hold the feet of those authorities to the fire—you can ask where he or she got that authority. For example, virtually every day since September 11, the American people have been told by authorities that terrorism is a great danger, and if it takes the surrender of individual liberty to combat it, that's the price that has to be paid. Of course, terrorism is a danger, but surely it is not more of a danger than the rise of new strains of infectious diseases across the world or increasing poverty in the United States.

THE ROLE OF TECHNOLOGY AND THE LIBERAL PROJECT

If technology is a tool of violence in the way people are organized or the hardware they use, then technology will not be an instrument of either democracy or freedom. And it will bring more difficult—even species-threatening—problems.

An argument might have been made that Newt Gingrich was a conservative futurist who believed that conservatives should be optimistic and progressive. But for him progress was related to the kind of technological progress that the huge defense contractors believed progress was, namely, better war-fighting capability. As Bush II once told graduates of the Naval Academy, "Revolutionary advances in technology are transforming war in our favor."[5]

One of the extraordinary questions is to what extent technology should be considered a part of a moral philosophy. If it is part of a moral philosophy, what should that moral philosophy be? Although this question has been raised in different times and in different ways by various philosophers, they have never answered the question. Perhaps it can't be answered. Or at this stage, perhaps it is those people engaged in technology, in organizing things and people, who can best answer the question. After all, they can pretty much invent what they want, governed only by financial resources and the malleability of nature. That may explain why the scientists and technologists see themselves as evolutionary saviors. Certainly, the assumption of capitalism and socialism alike was that modernism—science and technology—was going to save us; if we can put a man on the moon, we can fix this and that here on Earth.

Nineteenth-century romantics doubted the sciences, but their alternatives had deep and frightening conclusions. At the extreme, they manifested themselves in the politics of fascism—represented by German poets such as Stefan George, whose interest in purity demanded a society of the Ideal, which had nothing to with everyday life or people. It pursued the Superman myth and accepted the Master-Slave view of humanity.

Therefore, given that this romantic direction is not one that anyone should favor, and given the problems science and technology cause (nuclear waste, nuclear death), what is the overall direction in which science should go? What are the consequences of particular experiments and where will they take us? Should there be boundaries on experiments and science? If so, what happens to free speech? What happens to freedom in general?

These are hardly new questions. They can be found in Plato's *Republic* with answers that are not acceptable to us. In the eighteenth century, Rousseau asked if science and technology dominated, would people be happier? He concluded that they would not.

The question of the benefits of scientific knowledge to humanity became a very important element in the modern understanding around which ideology—capitalism or socialism—was the real scientific engineer that could drive progress for the world. Science and technology represented progress, always with the unstated notion that progress meant happiness.

One must look more closely at the kind of technology and science that is being pursued. This is as true in very poor areas of the world as it is in our country, where our foundational literature such as the Constitution makes clear that happiness and technology are inextricably intertwined with patents, that is, private ownership against competitors and the public.

This linkage may strike some as trivial, but changes in the patent laws would lead to the reconstruction of the hierarchic and authoritarian and economic bias against worker community-shared production and responsibilities—to the extent that they can approach or become nonhierarchical—thus ensuring lives of decency and participation in all avenues of life, including the economy. In a nutshell, that is a fundamental project for modern politics. But achieving this depends on the actions that people take and the scale in which they undertake them. Admittedly, this is a hard standard, for so many of our institutions are predicated on hierarchy and unshared authority. But at a minimum, the linkage of political and social scale gives rise to various social movements and makes room for the continuous struggle necessary to demonstrate the power to keep or extend freedom.

The place to start is with the people who design technology because they can be either humane of destructive. When science and technology are used for modes of control over people, it defeats the whole notion of what human beings can be, and therefore it defeats what the Liberal Project is and turns progress into such a nightmare that no technological fix will help us in our attempts to wake up before human disaster becomes irrevocable.

SOCIAL MOVEMENTS AND THE LIBERAL PROJECT

The Power of Protest

Protest movements, which combine freedom of speech and peaceful assembly, by their nature make demands on the system to bring about change. But these movements often lack reconstructive elements because the choice of what is to be done and how to answer or not answer the complaint of the protest movement is in someone else's hands, namely, the powerful and the established whose interest, obviously, is in keeping the status quo of the pyramid of power. For example, peace organizations will remain politically weak until they reject the nature of the National Security State. At this point, however, they just want the state's leaders to repudiate nuclear testing or adopt so-called coercive diplomacy as against war making. Sometimes, they adopt the language of the Pentagon, talking about arms control rather than disarmament. So the system remains in place without much change and with essentially the same kinds of leadership regardless of political party. Thus when Lyndon Johnson, the Democrat, surrendered his presidency because of his failed Vietnam policy, his successor, Richard Nixon, the Republican, not only pursued the same policy but kicked it up several bloody notches.

Some movements have within themselves the seeds of projects that challenge the ongoing dominant system's managers and elites to act differently and even be catalysts to help in transforming the system and its institutions. Demonstrations in which we exercise free speech and association provide lingering memories that catalyze surprisingly "unintended" but positive consequences. In the 1960s, as part of the effect of the demonstrations against the war in Vietnam and the civil rights movement, free street medical clinics began to spring up. There was a powerful existential quality to the clinics in which the person or persons who began the projects lived them, which meant they were prepared to be the object of their projects, defending them and sharing their fate if they failed. The problem comes when the initiators of projects feel isolated and without much of a social or financial base and support group. So while the clinics help to alleviate, assuage, and confront the deeper systemic problems involved with medical care, those problems were not solved by a few free clinics.

But often these projects fail as a challenge to the system. They are either co-opted or overly praised, giving lip service to its aspirations but without immediate reform or systemic change. Surprisingly, the exercise of free speech figures into this calculus in a negative way. Free speech can serve established forces in a democracy that "invites" alternative voices to let off steam with the purpose of not changing the power structure or even particular policies that people are protesting. So while the massive anti–Iraq War protest marches in New York, Washington, and other U.S. cities in 2003 may have had the appearance of free speech (forget that the entire weight of the police and surveillance apparatus was used to curtail and diminish such demonstrations), they may have served the government's purposes by taking pressure off the establishment in a period of great tension.

Does that mean that protests and demonstrations such as those in recent years against war and economic policies of the World Trade Organization and the World Bank should be disbanded in despair? On the contrary, they should be expanded but with an important qualification: the projects must have practical visions that are tested and fought for. Demonstrators need not become well-intentioned marching societies that fall back to where they were before they took the first step. By their purpose, these movements may have arrived at systemic change without plan or intention.

The Power of Boycott

There was a glimmer of hope in 2005 that the worker tool of boycott was not quite ready for burial in America, problems of secondary boycott notwithstanding. The Coalition of Immokalee Workers, a farm worker organization made up largely of indigent immigrants who pick tomatoes in southwest Florida, called off a four-year national boycott of Taco Bell after the company agreed to increase the amount it pays for tomatoes (which it uses in prodigious quantities) by a penny per pound. The increase will go directly to workers' wages. Taco Bell also said it will help the workers' efforts to improve working and living conditions. As part of the agreement, Taco Bell's parent company, Yum Brands, which also operates KFC, Pizza Hut, A&W, and Long John Silver's, said that it will help to ensure that none of its tomato suppliers employ "indentured servants." Colleges and high schools across the country were instrumental in the boycott's success in the movement to "Boot the Bell" from their campuses.[6] (Here we see a crucial institution in the civil society—the university— challenging global corporatism as a result of internal pressure by students and unionized workers. This represents a model that will expand as universities are increasingly forced to choose sides in the delineation of morality and capitalism.)

The Power of Nonviolent Confrontation

As wages of workers continue a downward trend, education costs increase, and analysis in economics seem irrelevant to managing local and international economies for a recognized common good, popular protest may lead to changes in labor-corporate relationships and new contracts— without the engagement of government.

A version of nonviolent protest organized late in the last century, which owes its existence to free speech, has yielded important changes in consciousness. This project (which continues to expand) confronts global corporations and the military. It quickly grew from a handful of people into an international movement that challenged the imperial ideology of globalization with alternatives that featured human rights and dignity at the center of the economic and productive process. This is a natural progression to the emergence of a global peace movement that shows the linkages between the needs of societies; perhaps it will even lead to an understanding of the deep and economic causes of war that will help define what we mean by "peace" in the absence of wars without end. (It is significant that movements from the Left in Latin America in 2005 and 2006 have gained sufficient strength to change the direction and policies of their governments, moving them against oligarchy into democratic forms, hopefully adopting the moral pragmatists' view that the means define the ends.)

The Power of Imagination

Free speech (and sufficient funds) allows for the exercise of imagination and expanding social spaces for projects that change everyday life. This has been demonstrated in arts and science projects that may not be on a grand scale but serve as the building blocks of a transformed society. Take the Music Carry-Out project in which people could come in off the street to make music together on the spur of the moment. Or the Neighborhood Science Center where people also came in off the streets and did simple scientific experiments helped by graduate science students. There are any number of actions that one can conceive and that carry the seeds of a different or parallel society outside of the way the establishment usually does things. These projects, in which risks are taken to begin and then defend, are collectively the roots of a transformation as powerful as innovation for economic profit.

In a similar vein, one can imagine individual ownership of books in such a way that children get books and perhaps computers from outlets such as the Library of Congress, thereby building up their own libraries.

The Power of the Catalyst

Often a project that starts out small can open the door of possibility for others. One example is the Cities for Peace project, in which some 165 city councils across America voted against Bush's war in Iraq months and weeks before the invasion. Many city councils were against the war unless there was a specific involvement and sanction of the UN, others totally opposed the war. Historically, cities have borne the burden of the king's sport of wars. This is as true today as it was in the palace courts of the French and British. American city councils are catching on to this troublesome reality, which explains the success of this political project.

Cities for Peace in turn was the catalyst for Cities for Progress, a network that loosely united some 134 Republican and Democratic mayors to push issues on a local level that the Bush II administration and Congress either could not act on or refused to act on, such as meeting the Kyoto Protocols greenhouse emissions goals and pushing Wal-Mart to pay livable wages and reasonable benefits. The project makes use of local colleges and professors, city councils, and Citizen Budget Juries to assess current needs and funding allocations and town meetings.

In the 1980s and 1990s, thousands demonstrated at the South African embassy in Washington—and many went to jail—to end support of the apartheid regime and American trade complicity with South Africa. The strategy of nonviolence was successful and U.S. policy changed to enforce an embargo against South Africa. This important shift in policy was a catalyst for the liberation movement in South Africa. A generation earlier, the CIA fingered Nelson Mandela for the South African government; he was then arrested and imprisoned. This was a "hot fact" just as the assertion that there were no weapons of mass destruction was a "hot fact" that shifted the debate on Iraq.

The Power of "Hot Facts"

The way in which Americans get information about their government, as well as the quality of that information, can determine how long they must wear the yoke of authoritarianism.

Hot facts, while harder and harder to come by from mainstream media, are perhaps the most important information. Paul Goodman invented the term "hot facts." It means to look at reality carefully in an empirical way, evaluate facts that no one else has noticed, see connections, and thus gain insights about a situation others have missed.

A hot fact comes through research—though not necessarily heavy, intensive research. Sometimes it comes through insight or intuition. A child sees the emperor and says, "Look, that guy has no clothes." A hot fact can change the reality that everyone lives by.

Goodman urged that such facts should be pressed forward, which could bring forward a new social reality and allow us to frame the way we look at the world in different ways. Or a hot fact would cause us to do specific things to correct problems that previously we thought did not exist. For example, until recently, experts thought that the chemical analysis that was done on hair in criminal investigations was virtually foolproof. But as it turns out, it is actually fairly hit and miss.

In political matters, hot facts are necessary to reshape consciousness. Again, for totalitarians, the question is, how do you manipulate and control the consciousness of the nation as a whole? For Joseph Goebbels, it was by inundating Nazi Germany with lies, over and over, and using the lies to destroy opposition. This technique could be called "hot lies."

Is this much different from the elaborate shades of lies our government, whether controlled by Republicans or Democrats, has given us for a very long time? In American society, manipulation takes a far more benign form than it did in Nazi Germany; it happens through the kind of boosterism that endlessly assures the public that we are the best, most free, richest, healthiest, best-educated, most powerful nation in the history of the world. And our Gross Domestic Product (total value of final goods and services produced within U.S. borders in one year) is dependent on consumption.

Consumerism and its bottomless desire are equivalent to patriotism—so long as the nation does not get into major wars. Then consumerism must give way to guns. Remember, the Democratic liberal slogan in the 1950s and 1960s was that we could have guns and butter. But Hermann Goering's (Hitler's second in command) slogan was guns *before* butter. Why are these slogans important? For the Nazis the answer was clear. Military expansion was their first purpose, although ironically Hitler was careful not to impose rationing on the German middle class until his loss at Stalingrad.[7] The American view was that we were so rich we could have both—guns and butter.

There is a negative aspect to the information citizens gather and that aspect should be carefully assessed. Information about politics is presently in the form of "politainment," the modern union between politics and entertainment. This means citizens may come to see politics as unrelated to them or their daily lives. Rather, they see it played out on television and radio as a spectacle or, worse, a spectator sport. Conservatives discovered this new kind of power years ago, broadcasting their fairly unified message through popular radio and television talk-show personalities such as Rush Limbaugh (who reaches 20 million people a week) on hundreds of local and regional stations that advocate belief in family values, Christian fundamentalism, antiabortionism, prayer in the schools, creationism, and militarism, all paraded under the banner of patriotism.

Against this background, an information inversion is taking place. While government and large corporations seek to hide information about themselves and their entities, claiming all sorts of privileges to the point at which they claim a kind of "right of privacy" for themselves, the individual citizen is stripped of more and more privacy and is left wandering in the neverland where a citizen's deliberations are thought by the government to be outside the purview of the citizen! Trying to get information from the bureaucracy, whether federal, state, or local, is an enervating task, and some people simply give up trying, especially if they tire of being surveilled or having their photos taken at rallies, opening them to investigations.

Suppose information people *do* receive is wrong? Governments view their task as educating the public, but all too often it is education for the purpose of reinforcing hierarchic authority and judgments that will exempt authorities from cross-examination. (Authorities will have a much more difficult time attempting this maneuver when there are Citizens Budget Juries.)

Suppose citizens can't access information on major issues—information that they are entitled to as taxpayers—because the government routinely stamps information "secret" or makes it difficult to obtain even through the Freedom of Information Act? There are ways around this, too.

As most know or are beginning to discover, you can find out a great deal of information without breaking the law because the information is available at countless Internet Web sites, including government sites that are full of raw data (for example, data on the federal budget). If you want to learn about certain things, say, what is going on in Colombia with respect to drugs or dictatorships, you might be able to learn what the government knows about it by going through an international network of trustworthy organizations that almost always post information on the Internet. These sites are often linked to other groups that work on research and legislation. For example, look under AIDS on the Internet and you will find groups that are political on the issue such as Act Up and Global Alliance. Then you can share information and opinions with still others over the Internet or in person.

But there are ways of getting information that government and corporations might like to restrict but can do nothing to stop. One form that should not be minimized is a person's instinctive understanding that however outwardly sincere or inept leaders may appear, many are skilled at manipulating symbols to preserve the status quo—as long as the status quo favors them. They do so, for example, by keeping the poor in their place while lowering taxes for the rich. Those in power cannot stop the average person from seeing that they preserve the status quo to keep the poor in their place while changing it to lower taxes for the rich.

Another form of information is what we may learn from critical thinking. We can learn from easily accessible sources of information including newspapers, radio stations such as NPR and Pacifica, and television to a lesser degree, as well as magazines and books. And do not underestimate how much families can learn from each other when there is real discussion and debate about what is reported by the media and other sources. It may seem almost old-fashioned in the Information Age, but we also learn from relationships with friends, whether it's after school, in offices, on the assembly line, or at dinner. Just as there are Bible study groups, there could be public affairs and reconstruction study groups that focus partly on study and partly on action projects.

The Power of the Whistleblower

Whistleblowing happens when people on the inside of corporations or government find they can no longer do what their jobs call for them to do because they believe that particular organizational actions or policies are unethical or illegal. Whistleblowers feel morally compelled to go public with their information even though they may be seen as snitches by the rest of the bureaucracy and may risk their reputations and their livelihoods. They are often kicked out of their workplaces and lose their pensions. Nevertheless, some courageous people press on with what they see as either a matter of personal conscience, responsibility owed to the citizenry as the sovereign authority, or to their professional calling. For all whistleblowers, those who become famous and those who work in anonymity, free speech is crucial for their truth-telling.

Daniel Ellsberg, a Vietnam expert for both the Defense and State Departments, blew the whistle on Secretary of Defense Robert McNamara's top-secret study of dubious U.S. decision-making in the Vietnam War, a study that Ellsberg himself had worked on. Hoping the release of the material to the public might help end the war, the material was published in the *New York Times* and *Washington Post* in 1971 as the "Pentagon Papers."[8]

A. Ernest Fitzgerald, an industrial engineer who served as a cost analyst at the Pentagon, became something of a celebrity during the Vietnam War when he blew the whistle on Pentagon waste, saying: "Within the Pentagon, when people are being candid, I'm told bluntly that we have no need for cost control or cost reduction, that we can get all the money we need."[9]

W. Mark Felt, J. Edgar Hoover's second-in-command at the FBI, who had also participated in covert operations against anti–Vietnam War protesters, blew the whistle on the Nixon administration by giving clues about its criminal activities to the *Washington Post*'s Bob Woodward. Until 2005, when Felt went public, he was known as "Deep Throat" in print, history, and lore.[10]

People working in nuclear power plants have been whistleblowers who successfully prosecuted their cases through the Government Accountability project in Washington.[11]

Those who blow the whistle quickly find that their patriotism is questioned. Fitzgerald was told that his promised civil service tenure was a computer error, and his department was restructured to eliminate his position. It took four years and nearly a million dollars in legal fees to win reinstatement to his office.[12] Ellsberg was prosecuted by the government on twelve felony counts and could have received a possible sentence of 115 years, but the suit was dismissed in 1973 on grounds of governmental misconduct against him, which led to the convictions of several White House aides and figured in the impeachment proceedings against Nixon. Three whistleblowers were *Time* magazine's "Persons of the Year" in 2002. Cynthia Cooper blew the whistle on WorldCom's fraud, Sherron Watkinson on Enron's fraud, Coleen Rowley on the FBI for its failure to take seriously the case of Zacharias Moussaoui before September 11. They were treated with disdain by their bosses and colleagues.

The government continually tries to preempt whistleblowing before it can happen. In 1981, the Reagan administration created Standard Form 189. If federal employees refused to sign this gag order, they would lose their security clearances and thus their jobs. If they did sign, they could be punished for security violations, even for the release of *unclassified* information that had been retroactively reclassified as top secret. Eugene Scalia (son of Supreme Court Justice Antonin Scalia), the first Solicitor for the Labor Department in the Bush II administration, tried to undermine legal protections for whistleblowers in both government and industry.[13] Under Bush II, Homeland Security employees and contractors were made to sign pledges barring them from telling the public about sensitive but unclassified information.[14] Yet without the courage of a government whistleblower (perhaps more than one), U.S. citizens would not have learned in 2005 that the Bush II government, through the National Security Agency, had been spying on them for years. In 2006, a front page story in the *New York Times* reported that James E. Hansen, the top climate scientist at the National Aeronautics and Space Administration (NASA), said that the Bush II administration tried to silence him after he called for prompt reductions in greenhouse gases linked to global warming. (Hansen, who as chief of the NASA Goddard Institute for Space Studies in New York had simulated global warming computer models for years, released data showing that 2005 was the warmest year in at least a century.) It did not sit well with the Bush administration when Hansen said in a lecture in San Francisco that significant emission cuts could be achieved with existing technologies, particularly automobiles, and that without leadership by the United States, climate change would eventually leave the Earth "a different planet."

Hansen ignored restrictions placed on him by NASA, claiming that "communicating with the public seems to be essential because public concern is probably the only thing capable of overcoming the special interests that have obfuscated the top."[15] What made this scientist so courageous? Hansen believes the Earth's climate is at a tipping point, from which it may not be able to recover. The Earth's average temperature has risen nearly one degree Fahrenheit over the past thirty years, he says, and another increase of about four degrees over the next century would "imply changes that constitute practically a different planet. It's not something you can adapt to. We can't let it go on another ten years like this. We've got to do something."[16] A week after NASA tried to silence Dr. Hansen, they seemed to back down. In the meantime, other NASA scientists and public affairs officials have said that beyond Hansen's case, there were several "other instances in which [Bush II] political appointees had sought to control the flow of scientific information."[17]

But there is another side of the coin, literally: the False Claims Act was originally signed into law by Lincoln to combat fraud in Civil War contracts. People blowing the whistle on modern-day fraud in the government are promised a 15 percent to 30 percent share in any financial recovery. Since 1986, hundreds of whistleblowers have shared in over four billion dollars.[18] So while government and corporations may try to intimidate whistleblowers, fortunately for the country, they cannot gag them entirely. But the success of the whistleblower is dependent on free speech and the realization that a government or corporate civil servant owes his or her allegiance to the public at large when harm could come to the public.

SLEEPING ON YOUR RIGHTS

There can be as many Liberal Projects as there are citizens willing to take back their freedoms from authoritarians or expand freedom where it is still an aspiration. Projects described here and those that will be created in the future have the same duel objectives: putting the brakes on the actions fomented by authoritarians and reconstructing the government and the corporation so that they are opened to individual dignity, liberation, cooperation, and justice.

None of these projects was without personal risk, and there is no reason to think that such risk will disappear in the future. Nevertheless, there is cause for optimism here because the modern democratic form encourages these objectives. They are made available, sometimes through technology but invariably through struggles in which there are practical ends in view and a determination to secure a preferred direction.

However, the reconstructive method can only be derived through free speech and projects that show the type of lived reality that citizens care to bring into existence. There is sufficient evidence in modern liberalism that this is its purpose and that it works—but not without a struggle. For example, there was a long and honorable history from the last days of the nineteenth century through FDR to control corporations. Various ideas have surfaced since the nineteenth century, including corporate chartering, election of employees to boards of corporations, even worker-community sharing of responsibilities with corporate management for what goes on in the everyday life of corporations: their profits, investment allocations, and behavior with regard to environmental, social, and economic justice issues.

Thus there are definite things that the American people can do to help themselves, to think about, and to act on, but there is no chance of this working unless people have the will, unless they organize for broad objectives that are beyond single-issue organizing or single heroic acts, unless they *remain* organized and exercise their right of free speech. This may go against human nature and the individual's understandable preoccupation with the time and energy required for his or her economic survival, but there is no other way.

Big corporations and the "economic royalists," as FDR called them, came under fierce attach and scrutiny in his first two terms in ways that had not been known since the Progressive Era before the United States entered the First World War. The claim was that avarice and speculation have reached similarly dangerous heights masked by misleading economic statistics, unaccountability, and inequality.

Reasoned public action for broad objectives such as the restructuring of the corporation can no longer be contained in a locked box of unfinished business. It is free speech catalyzing new thoughts and new movements that unlocks practical programs and the redistribution of justice.

Ironically, in the discussion of free speech, silence is a major feature missing from liberal attempts at securing freedom and social reconstruction. Silence may be a religious cleansing for one in a monastery, and it is obviously crucial to protect the accused against self-incrimination. But in a free society silence means surrendering the public debate and accepting the legitimacy of injustice and stupidity that leads to annihilation.

If we do not secure free speech by using it, we are giving up that right and power to those who have shown no interest in the common good, who will say—are saying—"well, you never spoke out before; why are you bothering us now?"

Part Two

Freedom to Worship

In the future days which we seek to make secure, we look forward to a world founded upon four essential freedoms.... The second is freedom of every person to worship God in his own way—everywhere in the world.

—Franklin Delano Roosevelt, January 6, 1941

Chapter 9

Our Religious Sea Change

GOD'S HELP

When Franklin Roosevelt proclaimed the second of the Four Freedoms, he was really saying that it is not freedom of religion—as most still mistake it for—it is freedom to *worship*. What this means is the freedom to worship the way you choose—worship that which you value, have a connection with, or wish freely to subordinate yourself to. That is the essence of FDR's freedom to worship.

FDR left open the question of *how* to worship God. And he does not talk about freedom of disbelief—the freedom not to believe—or, for that matter, the freedom *not* to worship God. He would have probably been aware from his own experience that while religion was a significant part of life—certainly his—there was a negative side, framed by the nineteenth-century writer and activist Horace Greeley:

> To the conservatives...religion would seem often a part of the subordinate machinery of Police, having for its main object the instilling of proper humility and contentment into the breasts of the down-trodden, a sacred reverence for property.[1]

Both Roosevelt and Greeley would have known the roots of the American colonies, some of which were absolutist and Puritanical. Roosevelt would have known politically that the states were deeply influenced by particular religions, as in the case of Pennsylvania (Quaker, Catholic, and Protestant), New York (Jewish, Protestant, and Catholic), or Maryland (Catholic). From these groups and multiple sects of different Protestant institutions, any politician (certainly Roosevelt) was aware that in a democracy a continuing truce was necessary among the institutions, especially if they sought dominance one over the other, were expansionist, or poached on the religious territory of the other.

Whatever religious term is applied to American civilization, it is essential to see religion as a disestablishment idea that recognizes the danger that establishment of religion can cause for a nation. Look no further for proof than the terrible troubles the Sunnis, Shiites, and Kurds have had among themselves for centuries, in lands that did not become "Iraq" until the early twentieth century, not only because of control over material resources but because of religion. Note the attempts at theocracy in such nations as Saudi Arabia and Iran, which placed harsh burdens on people, especially women. Note the troubles Israel has suffered for decades, not only with the Palestinians and other Arabs, but also with themselves, the ultra-Orthodox Israelis versus the secular Israelis.

With religious nonfundamentalist Jews, part of their insight is also part of their dilemma: each statement in the Talmud is something to be debated—endlessly debated—and reinterpreted. Martin Buber, the twentieth-century Jewish scholar, philosopher, writer, and Zionist leader, had an answer. He believed that God is to be questioned. But he also thought that Jews can and should have a *dialogue* with God and that dialogue, in fact, is not authoritative but a continuing form of worship often framed as a series of doubts and questions. However, that is not the way it comes down nowadays in political terms when a political party's "God platform" (and multimillion-dollar media expenditures to market it) boldly claims: "*We* have the answers, this is the way it's to be."

Buber had a political solution to at least calm the Middle East strife: a binational state in Israel-Palestine between the Jews and the Arabs. He pressed very hard for this, but the concept was moved aside by the arrangements made between the Israeli leadership and the proponents of Jewish orthodoxy. The process of political accommodation touched all religions. Once the Catholic Church made converts of emperors and vice versa, the church changed in terms of political organization, and Jesus became a commodity of ritual, ornament, and symbol.

But the politics of survival for religious groups and their willingness to succumb to expedient tactics still leaves open the question of worship and religion. Organized religion might cater to the needs of human beings in their anxiety. They might sign concordats with the state whatever its ideology. But worship really does not change. Worship can be private or public, silent or hollering, bowing down or dancing, in cathedrals or storefronts. Religion is organized through institutions *outside* the person. God is not necessarily in the person. Worship may insist that God is *inside* the person irrespective of external religious institutions and their claim of external loyalty to the institution's tenets. Down the road, some may want to worship many gods, which was the way much of the world worshiped before Christ.

Freedom to worship can be interpreted as just that possibility in a democracy, which suggests that one of the Four Freedoms should read: "Freedom to worship any or many gods, or no gods." As Thomas Jefferson put it: "But it does me no injury for my neighbor to say there are twenty gods or no God. It neither picks my pocket nor breaks my leg."

This meant that religious people could believe what they wanted, but like the rest of society they were bound by their conduct, which was decided by secular authority.[2]

In America, we have passed through several stages of how we perceive ourselves. First, we were a Christian civilization, then we were a Judeo-Christian civilization. Now there may be more Muslims in America (some two million according to one study and seven million according to another study)[3] than Episcopalians, leading some to say that America is no longer a Western country but a Judeo-Christian-Muslim—maybe even also Buddhist-Agnostic—civilization. The term "Abrahamic tradition" covers any group tracing its theological heritage to Abraham, meaning Muslims along with Jews and Christians. So we are witnessing and perhaps taking part in an extraordinary homogenization that will probably continue well into the future. It will include Muslims who may seek cultural and religious control over their identities in Western nations but who will still be integrated into the American "rainbow."

Nevertheless, we are bound to see the unpleasant fallout of various Arab and Muslim groups attempting to protect themselves against irrational fears generated by extremists within the present dominant American culture. The belated discovery of Islam and awareness of Arab nations as more than the humiliated has caused a certain amount of panic in the United States and Europe, beginning with prison officials and police. They are now concerned about the massive prison population, especially in the United States, which has turned to Islam. Police use the opportunity of Islamic conversion in the prison population as a means of increasing their surveillance and applying Draconian rules for prisoners, adding to resentment and alienation. But since Muslims are no more criminal than Christians and Jews, Islam will become an issue politically in the United States, as Muslims want to be heard just as Asians and their various sects want to be heard outside of their religious ghettos. They attempt to assimilate into American society, but they are fearful of Americans and conflicted as they attempt to keep aspects of their own religion and culture. They are similar, in terms of their social place, to Japanese detainees in internment camps whose sons fought for the United States as soldiers in the Second World War.

While it is true that the United States prided itself on openness, its twentieth and twenty-first century leaders have had no problem assigning enemy-other status to particular groups that were either expelled or found themselves in internment camps albeit for nonreligious reasons. In terms of religion, it is the turn of the Muslims in the United States to be the "Ashcroft vision" of the enemy-other, even as Bush II praised the Muslim religion as a peaceful religion while also calling for a crusade against Muslim-dominated nations such as Iraq and Afghanistan. Muslims will remain in this suspect category if there are further terrorist acts in the United States, if terrorism occurs abroad as the London subway bombings in

2005 demonstrated, or if the United States continues to take seriously the idea of permanent war, especially against those who are dark-skinned. Then freedom to worship for Muslims will suffer as their mosques are surveilled and Muslim ghetto communities are spied upon and infiltrated.

Nations will be nominated as enemies of the United States even though they have no direct connection to terrorists. Generally, states need other states to fight, and it is better and, frankly, politically convenient to see particular nations as the origin or site of terrorism than it is to see terrorism as free-floating and without a command structure, which means it is not easily dissected. Still, such an enemy creates the possibility of claiming the need for a "total force," as the Defense Department has put it, to confront terrorist gangs and nuclear war.

It is also worth reminding ourselves that the way peace was kept in the American society, to the extent that it was kept, was through a hegemonic position that was defined in most public and commercial institutions by white Anglo-Saxon Protestants (WASPs) during the nineteenth century and a good part of the twentieth century. (While it may feel like an uncomfortable parallel, Saddam Hussein arranged for a hegemonic position for the Sunni's that allowed for religious diversity—after repression of Shiite challengers—and women's rights.) The Protestant hegemonic position in the United States was broken by immigration and the emergence of democratic city politics in which Catholics played a strong role in shaping the character of the Democratic Party with the continuous involvement of an expanding Catholic Church.

What effect this has had politically in the secular realm is not yet clear. Catholic Church leaders for the most part have weighed in on the abortion issue, as well as on a social welfare program that is not based on capitalist principles.[4] Whether their views on social welfare will prevail is yet to be determined and is linked to the economic condition of the nation as a whole and to the economic condition of Hispanics who are often Catholic in orientation.

Non-Catholic American universities by and large are reflective of the WASP tradition, even though at this point, many of the elite schools are administered by Jews. Protestant attitudes presently do not contradict striving and class, nor do they contradict toleration and openness—quite the contrary. In the process, the universities emphasize modern values that they want to uphold in the larger community and that seem to fit well with an updating of the dominant Protestant elite education. For economic and social reasons, parents want very much to get their children into universities that are governed by pluralism. This is true even for those parents who have discovered their own religious traditions being questioned at universities. Nonbelievers, that is, those who subscribe to ideas such as secular humanism, seek pluralism and pluralist education!

Conservatives in recent years have claimed that the greater enemy of God and the American way—greater than communism was—is secular humanism, by which they mean those who believe that an ethics can be developed without a God. Secular humanism is an ethics that derives from the actualities of daily life and what can be learned from the human past, so, almost by definition, secular humanism has to be very nuanced and is sometimes maddening in its intricacies. This is a problem for absolutists who are assaulted in everyday life by impure thoughts and images that upset the stability of the family. On the other hand, Roosevelt stood for Christian humanity seeking to bring together generosity with an awareness of suffering bounded by the pragmatic limits of political power to bring about positive change.

THE GOSPEL ACCORDING TO THE WHITE HOUSE

Roosevelt's own background was tinged with a type of Christian responsibility that probably came from his days at Groton, the New England prep school, where the upper-class boy was to live a life of obligation and duty, accepting Christ as the exemplar. Roosevelt was never far from this creed. Even as president, he wrote to his Groton headmaster, Endicott Peabody, in ways that made clear that religious fervor was not far from his ideological thought, which was combined with scientific pragmatism, such as repairing nature and showing respect for it.

It is important to the story of the Four Freedoms, however, to remember that while the Puritans and others fled Europe to escape from religious persecution, the Puritans themselves were not above an absolutist position toward the flock. It is one reason that Rhode Island and other colonies broke away from Massachusetts.[5] Persecution and bias have always been part of the social, economic, and political fabric in the United States, coming to a head (but never really disappearing for long) during Franklin Roosevelt's presidency when progressive New Dealers sought to escape religious fundamentalist belief through the acquisition of scientific knowledge, pragmatism, and secular humanism.

In his personal environment, FDR grew up at a particular time and in a particular class in which anti-Semitism was taken for granted and some may well have rubbed off on him, but he was certainly far less anti-Semitic than any leader of the time, including those in his own State Department. A turning point for FDR probably came during the Second World War when he talked publicly about the Judeo-Christian tradition. That was vital not only for the inclusive reference to Judaism but also because the word "Christian" included a long history of negative connotations in America. "Christy" was used as a pejorative for certain people in the government who came off as holier-than-thou. Christian crusades in the United States of the 1930s were identified with anti-Semitism and lynchings of black Americans, and sometimes with anti-Catholicism, although the Catholic hierarchy in the United States and other nations was nurtured by anti-Semitism and racism as well.

For Father Charles Coughlin, Father Feeney, and others, being Christian Catholic was an important authoritarian dogma used to simultaneously attack and defend themselves against Protestant power. Coughlin, called the "radio priest," capitalized on the new power of national radio to broadcast his creed from his small parish in Royal Oak, Michigan, to some thirty million listeners on Sundays (stations in London, Rome, and Madrid also carried his program).[6] He used anticommunism and anti-Semitism as the bait for a poor and lower middle class that needed answers linked to traditional unquestioning beliefs. This form of faith was rampant in Europe and in certain parts of the United States where Eastern European and Irish immigrants huddled around the mines of Pennsylvania and West Virginia and the steel mills of Gary, Indiana, Pittsburgh, and Detroit.

By the mid-1930s, President Roosevelt and the Catholic Church held some similar social purposes, including campaigns against unemployment, unfair labor practices, poverty, and discrimination. Father Coughlin, an early supporter of Roosevelt, ultimately turned against FDR and accused him on his radio show of being sympathetic to communism. Coughlin was difficult to control, and Roosevelt's popularity began to dwindle because of Coughlin's attacks. Eventually, the United States and the Vatican reached a quid pro quo agreement. According to author John Cornwell, Roosevelt wanted Coughlin silenced in return for renewed diplomatic relations. Eugenio Pacelli (Vatican secretary of state before he became Pope Pius XII), in turn, is alleged to have desired diplomatic relations with the United States as an assurance of U.S. friendship in the face of Soviet power in eastern Europe. In exchange, FDR arranged to have a personal emissary to the Vatican from the United States. Coughlin was finally silenced, the Vatican got its first American representative, and Roosevelt escaped the wrath of the Senate, which up to then wanted no representative to the Vatican.[7]

In terms of the politics of the Catholic Church, Pope Pius XII saw anti-Semitism as a tool of church protection and a belief system. The Jews were the enemy of his notion of Christian civilization and Catholicism. After all, the Catholic Church for most of its history was anti-Semitic and portrayed the Jews as the Christ killers and the enemy.[8] Even before he was pope, Pacelli negotiated with Hitler in an attempt to assert Vatican power over local churches, which in many cases tried to resist Vatican authority. The churches finally accepted the Vatican-Nazi concordat as a means of the Catholic Church protecting itself. One result was that the Jews went off to the death camps. Local bishops and nuns protected Jews in many cases. Pius XII had other concerns as well. Communism seemed to be expanding, and Germany was needed after the Second World War as a buffer against Soviet expansion. In the meantime, he sought ways of accepting fascism as a tactical and strategic matter to protect the power of the church. Distaste for Jews in this case was a mode of convenience to appease Hitler.

In the United States, the Catholic Church was closely linked to the Democratic Party and Congress as well as to executive power. Even as the Catholic population grew in numbers, most of its members saw religious doctrine as another story that need not be believed. Instead, a secular humanism challenged the religious believers, pointing out severe contradictions in their beliefs and even the immoral character of what they believed.[9]

People forget that Christian churches organized their doctrines for well over a thousand years on the basis of anti-Semitism and hatred of the infidel. And once the bishops of the church, including the heretic Martin Luther, weighed the political power between the wretched or the rich and the princes, they had no trouble throwing in with the princes and the rest of the oppressor classes, which is how Western religion and economic and military power organized itself to dominate infidels and reinforce hierarchies and order, while exploring and dominating the nonwhite world.

In the American context, the word "Christian" was taken over by the extreme Right. There was Coughlin's Christian Front, the Christian Crusade of Fred C. Schwarz, and the hatemongering of the anti-Semitic Gerald L. K. Smith in the 1930s, which lasted until the 1960s. Here, their religious stance served as the glue for the conservative program, which by the time of Nixon and then Bush II morphed into a new kind of extreme conservatism that in some cases included the Rightist Jews who favored the expansionist policies of Israel.

At the beginning of the twenty-first century, if you were "mainstream" religious, you were acceptable for high political appointments; thus, five out of nine members of the Roberts' Supreme Court are Catholic. Catholics in the early part of the nineteenth century in certain states such as New Hampshire were barred from holding public office, yet it is important to note that the towering figure of the Supreme Court, Chief Justice John Marshall, was a Catholic. The federal government had no qualms about sending in troops to the Utah territory to stop or at least inhibit the Mormon's practice of polygamy. And American Indian religions are still not accepted. But, generally, exercising power and having political authority irrespective of one's religion came to be a twentieth-century phenomenon in the United States. As Professor Marcia Hamilton pointed out, the Supreme Court "toyed" with the idea of a very special exemption under the assumption that churches were "moral."[10]

Politicians who aren't particularly religious know they have to have the support of religious figures and religious organizations. It would be surprising if any member of Congress did not identify himself or herself with a religion as a way to win votes or placate constituents. Few American presidents, whether great, unremarkable, ineffective, or corrupt, have not spoken of their faith or have been averse to wearing it on their sleeve if they thought that it would result in political benefits. Sometimes, there is more to the reality of belief then advantages of personal ambition.

George Washington believed that it was "impossible to rightly govern the world without God and the Bible,"[11] thereby excluding Indians. Lincoln famously said, "My concern is not whether God is on our side. My great concern is to be on God's side, for God is always right."[12] Herbert Hoover's ideas of responsibility came from his Quaker background, as when he declared, democracy's "highest embodiment is the Bible; on the political side, the Constitution."[13] Woodrow Wilson's strong Presbyterian roots gave him a religious mission to fulfill his political vision. Jimmy Carter talked about his "intimate" relationship with Jesus Christ. (Carter's favorite theologian was Reinhold Niebuhr, but it is doubtful that Carter ever mentioned Niebuhr's warning that "religion is more frequently a source of confusion than of light in the political realm. The tendency to equate our political with our Christian convictions causes politics to generate idolatry.")[14] Nixon's mother was a Quaker and while he spoke about a generation of peace and establishing a structure of peace, his interest in the Quaker tradition and its teachings was not much in evidence during his presidency, although he supported the treaty against developing and stockpiling chemical and biological weapons. He even championed the SALT One Arms Control Agreement limiting the number of strategic missiles but not warheads the United States and the Soviets could have on each missile. But for Nixon, religion was a prop until he fell to his knees and asked his Jewish secretary of state, Henry Kissinger, to pray with him when God and the Republican Party turned against him during the Watergate scandal. (During the bombings of Hanoi and other cities, Nixon was concerned that the United States should not bomb on Christmas because of the way this would look to the rest of the world.)

The president who has not publicly asked for God's blessing to guide the country in times of war or economic depression is the exception, and FDR was not that exception, as when he said, "Where we have been the truest and most consistent in obeying [the Bible's] precepts, we have attained the greatest measure of contentment and prosperity." FDR asked for God's divine protection of allied troops the day of the invasion (D-Day) in France, which began the end of Nazi power in western Europe. General Eisenhower, the Supreme Allied Commander, later called this effort the "Crusade in Europe."

Roosevelt also knew that the United States was becoming multicultural and therefore a nation in which diverse religious and ethnic tribes could turn on each other. Since FDR, politicians have tread lightly on doctrines of difference between the various religions and sects, especially in the Protestant Church. Politicians are aware that religious institutions play an important role in shaping the consciousness of the nation as it attaches to shame, guilt, and other more practical matters such as sex, power, and race. Since the Second World War, these all have created enormous social tensions in the churches. But the question for the state is also the use of force, which religion does not have direct access to.

It appears, however, that in the twenty-first century, war presidents who may fight aggressive wars and their version of the crusades are doing so as tyrants ready to use the citizens for the greater power of the tyrant and his clique. Religious institutions are needed, for God becomes the state's instrument for rationalizing and directing aspects of our lifestyle, which includes war. George W. Bush began a careless war for his glory, saw it go badly, and continued to throw more soldiers onto the funeral pyre, even as he met with a few (a very few) of their families to tell them how sorry he was. This attitude has nothing to do with worship of God and everything to do with hubris and stunted maturity. Once in power, it is how authoritarians play with the latent religious feelings of a populace as a means of masking their intentions.

Carter may have been America's first born-again president, but Bush II is the most overtly religious president in U.S. history—he sees war as the means to proselytize for his blessed mission. For Bush II, the state and religion are not distinct. It is why he favors faith-based initiatives from the executive offices of the White House. As the ACLU saw it, this meant faith-based federal spending, federal judges, federal laws, constitutional amendments, and public education.

Others under Bush II's command really did proselytize. The Evangelical General William Boykin, undersecretary for intelligence at the Pentagon, who was involved with Guantanamo and Abu Ghraib prisons, "allied himself with a small group called the Faith Force Multiplier that advocates applying military principles to evangelism. Its manifesto—Warrior Message—summons 'warriors in this spiritual war for souls of this nation and the world'." General Boykin often appeared at churches in dress uniform and polished jump boots when he preached: "Satan wants to destroy this nation, he wants to destroy us as a nation, and he wants to destroy us as a Christian army"; they "will only be defeated if we come against them in the name of Jesus."[15] Boykin's actions drew sharp protests from parts of the public and media, but in the end, he received only a mild reprimand.

In a similar vein, a 2005 report from Americans United for Separation of Church and State concluded that going back to 2001 the United States Air Force Academy at Colorado Springs frequently pressured cadets to attend chapel and take religious instruction, particularly in the evangelical Christian faith (whose chaplains are a growing force in the military); that prayer is a part of mandatory events at the academy; and that in at least one case a teacher ordered students to pray before beginning their final examination. The report said it found that non-Christian cadets are subjected to "proselytization or religious harassment" by more senior cadets and that cadets of other religions are subject to discrimination, such as being denied passes off-campus to attend religious services.[16] But does the Right, rather than fearing such questions, regard them as evidence of sublime conduct?

THIS PRESIDENT IS THE RELIGIOUS RIGHT

Strangely, Bush II's background, while obviously very different from FDR's (although both, it is claimed, had dominating mothers), is more important to the ongoing story of the Four Freedoms. For at least twenty-two years, until he turned forty in 1986, George W. Bush by his own admission was a "heavy drinker," the polite term the rich often use for an alcoholic. His drinking life (and some believe his drug-abuse life as well) began at an Eastern prep school, continued at Yale and Harvard, and apparently ended when evangelist Billy Graham, a Bush I family friend, convinced Bush II to overcome his alcoholism to become a "born again Christian." (Graham may have been "America's pastor," as he was called, but he was clearly the "Zelig" of all modern presidents, invariably at their side for a photo opportunity and rallying believers to the side of decency. American Jews in established Jewish organizations thought of Billy Graham as a good friend. However, Nixon's White House tapes, released in 2002, included a conversation between Graham and Nixon in which Graham disparages Jews, saying, "They're the ones putting out the pornographic stuff" and their "stranglehold of the media has got to be broken or the country's going down the drain." Graham added that the Jews "don't know how I really feel about what they are doing to this country." Graham claimed to have no memory of the conversation.)[17]

The public never learned much about Bush II's alcoholism. As president of the United States and commander in chief of the country's armed forces (and by extension much of the Western world's armed forces), his past should have been an open book. But Bush glossed over or left out important details of his life beyond even his drinking and questionable service in the Air National Guard that may have influenced his policy decisions as governor and president. Mostly, the media gave him a free pass. During the 2000 presidential campaign, when Oprah Winfrey asked him about his drinking, he said he stopped because his wife told him he needed to put his life together. End of story. When Oprah asked him in another interview about his reported drug use, he said, "I'm not going to talk about what I did 20 to 30 years ago."[18] And he did not.

Bush's temperament in office fits the pattern of what Alcoholics Anonymous and substance abuse counselors call a "dry drunk," a recovering alcoholic who is no longer drinking, one who is dry, but whose thinking is clouded. Such individuals are said to be dry but not truly sober. As a psychological profile, people like Bush tend to be rigid in judgment and outlook and impatient; they also tend to overreact and reach decisions out of personal certitude.[19] And it was in this context that

Bush II was saved by his ambition, which he melded to the symbols of good versus evil and Jesus.

Dry drunk or reformed sinner, Bush II flaunted his newfound power. In 1993, just before running for governor of Texas, Bush hinted at the certitude he would bring to public office when he allegedly told a Jewish reporter that only believers in Jesus go to heaven. Yet one writer wondered how Bush as president, eighteen years after disciplined sobriety, could be "so fumble-tongued, incapable of stringing more than two coherent sentences together, snippily irritable with anyone who dares disagree with him or even ask a question, poutily turning his back on the democratically elected president of one of our most important allies because of something one of his underlings said about him (Germany's Schroder [sic], of course), listlessly in need of constant vacations and rest, dangerously obsessed with only one thing (Iraq)."[20]

Bush's record of public religiosity, however, is quite clear. He was not shy about using his faith as a political weapon and personal cleanser. Preparing to run for president in 1999, he assembled leading pastors at the governor's mansion in Austin for a "laying-on of hands" (a covenant rite in the Bible, the method used to bestow a special divine blessing or a special form of recognition), revealing to them that he had been "called" to seek a higher office.

Bush stopped the show during the 2000 television debates with Gore when he said his favorite political philosopher was "Christ, because he changed my heart."[21] (Not to be outdone, Gore, who spent a year taking religious courses at Vanderbilt University, said as president he would ask himself, "What would Jesus do?") Bush's answer obviously was calculated because that kind of question was bound to come up in much the same way candidates are asked: "Who is your favorite writer?" "Who is your favorite president?" (In fact, Bush used the same answer almost a year before when he was the Republican front-runner.) But Bush really seems to believe that Jesus *is* his man. Jesus was an interesting choice because Jesus did not write anything, so all we have is what others say about him. Most people learn by word of mouth—storytelling and oral traditions—from family and friends. One suspects this is the way Bush learns. So one can make fun of the parochial religious influence on Bush—his having God in his back pocket, so to speak—or see it as something of a put-on in American life, but such an attitude has been shown to be a mistake. Storytelling and oral traditions are central to the way humanity centers itself, including the way we use elections, illegitimate or not.

As noted, Bush began his presidency under a cloud after losing the popular vote in 2000, nevertheless believing in God's will that he be president. Once he was ensconced in the White House, his intentions became obvious. He set out to destroy any vestiges of Roosevelt's New Deal and Johnson's Great Society, proclaiming the United States as the supreme warrior nation, and preaching the kind of moralism one might find coming out of the mouth of a reformed alcoholic or addict. His speeches were laced with Biblical references, absolutes, repentance, and state-sanctioned violence:

- "The liberty we prize is not America's gift to the world, it is God's gift to humanity."[22]

- "We Americans have faith in ourselves, but not in ourselves alone. We do not know—we do not claim to know all the ways of Providence, yet we can trust in them, placing our confidence in the loving God behind all of life, and all of history"[23]

- "We can also be confident in the ways of Providence, even when they are far from our understanding. Events aren't moved by blind change and chance. Behind all of life and all of history, there's a dedication and purpose, set by the hand of a just and faithful God."[24]

- "Freedom and fear, justice and cruelty have always been at war, and we know that God is not neutral between them."[25]

Bush II left no doubt that his purpose was to meld the force of God with the God of force. He wanted to move in a very different direction from that which is healthy for a modern democracy. Though a believer in being reborn, his views on religion did not seem dissimilar from those held by twentieth-century dictators Antonio Salazar of Portugal and Francisco Franco of Spain, patriarchal authoritarians whose religious fervor was aimed at stability and a hierarchy of power and command that fit well with Catholicism of the type favored by Pope Pius XII. David R. Gergen, who worked in four preceding administrations, observed that Bush "made it clear that he feels that providence intervened to change his life, and now he is somehow an instrument of providence."[26] And as an instrument of providence, Bush is absolved of responsibility for an aggressive war in which tens of thousands died.

Did Bush really believe that he was an instrument of providence, or was he simply the ideal politician to pander to evangelicals and born-again Christians who, with sixty million adherents, represent one of the most powerful voting blocs in America? Probably both. As a Bush cousin said, "I always laugh when people say that George W. Bush is saying this or that to appease the religious right. He *is* the religious Right."[27] As the country saw, with the Rightist president, the religious Right can have unprecedented influence on the making or unmaking of federal policies such as legal abortion (against); HIV/AIDS prevention and cure programs (generally against); stem cell research (generally against); faith-based programs (for), strict conservative judicial appointments (for), and teaching creationism in public schools (for; Bush thinks the jury is still out on evolution).

Bush II is the example of the hedgehog in Isaiah Berlin's essay "The Hedgehog and the Fox." He is the hedgehog who seems to know one thing: he was chosen by God and therefore has power to decide the reality that he has chosen to construct. Of course, there is much that is beyond his blasphemy, for there is nothing in his statements that has the slightest bit of doubt or modesty, even in the eye of war or (God-invoked?) hurricanes. For that matter, there is nothing in Bush II's statements that is intended to withstand scrutiny. They are shallow statements, which only have meaning insofar as they appeal to triumphalism and the assumptions that he defines: Christianity, God, and good and evil. Public policy in this context means little except to the extent that it promotes attitudes and frames questions that characterize even the most virtuous of men as cowardly.

What sustained Bush II for a surprisingly long time was the modified hedgehog attitude that one hears from some Americans: "Don't confuse me with the facts." Certainly, Bush had little interest in being confused by reality or facts. He came armed with cliches and platitudes, inscribed as "higher values," that had little to do with the multiple realities, some of which he unwittingly created, that now befall humanity. The applications, in one form or another, have found their way into national attitudes and created in the public a puzzlement that was intended to be placated by his leadership—and will be around long after he is not. (Bush II dared to conflate God's voice—his thin silence—with his own. And if this were not enough, he asked the citizenry to undertake actions that had no humane or ethical basis, thereby undercutting our own law and the fragile international law that Roosevelt sought to bring into existence.)

THERE IS A RELIGIOUS LEFT

Evangelist Jerry Falwell, the 1979 founder of the Moral Majority who once announced that had had "a Divine Mandate to go into the halls of Congress and fight for laws that will save America,"[28] and televangelist Pat Robertson, founder of the Christian Coalition in 1989, introduced Christianity as a Rightist political movement.

With so much talk about the religious Right, or the Christian Right as it was known in the beginning (the two names are used interchangeably today), many Americans are unaware that there is also a strong religious Left in the country that has been underreported for years but in fact was on the scene *first*, going back at least to John Brown, who believed in his role as the avenger of the sins of slavery.

Beginning in the 1920s, a mission of Protestant ministers used the teachings of Jesus as a means of confronting industrial capitalism in the United States. This was an important change because through the First World War and beyond, most of religion, primarily Episcopal and Presbyterian, fit perfectly with exploitation as the instrument to keep the people in their place. Clergymen like the radical A. J. Muste and Reinhold

Niebuhr began organizing industrial missions in Detroit to change the conditions of factory workers. This carried over for a long period of time in the American tradition, past the Father Coughlins and Gerald L. K. Smiths, to the pacifist tradition around the confrontation of war led by clergymen such as Martin Luther King Jr., the Berrigans, J. T. Vivian, A. J. Muste, William Sloan Coffin, and religious sects such as the Mennonites.

The religious political Left today is represented by such people as Reverend Barry Lynn, executive director of Americans United for Separation of Church and State (founded in 1947), probably the major organization fighting to maintain the wall between church and state. Many other religious groups on the Left fight for justice with their voices and pocketbooks, including the Fellowship of Reconciliation, the largest and oldest interfaith peace organization in the country, whose mission is to "replace violence, war, racism, and economic injustice with nonviolence, peace, and justice," and Americans for Peace Now, which has worked for decades to strengthen Israel's security through peace with Palestinians. The Sojourners, founded in 1971 by Jim Wallis, describe themselves as a voice and vision for social change. Wallis battles to provide an alternative perspective on faith, politics, and culture. Usually a critic of the Right, he holds views that are independent of the Left. American Jews plagued by affection for the ideal of Israel, nevertheless are committed to social and economic justice. This sentiment is continued by the work of Rabbis Arthur Waskow and Michael Lerner (the latter through *Tikkun* magazine), who seek to meld social activism with religious purpose.

Their task is to ensure that actions taken are integral to a moral means and are also linked directly to the explanation of ends that a society quickly sees as a common good.

One can choose Reverend King, who would say that violence is not a complement to peace and love, or Reverend Falwell, who opposes the SALT treaties, nuclear disarmament, gays, and feminists. Both should be protected in their freedom of speech, association, and religion, but most would consider King (his philandering notwithstanding) the moral one, for he celebrated humanity in this world. He confronted ruling oppressors and proposed living life in such a way that there is no need for an opium of the kind that shapes a heaven of perfection after death while others suffer in this world.

King moved toward leadership and the crucible of suffering in civil rights because, in an existential sense, that was the problem he was directly confronted with. Politically, he hoped that the notion of civil rights defined as "one person, one vote" would open other doors, for example, to ending economic injustice. In his own way, Lyndon Johnson thought that the right to vote could change the distribution of economic and political power in the nation, but King found out that it only goes so far.

So religion as a political instrument is not a so-called black-and-white issue. It is a question of religious interpretation and ethics and how they fit with the direction of the active social forces that move society. It is unlikely that even among the most fundamentalist readers of the Bible, who look to it for guidance in daily life, there would be any who praise the institution of slavery. But not many would read the Ten Commandments as countering slavery because slaves were once considered private property.

ONWARD, CHRISTIAN SOLDIERS ...

The religious Right with their neoconservative complement are certain that whatever the reason or pretext, war against the infidels (twenty-first century Crusaders versus Moslems) is a necessary war. Like Bush II, they believe that using their faith as a call to arms is not only moral but a call from God, who demands that they act on his silent command. This may require permanent revolution, but it is a price neoconservatives are prepared to pay for their view of the good.

The religious Right never questioned the rationale for the invasion of Iraq beyond the cooked-up notion that it actually had something to do with September 11. It did not question the war in Afghanistan or our treatment of prisoners. So on June 1, 2002, some nine months before the contrived invasion of Iraq, it was entirely fitting for Bush II to address the graduating class of the United States Military Academy in the typical absolutes of American triumphalism fortified by the simple message of the religious:

> We are in a conflict between good and evil, and America will call evil by its name. (Applause from cadets.) By confronting evil and lawless regimes, we do not create a problem, we reveal a problem. And we will lead the world in opposing it. (Applause.)[29] [Note how Bush II calls on revelation, and adopts God's directing hand for the rest of us.]

And at the National Prayer Breakfast in Washington on February 6, 2003, a self-assured Bush preached:[30]

> Events aren't moved by blind change and chance. Behind all of life and all of history, there's a dedication and purpose set by the hand of God. [Bush II makes clear he is a fatalist and determinist, an instrument of God.]

Of course, one can pick and choose Biblical verses to suit one's beliefs and intentions, but it does seem curious that missing from the presidential pulpit is a modicum of introspection—something along the lines of Psalm 55:21:[31]

> The words of his mouth were smoother than butter, but war was in his heart: his words were softer than oil, yet were they drawn swords.

Or Psalm 68:30:[32]

> Rebuke the company of spearmen, the multitude of the bulls, with the calves of the people, till every one submit himself with pieces of silver: scatter thou the people that delight in war.

Or the old reliable of church and synagogue, Isaiah 2:4:[33]

> And he shall judge among the nations, and shall rebuke many people: and they shall beat their swords into plowshares, and their spears into pruning-hooks: nation shall not lift up sword against nation, neither shall they learn war any more.

But when services are over, the United States remains a warrior nation, and many of our leaders seem to prefer taking their marching orders from the enduring 1865 hymn sung at the State funeral of Dwight Eisenhower:

> Onward, Christian soldiers, marching as to war, with the cross of Jesus going on before. Christ, the royal Master, leads against the foe; forward into battle see His banners go![34]

Chapter 10

Holier Than Thou

ORIGIN OF THE SPECIES

Pat Robertson's Christian Coalition claims to represent more than two million people of faith; even though some critics say it represents closer to four hundred thousand, the organization is still alive—and kicking liberals and anyone else it believes gets in the way of its goals.[1] Robertson's spiritual leadership showed itself when he advocated the assassination of the left-wing elected president of oil-producing Venezuela because it would be cheaper than going to war with that country.

Even more fiery groups have emerged to claim their share of religious leadership and the power to affect secular issues. Focus on the Family, led by James C. Dobson, produces his syndicated radio programs, which it says are broadcast on 3,500 radio stations in the United States and more than 5,000 stations in 163 countries.[2] Dobson protégé Tony Perkins, head of the Family Research Council, hosts the weekly national radio program *Washington Watch Weekly*. He also appears on mainstream television shows such as *Today* and *Good Morning America*. Perkins feels he "has a tremendous burden to reclaim the culture for Christ."[3] Like fellow religionists on the Right, Perkins often makes news when he goes after the federal courts, as he did on his group's Web site. He wrote that "the liberal, anti-Christian dogma of the left has been repudiated in almost every recent election, the courts have become the last great bastion for liberalism. For years, activist courts, aided by liberal interest groups like the ACLU, have been quietly working under the veil of the judiciary, like thieves in the night, to rob us of our Christian heritage and our religious freedoms."[4]

Many small groups and vocal individuals with a fire-and-brimstone message in person and via spirituality Web sites have roles in the religious Right. Jay Sekulow, a Christian radio host, is chief counsel of the American Center for Law and Justice. Randall Terry, a virtual one-man show, has fought in the religious Right trenches for years. The acerbic William Donohue is the long-time leader of the Catholic League for Religious and Civil Liberties.

Whatever personal differences and jealousies various players on the religious Right may have with each other, they generally come together to try to frame their message in terms of good versus evil. Politically, it is a message that leads to the eradication of the adversary by making him or her both morally wrong and inhuman. The religious Right will pressure producers and advertisers to censor movies, plays, songs, and television and radio shows whose values they abhor. (They bullied CBS into canceling what they said was a critical docudrama on the Reagans in 2003; it was later shown to a smaller audience on cable.) They will pressure public libraries to ban and remove adult and children's books they say undermine their definition of family values. They are in the thick of the battle over judicial nominations. They have attempted—with some success—to turn the courts into instruments that will countenance the breaking of the wall of separation between church and state.

In all of this, Rightist conservatives of the Bush II stripe believe that they are heeding the teachings of Jesus and see nothing contradictory in the fact that the United States spends trillions on war, nationalist triumphalism, and nuclear weapons, while refusing to change the status quo regarding even a modicum of wealth distribution to help raise up the poor. Nor do they find it inconsistent that they want to dictate not only how the society lives but also how it should die. Such thinking is an article of faith for them.

While not standing on this past tradition, conservatives feel quite comfortable with that part of the Christian heritage that embraces the absolutism of those who call themselves "God's servants." Their values revolve around patriarchal family, the state, and private property. Their origins are not pretty.

Such ideas had their own roots in America in the racist ideologies of organizations such as the Ku Klux Klan. At its height in the 1920s, the KKK had between three and five million members who were predominantly poor whites.[5] But it actually had support in the universities as well, where study was given over to reinforcing racism. Anti-mongrelization also had its supporters in the university system. Before the work of Franz Boas, a Columbia University professor of great eminence, Columbia was a prime example of racist thought. There are earlier statements of the Supreme Court that America could afford to be color-blind because, in the last analysis, it was a white nation. Such ideas are part of the residue of American social thought, so it is not surprising that Christian fundamentalism is often related to racism. But it has other features.

The ideology of modern fundamentalism is often related to patriarchy. A wife must be alluring and a good manager in the household where she might appear to reign supreme. But outside of family, nonworking wives are not to have a voice unless they champion submission. The Right makes patriarchy a fundamental, invariant part of life. This was not disputed by one of the few women celebrities on the religious Right, Phyllis

Schlafly, founder of Eagle Forum, when she fought against the Equal Rights Amendment. (It should be noted that men on the Left did not take women's rights seriously until women organized for themselves.) For his time, FDR was progressive on women's issues, having found that his wife Eleanor was his ambassador to America's Left and dispossessed. His secretary of labor was Frances Perkins, the first woman in U.S. history to serve in a cabinet post. Roosevelt lived through the women's suffrage period, and he comprehended that with votes might come the need to pay attention to women as political actors. He also saw that Woodrow Wilson had no choice but to capitulate to the women's right to vote once they began chaining themselves to the White House fence in protest.

When it comes to conservative worship, it would be well to recall that some churches were started by street missionaries that were not at all conservative—like Jesus himself. John Wesley (founder of the Methodist Church, leader of the Evangelical Revival in the early 1800s) and the people who followed him are an example. They supported ending slavery and helping the working class find new kinds of decent and dignified lives.

It is hard to predict what the dominant strain in a church is at any one time because a church as an organization is just as prone to political pressure and the winds of change as any other institution. During the Vietnam War period, parts of the antiwar movement were very much allied with religious institutions, including the Clergy and Laity Concerned, the National Council of Churches, and strong elements in the Catholic Church such as that represented by Bishop Thomas Gumbleton, who sometimes had the support of the Vatican, and Father James Groppi, a prominent Milwaukee civil rights activist. It would be a mistake to not comprehend the stunning effect Pope John XXIII had on the church in the 1960s. This showed itself among the nuns who left the cloistered world of convents to take political stances from the Left, sometimes spending long periods in prison because of their hatred of war and nuclear arms, sometimes embarrassing their more conservative male counterparts as they worked for the end of that war.

In general, those are not the views of the Right, but if Christianity is looked at as a whole, those *were* the views taken by churches in their struggles to be morally relevant in the way that Jesus was politically relevant during times in his life of great stress and social crisis. Even in the case of Christian fundamentalism, there is a series of political issues about which there could be agreement to some extent with liberals. At least a fruitful conversation could be held, especially where there is a willingness to suspend the belief that God's voice can only be heard by those who claim to have access to His perfect knowledge. For example, large numbers of Christian fundamentalists dislike the advertising and violence on television, and it is undoubtedly true that there are a number of people on the Left who also feel similar revulsion. Both argue that "family values" are being distorted because such advertising and programming idealize pornography and violence. It is not just the sexual titillation that bothers them; it is the assumption of official violence in order to beat out confessions from the detained as exemplified by the long-running police program *NYPD Blue*, which, in syndication to hundreds of local television stations and independent channels, continues to be both racist and fascist. Such programs promote the belief that evil can be done for the sake of the good, as in the case of beating witnesses or potential defendants.

Like many on the Left, a great number of those on the Right also see what happens on television as a crude manifestation of capitalism and they, too, feel disenchanted. The corporations (perhaps their own) want to turn bedrooms into a bazaar, selling everything they can. So too with members of the Hollywood film and video industry, which does not shirk its commercial responsibilities for profit, using sexual violence as means to a profitable end. It is not as if Christian fundamentalists are not capitalists, and zealous ones at that. Many are highly successful entrepreneurs. And many have brought their born-again beliefs directly into their businesses, in some cases imposing them on employees in the workplace— and sometimes at home. Indeed, one fundamentalist preacher said that he did not favor abortion because it cut back the number of customers in a consumer society such as ours.[6]

PICTURE OF THE FAMILY THAT NEVER EXISTED

The religious Right can preach about family values (which happened to be a code word coined by the Right for patriarchy—and too often abuse in the family), but the fact is that *half* of all first marriages in the United States end in divorce. Churchgoers probably will not hear from charismatic ministers of the new megachurches (one can hold 16,000 worshippers) that, according to the George Barna Research Group (described as a born-again Christian company by the Boston Globe), born-again Christians have the highest divorce rates—or that liberal Massachusetts has the lowest![7] Or that the consequence of the unholy state of matrimony in the twenty-first century is an army of single mothers and single fathers. So the religious Right's picture of the family does not quite exist in reality today—nor did it ever. One need only use the Bible to show the dysfunctionality of family structures with their high incidence of rape, incest, assault, and murderous competitions.

And there are other contradictions. One has to do with the velocity of social change. Fundamentalism and orthodoxy, perhaps more than other groups, feel the need to hang onto some fixed principles and values that its followers can call their own and can teach their children. That usually comes through a belief in the Bible or creationism where the world and humanity's place in it are fixed.

Aeronautical engineers and missile engineers, from the Southwest principally, are found in surprising numbers among Christian fundamentalists.

They seek a rootedness they do not find in their daily work. American technologists understand very well the velocity of change because they are bringing it about, and paradoxically they are also looking for a set of fixed principles or boundaries—not dissimilar from the orthodox yearnings found among Muslims and Jews—in their attempt to make sense of the human condition in a period of intense flux.

The question of the religious Right fighting for their beliefs, as reactionary as they might be in practice, is not the central problem of American politics. (Some feel otherwise, for they believe that beneath all the pretty talk clerical fascism is alive. This thesis will be tested as it relates to the repression of Arabs, Muslims, and immigrants generally.) The practical question is whether there is rampant racism on the religious Right—structural and personal—and similarly rampant anti-Semitism. There are some ironies as a result of American society's heterodox and surprising character. Thus the religious Right is attempting to recruit more blacks and Latinos to their cause and has been supportive of the right wing in Israel. Christian fundamentalists have given money to the Israeli Right. Both groups have overlapping and supportive constituencies among members of Congress. Unlike most American Jews, some fundamentalists traveled to Israel during the height of the Intifada—the Palestinian suicide bombers. Jerry Falwell was particularly supportive of Sharon and the Likud Party, a relationship that began during the Reagan period, as was the case with Tom DeLay when he was Republican Majority Leader in the U.S. House of Representatives.

It is not churlish to ask how much of the work of the Christian fundamentalists is really religious and how much is for acquisition of political power. The United States, at this point, is way beyond questioning that Christian fundamentalists want political power; they *are* in power in many places. When the moderates of the Republican Party and on the Left were not paying attention, as religious scholar John Green pointed out, many local religious Right "activists gravitated into the Republican Party as chairmen and campaign consultants. Once an independent force hammering at the president and Congress, they are now an institutional part of the party base. They must be kept mollified—but in balance with other parts of the coalition, like business, and within bounds of what a majority of voters will accept."[8]

But what if the religious Right is *not* kept in balance and over time seeks a theocratic state in policy prescriptions augmented by militarism and corporate oligopoly? Suppose the radical Right cloaks itself in moral values and faith? What is the rejoinder? What is the secular answer? The problem is magnified if the Democratic Party leadership embraces the moral values that favor big business, "prudent" wars, and balanced budgets paid for by the poorer classes, while presenting these ideas as if they have high ethical value.

Chapter 11

Religious War without End:
The Church Crosses the State Line

The separation of church and state is intensely political in the most basic sense because it goes to the heart of how pluralist communities can be maintained without real civil war erupting—a civil war that could deal a terrible blow to freedom to worship and bring down the other freedoms with it. In an everyday sense, the question is: how much independence from secular law should religious communities and institutions such as churches have when it comes to secular control of criminal law, taxation, and free speech?

When the Supreme Court gave Bush the election in 2000, Republicans in Florida taunted Democrats with "You lost, get over it, put it behind you." But conservatives cannot overcome the Senate's rejection of Reagan's Supreme Court nominee, Robert H. Bork, whether as a cynical political device or a deep-seated need to never give up on *anything*.

Bork illustrates not only the state of conservatives in this country but also the state of those disagreeing with conservatives. Bork seems to have spent his life searching for meaning, which he found in authoritarian order backed by the violence and purity of the state. In his student days at the University of Chicago in the late 1940s, he was a Trotskyist believing in world revolution. Later, he became a member of the Catholic Church's most conservative organization, Opus Dei. After Bork was denied a seat on the Supreme Court, he retained public prominence as a "shadow justice" for social conservatives. In 2005, he lashed out against the opinions of Justice Anthony Kennedy, the Republican who got the job he coveted, charging that Kennedy typified a Supreme Court "no longer sticking to the Constitution" but "enacting a political agenda."[1] (As if an ultraconservative reading of the Constitution has no political agenda or the Constitution is not a political document understood as such by its postrevolutionary drafters. Why else were the doors to the Constitutional Convention padlocked during deliberations?)

The Supreme Court, for Bork and for many other conservative judges and politicians, had become "the enemy of traditional culture" in "speech, religion, abortion, sexuality, welfare, public education and much else."[2] So much ill will and rage has now built up on both sides over religion, family values, abortion, subsidization of religious schools, gay rights, the death penalty, pornography, the display of the Ten Commandments in the public space, and school prayer—each one cunningly exploited as a "wedge" issue by Rightist conservatives, especially under Bush II—that it would take knowledgeable and deeply sensitive leaders, who may or may not be conservative or liberal, to step back from the church-state line that has certainly been crossed by the Right.

And what if leaders do not step back? Then a religious civil war is not unimaginable. There have been very good examples all through the history of other countries in which war occurred between different sects, indeed over how religion was to be practiced in different areas of one country, including Iraq and our own.

A critical element fueling such a war is the fact that religion, when it is not a universal conception that allows for inclusion of different beliefs, becomes a system for *exclusion*. It can say that those people who are not part of one's particular sect are evil, or they are infidels, or something else is wrong with them that is outside the boundary of that religion, and its members must fight against them.

Conflicts between different religious sects and religions have been one of the most critical and horrifying problems humanity has found it necessary to live through and confront. It does not matter when or where it occurs, whether it is the struggles between Ireland's Protestants and Catholics, the struggles between Shias and Shiites, the struggles within and against Judaism, the struggles of Huguenots and Catholics in France, or the Greek and Russian Orthodox confrontation of the Western churches. The line between culture and religion disappears, ultimately finding its way into a violent mode unless directly and specifically considered. (From the point of view of policy, it is important to be aware that some cultures and nations such as Iran and Iraq have had public views that conclude that the disaggregation of religion from secular affairs will be considered.)

In recent years, religious extremists in America have routinely walked right up to the line, tormenting abortion rights advocates, and they have sometimes crossed it and murdered for their beliefs. A former close associate of Randall Terry (Terry was a spokesman for Terri Schiavo's parents) is serving time for murdering a doctor. The Florida judge in the Schiavo case received death threats and required armed bodyguards.[3] When Schiavo died, Majority Leader Tom DeLay's threat seemed like more than rhetoric: "This loss happened because our legal system did not protect the people who need protection most, and that will change. The time will come for the men responsible for this to answer for their behavior, but not today."[4] Six months later, it was DeLay who had to answer for his behavior when he had to step down as Majority Leader after he was indicted by a Texas grand jury on criminal conspiracy and money laundering charges. Another Texas Republican, Senator John Cornyn, fed the fire when he warned that judges might invite physical attacks with controversial decisions. Legislators who cut Medicaid with abandon[5] and make war with alacrity could hardly make up for it with their crocodile tears and their support of Ms. Schiavo in her last days. Similarly, the Catholic Church's attempts to shield pedophile priests on the grounds that such matters were outside the jurisdiction of the state became indefensible and outside the church.

Fundamentalism as it relates to abortion is part of the culture wars based on faith, opportunism, and dominance, that is, the wars that decide who and what sets the agenda for society. Such a conception, which may be muted, reflects a real war between groups in this society nonetheless, just as, for example, there is a very different sense in different parts of the United States with regard to religion and exclusion. What is involved in the drive from the religious Right to teach creationism in the public schools—going back to the Scopes monkey trial in 1925—is not only a difference in point of view about the Bible but also a difference in point of view about culture and how people are to live, which is always subject to change in a democracy. One of the more divisive current examples is the struggle of gays in various church denominations, not just for the right to legally marry but to openly exist as gays and to pray as gays (or as human beings who happen to be gay) within their religion of choice.

Thus we should not assume that churches are impervious to radical change in their own actions and internal cultures. Not long ago, it would have been unheard of that a woman could be a bishop, and now women are bishops in the Episcopal Church and other churches as well. Before the civil rights struggles of the 1960s, it was said that the most apartheid part of American life was on Sunday morning in the Southern white churches because so many worshippers were members of the racist White Citizens Councils and blacks were not to worship alongside whites. So there was a conflating of universalism in values that were predicated on desegregation. Fights went on in the churches around it as a political matter. But in the end, universal values of dignity won if only by a razor-thin majority in some churches.

However, there is no reason to assume in history—surely not in American history—that certain things are always settled. In the twenty-first century, conservatives now have the money, organization, and will to fight by presidential, legislative, and judicial means on any issue they wish to pass or prevent, and they have demonstrated that they *will* fight whether it takes one year or twenty years. A conservative senator from Alaska summed it up after his bill to drill for oil in the Arctic National Wildlife Refuge was defeated in 2003: "It's never decided until we win." That is the reigning conservative process that liberals and moderates have been slow to grasp in their attempts to create consensus.

A BASE FOR THE FAITHFUL IN THE OVAL OFFICE

In the 1960s, liberal churches received government funds to operate Head Start and some low-cost programs. Attempts were made—not always successfully—to separate religious instruction from secular activity. Under Bush II, attempts at separation were replaced by a doctrine of commingling religious activities with a White House office on faith-based activities.

Nine days after his inauguration in 2001, George W. Bush issued his first executive order (a device presidents, including FDR, often use to avoid the arduous task of seeking legislation from Congress which a president fears he would not get): establishing the Office of Faith-Based and Community Initiatives. Bush II had kept a campaign promise—or so it seemed to the faithful—to allow religious groups to distribute grants to the poor directly from the White House, something no president had at least overtly attempted. Eight billion dollars was earmarked for the first year. Bush called the faith-based office "one of the most important initiatives" of his administration.[6]

Admitting that "more than one out of six American families with children live on an annual income of $17,000 or less" (the government's definition of poverty at the time was $18,660 a year, a very low calculator) Bush acknowledged that "our nation has a long and honorable commitment to assisting individuals, families, and communities who have not fully shared in America's growing prosperity."[7] Then came his proselytizing:

> Government can write checks, but it can't put hope in people's hearts, or a sense of purpose in people's lives. That is done by people who have heard a call and who act on faith and are willing to share that faith. And I'm not talking about a particular religion—I'm talking about all religions under the Almighty God. And we should not fear those kind of programs.[8]

The faith-based program did not escape criticism. Some critics said it was a cynical political program to win the votes of the religious Right. Others said it was straight-out interference by the state in religion. The office raised the hackles of many of the religious groups it was supposed to help or count as supporters. Many African American denominations were nervous about the newly blurred church-state line. For some Jews, the born-again influence inside the White House opened up the preeminence of Christ—which was interesting considering that Jews held powerful positions in the Bush administration: Paul Wolfowitz; I. Lewis Libby; Michael Chertoff; Douglas Feith, Rumsfeld's undersecretary for policy; Dov Zakheim, undersecretary of defense; Richard Perle, once chairman of the Defense Policy Board, Rumsfeld's unpaid advisory panel; and Press Secretary Ari Fleischer. (Bush was able to scar over some of the old sore with his commitment to the Sharon government in Israel. Many American Jews also seemed quite forgiving of born-again Christians—as they were of anti-Semitic leaders like Nixon—so long as the United States supported the Israeli government's West Bank and Gaza strategy of the moment, which usually included elements of the claim of many orthodox Jews that the West Bank is rightfully part of the "Land of Greater Israel," whose origin they trace to ancient Judea and Samaria, while other extreme orthodox Jews claim that Israel should not exist as a nation-state—until the Messiah comes.)

No matter the religious affiliation, money became an issue. Traditional Protestant denominations, a vanishing majority in numbers, felt that if "smaller" religions got a share of faith-based money, there would be less of the pie for them. Pat Robertson, a Bush ally, nevertheless warned his "700 Club" legions that the faith-based initiative could be a Pandora's box: "What seems to be such a great initiative can rise up to bite the organizations as well as the federal government." He was particularly concerned that religious cults (competitors for money and souls) such as the Church of Scientology, the Hare Krishnas, and the Moonies could receive federal funds. Robertson was right to worry. The *San Francisco Chronicle* reported that at least four longtime operatives of the Reverend Sun Myung Moon, the Korean evangelist and self-proclaimed new world messiah, were "on the federal payroll or getting government grants in the administration's Healthy Marriage Initiative and other 'faith-based' programs."[9] Robertson became a convert to the faith-based idea when his Operation Blessing received a half-million-dollar faith-based grant from the Department of Health and Human Resources, proving again the Russian adage, "Where money speaks, God keeps his mouth shut."

The Faith-Based Office never got all the money Bush promised, but over the next few years it managed to dole out several billion dollars to religious groups. Some groups complemented to their own proselytizing. Clergy who endorsed Bush in 2000 received generous grants. The charitable operation of Reverend Herbert H. Lusk II's Greater Exodus Baptist Church in Philadelphia got $1 million.[10] When the Luther House Foundation of Southern Chester County, Pennsylvania, was awarded $10.3 million to build an apartment building for low-income older people, the group's past president said, "We won't have to say, 'Oh my goodness, is it terrible to have a cross hanging on a bulletin board?'" Some grants, although comparatively small, seemed to serve a higher purpose. A group called Life Connections at the federal penitentiary in Leavenworth, Kansas, was given fifty thousand dollars "to help inmates about to be freed who volunteer to participate and pick one of six religious programs to follow. Activities include a two-week spiritual retreat and six weeks of intense religious study."[11]

Seven months into the faith-based office's first year, its first director, John Dilulio, a University of Pennsylvania professor credited with putting the faith idea in Bush's head during the campaign, quit. In an interview for an *Esquire* magazine article by Ron Suskind a year later, Dilulio said, "I heard many, many staff discussions but not three meaningful, substantive policy discussions. There were no actual policy white papers on domestic issues. There were, truth be told, only a couple of people in the

West Wing who worried at all about policy substance and analysis, and they were even more overworked than the stereotypical nonstop, twenty-hour-a-day White House staff."[12]

The article continued: "On his primary mission—push forward ideas and policies to partner government with faith-based institutions—Dilulio says that he saw the beginning of what was to become a pattern: The White House 'winked at the most far-right House Republicans, who, in turn, drafted a so-called faith bill that (or so they thought) satisfied certain fundamentalist leaders and Beltway Libertarians but bore few marks of compassionate conservatism and was, as anybody could tell, an absolute political nonstarter.... As one senior staff member chided me at a meeting at which many junior staff were present and all ears, 'John, get a faith bill, any faith bill.' Like college students who fall for the colorful, opinionated, but intellectually third-rate professor, you could see these twenty- and thirty-something junior White House staff falling for the Mayberry Machiavellis."[13]

Dilulio, wrote Suskind, defined the Mayberry Machiavellis as political staff—Karl Rove and his people—"who consistently talked and acted as if the height of political sophistication consisted in reducing every issue to its simplest black-and-white terms for public consumption, then steering legislative initiatives or policy proposals as far Right as possible. These folks have their predecessors in previous administrations (Left and Right, Democrat and Republican), but in the Bush administration, they were particularly unfettered."[14]

Not surprisingly, Ari Fleischer dismissed the *Esquire* article as "groundless and baseless." Dilulio stood his ground—for a while—then withered and issued an apology. *Esquire* stood "strongly behind Suskind and his important story."[15]

But funding for the faith-based office remained an issue. From the beginning, Bush wanted to make the faith-based office and ten similar federal agency offices a permanent part of the federal government. Various bills were introduced in Congress. Democrats balked at mixing church with state. Many Republicans saw it as a new federal welfare program. To keep the office running, Bush issued a second executive order in 2002; indeed, the office continued to run on executive orders. (Bush is the executive order champion. He issued number 183 in his first year, more than Clinton, Bush I, and Reagan combined in their first year.)[16]

Equally damning were the revelations of David Kuo, deputy director of the faith-based office for much of Bush's first term until he, too, quit in frustration in 2003. Kuo has written, "There was minimal senior White House commitment to the faith-based agenda. Capitol Hill gridlock could have been smashed by minimal West Wing effort. No administration since [Johnson's] has had a more successful legislative track record than this one. From tax cuts to Medicare, the White House gets what the White House really wants. It never really wanted the 'poor people stuff.'"[17]

THE CHURCH-STATE WALL BEGINS TO BREAK DOWN—IN 1774

The faith-based office is the latest proof that the line between church and state was crossed in various ways long ago. Congress opens each day with a prayer from a chaplain, a carry-over from the first Continental Congress in 1774. The Declaration of Independence states that "all men are...endowed by their Creator with certain unalienable rights." "In God We Trust" has been printed on U.S. currency since the 1860s and has been engraved on postage stamps. A marshal intones, "God save the United States and this Honorable Court," as the Supreme Court enters its courtroom. And in 2004, the Supreme Court found that it was not an endorsement of religion for children and others to say the Pledge of Allegiance with the "under God" phrase. "Ceremonial deism," Justice O'Connor wrote, is "simply not religious.... Certain ceremonial references to God and religion in our nation are the inevitable consequence of the religious history that gave birth to our founding principles of liberty."[18]

There is another point at which the state crosses the "church" that one does not usually consider. Armed forces chaplains are paid by the military, which means that chaplains are under the protection and control of the military, not the churches. But suppose that during confession a soldier reveals to the chaplain a military secret whose potential consequences have made him feel uneasy or guilty. Who then has access to the confession: the military authority or the religious authority? So, in effect, the line between freedom of religion and the establishment of a state religion is crossed once taxpayers begin paying directly for religious services rendered by the state. This has already seriously affected Muslim chaplains in the armed forces, as the country saw in the case of Captain James Joseph Yee, the army's Muslim chaplain at Guantanamo during part of the Iraq War. Yee was arrested on suspicion of spying and held for more than two months while "the military dragged his name through the mud" (as the *Washington Post* put it), but he was never charged with more than mishandling of classified materials. The army finally dropped all charges against him—except administrative sanctions for adultery and downloading pornography from the Internet. Subsequently, Captain Yee got the army to remove the reprimand from his record, but they never apologized.[19]

The Guantanamo situation is repeated in different guises throughout the U.S. prison system: who does the prison chaplain serve, the prison officials and guards or the prisoners? The management of American prisons can be a never-ending struggle between wardens and guards on the one hand and prisoners on the other. For example, different sects and religions seek "accommodations" for inmates in regard to food, dress, hair appearance, and segregation at prayer from fellow inmates. In the setting of the prison, it is obvious that the power of the state, in its most raw, most coercive form, governs. However, religious practices and their blanket denial can result in an undertow of prisoner rebellion resulting in riots.[20] Such matters are of great concern to prison officials. What is important to note is that in institutional settings such as schools, military institutions, and prisons, religious institutions and religious workers seldom, if ever, challenge the authority of secular power. They see their roles as "help-mates" to reigning civil power.

The army rank of general is frequently used in nonmilitary positions without most people thinking that it mixes church and state. During and after the Second World War, Cardinal Spellman of New York was also the vicar general of the armed forces. When Bush II introduced his Faith-Based program, he told the country that he wanted to "rally the Armies of Compassion." Military descriptions for religious good works, such as the Salvation Army with its hierarchy of officers, seem jarring to a great many people, but probably just as many consider such ceremonial phrases a harmless ritual, for so much of religious practice is predicated on linguistic manipulation of symbols. It is noteworthy when a society cannot find a vocabulary of action for the good except through the use of military terms. The concept of the military includes many functions from command to defense to changing boundaries. Our boundaries are constantly changed by words and metaphors into different, seemingly contradictory foreign territories, such as the use of public funds for Catholic universities that receive National Science Foundation grants for individual research.

People may ask, what is wrong with that? Perhaps nothing as long as citizens realize that in giving money the linkage between religion, the state, and the purse is *reinforced*. So the idea that a wall exists between church and state—and here the conservatives are right—is not true. The wall is thin even though the assumption of early thought on the constitutional separation of church and state struggled mightily to recognize its impermeability as necessary for the health of both. The state, however, never surrendered its power to ensure that religious institutions were law abiding, whether questions had to do with polygamy or the use of obnoxious racist standards.

In practice, religious institutions are respected because it is believed that, in the main, religion brings together positive, ethical values that a capitalist society needs in order to balance desires created through marketplace excesses and resulting in individual selfishness. Simultaneously, religion also blesses the rich as God's reward for living a successful life. How else can we explain Henry Ford, J. P. Morgan, Andrew Carnegie, or Texas oil tycoon Sid Richardson for that matter, except that capitalism and religion are linked to the benefit of both?

Some Marxist thinkers believed that religious conflicts are, at the root, struggles over resources, including possession of land or control over productive assets. Historically, what is hidden behind religious freedom *is* property and the power to tax religious property. Exempting religious property from taxation is a very old practice going back hundreds of years that turned out to be both a protection for religion and a protection for the *power* of religion, that is, for the people such as the monks who ran the churches. What the churches did, in effect, was lop off land for themselves and then the kings had to figure out how to get some of that land back without incurring the political wrath of church hierarchies. The solution was tax exemption for church lands.

In the United States, tax exemption has been a way of life, and there have been few strong moves publicly to take back lands or tax land from the churches. (Note that churches can be taxed for profit-making businesses they own.) This question becomes more real when hard-pressed municipalities and states struggle to find sources of badly needed revenue to pay for basic services, such as fire and police protection, sanitation, or just to keep public libraries open. On the other side, vast properties of churches, synagogues, mosques, temples, and any organization defined by the Internal Revenue Code as having "church-type" characteristics, have been removed from the tax rolls. Thus a religious organization likely pays no property tax on buildings and property it owns, such as land, houses of worship, schools, cemeteries, camps, and hospitals. Does this constitute an indirect form of taxation without representation for nonbelievers or even those who *are* religious?

Of course, there would be a big fight if a municipality or state tried to tax religious property—even though that idea has been floated without success since the beginning of the republic by powerful politicians such as James Madison and Benjamin Franklin. Perhaps their views can be implemented in modern form if it is shown that these church properties are not passive; they should be tithed by the municipality. They would be able to receive some credit for work with the poor, homeless, addicts, and those suffering from abuse.

Most churches would argue, "We already do that sort of thing." But they do so only in part. One way to think about this is to ask: How much does a particular church *really* provide for the common good of people living in the surrounding community, regardless of the varied religious beliefs of that community? Or does the church just take care of itself? If it just takes care of itself and has no commitments to the community at large other than saving of souls in preparation for a life after death, should the tax collector or a joint board of state and religious representatives make that determination? If religion is treated like doctors who are taxed on their good works—saving the person's body—perhaps churches should be taxed as business corporations in the business of saving souls. And should a person be taxed for providing sustenance to his or her soul just as we expect to be taxed on food we eat? These questions, when they are mulled over, may not be implausible for a nation that claims it is so religious, while basic needs go unmet in this world.

HOW MUCH POWER AND GLORY?

In the 2004 presidential campaign, some American cardinals, bishops, priests, and the Vatican itself publicly stated more than once that Catholic politicians should be denied communion if they supported a woman's right to choose to have a legal abortion. It was, of course, an infringement on the politicians' freedom to worship by the very people who claim they are responsible for what to believe and worship.

The church's stance was a transparent threat against Catholic John Kerry, not because he personally favored abortion—he stated publicly that he did not—but because he supported the right of a woman to act according to her conscience as well as her physical and mental condition. (The church had more quietly sought to make the same case against Governor Mario Cuomo when he considered running for president.) A few cardinals and priests came to Kerry's defense, and he found churches in which to take communion. But the big headlines were given to Catholic (and evangelical) clergymen who denounced Kerry from their pulpits throughout the campaign although, as Garry Wills pointed out at the time, "Modern 'right to life' issues—abortion and contraception—are nowhere mentioned in either Jewish or Christian Scripture." Wills added, "The bishops have no special mandate from their office to supplant the individual conscience with some divine imperative. For them to say that this is a matter of theology is, simply, bad theological reasoning."[21] It may be bad theological reasoning, but it enables the churches to ensure that they have future parishioners and supporters.

Was Kerry denounced by his own church because of his views, or because the church was following the political line of the religious Right, or a little of both? It is probably impossible to accurately measure whether the church denunciations influenced the election or whether the priests were simply playing the guilt-and-control card over women and men. In any case, here the hierarchy of the church was exercising its First Amendment guarantees while making clear that those who are believers must change their conduct in order to enjoy the benefits of the church. However, no one would think that Catholics should be forced by the state to tell Catholics to do what the hierarchy said they should do. Even the most liberal-minded of the Catholic (or any religious) hierarchy have not argued that the religion should withdraw its support from legislative and executive actions that cause war or actions that might contradict the religious teachings and hierarchy of particular churches.

But secular authorities pay no attention to statements of church leaders unless they directly confront the state through conduct. In 1977, American Catholic bishops came out very strongly for general nuclear disarmament, and they wrote a very useful paper describing their position, which was, yes, deterrence is acceptable—that is, nuclear weapons are OK as a passive threat—but this doctrine is only a way station to general disarmament. In effect, the bishops claimed that if the commitment to nuclear arms continued, those participating in the enterprise were in mortal peril of committing horrendous war crimes. These were strong words that would seem to have universal appeal. The same sort of document then came from the Methodists. Their effect on politicians was negligible, if it existed at all. No one in the military or defense industry was excommunicated or threatened with shunning.

Several years later, the Catholic bishops took the position that capitalism was not perfect, that there were too many poor, and there should be a redistribution of wealth. The response from politicians: silence. And the church continued to welcome the rich and powerful in private audiences with popes. But churches sometimes remain undaunted. They have a sense of where things are going, and they can take a position that may not be adopted today but may be adopted ten years from today. They might act as the cultural seedbed to or protector for those committed to antipoverty and race issues.

But suppose the cure is more damaging than the illness? Machiavelli might have said that if it serves the cause against oppression and yields something better, you must do whatever you can. However, there is a very big *if* in the fight against oppression: people must then be careful and be sure that the method of getting rid of an oppression is not itself an oppressive system that will end up being *more* oppressive because all the instruments that are oppressing the people remain in place, and new ones are added.

This was not the case among some Latin American clergy who struggled to have consistent means and ends. The Liberation Theology movement, with its emphasis on standing with the wretched and as an organizing base for communities, swept much of that continent. It excited nuns and priests whose Christian beliefs turned radical in the face of human suffering. They said, "look, the church has to identify with Christ and what Christ meant for the poor, and that is who we identify with." That was a bold reiteration of faith, as was that part of the Catholic Church during the Second World War that was committed to helping people who were running from the Nazis. Or those like Dorothy Day, who saw the church as a shield against indifference. Or French priests in the 1940s who represented the worker-priest movement, which emphasized how people could live lives of dignity. It seems clear that had Martin Luther King Jr. and his religious followers not been Baptists, they would have adopted Liberation Theology because so much of the doctrine beyond ritual was similar. Contrast these examples with various forms of religious orthodoxy throughout history reflective in, for example, the Catholic Church, Torquemada and the Inquisition, and during the Second World War when other parts of the church used Jesus Christ as a moral symbol to aid Nazism in their quest for safety.

As the German theologian Dietrich Bonhoeffer put it, the worst sort of evil is the one that parades as the good. (The Nazis hung Bonhoeffer for his strong opposition to Hitler.) One would be hard-pressed to claim that the actions and purposes of Liberation Theology were evil. Yet conservatives seized on Liberation Theology and promoted it as a sinister communist movement lurking on U.S. borders because its purpose was ending oppression and poverty, and its methods, consistent with those ends, necessitated challenges to the hierarchic structures of churches and doctrines that did not yield the bettering of the human condition. Just as the other institutions, such as the nation-state, seek a foothold in the whirlwind of change since the middle of the twentieth century, so too religious institutions seek a role for themselves that privileges faith and good works without challenging rationality (i.e., modern science) at its core and political structures that impede good works, even voluntary ones. But perhaps worship has different functions, not necessarily public ones.

Chapter 12

How Silent Must Prayer Be?

SETTLED QUESTIONS THAT WILL NOT GO AWAY

Roosevelt never suggested that prayer could be an official part of the day in public schools, but he would have understood people who thought it necessary to begin the day with a silent prayer. And so why not the children as well?

Along this line, a case could also be made for the nonreligious benefits of prayer. The French philosopher and mystic Simone Weil, a Jew who flirted with Catholicism, believed that prayer was a good thing because it allowed for the discipline of silence, which emerges from prayer. No one is going to talk back to you, and if you are able to pray and do it regularly there is a quieting of the nerves and a coming together of something that is much needed in modern life, which is to be able to both be silent and concentrate. But concentrate on what? And here the public-private questions touch on one another even in silent prayer.

So-called silent prayer time can be seen in a much more instrumental way than just organizing one's self in relation to God during those silent moments. Thus, if the teacher says, "Think about anything you want, recite a Psalm to yourself if you wish, but you have to be quiet for thirty seconds," that may calm down a boisterous class.

Aspects of prayer have become a routine part of everyone's life whether or not we participate or approve, yet questions that were supposed to be settled have grown more contentious. For example, is there really a difference between a teacher allowing the class a few moments for silent prayer and leading them in the Pledge of Allegiance with "one nation under God?" No doubt many people would answer that there is no difference and would abolish both silent prayer and the Pledge of Allegiance because they still believe that they are unconstitutional; others would answer, "Don't pray or pledge if you don't want to, but get off the backs of those who do."

In June 2002, Michael Newdow, an atheist, convinced a federal appeals court that it was unconstitutional for his daughter's school to require her to recite "under God" in the pledge or hear it uttered by others. Newdow lost when the Supreme Court dismissed his case, ruling that since he did not have custody of his daughter, he lacked standing to bring the case on her behalf. (See *Elk Grove Unified School Dist. v. Newdow*.) The Court may have skirted the Establishment Clause question, but the sum and substance of their "silence" was that in public places we believe in God and hold no brief for atheists.

"God" is an amendment to the Pledge of Allegiance. It was not inserted until 1954, when President Eisenhower's minister and religious groups convinced him that including it would fight the godless communists. The pledge itself goes back to the 1890s. Apparently, the primary motive for it was to ensure the loyalty of the white South to the Union after the Civil War. That is also why the flag became so important. Again, these are ritual statements but hardly for the first time in history.

In the seventeenth century, successful attempts were made to distinguish the state from religion. Even the philosopher Spinoza, a Jew excommunicated by the Dutch Sanhedrin (the highest Jewish governing council), took the position that religion could be regulated by the state but that freedom of *thought* was outside the purview of the state. On the other hand, America's first colleges were started as part of church denominations whose task was to teach the right moral attitude because one could not really trust the natural inclinations of man.

The Presbyterians were split on this question. John Witherspoon, a distinguished Presbyterian minister in Scotland, was implored to take the presidency of Princeton University, where God and religion were given their due, but in the context of promoting a spirit of free inquiry. Free inquiry is not exactly the same as doubting God and religion, but it does guarantee great diversity and pluralism that invariably crosses boundaries of class and race.

There has long been an uneasy truce in American life between those who are thought to desert God for reasons of hubris and science and those who believe that the public display of religion is nothing more than a ritual and a time-killing project, sometimes helpful in keeping public order, and other times useful in the process of grieving and dying or seeing war by the state as a holy war.

When we talk about the Pledge of Allegiance, we are also talking about a political yoking of all citizens to God and the state, thereby making a holy trinity of power, the state, and the individual. Encouraged by political and religious leaders, "under God" is a phrase intended to reinforce the state's role in religion and that of individuals who are pledged to the state and religion, using one public prayer for the purpose. And it reaches to sports, in which owners and coaches see a value to prayer—at least a cash value as well as one that secures discipline for authority. However, the courts have ruled that public spoken prayer at such events as public high school football games and graduation ceremonies is illegal, yet many school officials, often in the South, "wink" at the law, and prayer goes on just the same.

It may well be that the "wink" is given to judges to interpret the law, but it is a curious business. In the first place, we should distinguish between laws and judges. Winking at what might be called "small" laws that may be offensive to some falls under prosecutorial discretion. An unsavory example nevertheless explains the principle: say it is against the law to spit on the street and you spit anyway and a policeman sees you. The policeman thinks, "Well, I'm not going to bother with this guy because it's too difficult, I have to take time off from my work, I have to go into court, this guy might fight it, it's only a minor thing, and all the people in this area spit in the street anyway." So there is a discretionary piece to this whole story. (On the other hand, imagine a judge who upholds the law against a twelve-year-old *arrested* in a Washington Metro station for eating a French fry, as did Judge John Roberts, who went on to become chief justice of the United States.)

The story gets nasty when some people in the minority object and say, "Look, prayer at games can't go on because what you are doing is putting me and my child up against the wall of other people's religious beliefs." This is not the same as spitting on the sidewalk. This question raises a number of problems. The first is that the public ritual of saying the Pledge Allegiance or singing "The Star Spangled Banner" before the game is a means of tying America together. Sports, the pledge, the national anthem are all linked together to say: "This is what it means to be an American." So when various people object to that, what they are saying is: "This is *not* what it means to be an American, and we don't like it." That is where the conflict occurs because in a plural democracy—others will say that this is exactly what it means *not* to be an American. Pluralism means choice. Such choices also may extend to religions in which statements are made through clothes and in which children use dress as a system of messages and boundaries.

In 2002, the Supreme Court ruled that it was constitutional to use vouchers for private and religious schools. ("Whenever we remove a brick from the wall that was designed to separate religion and government, we increase the risk of religious strife and weaken the foundation of our democracy," wrote Justice Stevens in his minority opinion.)[1] Do parents who benefit from vouchers, which are paid from public taxes, have a legitimate complaint that they still have to pay taxes to a public school system their children do not attend?

Believing in the First Amendment, the answer must be "no" because in one case it is your *privilege* to send your child to any school. In the other case it is your *right* to have your child go to a school supported by the taxes of the citizens. That is not the same thing as saying that you have a right to practice religion in the school, before school, or after school.

If you have a pluralist school system, one of its purposes should be to teach tolerance and toleration. If a public school capitulates to religious symbols and doctrine, a serious question is raised. If a child has to sing, say, "Adeste Fideles" at Christmas time and it is done to honor Jesus—not as a teacher but as Christ the Son of God, who is an authoritarian figure—then you have an unwholesome situation. For young minds, it is an adult attempt to link what is politically and religiously correct. Similarly, if a public school adopts "praise to Allah" in Muslim prayer during the day, an encroachment of religion on the public space will become a new religious battleground.

Of course, privately, religious groups and their secular representatives would admit that much of what is claimed to be a religious question is really a *power* question to bring the state in line with their view of religion and religious practices. When this occurs, democracy in the pluralist sense is closed down because those who don't believe in God or a particular religion must count themselves as part of the excluded, which is often a short step from being seen as the enemy of others.

Chapter 13

Faith, Science, and Rationality

THE MODERN TRINITY?

Whether religion is more than a comfort blanket has yet to be proved to skeptics. But not everything has to be proved. It is enough to understand the political practice of religion. Churches, synagogues, mosques, and temples are human institutions related to the distribution of power and privilege. Sometimes they may be designated as moral.[1]

The question is: do these institutions get their power from God, the state, or the populace that believes and financially supports the institutions so their adherents can live forever or go to a better place where they can live without oppression?

What *is* clear is that religious institutions occupy an important place in human existence. When the Bolsheviks began burning churches in Russia after the Soviet revolution in the hopes of cutting out the heart of an alternative power center, the institution turned out to be more important than the Soviets suspected. The Bolsheviks then tried to make an accommodation with the churches but failed and had to reopen the houses of God. And, of course, the Soviet system failed even though it proclaimed itself "scientific."[2]

In its truest sense, the relationship between religion and science has been a dialectical one. Natural philosophers were fond of talking about nature as the second book—a Bible in which what was learned would in fact evoke the word and wonderment of God. Scientists were the priests who, through their concern with knowledge and wonder of things, would bring us back, at least partially, to what God had intended for Adam in the Garden of Eden. Science unlocked the secrets of nature through its revelatory means.

The relative power of the church diminished as scientists argued that *they* were the ones who discovered the motions of the earth. Through mathematics and the then recently invented telescope, Galileo discovered ways of unlocking the secrets of the universe. Several centuries later, scientists claimed that they had discovered the secret of life, if not what the living were doing here. Such notions were understood by certain of the religious as evidence of pure presumption and a grab for power that had to be defended against. In Galileo's case, his former protector and friend, Cardinal Bellarmine, sought to protect the role of the church by working out an accommodation with him that would allow for different interpretations of life. However, the effort failed; Galileo would not accept compromise. Soon, the church saw his stance as a direct attack on its authority, not only in "hypothetical" scientific matters (Bellarmine told Galileo) but also in matters of politics, and Galileo was sentenced to house arrest and threatened with excommunication.[3] The battle between religion and science went on for hundreds of years, retaining its animus as both struggled for state power and cultural dominance. This is exemplified in the struggle over education and what should be taught in the public schools concerning evolution, which, as Pope Benedict XVI has made clear, remains an open question. The discoveries of science and the power of technology seemed to relegate the power of worship to beliefs that could not be explained, were miraculous, or were represented by powerful rituals, saints, and lesser bodies within the many religions that sought to explain origins and ends.

Many might think that science conflicts with worship. Yet atomic scientist Robert Oppenheimer grandiosely spoke about "becoming God" when the first atomic bomb test went off successfully in New Mexico in 1945. (The code name for the test was "Trinity.") Science historian David Noble has traced this human propensity for discovering God in genes and nuclear explosions.[4] For Christian fundamentalists, it is a nuclear Armageddon that brings about the end, and then God appears. Similarly, Faustus-like scientists have a habit of asserting that their discoveries or manufactures prove God. And while there is great disagreement between the creationists and the evolutionists, underneath it all *both* believe that they are speaking for God.

For Christians, the question is whether Jesus is the son of God or the son of man. If he is the son of man, he, too, can be judged and emulated. As the only son of God, it is doubtful if Jesus or God can have a palpable meaning except as myth or fable intended to overwhelm, just as the rituals of scientific knowledge are intended to overwhelm. The National Academy of Science in Washington is an example of architecture meant to overwhelm visitors. It is built as a temple, literally; one feels as if he or she has entered an inner sanctum peopled by high priests, even though most scientists are workers in the corporate-military structure.

HIROSHIMA MON AMOUR

The atomic bomb first entered the consciousness of people outside of the laboratory with the destruction of Hiroshima and Nagasaki. Attention must be paid to a "technological improvement" that could kill almost instantly 200,000 people, mostly civilians. The truly religious outside of the church's mainstream saw the atomic bomb as a sign of the end of the world and the beginning of the return to Christ. In the same way, science saw itself, as now, if not on top, at least on tap to replace religion as the major consultant to power.

Thus science found itself in the business of "how" and not "why," which was left to metaphysics and religion. Even in an advanced technological nation, engineers looked to other explanations beyond what they had in the fulfillment of their own work. The division of labor broke down in several ways. Einstein sought "why" explanations and an end to mysteries. Religion sought to press against what was legitimate to research and what explanations were forbidden. The uneasy truce ended by the beginning of the twenty-first century as some in science sought a cosmology of explanation and others in religion sought to break the hold that science had over the modern consciousness, which owned the idea of progress.

The question for society of what and how to worship called for the reevaluation and discussion of the boundaries between science and religion, perhaps leading to religions of openness and doubt and scientists defending and explaining what they thought they knew as part of a religious conception of awe. In both cases, the right to worship and define God in one's own way seemed politically realistic for a democracy aimed at explaining and reinterpreting seemingly incommensurable understandings into peaceful sharing of ideas. Here the issue is less a question of tolerance or toleration by one dominant group over another than a willingness to share power and authority under the idea that there are many mansions in the house of God that are equal and interdependent, some necessary for particular human functions and others necessary for more inexplicable functions.

This view still does not decide control over the public space in which what is taught as dominant rules. A cynic may argue that most of what is taught in schools in the social sciences, history, and religion are narrative fables. Adding one more outrageous fact and misguided fantasy can hardly seem to be such a serious problem if it were not the case that the political/religious Right intends to press its case against an evolutionary theory as the means of opening and dominating the possibilities of human progress. Thus humanity becomes stagnant and self-satisfied in terms of class, domination, and subjugation. The scientist loses his power to wonder for fear of being branded a heretic and worse. Science as liberator ends; religion as interpreter of mystery is relegated to the priests.

Scientists believe that theories are virtually facts. To deny them is an act of irrationality if not madness. The idea that there is a universe-creator who developed the world according to some cosmic design, placing in the middle of that design the human species, seemed wrong; yet this was believed by scientists during most of the nineteenth century. The attempts on the part of the Right and Christians to offer such a thesis as an alternative to Darwinism, after so much evidence to the contrary, seems to be the height of foolishness and impiety. But the question is a political one: one of power.

If scientists lose their grounding, either in moral purpose or awareness of consequences and therefore clarity about their activities, and the religious fundamentalists seek a new, growing constituency, what happens to democracy, freedom, and scientific inquiry?[5]

INTELLIGENT DESIGN

The question of "intelligent design" is the latest attack on evolution in the political arena. Since Darwin's studies on the origin and evolution of the species, science has been freed from those who believe that God's word about the nature of the human species bound men to their category and place in the universe. The idea of the immutability of categories was thought of as changeless and it was thought that nature impelled the "acorn into becoming the oak tree." And surely it is true that for thousands of years this was the idea of thinkers, theologians, and those concerned with origins and purpose of life without necessarily being concerned with how life is lived, what institutions do, the human species, and whether progress in the sense of knowledge, its distribution, and its programs, leads to more progress.

At first it appeared that scientists limited themselves to how and not to ends and origins. But this idea was never as psychologically fulfilling as the quest for certainty. Thus Einstein's claim against statistical mechanics that God does not play dice was, whether or not he cared to admit it, a strong belief in his definition of God's "intelligent design." However, that belief is a far cry from the idea that humanity is set on an immutable course in which institutions don't matter. Or accidents that change the character of variety of the human species are unimportant. Or that there is a God-given moral standard that is far more important to the divine than is the humdrum world of people understanding their situation and preparing to use and deepen their knowledge in order to eliminate or ameliorate some of the worst tragedies of modern times, such as the proliferation of nuclear weapons, or fictions that demean human dignity.

There is no way for the species to surrender its wonder about origins and purpose. And here again is the place of freedom to worship. The revolution of science since Darwin in social terms is that scientific evidence, logic, and other criteria of proof that reject absolutist statements remain open theories inviting correction. In a democracy, *that* freedom of thought must be protected and expanded. This does not mean, for example, that at the university all manner of belief systems are to be taught as if they have overwhelming evidence behind their statements when they don't. It does open the question of reconstruction of knowledge that in a social sense will yield some of the hopes of the changing world that Roosevelt, and others, foresaw in the middle of the twentieth century.[6]

For now, American civilization is fortunate in having a pluralism that keeps in check one religion against another and, at the same time, causes them to accept the costs of progress. After all, it isn't sinful, and it is probably progress to hold priests and ministers accountable for racism or sexual abuse or even to allow people to worship one God, his or her emanation, or, for that matter, many gods.

A SPIRIT FOUND IN REALITY THAT CHANGES REALITY

There will be those who believe that the gulf of belief is so great inside nations and is so great between nations that there is no reconciling differences in order to protect the idea of freedom of worship and traditional, fundamental views about worship and different religious institutions. In the latter part of the twentieth century and now in the twenty-first century, there is a fear that what at least was an unstated relativism, which accepted different world religions, has exploded into differences that were central in making war between people and states. In the Western nations in recent history, politicians could point to irreconcilable differences that fueled the anger of Shiite Muslims against Sunni Muslims, as well as anger bordering on hatred against Christians and Jews. For many, these hatreds were based on absolutist's beliefs that confronted putative enemies of other beliefs but were against modernism and the project of science and democracy, the latter more a shibboleth than a reality when applied to the conquered among poor nations.

In many cases, this anger and hatred were fueled by three social conditions: (1) the idea of superiority of one group against others; (2) the feelings of humiliation that one culture had to endure against another culture where one group of nations had a superiority of weapons and found means to extract resources from the poorer nation or group; and (3) the mutual feelings of distrust based both in fact and in fearfulness of the other. This set of circumstances, some having to do with belief, others having to do with the problems emerging from poverty, want, and global strategies to control resources, cannot be wished away easily. It must be remembered that the United States in the person of FDR traveled to meet with King Ibn Saud of Saudi Arabia to ensure that oil would flow without interruption and at low prices to fuel American needs at the end of the Second World War (with American corporations becoming the dominant factor in oil in the Middle East). Clearly, it did not matter to Roosevelt what garb Ibn Saud wore, whether he had as many or fewer wives than the Utah Mormons of the nineteenth century had, or whether he had contempt for Muslims who did not visit Mecca at least once in their lives; oil is what mattered to FDR.

But there is another side to this story, which is immediately relevant to our present world condition and specifically that of the United States if we were able to see more clearly. The underlying thesis of this chapter is a statement of the *is* and the *ought* and how one emerges from the other. This is not so easy to assess, for what is new and different may appear irrelevant and marginal especially as written in the present. But the question is from whence does the *ought* now stem? Is it to inhere in a world struggle around the many faces of religion, the question of who controls markets, or is there some other force present in the freedom to worship and freedom from want and fear that can be found in the coming together of worship, religious institutions, and world civilization. Here the tentative answers can be seen in certain outlines that emerge as undeniable once noted. This is not to argue their immediate success; it is, however, to argue their very practical utility.[7]

Although there are efforts—some successful, others bogus—for globalization of capital through markets and the breaking down of customs so that customs are shared as well as bedmates from different cultures, certain things become clear. Gandhi and Martin Luther King have lessons for this period in regard to the use of nonviolence as a tactic between nations and peoples. But in every case, for this system to work, a socially shared epiphany is needed; in this stage of history, that epiphany is that there is nothing to be gained through force of arms, even for those who are or think they are exploited (and often the exploiter thinks that they, too, are exploited). The success of nonviolence in the United States, an extraordinarily violent nation in its culture and attitudes, tells much about the possibilities of nonviolence and the willingness of one group to listen to the other group's complaints. While it is true that the United Kingdom found itself greatly diminished by the First World War and no longer able to afford to control India, it was the movement of nonviolence that was key to ending its control over India. And it was also through nonviolence that South Africa (admittedly with some violent means) ended apartheid.

What then are Americans supposed to think about those who practice different religious methods and perpetuate different customs? It remains a continuous tension in American life as to what to accept and what space religion as an institution should occupy. What is clear, however, is that beliefs come in different varieties, although their causes may vary. Internationally, if one nation presses democracy or capitalism or any system on another nation or culture, there is bound to be resistance—often it is extreme resistance. Similarly, where there is great poverty, a sense of powerlessness and humiliation with no way out, there will be a kind of religious fervor that is easily manipulated whether by the exploiter or the exploited. Thus the question of worship of a God or Gods takes on material meanings which, if confronted, can turn religious beliefs away from murderous consequences. The American policies in the Middle East, for example, with regard to keeping troops in Saudi Arabia when the Wahabi sect objected, claiming sacrilege, was surely one important reason for the rise of bin Laden, a creation not only of his religion and family wealth but also of the American geopolitical struggle with the Soviets in Afghanistan (1979–1989), where Osama and his supporters were allied with the United States.

The question is whether there is much that worship, beyond what it teaches the individual, can teach humanity. Buber, Gandhi, Karl Jaspers, and King believed in a spirit that had to be found in reality as the means for *changing* reality. To the extent that religious institutions comprehend this spirit, they lead by example, which one would hope could help to change basic attitudes and consciousness of the world. And humane scientists also are engaged in a similar project.

By the last year of his life, Roosevelt concluded that international politics needed a New Deal. It had to be more than the exercise of coercion by the colonizers over the colonized and the strong over the weak and humiliated. Just as FDR understood in the early part of the New Deal that there was a floor of decency and adequacy that had to be achieved and maintained in a democratic society, so it was that after a horrible war human affection had to be repaired in order to be shared in other parts of the world as a means of keeping the peace.[8] Then there would be a reasonable chance that power could be held in check by international law and justice and conciliation could be promoted. That, in turn, would stimulate finding nonviolent solutions to immediate and long-term problems that would be sure to emerge in the politics of nations. Established groups and new ones would ameliorate difficulties through the United Nations (as flawed as it was) and its various organizations.

In the post–Second World War era, as European empires were breaking up, there were profound divisions between the five permanent members of the UN Security Council—divisions even greater than those that exist now—and such notions seemed to be irrelevant to so-called pragmatists. Yet those notions turned out not to be irrelevant. True and able statesmen knew that practical solutions to peace required a measure of comity, trust, cooperation, and affection—at least respect for differences among people. Without these features and ways to organize them practically, sovereignty would become a dangerous conception and, worse, the permanent enemy of the people—as we have seen again and again more than half a century later—and religion would become a tool of humanity's destruction in the hands of fools and "saviors" such as Bush II, who claimed he was doing God's work through aggressive war.

Part Three

Freedom From Want

In the future days which we seek to make secure, we look forward to a world founded upon four essential freedoms.... The third is freedom from want, which, translated into world terms, means economic understandings which will secure to every nation a healthy peacetime life for its inhabitants—everywhere in the world.

—Franklin Delano Roosevelt, January 6, 1941

Chapter 14

The Business of Hunger

THE GOVERNMENT FEEDS THE POOR—AND CHANGES THE WAY EVERYONE EATS

A passage from Roosevelt's second inaugural address in 1937 was the prelude to the third of the Four Freedoms five years later:

> The test of our progress is not whether we add more to the abundance of those who have much; it is whether we provide enough for those who have too little.

Lofty words perhaps, but Roosevelt had two pragmatic objectives. First, the New Deal sought to prove the superiority of democratic capitalism—really social democracy over the competing totalitarian ideologies of that time. FDR wanted the United States to lead in ridding the world of hunger, poverty, and disease. There was also an intermediate goal. In 1937, he was primarily concerned with feeding our own people so that there literally would not be starvation; millions of Americans were still suffering from the effects of the Depression, and countless numbers were destitute.

The principle of freedom from want was highlighted as a social objective at the end of the nineteenth century by various radical movements, which in turn had religious roots in the West. As public policy, the idea made its way into established circles, including the University of Chicago in the 1920s, where leading political scientists such as Charles Merriam, who served as a chairman of President Hoover's commission on the nation's future, argued that the country could not afford the luxury of having starving people in its midst. Christian charity was not enough in an industrial society. Freedom from want had to be an absolute *right*—indeed, an entitlement—and by implication government had to intervene to ensure this objective.

To fulfill this purpose, Roosevelt understood the need to drastically change the role of the federal government. No longer could or should the political economy of the United States be run out of the Union Clubs and other blue-blood sanctums—the hungry needed to feed themselves with more than the nostrums of laissez faire market ideologies. For him and for much of the New Deal, liberal thought was predicated on the belief that democratic government should have an important role in helping to give people lives of dignity and decency, and so the government would now have the most to say about changing the situation of the poor in material terms; volunteerism would, for the most part, be replaced as a primary source of aid to the poor. Where people need a helping hand, as Lincoln had said, the social contract obligated the government to give it to them. This would be achieved through democratic means of redistribution of responsibilities and equity over the fruits of labor: FDR's version and vision was freedom from want for all, but this was not everyone's view. During the Depression, however, the New Deal point of view led to enormous conflict with Southern plantation owners, who had no interest in sharing subsidies from the federal government with poor black tenant farmers and sharecroppers.

Once the Second World War broke out, Roosevelt saw, as did others, that hunger was not only a problem in the United States, it was a worldwide problem. This led to the second project of consequence: an export trade strategy for the United States in which agriculture played an important political role. American farmers needed new markets, especially as mechanization made them more productive. So Roosevelt's two-pronged attack was a chance to feed the hungry and, at the same time, aid the country's farmers by expanding agricultural exports.

The conservatives scoffed at FDR's goals as impossible, arguing that they would mean an expansion of government that would become an all-consuming albatross.

Despite all of its experimentation and disorganization, New Dealers were committed to organization and management as the way to solve problems. In fact, many New Dealers had been advisers to big business and helped to promote the value of managerial efficiency. So the export strategy was not new. It was talked about in Democratic Party circles before the administration of Woodrow Wilson, who himself was an advocate. As part of U.S. export strategy after the Second World War, both the Truman and the Republican Eisenhower administrations gave agricultural surplus to poor nations. Under Public Law 480, renamed the Food for Peace program under President Kennedy (its most successful director was George McGovern), food was given to millions of people who might otherwise have starved. It is still hailed as one of the government's great humanitarian programs.

But feeding the poor had surprising consequences. FDR's New Deal and Truman's Fair Deal programs in agriculture helped to change the growing and eating habits of America and the world, but it also signaled an end to traditional farming at home and abroad. Until the 1950s, fruits and vegetables were locally grown and consumed, as were livestock and chickens. (Chickens in those days roamed free, outside; they were "free range" without being called that. The notion of raising chickens by the thousands, penned up in small cages, in huge artificially lighted buildings, would have seemed crazy.) The long-term trends became clear. As it became harder for small farmers to have a decent living standard, they were forced to sell out to the new, highly efficient corporate farmers or end up as day laborers or tenant farmers. What is now called "agribusiness" seemed to grow overnight from birth to industrialized food conglomerates that shipped fruits and vegetables grown in California (and eventually Mexico and Latin America) to markets throughout the country. Seasonal produce became available year-round, even as the taste and quality of some produce suffered as a result. Such a pattern governs the American agricultural system at the beginning of this century.

By 2002, 3 percent of the country's big farms and ranches (70,600 with annual sales of more than $500,000) produced about 62 percent of U.S. agricultural goods, up from 56.6 percent in 1997. During the same period, there were 87,000 fewer farms.[1] In 1998, with the elimination of many government regulations on production, small farmers were subjected to market forces they had not faced since before the New Deal.

As a result of the markets changing, the situation of third world farmers in Africa and the Americas also changed. For example, in Latin America some farmers ended up growing flowers for an international market rather than the food their own people needed in order to survive.[2] Unintended consequences also changed eating habits, and these changes were not always for the best (for example, people began eating much more beef). Local hangouts where one dropped by for an occasional hamburger were replaced by fast food chains where kids and families regularly ate breakfast, lunch, or dinner. The national body grew fatter. Agribusiness interrupted basic needs by switching many consumers to nonpowdered milk and, in the case of American and African mothers, pushing products such as canned milk, which replaced their breast milk.

So the character of agriculture changed enormously in the twentieth century and accelerated in the twenty-first. Along with it, a very strong agribusiness bloc emerged in Congress, which helped secure huge federal subsidies. Under the Bush II administration, some thirteen billion dollars went to roughly seven hundred thousand farmers in 2002. Yet despite the money and technological advances, the conservative Hoover Institution predicted that the United States could soon become a net importer of food for the first time since the 1950s![3]

The number of people who have left the farm substantially changed the character of American life itself, from half farming, half urban before the First World War to farmers only amounting to about 3 to 4 percent of the population. The question for the future is whether or not a substantial number of people will ever want to leave the cities and go back to small farm agriculture.

In the 1930s, Wisconsin boasted that its traditional small dairy farms were in fact "America's Dairyland." The motto was on the state's license plates and had an important political meaning: it showed the dominance of rural Wisconsin over the state's urban centers of which Milwaukee was the only one of substantial size. Then California began corporatizing its dairy farms. They were called "factory farms." As a result, dairy farming became a cold but efficient business and, in effect, California became "America's Dairyland."

The "Cow Case," one of the famous cases studied in law schools, defines the dilemma increasingly faced by some farmers and consumers.[4] The case concerns a transaction between two farmers. One farmer buys a cow from another farmer. The cow is not noticeably pregnant at the time of the purchase. Months later, however, the cow has a calf. Law students are asked: who owns the calf? The first farmer says, "Look, I bargained for everything that I got, so I own the calf." The second farmer says, "No, you just bargained for the cow and the calf belongs to me." That question puzzled many law professors and students over the years. One day, a professor put this question to an eight-year-old boy who said that the real issue is, "Who will take better care of the calf?" His stunning answer goes to the heart of the question of what we mean by efficiency and inefficiency in agriculture—and to what end? Profit is one obvious answer. But profit, of course, goes hand-in-hand with the thoughtless ways we fatten cattle with growth-promoting hormones and slaughter them as if they are assembly-line products.

Despite all the press in recent years concerning healthier eating, only a minority of Americans seem concerned about healthier eating habits or whether their food is free or substantially free of hormones or pesticides by government standards. Indeed, the way cows, chickens, turkeys, and other animals are treated prior to their slaughter is not of much concern, yet there is a changing consciousness and awareness for the economically higher classes who emphasize "organic" foods in their diets. But their awareness is hardly enough given the consumer's minimum knowledge of what "organic" means.

Healthier eating will truly become a national standard when enough people have a political program that finds its way into the public space through social movements or ideas—one in which linkages are shown between food, ecology, and the air we breathe and in which a different kind of medical practice whereby people who were once thought of narrowly as doctors now factor into their practices *all* aspects of food and therefore of farming.

Is this likely to happen anytime soon? It will if the food reactionaries and the technological "progressives" who care more about the bottom line than the consequences of their actions are outsmarted by moderates and the Left. Sometimes, tedious, commonplace tasks must be undertaken. A good place to start is by scouring the fine print of every piece of legislation that could be harmful to good agriculture standards. In 2003, for example, a Republican congressman from Georgia with the Dickensian name of Deal slipped a small item into the three-thousand-page spending bill that changed the law so that poultry, meat, and dairy products from animals raised on nonorganic feed can be labeled and sold as *organic* even if pesticides are used.[5]

One person who bypassed big agriculture is Alice Waters, who has created a small but meaningful food revolution. Beginning in the 1970s, she persuaded small farmers in the San Francisco Bay area to grow organic lamb, beef, chickens, and seasonal produce for her new Berkeley restaurant, Chez Panisse. ("Eating is a political act," Waters announced. "We make choices that affect our social and ecological environments every time we sit or don't sit at the table.")[6] Her idea has kept many farmers in business, while offering her customers cuisine that has set a high standard for American restaurants. As a result, other well-known restaurants on the West Coast followed suit. Small farmers in the Hudson River Valley have been similarly sustained by prominent New York City chefs and the city's farmer's markets. And a "back to nature" movement continues in Vermont, where there are successful family farms, but these examples do not reflect the direction of American agriculture.

The public should also be clear about any so-called technological advance: such an advance is *never* an absolute good. It may only be a relative good for some and must be so judged because the consequences can be disastrous, as was shown by decades of spraying DDT on crops. DDT was banned in the United States in 1972, but some want to use it again, arguing that its benefits outweigh the risks of its long, poisonous record, especially in malaria-infested areas of the world.[7]

WHO'S ASSESSING THE RISK OF WHAT YOU EAT?

A child growing up in the 1940s had a much better chance of not getting sick from contaminated food than a child today. According to the Centers for Disease Control and Prevention (CDC), the frequency of serious gastrointestinal illness, a common gauge of food poisoning, is 34 percent above what it was in 1948. "After eating contaminated food," the CDC said, "people can develop anything from a short, mild illness, often mistakenly referred to as 'food poisoning,' to life-threatening disease." The CDC estimates that each year "76 million Americans get sick, more than 300,000 are hospitalized, and 5,000 people die from foodborne illnesses."[8] A congressman who advocated increased food inspection wondered, "If a terrorist had been responsible for killing those five thousand people, don't you think we would be mobilized?" Maybe. But that sidesteps two other questions: Wouldn't a knowledgeable terrorist be able to poison some part of our food supply fairly easily? And what is the government doing to protect the public from such risks? Fear of a terrorist attack from the outside is certainly real enough. But there is substantial "terror" from parts of the agribusiness that too often favor profit over protected food. Not surprisingly, agribusiness hires the best Washington lobbyists to *protect* their profits.

Take the brief, sordid history of Mad Cow, a disease that can kill human beings who eat the meat of cows fed with the spongy brains of sheep and other cows, and compare the public policy of Great Britain to that of the United States. David M. C. Bartlett of the University of Leeds traced British history with Mad Cow to 1979, when Margaret Thatcher became prime minister of Great Britain. Thatcher's conservative government, Bartlett writes, was

> ideologically committed to deregulation and removed many of the state's previously established regulatory procedures. The policy permitted important changes in the structure of the meat rendering industry and in the processes employed by it. These changes were directly responsible for the spread of BSE [Bovine Spongiform Encephalopathy] through the British cattle herd and led to a rising incidence of the human form of BSE-variant-CJD [Creutzfeldt-Jakob disease]. The British Government—and particularly MAFF [Ministry of Agriculture, Fisheries and Food]—sought to defend the meat industry by denying—until March 1996—both the seriousness of the BSE epidemic in cattle and the possibility of a species jump from cattle to the human population. Ministers and officials insisted that beef was safe to eat and underpinned this stance by providing misleading or inaccurate information to Parliament and the public.[9]

Then, in 1996, eighty Britons died from eating Mad Cow meat, and thousands of cows that might have been infected with the disease were killed and their carcasses burned—in full view of American television audiences.

In the meantime, American ranchers and farmers continued feeding spongy sheep brains to their cows. The U.S. government seemed to echo the beef industry when it assured the public that American beef was safe. Business as usual continued—until December 23, 1997, when the government revealed that a dairy cow in Washington state was infected with Mad Cow, the first known case in the United States. According to People for the Ethical Treatment of Animals (PETA), the diseased animal had been killed thirteen days before and had passed through *three* processing plants before the problem was discovered. A ban against feeding the spongy sheep brains to cows finally went into effect. But as late as 2001, the government said that there was widespread violation of the feeding regulation. The same year, two hundred sheep raised for dairy on a Vermont farm were killed on suspicion that they were infected with their species' equivalent of Mad Cow disease. And Chronic Wasting Disease, which is related to Mad Cow, has been widespread in deer and elk in western Canada and the United States for years and is suspected of infecting hunters who may have eaten meat from sick animals.

The diseased Washington state cow played in the media for weeks. Those who did not stop eating beef worried that the beef they were eating could be infected. U.S. beef exports plunged. The Department of Agriculture promised better testing for Mad Cow.

A second case of Mad Cow was found in Texas in 2005 but *apparently* did not get into the food supply. A third case of Mad Cow was found in Alabama in 2006. Apparently, it did not enter the animal or human food chains. Was it luck? Was the U.S. inspection system that good after all? Or had American beef eaters, ranchers, farmers, meat processors, butchers, supermarkets, and restaurants assumed both the benefits and risks of eating beef? The Department of Agriculture did not see it as a risky business. In July 2006, it said that it would cut Mad Cow testing by about 90 percent because the low number of infected animals did not justify the current level of surveillance, which was about a thousand tests a day, or less than 1 percent of the thirty-five million cows slaughtered each year. The secretary of agriculture said that about one hundred tests a day would be conducted, saving taxpayers millions of dollars.[10]

Up to the early 1900s there was no real inspection of food in the United States. The point of progressive reform in the twentieth century was to make sure that our food and drugs would not be rancid or poisonous to the extent this can be avoided. That was why the Food and Drug Administration (FDA) was established and why the United States instituted national reinspection.

But deregulation at the FDA, which was begun by several Democratic administrations, shifted into high gear under Bush II with his emphasis on two principles: trust the corporation to do the right thing with regard to the safety of its product, and let regulations wither. The FDA was starved for funds. The *New York Times* reported that the federal agency had slashed "its laboratories and network of independent drug safety experts in favor of hiring more people to approve drugs—changes that arose under an unusual agreement that has left the agency increasingly reliant on and bound by drug company money."[11] Safety has already been compromised. As startling as the revelation of the dangers of the painkilling drug Vioxx were, it was only the first case of the bitter fruit of deregulation. (Merck, manufacturer of Vioxx, could end up paying millions of dollars in consumer lawsuits.)

The FDA has other serious problems. It oversees some 80 percent of the food supply, but has only about a quarter of the total federal budget on food safety inspection. Food reporter Marian Burros pointed out in 2001 that "15 separate federal agencies oversee the production, importing and distribution of food. Each agency has its own set of rules, which sometimes conflict with the rules of others. And the level of vigilance varies wildly.... For example, the F.D.A. allows more than four times as much methyl mercury in fish as the E.P.A. does.... Meat and poultry processing plants cannot operate without an Agriculture Department inspector on the premises; the F.D.A. inspects fish processing plants about once a year. The system is so antiquated that it has been described as the regulatory equivalent of the Model T."[12]

Furthermore, the General Accounting Office said in 2002 that Department of Agriculture inspectors were poorly trained to evaluate the production process, meat testing was inconsistent, and when problems were discovered, companies were seldom punished and processors were not actually forced to shut down, even though the plants then took several months to come into compliance.[13]

Why doesn't the United States reduce food-borne illnesses as Sweden, Denmark, and the Netherlands have done? Why does our government keep cutting the food inspection budget? Again, it appears to be a case of risk assessment, as in 2002 when Wampler Foods in Franconia, Pennsylvania, had to recall 27.4 million pounds of cooked turkey and chicken products because it was very likely contaminated with *Listeria* bacteria. This followed an outbreak in the Northeast that caused seven deaths and made dozens ill. The same year, nineteen million pounds of ground beef from ConAgra Foods in Greeley, Colorado, were recalled after sixteen people became ill from *E. coli* bacteria. In 1998, fifteen million pounds of hot dogs and deli meats by Sara Lee Corporation were recalled after *Listeria* contamination from a Bil Mar Foods plant in Borculo, Michigan, were linked to twenty-one deaths and one hundred illnesses.[14] The agribusinesses, together with the government, seem to be saying, if a few hundred people are stricken with serious food poisoning, it's just business.

One of the problems of industry is that engineers are governed by their management's bottom line. Thus they do not always turn out the best-made product or the safest product or even the most efficient. What this means is that it is no longer just the actions of a particular corporation or the U.S. government that come into play. Risk assessment, or "accumulative loss" as business sometimes calls it, becomes a social determination of how much the corporate bottom line costs the society as a whole. Loss of life and illness, whether in food production or automobile manufacture, is based on turning economic calculations into arguments that limit or erase legal risks, health standards in food, and toxic substances, not the health concerns of the public. One can only marvel at how the gas disaster in Bhopal, India, in 1984, which killed some seven thousand people in a matter of days, was finessed by those responsible for the tragedy: the Union Carbide Corporation (since acquired by Dow Chemical), the Indian government, and U.S. courts. Bhopal is the worst industrial disaster in history. "Over the last 21 years exposure to the toxins has resulted in the deaths of a further 15,000 people as well as chronic and debilitating illnesses for thousands of others for which treatment is largely ineffective," a 2004 study by Amnesty International reported. "Toxic wastes continue to pollute the environment and contaminate water that surrounding communities rely on.... Despite determined efforts by survivors to secure justice, they have been denied adequate compensation and appropriate and timely medical assistance and rehabilitation."[15]

FREEDOM FOR BASIC NEEDS

Freedom from want for Franklin Roosevelt was also a statement: "Those who have are going to have to contribute." In his eyes, this freedom was not only a strategy for feeding people, as well as a trade strategy, an unemployment strategy, and an aid strategy, it was ultimately a cultural strategy that included artists, writers and musicians who "fed" the quality of life of a nation. That was to be mediated through one's own belief about tithing, contributing voluntarily, and caring. The concept of tithing, which was a big part of Roosevelt's Episcopal Church, was embedded in the aid system as an ethical guide to public policy. The caring concept meant that the United States would not destroy the land and well-being of peasant farmers.

By the Depression period, churches could not be counted on for voluntary contributions. The New Deal strategy for democracy demanded that government involve itself directly and that citizens understand that people were entitled to basic human necessities.

Want included the protection of basic needs, and this raised serious policy and ethical questions for determining a common good: How much of want and basic needs is necessity? How much of it is want and how much is desire? Obviously, each question runs into the other. What is clear is that there are necessities such as clean water, clean air, shelter, and uncontaminated food, which may precede other wants of all societies. Freedom as a shared need can only be supplied for communities through collective action (that is, organized, sustained social action) brought about through legitimate state intervention within the law and with the aid of voluntary activity. Water, for example, cannot be supplied for everyone by faddish substitutes such as bottled water. The only result is greater inequity and disparity in health and social terms as well as corruption and phony science.

Similarly, there is recognition that necessities reflect the staples of life. This raises two public questions: How much indignity must a person endure in order to obtain the necessities? And further, who sets the standards for what constitutes a necessity? This latter question is used by conservatives to prove the difficulty of ascertaining a just meaning for necessity because of the variations among human beings. This is a kind of evasion that one might expect to hear among economists or professors, but it has nothing to do with people's everyday lives in most of the world, where countless numbers of people live on the equivalent of a dollar a day. Even in the United States, workers are not exempt from subsistence and poverty wages. Thousands of studies make clear what is necessary to support adequate life, though there will probably always be some conservatives who make the classic argument (privately, of course) that hunger is necessary to get people to work. This argument is only one step above those who argued that slavery was a beneficial condition for the slaves.

———————

"Have-nots" are usually thought of as the poor class. But when the economy touches the edge of depression, as it did at the end of the the dot-com boom of the 1990s, the haves who lost their jobs and were overextended on credit often tumbled into the have-not class of the working poor. Barbara Ehrenreich demonstrated that the working poor trying to live on jobs paying six or seven dollars an hour are not even coming close to making it, often not even with two jobs, especially if they have children. (One of many examples of the gulf between haves and have-nots in America can be found in the glorious hills of Berkshire County, Massachusetts. It probably does not cross the minds of most affluent second homeowners from New York and Boston or the hoards of tourists who make the summer pilgrimage to the Tanglewood Music and Jacobs Pillow Dance festivals that nearly 10 percent of the county's 134,953 citizens and 6.5 percent of its families live below the poverty line.[16] These citizens include the working poor who serve the haves at the area's expensive restaurants.

World conditions are worse now than when FDR said that freedom from want should encompass people *everywhere* in the world—as the following grim statistics from the United Nations demonstrate:[17]

- In 1990, more than 1.2 billion people—28 percent of the developing world's population—lived in extreme poverty. These were the poorest of the poor, struggling to make ends meet on less than a dollar a day. Some three billion people live on under two dollars a day.

- Hunger is nearly as pervasive as extreme poverty. In 2002, an estimated 815 million people in developing countries had too little to eat to meet their daily energy needs. The lack of food can be most perilous for young children since it retards their physical and mental development. Over one hundred and fifty million children under five in the developing world are underweight, a factor contributing to over half of child deaths and lives of recurring illness and faltering growth. Child malnutrition is caused not only by food deprivation but also by infectious diseases and lack of care.

- More than one billion people lack access to safe drinking water, especially in rural areas of Africa and in urban slums. It is estimated that by 2050 between two billion and seven billion people will face water shortages.

- Nearly one billion people worldwide—almost one in three city dwellers—live in slums, and about two hundred million new slum dwellers were added to urban communities between 1990 and 2001, representing an increase of 28 percent.

- An estimated 2.6 billion people—representing half of the developing world—lack toilets and other forms of improved sanitation. If the 1990–2002 trends hold, close to 2.4 billion people will still be without improved sanitation in 2015, almost as many as there are without improved sanitation today.

- AIDS has become the leading cause of premature death in sub-Saharan Africa [It is Africa's single most deadly disease.] and the fourth largest killer worldwide. More than twenty million people around the world have died of AIDS since the epidemic began. And at the end of 2004, an estimated 39.4 million people were living with HIV—the highest number on record. Nearly two thirds of them live in sub-Saharan Africa, where the prevalence rate among adults has reached 7.2 percent. Globally, the epidemic shows no signs of slowing: 4.9 million people were newly infected with HIV in 2004, and there were 3.1 million deaths due to AIDS (five hundred thousand of them among children under fifteen). In the worst affected countries of southern Africa, AIDS is an increasingly significant cause of death for children under five.

- Nearly half of all people living with HIV are women. But as the epidemic worsens, the share of infected women and girls is growing. In sub-Saharan Africa, 57 percent of those infected with HIV are female.

- AIDS is not only a source of extreme human suffering. It also strains social services, exacerbates gender inequalities and child labor, and drains the labor supply. Workforce losses due to HIV/AIDS are expected to reach 28 million by 2005, 48 million by 2010, and 74 million by 2015 in the absence of widespread access to treatment.

- Many other diseases are quietly draining the vitality and hope of people in the developing world. Malaria claims the lives of a million people a year, mostly young children, and is estimated to have slowed economic growth in African countries by 1.3 percent a year.

Much of the African continent is haunted by despair, sickness, and death. Yet Africans, especially women, have survival and technical skills that are greater than many Americans, who seem to be dependent on consumer acquisition and indebtedness for their survival. There is an important underlying reality in Africa and elsewhere: internationally, poor women are seldom heard collectively. They have virtually no voice in international negotiations regarding agricultural production, land reform, pesticide use, food marketing, and the production of reasonable diets. (The irony, if it can be called that, is that so many of these women, and their husbands and children, suffer from near or actual starvation.) To the extent that agriculture exists, it is the result for the most part of women's labor outside the West. The same is true for women and children who work in virtual slave labor conditions making clothing and sneakers in Asian sweatshops run by corporations based in America, Europe, and Asia itself. (No one should be blind to the existence of sweatshops in New York, Los Angeles, and other American cities not very far from affluent neighborhoods.)

Yet some contend that sweatshops in which women work at least offer a precarious escape (for several years) from poverty. But what does that really mean? There is no clue in the sentence as to how the predecessor of Western globalization—imperialism— penetrated various countries and through the market system destroyed the local cultural life. This is not meant to romanticize any country's village system; it is meant to make very clear that the market, as defined by a particular kind of global capitalism, is highly destructive.

This problem, seen over and over, never goes away. Could it be that *men* don't want it to because they would rather keep exercising patriarchal power and oppression to the exclusion of women? After all, it is only in recent years that the World Bank has paid any attention to reports that women are oppressed in this fundamental way. There is a cruel sequel: if the women are not working fast enough for their few dollars (or pennies) a day, and the profits are not high enough in a particular country, the corporation will simply pull up stakes and move its factories and sweatshops elsewhere. What happens to the broken-spirited people, including those who live in the United States, who are left behind? Where do they go? What do they have left? The only option for many young women in Thailand or Romania who have the responsibility of supporting their parents is to become sex workers. So in that sense it is true that the women escaped the poverty of the village. But they may not escape death at an early age; life-spans in many areas of the world do not extend beyond forty years, which is not very different from statistics in the eighteenth century.

The public policy tragedy is that so many of these conditions are unnecessary. Tens of millions of children die of preventable diseases annually. In Washington DC, mortality statistics for young children and babies are as bad as in many third-world countries. Perhaps the bigger tragedy is that we know these facts but have neither the will nor the cultural knowledge to change these conditions. Instead, the former president of Harvard, Lawrence Summers, offered as an innovative recommendation (when he was chief economist at the World Bank) that Africa should take the West's garbage as a strategy for economic betterment of their condition.

Oppression and selfishness have their own rationale. That rationale is quite enough, especially when it is coated with the iron laws of capitalism as understood by robber barons, the oligarchic, and the "loving heart" of the colonizer, always ready to "guide" the muddled character of the government's aid policies.

But what if the United States actually practiced at home and abroad the principles of freedom from want (which does not mean dumping standard commodities on poor nations)? Aside from being the decent thing to do, wouldn't really helping the have-nots be a relatively inexpensive strategy for America's security? That is the theory, but whether or not that is true is a question. The historian Crane Brinton made the argument, which has a certain amount of at least surface validity to it, that revolutions do not occur when the economy is totally down, but when it is coming up. His argument was that people then had the space to look around.

But prudent liberals feel that the haves do not have the luxury of spending much more time contemplating arguments such as Brinton's before the international house of cards collapses. On the other hand, "compassionate conservatives" give the impression of having all the time in the world and the inclination to assess the implications of that statement for their policies and their interests. Perhaps they still hold the cynical view of their forebears that the upper classes give charity out of fear of the lower class; they give alms but not rights of economic justice.[18]

Chapter 15

FDR's Economic Bill of Rights

WHEN THE FUTURE HELD PROMISE FOR THE HAVE-NOTS

Even as Roosevelt was giving the nation the Four Freedoms, the experience of the Depression caused him to think ahead to what he would call his "Economic Bill of Rights." He described those rights at the end of the Second World War in his State of the Union address, telling the country that there would be "a new basis of security and prosperity [that] can be established for all—regardless of station, race, or creed":[1]

- The right to a useful and remunerative job in the industries or shops or farms or mines of the nation

- The right to earn enough to provide adequate food and clothing and recreation

- The right of every farmer to raise and sell his products at a return that will give him and his family a decent living

- The right of every businessman, large and small, to trade in an atmosphere of freedom from unfair competition and domination by monopolies at home or abroad

- The right of every family to a decent home

- The right to adequate medical care and the opportunity to achieve and enjoy good health

- The right to adequate protection from the economic fears of old age, sickness, accident, and unemployment

- The right to a good education

Roosevelt's Economic Bill of Rights, like so many of his legislative proposals, was the product of a sensitive and practical politician's mind linked to social movements seeking their idea of justice, all within the framework of regulated "progressive" capitalism.

In the 1944–1945 period, FDR publicly presented his ideas on a high rhetorical level at a time when he must have known that his life would soon end. (He insisted that his doctors keep his grave heart condition secret from others.) The Second World War was drawing to a close and no New Dealer wanted the nation to return to the horrific conditions of the Depression. Roosevelt understood that the federal government had to act to bring into political reality a vision of an America different from the social hardships the soldiers had left behind when they went to war. By 1944, he knew that the United States and its allies were going to win the war. In fact postwar planning began almost immediately in 1942–1943. Roosevelt saw the need to rethink and rebuild the social structure into a highly individualized society, and he was concerned with how to organize politically and socially for rights that would guarantee these new realities. So there is a democratic-ideological cast to what would come to be known as the "Second" Bill of Rights.

Roosevelt also had another purpose: some sixteen million men and women were under arms, they were coming back from the war, and it had to be made clear to them what they had been fighting for. Otherwise, he knew that he would have to face up to what happened with the Bonus Marchers in the early 1930s when First World War veterans—fifteen thousand strong—marched on Washington to demand bonuses promised to them in 1924. President Hoover called out armed troops, commanded by General Douglas MacArthur (with the aid of two future generals, Dwight D. Eisenhower and George S. Patton), to drive the veterans out of the city and burn their tents. This end for veterans of the First World War could not be repeated. Roosevelt would not risk not offering something to the divisions of new veterans.

The Economic Bill of Rights as laid out was remarkable for several reasons. First, it is remarkable how carefully drawn and how moderate some of the language is. Second, the economic rights seem so obvious and unobjectionable. Third, it is remarkable how far the country remains from fulfilling them.

Roosevelt would have been the first to admit that the Economic Bill of Rights was just the opening political salvo to free the nation's have-nots from their long history of economic abuses. No doubt this accounts for the restrictive language of the document that calls for "adequate" protection from the economic fears of old age, sickness, accident, and unemployment, while each family should have a "decent" home. But "adequate" and "decent" have very different meanings and very different levels of need that are to be fulfilled. Social Security is meant only to be adequate, not decent. Medical care is skewed according to class and increasingly is inadequate. Farmers who are left behind may not have an adequate standard of living, let alone a decent one. And the right to a "good" education is loaded in favor of the haves.

The Economic Bill of Rights, well-meaning as it was, did not go far enough in the 1940s and clearly is not nearly enough for the have-nots in the twenty-first century. Tragically, Americans have not achieved even the minimum of FDR's vision as a standard; in some ways, we have actually fallen backward. Where is "the right to a useful and remunerative job" in industries that have outsourced their labor and with it "the right to earn enough to provide adequate food and clothing and recreation"? And "the right of every farmer to raise and sell his products at a return which will give him and his family a decent living" and "the right of every business-man, large and small, to trade in an atmosphere of freedom from unfair competition and domination by monopolies at home or abroad" seem old-fashioned indeed. If you are a have-not in places such as El Paso, Texas, or in a prison, how hollow does "the right to a good education" sound? And if the credit-card-driven, foreign-financed economy of the United States goes from sizzle to fizzle, literally all bets are off for many who are classified as the haves but who know otherwise. In fact, in many cases, they are the debtor class, living on loans and credit cards, just as the United States is living beyond its means, increasingly indebted to China, Japan, and Germany in its balance of payments as imports exceed exports by hundreds of billions of dollars.

President Clinton—along with Senator Hillary Rodham Clinton—spoke of a bill of economic rights for the middle class, but that concept merely added to class divisions. President Clinton suggested nothing that made possible redistribution to the most needy. He had nothing to say about the equalization of expenditures between suburbs and the tax-starved cities where so many suburbanites make their living and enjoy the benefits of municipal services, including police and fire protection. Clinton did not show the linkage between his policies, the opportunities that were supposedly created, and actual outcomes, and he was uninter-ested in the government's role in sustaining collective action for social improvements, announcing that the era of big government was over. The political myth is that Clinton was a liberal. (It was a myth in part because he was not, in part because conservative propaganda said he was!) He was Gingrich lite; he believed in opportunity, especially for "the most deserving": the rich, the well-connected, and the opportunistic. In reality, he opened the door to greater suffering for the poorest in the society.[2] Bush II took Clinton policies and made things far worse, from health aid for the poor to the environmental degradation.

"REDISTRIBUTION"—NOT SO SCARY, AFTER ALL

People and their political leaders have become so fearful of suspicious-sounding concepts—many of which originated decades, even centuries, before they were born—that they robotically reject ideas such as "redistrib-ution." FDR did not see the Economic Bill of Rights as a zero-sum game.

Rather, he saw it as a framing device—not a way to take rights away from the rich but a way to distribute those rights more equitably and democratically to those who did not occupy the top of the financial pyramid.

In fact, we have had redistribution in the United States without realizing it for a very long time. Education is a mode of redistribution. Ending segregation and moving to integration was intended as a mode of redistribution in terms of economic and cultural possibilities and opportunities. Inclusiveness is important because in all likelihood it will result in greater redistribution of economic and property power. Voting can be a mode of redistribution. Persuading more of the lower and middle class to vote and run for office is one of the underlying struggles that is going on with regard to campaign financing, repairing the voting system, and moving away from the Electoral College to electing presidents by popular vote. These seemingly unconnected activities can lead to redistribution of power in the political and economic system but only if voting by the individual is understood as a small part of citizen participation.

It could be said that redistribution is the patriotic thing to do—or it would be if patriotism was something other than a legitimacy ritual that sanctifies continuous war. But the fear of redistribution is another of those myths used to stonewall egalitarian interdependence as the means of linking equality with freedom in democratic society.

The Economic Bill of Rights was a brilliant example of what some presidents are capable of, just as it was illustrative of the conservatives of FDR's day who had no interest in the democratic project. This situation does not seem all that different from the conservative position today. Why? Conservatives and others have always worried that a people that achieved basic necessities might "get ideas" and turn their attention to other matters such as the redistribution of *power* and *participation* in a political system that credits their existence as citizens but fears that they might open the floodgates of social concerns. Politics thus becomes the art of denying the public the kinds of social and economic justice that is necessary for a well-balanced democratic society.

On the other hand, progressive liberals remain unshaken in their belief that ensuring rights, dignity, and decency are possible in our lifetime. And tithing for the poorest populations inside and outside the United States is *not* an empty dream. In class terms, it may even be a necessity for ensuring the security of the better off. It is why these rights were thought by Roosevelt to have international implications without limits to particular national boundaries. To put it another way, people should and do have two classes of citizenship. One is that of their own nation and the other is that of the world, for whether some Americans like it or not, we are all in a quest for a world civilization that recognizes plural cultures.

However, can a good notion be translated into practical politics? This is a profoundly difficult question to answer, especially when the country is governed by conservative administrations. Ignoring what others think, presidents such as Bush II and their advisors believe that their mission is to spread their version of democracy, freedom, and open markets throughout the world. And they intend to use war as the instrument and propaganda as the opaque cover—at least opaque to the American people.

But Rightists have their own view of civilization. It is astonishing to read the White House's national security statement of September 2002. The first part was written in the triumphal language most American presidents have used since the beginning of the twentieth century. Democracy and freedom are both undefined in Bush's statement, but they are the mantra and the dogma of belief of today's Rightists, who have virtually no view of other cultures and their vision for the American people as a true exercise in democracy is still very much a work in progress with gaping holes.

The second half of that document essentially says that the United States can and will make war at its own instigation. We learn that civil liberties and other rights a president may decide to ignore are not of great importance, that terrorism, which is vaguely defined, overrides any guarantees to American citizens, and that the rest of the world had better beware of us, our purpose, and intentions. In the second half of the document, the velvet gloves come off and the present and future economic intentions of the United States are made clear.

Chapter 16

The Haves and the Have-Nots

AFTER ALL, IT'S "ONLY" THIRTY-SEVEN MILLION PEOPLE

On the eve of the 2000 presidential election, Governor George W. Bush of Texas told the wealthy and politically influential at the annual Al Smith Dinner in New York, "This is an impressive crowd, the have's and the have-more's. Some people call you the elite, I call you my base."[1]

While the future president of the United States was telling jokes (though in the coming months it would become clear that he really wasn't kidding), this was what life was like for the have-nots in his bountiful country:

- There were 31.6 million Americans living in poverty. By the time Bush was elected to a second term, the poverty rate had risen for four consecutive years to 37 million people—12.7 percent of the population.[2]

- Nearly half of blacks and 28 percent of whites called themselves "have-nots."[3]

- In 2003, according to the Children's Defense Fund, "12.9 million American children younger than 18 lived below the poverty line and more than one out of every six American children (17.6 percent) was poor. That is more children living in poverty today than thirty or thirty-five years ago. A child in America is more likely to live in poverty than a child in any of the eighteen other wealthy industrialized nations for which data exist."[4]

- "We are now living in a new Gilded Age, as extravagant as the original. Mansions have made a comeback," wrote Princeton economist and New York Times columnist Paul Krugman in 2002. "In 1998 the top 0.01 percent received more than 3 percent of all income. That meant that the 13,000 richest families in America had almost as much income as the 20 million poorest households; those 13,000 families had incomes 300 times that of average families."[5]

- According to a 2004 report of the Department of Agriculture, 11.9 percent of U.S. households, 13.5 million, were "food insecure." "At some time during the year, these households were uncertain of having, or unable to acquire, enough food to meet the needs of all their members because they had insufficient money or other resources. About one-third of food-insecure households (4.4 million, or 3.9 percent of all U.S. households) were food insecure to the extent that one or more household members were hungry, at least some time during the year, because they could not afford enough food."[6]

Nothing illustrates the widening gap between haves and have-nots more powerfully than the obscene difference in salaries and wealth between the heads of corporations and their workers for 2004:[7]

- Salaries for chief executives rose 290.7 percent, after adjusting for inflation, between 1990 and 2004, while the average worker's pay rose 4.5 percent. After adjusting for inflation, the minimum wage actually *fell* 6.2 percent over this period.

- The average total compensation of the top 370 CEOs in 2004 was $11.1 million, which amounts to 402 times the pay of the average production worker.

- If the minimum wage for production workers had increased as quickly as CEO pay since 1990, it would be $21.46 per hour, rather than $5.15 per hour (as of 2005). (Congress has not raised the minimum wage since 1997, but it has voted for nine wage increases for itself since then.)

These facts contradict the comfortable notion that somehow poverty in the United States is altogether different from poverty in the rest of the world—and not part of a worldwide shame. There are many features that American poverty as a social condition shares with the world. Hunger and homelessness shorten lives and limit access—if there is any to begin with—to cultural possibilities such as higher education.

Besides the extraordinary disparity between the very rich and the poor here and elsewhere in the world, there is a feeling that there is no control over the possibility of narrowing this runaway economic disparity. For the nature of capitalism, as it is presently understood, is the creation of desire and want over tending to the needs of feeding the hungry, administering to the society's food, health, and shelter. So the question about freedom from want and the relationship of this human aspiration to those who have, whose accretion of private wealth is more and more fenced off from the general public, can be toxic on every level of human existence.

Instead of being part of a world rights program of the future, what Americans now have is a runaway corporate system that, by its nature and behavior, cannot yield the common good. At the same time, individual nations are losing their own power to mammoth corporations. By its actions, the United States proclaims imperial law and doesn't even want to be bound by nations that favor the established framework of international law in terms of the world economy. The corporate powers are linking together through, say, the economic side of NATO, the Organization for Economic Cooperation and Development, and the economic side of the World Trade Organization, which—besides some words and intentions to the contrary—is virtually a cartel and corporate scheme for protection of the most powerful, adjusting differences between them.

All this lays the basis for a struggle between the haves and the haves, but it does nothing for the have-nots. "Haves and haves" is not a misprint. It means that unless the United States—regardless of the party in power—turns away from the imperialist road, it will continue to support "friendly" oligarchies, which it often refers to as "developing democracies." This policy would mistakenly set the frame of reference for the next fifty or one hundred years, thus allowing the United States to remain the sole superpower against the others—the others being Europe, increasingly suspicious of the United States. Their leaders will act as the "other Western civilization" competing with the United States and acting more civilly toward the third and the even less developed fourth world. Poorer nations have their own agenda, which is broadly comparable to positions taken by antiglobalization movement and found in various resolutions of the UN General Assembly on disarmament, antipoverty, and economic rights. American activists and scholars, empathetic and knowledgeable about the needs of the poor nations, have long pressed for controls over the global corporations through national and international chartering.

However, most Americans seem either bored or annoyed by what they see (and the line conservatives feed them) as the chronic dithering of the UN, especially after the wrangling of France, Germany, and other nations for refusing to give Bush II their stamp of approval for war against an obviously weak nation that had agreed to complete inspections in order to avert war with the United States and the West.[8]

American Rightists in recent years have insisted on the UN's marginalization and the flagrant exercise of our nationalism irrespective of international law. But perhaps the leading nationalist in post-Second World War Europe was Charles de Gaulle, who did not accept an anarchic international system that consigned the wretched to abject poverty. This does not disturb American conservatives or nationalist triumphalists. Around the world, however, even in China, there is a strong feeling for the importance of the United Nations and the role it could continue to play in raising people out of poverty if it had sufficient funds.

A system of international taxation would help poor nations to guarantee adequate incomes, health, and education to workers and their families and provide on-the-spot aid in terms of money and international emergency responders during natural disasters such as the tsunami around Indonesia in 2004 and the Pakistan-Kashmir earthquake in 2005. Gone would be a total dependence on particular nations to guarantee such funding.

It is hardly a far-fetched idea. In fact, there have been political answers that have been more than rhetoric. In 1960, calling on his own Catholic roots and ideas of moral justice, de Gaulle said that the countries that could afford it (he meant the West) should give 2 percent of their gross national income to the poor to rebuild the whole economic and social system around the world so that there would not be egregious disparity. In effect, this would be an international form of tithing. James Tobin, the economist and Nobel Laureate, offered a tax proposal on international travel to aid the poor. Shippers could contribute to such an international fund for each passage and movement of goods. Brian Urquhart, the former undersecretary general of the United Nations, and others have talked seriously about an international tax. Such notions fit well with the moral assumptions that support the political framework of the UN. In 2006, France established an international solidarity contribution from taxes on airline tickets, with part of the proceeds going to the International Drug Purchase Facility in the fight against pandemics.[9]

The disparity between the haves and have-nots is a moral question, which centers on practical implications, namely, distribution, price, and wages. There was a religious concept used by the churches called "just price/just wage" ("just" as in justice), which was to precede market distributions. "Just price" considers the actual kind of work done to determine what is a "just wage" that you need to live a decent life. This comes through very strongly in some Catholic literature. The influential Jacques Maritain, the "secret cardinal," advocated this position after the Second World War. But except as a slogan, a free market system, certainly as it operates in the United States, does not have as its purpose a just price or a just wage. Catholic charities have sought voluntary gifts from parishioners to help the poor. If the church let up on condemning the use of condoms to fight AIDS while committing itself to the sanctity of prebirth and used more of its considerable moral force to press for universal ideas such as "just wage," how much better off the have-nots would be.[10]

What was the response of the Protestant believer George W. Bush to these problems as a student-disciple of Jesus? The kind of government run by Bush II conservatives pretended to be in the picture but really sold the have-nots in America and the world a bill of goods. For example, Bush promised to create a new foreign aid program with the puffed-up name

Millennium Challenge Account. The United States, the administration's rhetoric went, would give five billion dollars by 2006 to assist countries that adopted "smart policies." By the summer of 2005, the Bush II administration had given exactly $117,500.[11]

So if charities alone can't sufficiently contribute, especially during lean years, and government by design plays a passive, even devious, role, are have-nots doomed to be permanently left out in the cold? In an affluent society, it does not have to be that way, but obvious wide-scale reforms are necessary. American legal scholars need to stop reading the Constitution as if it is a public relations document for free markets while protecting corporate power through the Fourteenth Amendment. A break with military Keynesianism is crucial for the long-term health of the society. Concepts such as "just price/just wage" and full employment that do not depend on war must be considered in the political arena.

Social and economic covenants such as the Universal Declaration of Human Rights show us what is *minimally* required of humanity.

THE WAR AGAINST THE HAVE-NOTS

A "Negro" soldier going home to America after the Second World War said, "Our fight for freedom begins when we get to San Francisco."[12] What has changed for have-nots of which blacks make up a large percentage? There have been outstanding victories, from civil rights lunch counters to selected executive suites to the halls of Congress, state houses, and cities, to athletic fields and the arts. But the overwhelming majority of blacks, as well as Latinos, and the dozens of other minorities who have come to America since that soldier returned from fighting the war, continue to wage an uphill battle for political and economic freedom—when they have the will.

Both political parties deserve shame, but conservatives, judging by their mean-spirited actions and not their disingenuous campaign words, seem bent on keeping the have-nots in their place, in low-paying jobs, and piling it on, as in 2003 when the conservative-dominated Congress, led by Newt Gingrich (eventually ousted as Speaker of the House for financial dealings around a book advance from Rubert Murdoch's media empire), removed a four-hundred-dollar credit that was vital to millions of working-poor families with children. This is not a new story, for the Right adopted these ideas as explicit policy along with idealistic sadism, states' rights racism, and the counterfeit notion of the "self-made" man: "I pulled myself up by my own bootstraps, you should pull yourself up by yours."

"Self-made" is one of the powerful myths in American life and one of the more ridiculous. It denies parentage, God, or other means of creation that most societies probably associate with life itself. The self-made seems to be a man or woman without strings or connections or good luck, as if each person is and always was utterly independent. It is a highly dubious proposition, but not to "family-made" people like George W. Bush, whose view, as Democratic Minority Leader Senator Harry Reid put it, is, "If you're poor, it's your fault. Go out and be part of America's success. Go out and get a job and be rich."[13]

The Rightists publicly declare their commitment to Christian ethics and morality, yet by their political actions it sometimes seems that they would like to put the have-nots, especially people of color, back on the plantation. As blacks know from family narratives and ultimately from personal experience, slavery is *still* the basis of a great number of American institutions. Without stretching the notion of slavery, look at the inverse number of blacks in prison: they comprise some 13 percent of the national population but half of all people incarcerated.[14]

U.S. arrest rates per hundred thousand inmates are far more than those of a number of western European countries. Our incarceration rate is the result of harsh sentencing, which, for the most part, is not tied to violent crime. It *is* tied to social control on the part of the state, which is used as a substitute for having full employment, universal health coverage, and continuing education—basic rights that are the only realistic means we have to rebuild society. But imprisoning people is not cheap. It can cost forty thousand dollars a year just to keep *one* person locked up, about what it costs to attend an Ivy League college for one year. And prisons are filled to overflowing. Some states, in the South particularly, have to release prisoners before they have finished serving their time because it is too expensive to keep them; room must be made for new prisoners.

Yet states continue to keep foolish laws on their books such as harsh sentencing for minor drug offenders and California's "three strikes and you're out," which, as one example, has put away a man for life for stealing golf clubs because that misdemeanor was his third offense. The United States Supreme Court upheld the California law.[15] The reason, when judged in terms of such consequences, is to control minority populations. (Perhaps some cost-benefit economists would argue that it would be less expensive if prisoners were executed, except that costs do not seem to be less when factoring in the appeals process.)

TWENTY-FIRST CENTURY KNOW-NOTHINGS

As noted, one reason the twentieth century was a period of some progressive reform was the fear on the part of the elites who ran the status quo nations and institutions that social and economic justice, from rhetoric to out-and-out radicalism, would transform the power structure in such a way as to open up the society to democracy that displaces overlapping economic oligarchies. The Right, especially big business, also feared that this would be just the prelude to the redistribution of resources, or at least access to them. These issues came to be seen in the context of what was thought to be the success of the Soviet Union, which made economic and social justice arguments for its deformed system. Enlightened officials in Washington held that the United States had better undertake social democratic policies as alternatives that worked inside of capitalism if capitalism was to remain the dominant world system that harbored the idea of natural affections among humankind.

But once the Soviet Union collapsed, interest grew in the United States and throughout the world in the victory of the capitalist market system (however much it, too, was deformed) in which people at the top no longer had to concern themselves with the people at the bottom. Which is not to say that it has not occurred to the privileged that they could face an actual uprising if have-nots managed to unite—and not for just a few fiery days like the riots after King's assassination or the beating of Rodney King by the Los Angeles police in 1991. Thus the wedge political strategy, to divide different groups with the same concerns from one another, has been an effective if well-worn strategy of the conservatives since Richard Nixon. Illusion and fantasy, the self-made dream, is used to encourage those who have entered the middle class to run from their roots and their unfortunate brothers and sisters. So in reality the have-nots are kept down through illusion and fantasy and by internalizing the idea that there is something wrong with them.

As usual at the end of any war period, the cold war in this case, there was a return to the idea of smaller government, at least in theory. It was to be a government that would step aside for corporate plunder such as that perpetrated by Enron largely at the expense of the have-nots and the insecure middle class, too often educated for gullibility. (Enron fooled Wall Street; Enron shareholders; Portland, Oregon; California; India; and nearly every Enron employee except for a few at the highest echelon before its fantastic Ponzi scheme was exposed.) Of course, if a nation has wars without end, the size of government will expand and corporations and the number of workers dependent on war will expand just as has happened with Halliburton's big stake in the Iraq War.

This kind of "let 'er rip" corruption policy did not originate with Bush II conservatives, but they pushed the idea of a corporate-controlled state to the limit as a partner to military expansion. Before this, the type of person who rose to the top of the Republican Party after Alf Landon in 1936, whether it was Dwight Eisenhower, Wendell Willkie, Thomas E. Dewey, or even Robert Taft, accepted the basic notions of the New Deal around such concerns as housing, welfare, and government regulation. This century's Rightist conservatives don't. Their prayer is that the market will solve all. In their political style they exhibit anger, arrogance, and disdain for facts. In that sense they are a kind of modern day Know-Nothing Party, many of whom are Christian fundamentalists who are committed to purity and fear of foreigners. The first Know-Nothings were "secret societies that flourished in the United States from 1852 to 1860. They were against immigration and the election or appointment of Catholics and the foreign born to official positions. When anyone who was not a party member asked a Know-Nothing any question regarding his policies, he replied, 'I don't know.'"[16]

Liberals through the years have known the score, yet their policies have often been seriously flawed. After integration, public housing in many instances became virtual internment camps for blacks that did enter or aspire to the middle class. Education became almost entirely "skills" education for preparation as workers in the corporate sector, rarely as inquiring citizens. Those on welfare were often seen as lacking skills, training, and the capacity to follow orders and as having no capacity to handle money. At the same time, they became the feared and reviled—often passive but feared.

History shows that the bureaucracy often zeros in on issues such as welfare, which can be understood in different contexts. Obviously, there are civil servants who want to give welfare to those in need, and they are appalled at the direction of shortsighted policy. Not only do they want a different policy, they see it as *necessary* for people to survive. Under both Clinton and Bush II, welfare spending plunged. A *New York Times* article (based on its request to the Department of Health and Human Services) said "the proportion of federal and state welfare money spent on cash assistance declined to 44 percent in 2002, from 77 percent in 1997. The proportion allocated to various types of cash assistance—training intended to help poor people get jobs and stay off welfare, for example—shot up to 56 percent from 23 percent in 1997."[17]

Few in political parties, except those who might favor a guaranteed national wage or income, would disagree that it is better to get people off welfare and into jobs. But if there are no jobs, or only minimal jobs that pay less than welfare, and if the ideologues refuse to rebuild the infrastructure of the government with governmental and nonprofit local entities leading the way, then what?

Dr. Pamela Loprest, a senior research associate at the Urban Institute, has an answer: "Fewer adults who left welfare recently [2002] are working than was the case shortly after welfare reform was enacted. More recent leavers have returned to welfare or are at risk of serious hardship because they are not working, do not have a working spouse, and are not receiving any government cash assistance. For those who are working, job quality is unchanged in recent years."[18]

So the have-nots keep sliding downhill in this richest of nations. For them, the American Dream becomes an American nightmare.

Chapter 17

The National Health

DIAGNOSIS: CRITICAL

This is a snapshot of the most costly health care system in the world. What a curious picture it is of the "super power" that thinks so little of its citizens in comparison to other industrialized nations when it comes to health care.

- "The fact is that the U.S. population does not have anywhere near the best health in the world," Dr. Barbara Starfield of the Johns Hopkins School of Hygiene and Public Health wrote in 2000.[1] "Of 13 countries in a recent comparison," Starfield continues,

  the United States ranks an average of 12th (second from the bottom) for 16 available health indicators. Countries in order of their average ranking on the health indicators (with the first being the best) are Japan, Sweden, Canada, France, Australia, Spain, Finland, the Netherlands, the United Kingdom, Denmark, Belgium, the United States, and Germany. Rankings of the United States on the separate indicators are:

    13th (last) for low-birth-weight percentages

    13th for neonatal mortality and infant mortality overall

    11th for post neonatal mortality

    13th for years of potential life lost (excluding external causes)

    11th for life expectancy at 1 year for females, 12th for males

    10th for life expectancy at 15 years for females, 12th for males

    10th for life expectancy at 40 years for females, 9th for
       males

    7th for life expectancy at 65 years for females, 7th for
       males

    3rd for life expectancy at 80 years for females, 3rd for
       males

    10th for age-adjusted mortality.[2]

- The number of Americans without health insurance stood at an all-time record—46.6 million in 2005 (15.9 percent lacking health coverage) according to the U.S Census Bureau. "It is sobering that 5.4 million more people lacked health insurance in 2005 than in the recession year of 2001, primarily because of the erosion of employer-based insurance," commented Robert Greenstein, executive director of the center on Budget and Policy Priorities.[3]

- The percentage of Americans who are uninsured rose largely because the percentage of people with employee-sponsored coverage continued to decline, as it has in the past several years.[4]

- One out of eight children—more than nine million ages eighteen and younger—have no health insurance.[5]

- Lack of insurance was much more common among those with low incomes. Some 24.3 percent of people with incomes below twenty-five thousand dollars were uninsured, almost triple the rate of 8.4 percent for people with incomes over seventy-five thousand dollars.[6]

- African Americans (19.7 percent uninsured) and Hispanics (32.7 percent) were much more likely to be uninsured than white, non-Hispanic people (11.3 percent).[7]

- Sixteen million adults were *underinsured* in 2003, meaning their insurance did not adequately protect them against catastrophic health care expenses. *An estimated total of 61 million adults*, or 35 percent of individuals ages nineteen to sixty-four, had either no insurance, sporadic coverage, or insurance coverage that exposed them to high health care costs during 2003.[8]

- The percentage of privately insured people who have problems paying medical bills has risen in recent years. Problems are particularly severe for low-income people with chronic health problems.[9]

- The United States is the only industrialized nation that does not ensure that all citizens have health insurance coverage.

The Institute of Medicine, an arm of the National Academies, estimated that this causes some eighteen thousand unnecessary deaths each year.[10]

Hundreds of billions of dollars are spent, often lavished, on health care in the United States each year. Certainly, breakthrough advances have resulted. The number of Nobel Prizes for medicine won by American scientists outstrips any other nation. But prizes do not change the fact that the U.S. health care system is incoherent in concept, wasteful, and often demeaning to patients and medical staff alike—afar cry from Roosevelt's belief that every American should have "the right to adequate medical care and the opportunity to achieve and enjoy good health."

Why has this been allowed to happen?

To make sense of America's senseless and chaotic health system—lamentably some sense *can* be made—start with an astonishing fact usually lost in the flood of high-tech medical treatment and the commercial and medical authoritarianism that grew up with it: until around 1912–1915, just thirty years before FDR's Economic Bill of Rights, there were almost no checks on who could practice medicine and the kinds of medicine they could practice! Was it a person who just hung up a shingle, or one who was spiritual, or some other variant?

There were different notions of what it meant to be a doctor, what it meant to really practice and administer medicine. From that point on, the U.S. medical system developed in distorted ways that were more apt to be hypocritical than Hippocratic.

It took a Carnegie Corporation study to show the people who practiced medicine that they had to have a much clearer technical understanding of what they were doing, that they should be accredited and certified, and that young people who wanted to be doctors should be *required* to go to medical school and obtain a particular certification, first the "bottom" certification, then for the specialities.[11] Eventually, certification was linked to the notion that "the doctor knows best." If you were really sick, did you know better? Of course not; you thought, "The doctor knows everything and I won't ask too many questions and I'll be safe." So you counted on the doctor's honesty, that if he (and as time went on and medical schools admitted some women, she) knew your condition on the basis of comparison with similar cases and the use of inductive reasoning, through cause and effect proved through empirical evidence, the doctor could deal with your problem. It was not long before the doctor became an authority figure pushed by medicine, personal ego, and the patient's fear and subservience. Even if the doctor could not deal with the patient's health problem but had a good bedside manner, the patient *still* felt better psychologically, and your faith in the doctor was undiminished. In this process, doctors and their medical associations nominated a whole group of non-medical-school professionals as "quacks." Quacks included trained and certified midwives and licensed practitioners of homeopathic medicine, which doctors saw as an economic threat. Most "quacks" had accredited college degrees, and many had advanced degrees. The same kind of healthcare practitioners—if anything, more of them—still serve countless numbers of people throughout the country and are still fighting the medical-political establishment for the recognition that they earned from *their* patients long ago.[12]

Doctors arrived on the scene politically when they were certified by the states. That gave them newfound political power as a group, but it collided with their personal code of individualism. So to get ahead, they were faced (and still face—despite some doctors organizing as unions in the twenty-first century) with being highly individualistic and with the necessity of being certified by the boards, that is, *groups* of doctors representing the state, in the new and advanced medical specialties. Most doctors tried to walk the high wire between the two and were highly successful, but in time the highwire broke and many doctors fell out of the medical profession.

Another element was added to the practice of medicine in the 1930s and at the end of the Second World War: the federal government attempted to set out certain rules and regulations that made it clear that doctors had to take patients because medicine was more than a volunteer activity. This was quickly labeled "socialized medicine" by opponents who resented the government trying to "control" doctors. That was the fear, and the politics, of the American Medical Association, which had become a powerful lobby in Washington.

As the system developed, health became an industry. Pharmaceutical companies not only became a big business—sales in 2004 topped a quarter *trillion* dollars for the first time,[13] some companies became "hot" stocks on Wall Street. (In recent years, pharmaceutical companies also developed cozy relationships with doctors. For example, nearly 10 percent of the nation's seven hundred thousand doctors signed up as consultants with a new segment of the investment industry: companies that act as the medical matchmakers of the investment world.)[14] The top twenty pharmaceutical companies accounted for 70 percent of the total market.[15] Even with a near monopoly, they kept prescription drug prices high for Americans, far higher than what people in other nations pay. The pharmaceutical companies claimed that increases were needed to cover the cost of research and development of new drugs; critics said it was mostly to keep shareholders contented and to ensure very high salaries for administrators. The reasons did not matter to have-nots, who were often forced to choose between paying for life-saving prescriptions or food or rent. To help needy residents, Illinois and Burlington, Vermont, began buying drugs for much less money from Canada. U.S. pharmaceutical companies and the Bush II government cried foul and succeeded in blocking some importation.

With the creation of more and more sophisticated technologies, costs continued to rise. Hospitals became much more complicated places. People became more dependent on what happened in hospitals. More people believed that there was no need to be sick anymore when they could get relatively well by going to the hospital or taking pills. Under a system of private enterprise, good health care to Americans meant technology made by the private sector with federal subsidy. It meant more engagement of other technicians and experts literally "on your case." It meant more tests, more batteries of tests that would have been unimaginable just a few years before, and more prescriptions written for the parade of new drugs from competing pharmaceutical companies, many of the drugs virtually identical, many directly advertised to the public. That was part of the dynamic that was driving the health system and driving up its cost into the stratosphere. Administrative costs became the chief culprit, accounting for 31 percent of health care expenditures in 1999, about double that of the Canadian single-payer health system.[16]

In the United States, health care for the individual became a social matter mediated either through Medicare, Medicaid, or HMOs. The result is that, every step of the way, a certain amount of profit is added to each procedure the patient receives but also for every bureaucratic activity that has little or nothing to do with medical care and everything to do with fees charged for the patient's care to keep a bureaucracy employed.

When a piece of equipment in a hospital is used for a patient's X-ray or CAT-scan, the hospital adds some profit to the procedure for each person who uses it. So for insurance claims, every body part has a value, a cost factor computed on the basis of replacement parts, pain and suffering, and not incidentally Wall Street's projections of the insurance company's earnings. Thus a knee is worth so much money, a heart is worth so much, a broken arm is worth so much. That each body part has become a cost and profit center is one of the social miracles of modern medicine and capitalist economics. And it is seldom feasible for a prospective patient to shop for the same service from competing doctors, especially when acute care is needed. (Indeed, the thought borders on the absurd; patients in an extraordinarily vulnerable condition are not in the business of comparison-shopping for their health care.)

In the 1980s, a substantial amount of the country's health care was taken care of by HMOs, which rarely fulfilled the promise of a workable private-public regulated system. Instead of fixing the system, what the country has gotten, as *The Nation* pointed out, is "two decades of managed care and government cuts [that have] left a depleted system with too few hospitals, overburdened staff, declining access for patients, rising emergency-room visits and an increasing number of uninsured."[17]

Without insurance the poor and the working poor depend on hospital emergency rooms for routine treatment, which further drives up costs as they overload the hospital system. Community health clinics, which were part of Lyndon Johnson's Poverty Program in the 1960s, try to take up some of the slack, but they, too, are hard-pressed for funds and are under continuous attack by a Congress ever on the lookout for any health service program that appears to be the backdoor to what they think is socialized medicine or coddling the poor. No money equals no care. Stories are told of patients who did not have health insurance, or have even modest health insurance, accepting death rather than being a burden on their families.

HMOs and the insurance companies *corporatized* the health system while at the same time making billions for themselves as they made the system more dysfunctional. A flagrant example of conflict of interest and deception is that of Dr. Bill Frist (unanimously elected majority leader of the Senate in 2002), whose family, including him, held millions of dollars of equity in the Hospital Corporation of America (HCA), the country's largest for-profit HMO, and who has speculated millions of dollars for personal benefit in health stocks.[18] (In 2003, HCA agreed to pay the government $1.7 billion for defrauding Medicare and Medicaid; it was the largest health care fraud case in U.S. history, according to the Justice Department.)[19]

Premiums for HMO services have increased far faster than their costs. In addition, there are many additional financial costs, including the unaccounted cost to patients (who are, after all, consumers) for time spent waiting in doctors' offices, hospitals, and on the telephone for doctors and insurance companies.

HMOs provide a special form of "negative" insurance. They make it hard on a daily basis for millions of people to get past the primary care doctor when a specialist is needed, that is, if you are not one of the millions of people with medical problems whom HMOs have excised from their rolls because they are too expensive to maintain. In fact, HMOs have long cherry-picked to get the healthiest people on their rolls, which, of course, is where they make the biggest profit.

Dr. Sidney Wolfe, director of Public Citizen Health Research, summed up the nation's unhealthy state when he asked why the government, instead of protecting citizens from HMOs, often protects the HMOs from public scrutiny and criminal prosecution, not to mention depriving citizens of benefits they thought they had paid for.[20] If all this were not reason enough to be nervous, the U.S. medical system has been further complicated by diseases once thought to be eradicated and by new diseases literally flying into the United States at jet speed. In 2003, it took just days for contagious passengers traveling from China to bring SARS (severe acute respiratory syndrome) and death to North America. Tuberculosis is making a comeback. There has been a shocking increase in AIDS in Asia, which—not coincidentally—has the world's highest rate of tuberculosis. Why? AIDS is a potent facilitator for active TB, which virtually ensures an explosion of active, transmissible TB. According to the executive director of the New Jersey Medical School National Tuberculosis Center, "since active TB is spread through the air, the potential for an airborne spread of TB to and within the United States is real and growing."[21]

IF THE SYSTEM IS BROKE, FIX IT

How much more of a health hazard does our health care system have to be before the chaos becomes overwhelming--particularly as more of the population enters old age? The humane public policies are there; whether the United States is prepared to sacrifice its superpower imperial role to take care of its own citizens remains to be seen.

There are several ways to transform the system fairly and with higher health standards that are fulfilled for less money than what we now spend.

The Need for National Goals

Responding to Dr. Starfield's article, a letter to the editor of *JAMA* noted that she had overlooked "a much more fundamental issue: the absence of nationally agreed-on goals and directions for promoting the good health of our citizens and the absence of a nationwide system for implementing health goals. Without clear health policy goals and clearly developed ways of directing the health care effort in a goal-directed manner, U.S. health care will be determined by 'the invisible hand' of a relatively unregulated health care market that values efficiency, economy, cost-saving, and the most diluted, adulterated product that the public will tolerate. These de facto health care goals tend to promote the financial interests of an industry (health care financing) in preference to the public's health interest."[22]

The Need for a New Social/Environmental Model

There is another reality that is less respectful of what doctors know and less respectful of the costs of straight medical advice that could result in an important change for the better for hospitals and surgeries—that is, *if* a different model of the human being is followed than the one that now undergirds medicine. In short, we need to have a far more developed view of *alternatives* and *mind-body-environmental-social connections* about disease and health, which must permeate medical and consumer workers' education. Many medical and health advocates recognize the need to change the emphasis from medicine to *prevention*. But what does preventive medicine mean in the twenty-first century? Surely prevention becomes social activity.

Where there is discussion of universal preventive medicine, its meaning must be expanded to include environmental and manufacturing factors that define the health of the person. The right to health care and prevention is easily defeated in economically depressed times in which the worker is forced to accept any kind of working condition just to have a job. As Norway and Sweden—and even Cuba—have demonstrated, health risks for individuals and their families need not be overwhelming and dislocating either for the individual or society.

More than a half century before American doctors began to be certified, Rudolph Virchow, a nineteenth-century German doctor and political leader, saw the importance of public health as the basis for individual health. Virchow believed that doctors had to be doctors of *social practice*, and he backed up his theory with action. He persuaded Berliners and Germans in the countryside that if they cleaned up their sewage and sanitation systems, they would be dealing with the problems of disease at the same time. They heeded his advice and their sickness decreased.

The same is true of our environment. We need doctors who understand the environment and the sickness that occurs as a result of what humans put into the environment: the toxic nuclear junk we have put into the air and water as a result of the cold war and the wars without end that followed; the grossly inefficient, wasteful ways we persist in heating, air conditioning, and lighting our homes and cities; and the grossly inefficient, wasteful way American auto manufacturers guide us to use and drive our cars. Millions of American drivers finally caught onto this and switched their allegiance to more efficient foreign cars, many made in the United States. Whatever Americans drive, it is one of the ironies of our time that the automobile, which began as a liberating technology, giving us freedom to go to new places and private spaces for romance, has become a virtual prison, making the daily grind of commuting unhealthy in its own way as freeways are gridlocked and nerves are frayed. But as Virchow showed, understanding is academic unless there is a concerted social health effort to eliminate the most obvious devastating harms, which often relate to public health matters such as water, air, industrial, and food pollution. As important as work is in the field of genetics (genes can certainly be damaged by social and political decisions, as is the case, for example, with radiation effects), there is little to suggest its total success in explaining critical aspects of life facing us as we breathe, drink, and try to keep warm and stay cool.

Research must comprehend the interaction between the social and the genetic and between the way we have organized basic systems such as transportation and different levels of industry. For instance, how is the hi-tech industry similar to industry now thought of as low-tech such as skilled repetitive work? Special studies are needed to comprehend the adverse effects repetitive work has on factory workers. The physical complaints may have changed, but they are still there, causing every manner of illness.

Schools of public health need to move in this direction, beginning with a branch of medicine that should be expanded: epidemiology. Unfortunately, epidemiology is held somewhat in disrepute because statistical correlations may not prove causal conclusions. Here, conventional standards historically adopted by mothers and people unfamiliar with modern means of cause could be helpful in tipping the scales of judgment for dealing with sickness. One may rebel hearing it, but "Dr. Mom" may have good health advice just as shamans and witch doctors are showing the way to pharmaceutical companies in regard to the use of plants from age-old forests that are then produced in pill form. And many in the West now take seriously the use of ancient Chinese herbs and acupuncture to ameliorate pain and even cure certain ailments.

The Need for a New Social Responsibility

If the United States had a fair tax system as do many European countries, we could get to FDR's vision of "adequate" medical care and better social welfare—that is, if there are proper regulatory and accountability controls and a different model of medical and social health for the individual. But to get to this point, Americans will have to swallow hard and comprehend that even in a democracy social responsibility is difficult to obtain.

What is social responsibility? The simple answer lies within another question: what responsibility do I have for somebody else? You could take the position that your only responsibility is to yourself or, if you have a family, perhaps to your spouse and children. But if you say, no, there is a much larger social responsibility that goes beyond the notion of, for example, sending your children to war, then this brings us to the question of how we live and how we may live with each other. That question reflects a moral consciousness and a definition of citizenship that allows for new boundaries, that gets away from selfish individualism, and that shows the responsibility people have toward each other's health and the need to support others who are less steadfast than we are.

An example: In the 1980s, a new idea was put forth by Reagan. The essence of the conservative view was: "Here I am in California, why should I be responsible for somebody who lives in New York? It's not my business. I only want to be responsible for myself and my family, and I certainly don't want to be responsible for anyone else. You in New York have your responsibilities within your boundaries." Tip O'Neill, when he was the Speaker of the then Democratic-controlled House, famously said of Reagan, "He has no concern, no regard, no care for the little man of America."[23] Modern conservatives and Rightists, whether they are social conservatives or Libertarians, have little if any interest in the collective responsibility to the poor and the elderly, who are seen as the nonproductive and who are supported by the productive.

Those who do not think it is immoral for a rich nation to allow a third of its citizens to be without health insurance or underinsured might consider that the haves, through their taxes, are paying much of the bill for the have-nots. This economic stupidity is rarely reported in the media or seriously debated in Congress. Yet the Institute of Medicine reports that the United States spends nearly a hundred billion dollars per year to provide uninsured residents with health services, often for preventable diseases or diseases that physicians could treat more efficiently with earlier diagnoses.[24] And unpaid hospital bills, mostly for the uninsured, cost the United States about forty-five billion dollars a year, adding about 8.5 percent to the health insurance bills for those who do pay, according to Kenneth E. Thorpe, a health-care economist at Emory University.[25] A more rationale single payer system would likely lower the actual costs of medical care to the middle classes.

Obviously, health right is a changing concept related to what a society is prepared to pay for decent--that is, beyond "adequate"--health care. If prevention is considered a health right, it will include those aspects of collective and industrial behavior that define individual health. "No smoking" bans are implicitly predicated on health rights and social control. Thus a health right is also expansive and necessarily leads to the question of those aspects of social and economic behavior that are detrimental to the person. Toxic water, nuclear waste, unsanitary foods, and unsanitary working conditions are all examples of activities that require a preventive health system. That is to say, the health right must be more than a safety net trigger employed after disaster occurs. It is a means to change environmental and industrial activities so that individual harm can be diminished. A health right becomes an expansive protective legal means to avoid the harm the society may encounter as a result of methods over which the individual may have little or no control. (An argument can be made in the Libertarian sense that the individual has the right to destroy himself or herself without government interference. This argument is only credible in a society in which the individual's choices are not predetermined by the economic and social system through education and propaganda.)

The Need for Affordable Health Insurance for Every American

Forward-thinking American doctors and health-care specialists have long advocated switching to government-financed insurance that covers all Americans and that has community involvement. Such a plan would be similar to universal (or single-payer) health care that Canada and most western European countries have had in some variation for decades. Canadians know their system is not perfect, but they continue to support it. One reason is that administrative and transfer costs under their system are cut drastically, which literally makes family and individual health costs affordable. Many American politicians and doctors disparage the Canadian system as unrealistic. As usual, they decry it as "socialized medicine" and use this rhetoric as a means to shore up antipathy for preventive health and medicine as a basic right. Of course, Medicare, Medicaid, subsidies for medical education, and publicly financed research are forms of socialized medicine.

The difference in speed of service by the medical profession in the United States compared with the allegedly long waits in Canada is vastly overstated. Every American knows that waiting for a doctor in an office (when you finally get an appointment, which often takes weeks) or in the emergency room can turn into hours. American doctors may be overworked and unclear about their status, but they are also invariably hard to reach, especially those who work on the HMO assembly line who are not supposed to spend more than twenty minutes or so with each patient. Patients often don't see the same doctor twice and may find themselves faced with a triage situation in which they are the last to get some care.

Part of the problem of patient care in the United States is related to limiting the number of medical schools in this country of 300 million to just 125. As a result of rigid controls over the number of students admitted to our medical schools, we are highly dependent on foreign doctors who then stay in the United States rather than returning to their native lands.

The Need for More Nurses

Hospitals, in fact, are run by nurses, lay nurses, and overworked interns, residents, and attending physicians. But anyone who has been in a hospital in recent years as a patient or visitor knows that there is a serious shortage of nurses. A study of 168 hospitals in Pennsylvania by researchers at the University of Pennsylvania found that you have a greater chance of dying after surgery in hospitals where nurses (and residents) are overextended—that is, taking care of more patients than they can reasonably or safely handle. This does not factor in tens of thousands of patients who die from infections acquired in hospitals, which have become some of the least sanitary places, or from the spread of drug-resistant bacteria brought back to military hospitals in the United States by American troops wounded in Iraq—and in Vietnam before that—that could pose a major problem for military hospitals and possibly for civilian hospitals.

How can we attract more nurses? The simple answer is also the correct answer: listen to the complaints of nurses. Make nursing hours livable, pay nurses what they truly are worth, increase government spending on nursing education, and increase space and facilities for teaching, which is sorely lacking.

WANTED: A POLITICAL PARTY WITH BRAINS, GUTS, AND EMPATHY

By now there can be no doubt about the state of health care in the United States. Yet the two major political parties fear a comprehensive overhaul of our health system because of the political struggle that would ensue. But if one did, a number of changes would be required for progress to be made.

- There would have to be direct confrontation with the insurance companies and the HMOs. This would require legislation conditioned on a universal health care plan and preventive medicine programs based on an analysis of work and environmentally related issues in modern societies, as well as insurance that paid for measuring risk factors and providing physicals and dietary and exercise counseling. This would bring down what are now the highest per-capita medical costs in the world.

- Legislation would also need to reinstate and expand a national health service corps so that health workers could work in underserved areas. This would include expansion of community health clinics and medical schools and reconsideration of medical education.

- A public pharmaceutical authority similar to FDR's Tennessee Valley Authority would need to be created; it would compete fairly with private sector drug and medical manufacturing corporations or, when necessary, recharter them as public corporations with heavy public and worker participation on their boards.

- The patenting system for drugs would need to be reconsidered so that their applications would be subsidized by federal contracts and grants.

- Community health boards would need to be linked to a public oversight jury system that would serve as a watchdog of the congressional budgeting process regarding matters of health policy and expenditures.

- Employers of large numbers of people would be asked to join in a national health insurance effort. (Are there progressive capitalists in the mold of Henry J. Kaiser, the twentieth century American industrialist, who was the first to care about the health of his workers?)

Americans should not fool themselves into thinking that even if a political party would stick with these points that reflect the common good, it would be very hard to get past the lobbying system that manipulates the levers of power with great effect regardless of the party in power.

Is there no solution?

Unless the country has a political party and a group of people in Congress who are absolutely committed to a program similar to that described here, it is not going to happen in any meaningful way. In Congress, over many sessions, a number of members, including John Conyers, Henry Waxman, and Ted Kennedy, have sought variants of these recommendations. What will be required in order to get lasting results is what was called "street heat" during the civil rights movement of the 1960s. Otherwise, the have-nots will not have freedom from want but eventually neither will millions of others who now consider themselves to be among the haves.

Chapter 18

Who Decides Who Gets Freedom From Want?

REMEMBER, OLIGARCHY IN A RIGHTIST AMERICA IS CONSTITUTIONAL

Democracy in our time is linked to freedom in the sense of choice, participation in the sense of inclusivity, and equality in the sense of equal voice. Participatory power would be relatively equally distributed in social, economic, and educational terms. Participation and access to resources are critical to the operations of a modern democracy. (Athenian democracy celebrated the freedom of the city-state in which people could debate and chose. But "people" did not include women, outsiders, and, of course, slaves. Nor did it include the relatively equal dispersion of property. Athenian democracy lasted for only 140 years.)

Democracy was a Jacobin concept going back to 1789. At the time of the French Revolution, this extremist French political group raised the idea of democracy as not just a class notion but a radical notion that includes different classes in addition to the poorest classes. Furthermore, the argument that was made during that period was that terror and virtue were linked. In effect, the Jacobins believed that governments or the Jacobians could hector people into becoming virtuous. (Similar to Bush II, some would say.) State terror and virtue were two sides of the same coin.

The Jacobins also talked about democracy in Rousseau's sense of a general will, which could be defined as what a society wants over a long period of time, not what it decides in the short-term because of a particular poll. So there would be a tradition of understanding what is really necessary for a life of freedom from want: a good education, a decent job, and affordable health care.

Even these basic rights are not always a given since the general will is determined by fewer and fewer people in the United States, even as the rhetoric of democracy becomes a propaganda instrument of a self-aggrandizing but Bourbon-like oligarchy. For example, if you don't agree with everything the government says about terrorism, you may be found guilty of being unpatriotic or *worse*! Suddenly, you may find yourself accused of associating with terrorists when it is the farthest thing from the truth.

So, there is a contradiction between what goes by the name of democracy and what democracy ultimately should be: tangibly related to greater numbers of people. There is a general will, but the definition of who interprets that general will turns out to be more and more narrow.

This comes back to the question of whether the United States is a republic or a democracy. We have struggled with this puzzle all through our history. Whether we are unsure or are simply sloppy in our language, we use the terms interchangeably. But by any constitutional definition on a National level, the United States remains a republic that is now *a system of aristocracy that has degraded into an oligarchy in which, in effect, a very few people decide the questions of the society and a national security organization of the government predominates.*

Thus the political question from the founding of the country has always been: who is a member of the political nation? This question is hardly distinct from the current degradation of democracy, where again fewer and fewer people decide particular questions. That is interesting because it really ends up the same way. The difference, at least so the founding fathers thought, was that if you were disinterested you could make objective judgments about certain kinds of policies.[1] And the people who were in the best position to make such judgments were property owners or those who had a stake in property.

The writers of the Constitution left no doubt about our form of government. The Preamble to the Constitution opens the door to a wider democracy. That is exactly the power of the First Amendment, which opens the door to articulating the meaning of the Bill of Rights. But the rest of the document (the Constitution without its amendments) is basically a plan for a republican form of government, which in effect says that we can recognize some of the rights of the people, but those people are really not the ones to decide the questions for the society. Stability is the objective and rule of law. In a business society such as ours, the rule of law, which means the protection of property, especially corporate property, is essential and is historically sanctioned by the courts.

If true democracy was not the concern of the Founding Fathers, it very much concerned the founding journalists and newspaper publishers who by and large were the real Democrats. They were thorns in the sides of the powerful, much as contemporary American journalists such as I. F. Stone, who exposed the McCarthy witch-hunts and the futility of the Vietnam War (and famously said, "all governments lie."), and Seymour M. Hersh, who exposes the deception and stupidity of today's defense establishment. The revolutionary journalists had little money but plenty of guts. Inevitably, some sold out to the highest bidder. A number of present-day conservative commentators seem to fit that description.

FORTY YEARS OF LOWERING THE BAR

Disparity and despair are hardly new in America. A paper written for the Bureau of the Budget in 1961 contained this observation, which is no less relevant today:

> The sad but true state of affairs is that technology and change have resulted in people of all ages not knowing what the few know, nor understanding how what is known by the few affects and changes the many. Continuing education becomes the only way to bridge the gap.[2]

More than forty years later, this gap—the democracy gap—has become a chasm that tens of millions of Americans do not and will not have enough education to bridge. An attempt to close the gap was made on January 8, 2002, with the bipartisan passage of Bush II's No Child Left Behind Act (NCLBA). The legislation focused national attention on the failure of many local schools to educate their children, particularly those in poorer districts, and its goals were not in dispute: provide all children with a quality education and close the math and language achievement gaps between rich and poor, black and white, native and nonnative English-speaking students.

But how much of the new law was genuine or even on the right track? By 2004, despite all the initial hoopla and promise, Bush II's budget under-funded NCLBA by tens of millions of dollars. Also eliminated were funds for some twenty-six existing education programs and funds critical to pro-grams such as those supporting after-school care and teacher quality ini-tiatives. As many as fifteen states were in revolt against the severe and irrational educational requirements the law suddenly placed on them without providing the necessary funding to carry them out. Liberal edu-cators worried that NCLBA was simply perpetuating "teaching to the test" on a national level which could become a form of rote learning. While this might result in higher scores in reading and math and let schools keep their accreditation it would not leave much time or energy for teaching critical thinking. In any case, the results have been mixed at best.

The troubling public school numbers continued, as reported in 2004 by the Children's Defense Fund (whose famous long-time motto, "Leave No Child Behind," Bush II simply swiped):[3]

- Seven out of ten fourth graders cannot read or do math at grade level.

- Children in the poorest families are six times as likely as chil-dren in more affluent families to drop out of high school. [Reasons for the high drop-out rate of students include low expectations about their future, distrust of the school system, boredom, and poverty—students frequently have to leave to make money for the family.]

- Seventy-five percent of the nation's public schools are in need of repairs, renovations, and modernization. The average school building is more than forty years old. Yet states spend on average almost three times as much per prisoner as per public school pupil.

- In forty-eight states, the cost of center-based child care for a four-year-old is greater than tuition at a four-year public college.

Since 90 percent of the nation's children attend public schools, it is instructive to note that Rod Paige, Bush II's secretary of education when NCLBA became law, said that he personally found Christian schools preferable to public, private, and secular schools for the values they teach: "all things being equal, I'd prefer to have a child in a school where there's a strong appreciation for values, the kinds of values that I think are associated with the Christian communities, so that this child can be brought up in an environment that teaches them to have strong faith and to understand that there is a force greater than them personally."[4]

Paige may or may not have realized that he opened up a wound that has lurked in American education since the nineteenth century. Schools and colleges often observed Christian doctrine. But with the rise of immigrant populations and different forms of Christianity, the idea of a secular American covenant took hold in the twentieth century as the means to ensure an American civilization that had a distinct multicultural hue. Public education was meant to accommodate all religions and cultures by absorbing them as the *new* America.

ORGANIZING FOR YOUR LIFE

Lack of education and its partner in crime, inadequate education, reinforced by claims of genetic inequality among people, is the new bar against democratic equality. One may work very hard or very little, but the fact is that the consciousness of the have-nots, and many haves on the margins, says: "This is all OK. I'm paid off through consumerism, watching television, and work that I don't believe in. This takes up my time and energy. It helps me escape, especially when supplemented by antidepressants."

Can this attitude of passive acceptance be changed?

One way to find out is to begin with an alternative program that has a chance of being heard. This will be difficult if the big corporate media is depended on as the catalyst for its own transformation as purveyor of passivity and consumerism. But if people organize across the country, through step-by-step grassroots organizing, they have a good chance of being heard and even reorganizing established political power for wide ranging changes. Roots are already there among teachers who do not tie themselves to the walls of classrooms. A complementary method of organizing would be study groups linked to bookstores, public libraries, religious organizations, labor unions, and community colleges, as well as retirement homes and prisons. A key is to use the hundreds of different smaller publications as purveyors of an independent culture. They should not be discounted because they add up, as does the Internet and its thousands of bloggers—writers of Web logs, or blogs—and some fifty-seven million American adults who read blogs.[5] "Communities on line," is how an official from MoveOn.org, the online liberal advocacy group with an e-mail list of 2.5 million supporters, described the new organizational process. (The Internet will become even more powerful when the digital divide is narrowed by putting inexpensive computers into the hands of more have-nots.)

John Cavanagh, director of the Institute for Policy Studies, has shown how potent grassroots organizing can be. When Clinton pushed hard for what the Left thought was his unfair "fast track" trade legislation in 1997, Cavanagh and a few others put together a liberal-progressive coalition that beat the president:

> We educated the public in two ways. One, some 40 million people belong to trade unions, environmental groups, Nader's group, family farm groups, student groups, various religious groups, all kinds of grassroots links, 100 disparate groups in all—the number is real—this is the Progressive Coalition. And they reach their members with newsletters and magazines which are well read. The other way we defeated fast track is that we really blanketed talk radio. I probably did a thousand radio shows all over the country. Our opponents won TV and we won radio. It turns out that radio is more important because you can't really educate on TV.[6]

One very important player in liberal issues is the Progressive Caucus in the House of Representatives that numbers between sixty and seventy members at any given time. Conservatives deride them, but this group generally sticks together and can provide the difference on close votes. They have an important ideological and elective role that may change the Democratic Party and nudge it toward the Left.

But Cavanagh is also critical of what he calls the plague of the Progressive community:

> Part of the plague is its timidity and its fear of jumping in and doing things. It's a fear for my generation, as opposed to the previous one because most of my generation [Cavanagh is 50] has never won anything. So people are in a sense happy to do their work and be marginal and be marginalized. But we have this brash sense at IPS and a few other places that we can do it and we know how to do it—shaming newspaper editorial boards into printing our Op-Ed pieces if we have to, but more often working with and developing relationships with people on the boards. And we know when we publish studies how to get press attention. Many other places spend 99 percent of their time writing stuff and 1 percent getting it out and they don't quite know how to get it out.[7]

So ideas must have "social legs." They must help to organize people now and in the future. That then gets people to think, ask, and act—for example, in study groups—on obvious but essential questions:

- Do I want to continue to be, in effect, a *noncitizen*?

- Am I only going to be a *spectator* in this story called America?

- Am I only going to be happy with my private life?

- Whose democracy do we want? Is democracy for everyone or just the few?

- How accountable should all levels of the government be to the public, and how is this all related to the educational divide and the digital divide between the haves and have-nots?

- How do we escape the prohibitive cost of the war system and imperialism, and what are the real costs to democracy if we fail to escape?

- What are my options?

In fact, there is only one option. If we are ever going to stop repeating the mistakes of the last half century and build on the successes of the movements that changed the American consciousness and some of its reality in a life-affirming direction, a large number of people must say:

> Yes, I *am* a citizen, and I am going to *change* this condition. I don't like these disparities because these disparities decrease the possibility and the capacity to be a full citizen. These disparities commit us to terrible policies that recreate some of the authoritarian tendencies found in other nations from the 1930s to the present.[8]

Simplistic as it may sound, the first step is to break the stranglehold of the status quo. It remains to be seen how long it will take to halt the damage to our freedoms that Bush II-Cheney conservatives have perpetuated and how long it will take to repair them, for it is much easier to destroy good ideas than to construct or reconstruct them. The fear is that the bad choices of the present (to put it mildly) will go unexamined by a future president and future American generations. Then authoritarianism will become more obvious and people will, without knowing it, accept the dictum that if you want to get along, go along, hunching your shoulders, keeping your head down, staring at your feet. These fears will be greatly increased because there is nothing to trust in, and therefore freedom itself is replaced by the habit of acceptance.

As if this were not enough, fears of insecurity coupled with our problem of self-deception have made Americans perpetually jittery—perhaps without knowing it, quite mad in some ways. Orwell would have seen our fears as driving us to self-fulfilling and horrible prophecies of

Armageddon. Reliance on our own weapons of mass destruction to make our weight felt in order to protect ourselves—or so we foolishly believe—verges on the pathological. And the state's willingness to suspend the freedoms of citizens is a thrust toward the American version of fascism. Indeed, very quickly an authoritarian government can and will manufacture insecurities. It would be the height of folly to think that somehow the United States is immune, as FDR knew so well.

Here, again, the result is clear. The ironic lesson of being frightened and insecure is that it forces you to turn to that which you distrust, beginning, sadly, with your social institutions, which are apt to easily fit into the authoritarian and fascist mode. That is what happened in Germany and Italy in the 1930s. Violence as permanent war is accepted, though people come to know the misery it causes them. They are told that their children—the troops—are giving and dying for a higher cause, and they come to believe it sufficiently enough that they help to silence those who don't. Obvious and reasoned choices are lost in the welter of propaganda. What is missed, therefore, is not only the freedom to choose, rightly or wrongly, but the freedom to frame the question along other lines so that we can concern ourselves with issues that seem intractable when considered in the wrong frame of reference—for example, the way questions of health, education, and environment are considered.

WHERE DOES THIS LEAVE LIBERALS AND MODERATES?

Liberals and moderates are left raising many old and some new issues. This is actually a big plus if there is continuous local conversation about the issues at home, in social and study groups, and at work, to develop answers and projects that will shift the practice of the largest institutions, namely, the large corporations and the state. Answers will come in time, but that can only happen when questions are reframed.

That leads to the hardest questions of all: How willing are citizens to do the difficult work of real democracy in order to make the country's institutions work for all? How willing are they to have a truly democratic Constitution that widens the scope of freedom and participation in all aspects of American life? How willing are they to go beyond voting? Some will argue that the democratization of all institutions would be a disaster.[9] According to this line of thought, there would be no room for minority opinion or beliefs. What those who argue in this way really are saying is that their property might be expropriated by the majority.

Obviously, there are many circumstances in which democracy might be cumbersome. These occur where one's skill, critical thinking, and judgment coincide—for example, in the case of a plane, these factors are in the hands of the pilot and not the passengers. What a nation seized by the idea of democracy can do is make collective judgments about what should be handled by the few so trained. People really are reasonable. They are not fools. They do not enter into activities that they cannot perform and for which skills training is necessary. And if there is a probability of such an occurrence, the people will compensate with laws that allow for *experts* responsible and accountable to the people in every aspect of governing and public life.

People understand boundaries and the importance of fairness. People also understand that want is not another word for avarice and greed. Democracy, when it is working well, emphasizes this irreducible fact. This is the major reason the public is increasingly appalled by government, most recently under Bush II. But democracy can only happen if and when the people keep their heads up and stop acting submissively, mistakenly accepting the idea that self-interest and selfish interest are the same. It can only happen when they stop believing that there is no common good or collective responsibility outside of war and its partners in fear—misguided defense and security—which leaders often force on the citizenry at the cost of citizens' freedoms.

Part Four

Freedom From Fear

In the future days which we seek to make secure, we look forward to a world founded upon four essential human freedoms.... The fourth is freedom from fear, which, translated into world terms, means a world-wide reduction of armaments to such a point and in such a thorough fashion that no nation will be in a position to commit an act of physical aggression against any neighbor—anywhere in the world.

—Franklin Delano Roosevelt, January 6, 1941

Chapter 19

The United States Goes to War
For Power, Peace, and Profit.
Subverts Constitutional Government.
And Makes Americans Fearful.

IN A WARRIOR NATION, FEAR COMES WITH THE TERRITORY

Hovering over the first three freedoms is the growing shadow of the lack of the fourth: freedom from fear. Many of us, in our daily lives, have been confronted by twenty-first century fears as we struggle to make sense of their maddening contradictions:

- Fear of terrorists attacks and fear of government surveillance
- Fear of the authorities and fear of rebellion in the streets
- Fear of criminals and fear of overzealous police
- Fear of God's wrath and fear of the political power of the religious Right
- Fear of losing money in investments and fear of not making enough
- Fear of redistribution of wealth and fear of not getting a fair share
- Fear of big government and fear of less government services
- Fear of the agenda of the Right and fear of the agenda of the Left
- Fear of racists and fear of blacks, whites, Latinos, and the immigrant poor

The list may be endless as new fears surface or are invented.

Americans have been very frightened since long before September 11. In 1949, Leonard Bernstein wrote his celebrated symphony "The Age of Anxiety," based on a work of the same name by poet W. H. Auden. Artists are often the harbingers of what cannot easily be expressed in prose or as nonfiction. These emotions can be expressed through music and art and are reflective of the politics of the time. Anxiety and fear were expressed by poets such as Auden, Stephen Spender and, to a degree, the conservative T. S. Eliot. William Butler Yeats told us that the center could not hold in 1939. And the end was being tolled for those who had not bought into totalitarianism.

After the Second World War, philosophic existentialists referred to different kinds of anxiety. One was the obvious: there is no escape from one's own death, although when it happens may be a question for negotiation and choice, especially for the economically secure. The other was institutionally caused anxiety. For example, the failure of political and economic institutions emanated from what seemed to be outside the person. This was the kind of anxiety that was and is both rampant and necessary to confront.

For the existentialists there were choices that could be made by the person and by humanity. Indeed, if you were to be free, you had to recognize that personal choices could be made. But to escape from egoism and narcissism, these choices could and must be made democratically for the entire society. Of course, if there is no freedom of speech, no freedom to communicate, there is no way that the choice can be anything but controlled by those with power who exercise it only for themselves if and when they so choose.

So the age of anxiety has not stopped. But in the twenty-first century it includes a great many more people who feel anxiety and depression. A terrible sadness has been added. No matter how many nuclear bombs and conventional bunker-busting missiles we have in our arsenal—or surveillance cameras or airport security checks or concrete barricades in front of public buildings or locks on our doors—we face a psychological level of fear previously unknown to our society: calculated, sweeping government secrecy, disinformation, lying, and the loss of civil liberties and civil rights. Our weapons have not created security. Neither did the cold war, nor did all of our wars and covert operations in the third world. Nor did the capture of Saddam Hussein. Would the capture or killing of Osama bin Laden or the next Osama bin Laden make Americans feel more secure?

Insecurity has become a permanent American psychological and political condition. Yet when our life-and-death fears—old fears of our existence and new fears daily—are added up, we will find that fear of war seems to have become the cancerous shadow of war.[1] Whether it is fear of nuclear war or fear of not having enough nuclear "protection" to supposedly prevent war, whether it is fear of not hunting down the terrorist before he or she can kill us or fear of waging futile wars in pursuit of those we think are terrorists, we reach the inescapable conclusion that the United States is a warrior nation, has been addicted to war from the beginning, and is able to sustain its warfare habit only by mugging American taxpayers—through the creation of an enemy other—and believing in its mission as God's chosen, whether or not one believes in God.

America's standing around the world plunged after the Iraq invasion and occupation, but the world's anger with us did not begin with Iraq. If we could begin to understand this, we would realize how it has made other people fearful and angry at us and why some have developed an outright hatred of us. Often—as in the case of Indochina or Central America, for example—they are the objects of our wars, even when innocent populations were minding their own business or had the misfortune of being in the wrong place at the wrong time. In the nuclear age, these actions only breed more fear in others, which breeds more zealots and terrorists, which breeds pride and joy among many have-nots (often led by their own upper-class firebrands such as Osama and Abu Musab al-Zarkawi, the latter, though killed by U.S. bombs in June 2006, seemingly destined to inflame a new generation of jihadis), which breeds more fear in us. This syndrome leads historically to mutual destruction for all sides.

How do we get off this treadmill? From the United States' and from the West's position, there is no choice but to change our relationship to the poor sectors of the society and the world. This means we will have to scrap our tortured foreign and national security policies, which in turn will require transforming and in some cases dismantling our war organizations and our deficient intelligence organizations. Doing so is not a simple process, for it includes shifting organizational purposes and encouraging the civil service and elected officials, including advisors, to critically reevaluate the American role in the world by examining America's history.

Even if nothing along these lines occurs, we will still be forced to withdraw from Iraq, just as we were forced out of Vietnam and the rest of Indochina by a people that had its own views of nationalism and development, just as the French were forced out of Vietnam and the rest of Indochina and Algeria, just as the Soviet Union was forced out of Afghanistan, Israel out of Gaza, the Russians out of Chechnya, and on and on it will go. There is an ongoing world revolution, and it will not fit into the procrustean bed of single superpower dominance. Some of these revolutions fit with modernism and the ideals of the French Revolution. Some are distinctly antimodernist in purpose with features of strict religious fundamentalism. Some take their cues from American struggles for economic, racial, and gender justice. Do free people have to be frightened of these tendencies?

WHY WE FIGHT

In his impassioned statement to rally a depressed nation, Franklin Roosevelt said, "We have nothing to fear but fear itself." But how should a free people react to war and preparation for war in the twenty-first century? Should we fear war, as Roosevelt and Herbert Hoover hoped, or are there rational and legal ways and means to create alternatives to war? This idea was the hope of pragmatists William James and John Dewey in the first half of the twentieth century, as it was for millions of people. Yet despite millions dead from war, alternative ideas have yet to take hold.

There is a terrible irony in Roosevelt's phrase about having nothing to fear but fear itself. Had he applied these words, rather than heeding those who insisted that the Japanese should be herded into internment camps for national security reasons, tens of thousands of Japanese-Americans would not have suffered severe indignity, incarceration, and loss of property. This kind of hysteria, which gripped otherwise prudent leaders in the 1940s, should serve as a cautionary tale. It is a profound error for twenty-first century democracy if the hysteria of that period, the egregious mistake of Roosevelt, and the other periods of fear, such as the McCarthy years, should overtake the nation permanently. That is why there must be constant vigilance in order to preserve civil liberties, for even the best of Democrats can suffer imprudent judgment and fear.

Why is this the case? The United States has shown itself to be inextricably linked to the talons of war throughout our history, and surely it has helped our expansion and created fear among others and respect among many.

But times change. Technology changes and, as it does, the concept of time changes. Formerly submerged people like those in China have become world players who do not care to be humiliated by the West. Nuclear weapons, an American creation, could, if used massively, end cultures and civilization in a day. And it is just the case that information makes many less ready to blindly accept the armchair heroics of those ready to expend the lives of others without reason, law, or moral justification.

At the beginning of the twenty-first century, humankind finds itself exhausted from the perverse ways it has concerned itself with fear. People are inundated with war and militarism, racism, class conflict (hidden for most Americans because of the pervasive ideology of individualism, personal opportunity, and desire, which Americans are taught to value), environmental degradation, disease, hunger, and national self-deception.

The human disaster in Louisiana and Mississippi in 2005 in the wake of Hurricane Katrina seemed for a moment to focus attention on poverty. For some contractors, awarded fat contracts without bidding or with scant competition, it soon became a bonanza as were the wars in Iraq and Afghanistan. Plans were put in place for the military to patrol New Orleans and other American cities because the military "works," according to Bush II. (But the military also contracts out the military functions to defense contractors who seem to operate with impunity.) [2] Plans were hatched with amazing speed in the conservative think tanks for a new test of a free market favoring the rich with guaranteed subsidy. These were meant to be the reality of governing and innovation. The kleptocracy—the government as a thief—advertised their wares as the solution to freedom from fear after a national disaster. (Nearly a year after Katrina, one could be forgiven for confusing New Orleans with the Baghdad of 2006: half of hospitals closed, 82 percent of public schools closed, 83 percent of local buses not operating, 40 percent of homes without electric service.)[3]

In a government, social conditions may change in relative importance in every administration, but together they are the political constant for all presidents when they raise their right hand and swear to "preserve and protect the Constitution." But what does preserve and protect really mean? All presidents know that the nation's quest for resources and raw materials has been and remains a central aspect of American politics and therefore the work of a president. The quest for commodities, markets, and resources such as land, gold, silver, water, uranium, and, of course, oil are necessary components of the American way of life, a deceptive phrase that was made very clear when President Lyndon Johnson visited the troops during the Vietnam War to buck them up. There are billions of them, he said, referring to the Indochinese as enemies around them, and two hundred million of us. "They want what we have and we're not going to give it to them."[4] This was Johnson's understanding of preserve and protect. In practical terms to preserve and protect in American history has meant to expand and keep.

The first and most important expansion of America took the form of continental resource wars with the Native Americans, who were systematically crushed by the American Army and pushed into reservations; hundreds of treaties were broken by 1871, and land was taken with no apologies or regrets.[5]

The definition of the American state from its founding is buttressed through war; indeed in our modern, technological age, the heavy hand of our warrior past is inescapable. How presidents concern themselves with this question determines the level of fear and well-being in the nation. No president wants to appear "unmanly" to the officials and citizens of his nation and other nations. (The feminist revolution notwithstanding, women who reach the highest levels of the U.S. government do not want to appear unmanly either. Perhaps secretaries of state Madeline Albright, a Democrat in the Clinton administration, and Condoleezza Rice, a Republican in the Bush II administration, feared that a public display of a little empathy would result in a loss of their power.) Thus citizens of the warrior state have been trained to live on the ledge of fear and war—and they are expected to. So the political leader must negotiate between war and protestations of peaceful intentions. But negotiation is usually skewed because it is compromised by preparation for war and participation in military conflicts that are invariably designated as fights for "freedom."

For war planners, politicians, and philosophers, war was to be made into a rational and spiritual process that is beyond the lived facts of war. Even the sainted Justice Oliver Wendell Holmes thought of war as a salutary process for much of his life. No wonder war is never far from the minds of astute political leaders, no matter how much they claim to yearn for peace. In the 2004 campaign, Democratic presidential candidate Senator John Kerry attacked Bush II for making war in Iraq, yet he was clear that he intended to prosecute the same policy but with more troops, more finesse, and therefore, he claimed, a successful conclusion. In other words, there is nothing to fear from war, and the state needs war to validate its existence. General Douglas MacArthur, an icon of the Second World War, was deadly serious when he preached that there was no substitute for victory. For the reportedly more advanced in this line of thought, there can be no such thing as defeat in the national lexicon. Our will is tested in war, according to Vice President Dick Cheney, who managed to obtain five draft deferments to keep him out of the Vietnam War. ("I had other priorities in the '60s other than military service," Cheney told a reporter in 1989.)[6] For President George W. Bush, defeat, whether in Iraq or on domestic issues, means the continuation of a life of personal failure. Being a loser in a society in which everyone is to be a winner is an intolerable burden for all, but it is unacceptable for a president.

Why is war so central to the public life of the United States? The political answer is as old as the struggles that engulfed ancient Athens. American politicians want to ensure that the various classes continue to feel themselves to be loyal to the same nation even though they live in totally different ways and in different classes with different religions and vastly different concerns. The more bellicose politicians, from Senator Albert Beveridge in the early twentieth century to Senator John McCain, point out that the success of the United States, its riches and territorial expansion, is directly related to its willingness to use force.

War, wrapped in the flag of ideals and patriotism, together with ameliorating the profound lingering problems of race, class, and ideals, is the political horse any president must steer lest he be trampled physically or politically. The task is not a simple one; there have been thirteen attempted assassinations of presidents, four of them fatal. So there may be something to the story that when presidents wander the rooms of the White House, they think about what their predecessors did in the hopes that they will learn from them and be able to justify their own actions and stay alive.

HIGHLIGHTS ABOUT WAR FROM OUR HERITAGE

Americans as a whole in their civil pursuits have been a reluctant warrior people. Dean Rusk, secretary of state under presidents John Kennedy and

Lyndon Johnson, intoned with a combination of resentment and regret that the American people had to be led kicking and screaming to war. On the other hand, when led to war by political leaders, the people all too readily follow. In recent years, it is members of the military who are most reluctant to go to war, knowing that they will carry the brunt of it, and if it goes badly, the civilian instigators inside government and the media will blame the military.

The influence philosophically for the American state as both a revolutionary and conservative entity was derived from the contrary views of John Locke, David Hume, and Thomas Hobbes. Of course, the Founding Fathers put their own spin on these thinkers. But in all cases, violence and war play a central role. For Locke, a social contract would exist as a clever fiction, giving people power and authority they did not have in a monarchy. But this fiction had real consequences. The person or group could revolt against the government if it acted against certain notions of decency. Locke seemed to be supporting the end of serfdom in Europe and therefore just war. For Hume, it was obvious that states had their heritage and impulse from violence and ambition. And it made sense for the state to defend against other states, whether legitimate or illegitimate. Hume's friend, Adam Smith, disliked the waste that war brought and the foolishness of colonialism, but he liked the economic importance of defense. For Locke's philosophical protagonist, Hobbes, there was no question that the sovereign had the power—indeed, the duty—to defend against outsiders and any grouping within the nation that organized and challenged his power. That is to say, the sovereign was honor bound to make war on the challenger and to escape the terrible consequences of civil war through concentrating the monopoly of violence in his sovereignty.

These ideas came to the United States in practical form. The colonists revolted against the British because the British took the side of the Indians in war and did not sufficiently protect the colonists fighting the Indians. Benjamin Franklin believed that the Iroquois Indians had a working democracy earlier than the learned gentlemen who prepared the Articles of Confederation and the Constitution did. The Iroquois nation of six individual groups prided itself on national consensus while guaranteeing free speech, political freedom, equality, and rights of assembly. Various founding fathers studied this document, yet Indians were thought of as savages to be destroyed if they got in the way of white settlers. So spoke General George Washington.

This idea of bellicosity accompanied by idealism has stuck with American leaders and soldiers in various wars. Perhaps the most poignant articulation of this idea was in the Vietnam War when a U.S. Army major claimed that his soldiers had to destroy a Vietnamese village in order to save it. This idea was described in the Preamble to the Constitution as the need to provide for the "common defense." This phrase was a softer way of describing in both a self- deceptive and accurate way the views of the

United States about warring. (It was one reason the Department of War was renamed the Department of Defense after the Second World War.) The way the United States fought against the Native Americans and the way generals William Tecumseh Sherman and Ulysses S. Grant ransacked the South served as a prelude to the Second World War in which the United States and its allies demanded unconditional surrender and then used the atomic bomb on a Japan already defeated, according to some American generals at the time.[7]

Until the presidency of Andrew Jackson, the United States was engaged in a series of aggressive and defensive wars against Indian nations and Great Britain that allowed for great expansion of U.S. territory. The wars themselves were aimed at showing the flag of sovereignty as the United States did on the high seas against the British who took American seamen off American flagships. Against the Native Americans, the wars were exercises in "white, civilized power" against tribes that faced extermination or an acceptance of conquest.[8]

Internally, President Washington protected the integrity of the United States by putting down domestic rebellions of soldiers eager to get some promised payment from the federal government for their service in war. That richer creditors were paid for services sparked an armed uprising of indebted farmers in western Massachusetts in 1786 that became known as Shays' Rebellion after its leader Daniel Shays. It lasted six months before it was snuffed out by federal troops.

The use of force and diplomacy was refined by Jefferson, who seemed to plead peace but, in reality, made war against the Barbary pirates, fought the British on the high seas, and, most importantly, more than doubled the size of the United States through purchase and then initiated the defense of the Louisiana territories against the Native Americans. Celebrated as the leading decentralist thinker and politician, Jefferson in fact centralized the government with his own brand of deception and claims of necessity. Jefferson bought Louisiana as an act of federal power, not for or through any one existing state but as a creation of the federal government.[9] During James Madison's presidency, war was recognized as a necessary concomitant of American power and expansion. The British understood the same reality.

Throughout American history, the British have been ambivalent in regard to American power and its existence as a state. Thus the British undertook to destroy the United States with the sacking of the capital (Washington) but lost their nerve. They were already spread thin militarily, looking for ways to protect their interests in Europe against an expansionist France. And the American navy, which was small but well constructed, was able to defend the pesky new nation smitten by its destiny. (It was not until well after the Second World War that the British adjusted to being a vassal of the United States.)

The United States, as a result of the Monroe Doctrine, authored by John Quincy Adams and issued by President James Monroe, feared the

Holy Alliance of Russia, Prussia, and Austria (organized by Czarist Russia), which seemed to threaten South America and the interests of the United States in protecting various republics. But the United States had another purpose: making it clear that South America was its backyard, an extraordinary act of bravado, until one realized that the British would lend their fleet against any attempts of the Holy Alliance to establish bases in South America.

It was Andrew Jackson who articulated most clearly the importance of war to the American state. Having commanded and fought in the battle of New Orleans, the most successful engagement of the War of 1812, Jackson became a hero and soon became president, doing so basically on a white, working-class, populist program of war, proslavery, anti–private national banking, anti-Indianism, and anti–foreign "intervention." These features were linked to Jackson's concern for the Spanish hold over Florida, where the Seminoles and Miccosukee tribes were settled, with Catholic missionaries. Perhaps more important was Jackson's ethnic cleansing of Cherokees, whom he had removed "for their own good" from Georgia into lands west of the Mississippi. Central to these questions was ensuring that ultimately Florida became a slave state. (Some leaders in political positions might confront their own class prejudices. Not Jackson. He started poor and ended as an owner of one hundred slaves, and he favored the expansion of agriculture and light manufacturing in the new territories. He also embodied a hatred of Native Americans—a powerful carryover from colonial times and the early years of the republic when Indians were allies of the British—yet he personally provided for a few Native American orphans.)

The role of the federal government was to defend and expand Jacksonian objectives. With the support of a greatly increased white male vote of the working class (women would not get the right to vote until 1920), Jackson kept and expanded the idea of populist imperialism. Whether his militant tendencies were greater than those of other presidents (Abraham Lincoln, Theodore Roosevelt, Harry Truman, Richard Nixon, and Bush II) is arguable. What is beyond dispute is that Jackson did not fear war but savored it—his interest was not in overturning slavery. But the question of war powers emerged in a new way in the generation prior to the Civil War and then during the Civil War itself.

FROM SEA TO SOMETIMES UNSHINING SEA

President James Polk took a border dispute with Mexico and turned it into an aggressive, so-called preemptive war with Mexico that he had no intention of avoiding.[10] His concerns about Congress' role were minimal. The Mexican War lasted two years (it ended just twelve years before the American Civil War) and greatly increased the size of the United States to include California, New Mexico, and Colorado. The war was a stunning defeat for the Mexicans, who have yet to recover from the loss of their lands and their pride. But the American excitement at the time of this great conquest was palpable. There were new lands to develop, shared as individual plots and ranches, and the possibility of riches from mining silver and gold. And there was the dream of Lewis and Clark (and Jefferson) reaching another ocean, which, in the minds of Americans, began to define the natural boundaries of the United States. It opened new frontiers to include commerce and conquest in the Pacific and would be called "Manifest Destiny" to manipulate a nation of hardworking landless farmers, speculators, and adventurers who linked personal acquisition to freedom.

Conflicting passions about the relationship between the Constitution and the executive branch's power to endow freedom was never far from the surface of American politics. In this sense, the argument of those who favored Manifest Destiny was integral to the abolitionists, for both the imperialists and the abolitionists believed in God-given rights of freedom; it was the American destiny—willed by God and assisted by a superior view of the rights of man—to bring this gift to all of the North American continent and eventually the rest of the world. The question under the Constitution was *who* had those rights and whether the war powers could be used to enforce freedom.

Such sentiments were easy to exploit. Needless to say, always present in the minds of Congress and the executive was the question of slavery. A major concern of American leaders was whether the Republic of Texas, which had proclaimed its independence from Mexico in 1836, would enter the union as a slave state. Another concern was whether Southern plantation owners and white owners of small farms could survive economically. (And there was a sordid feature: the sexual nature of exploitation and domination, which played a large part in American life, especially among white Southerners and slaves. Black women lived in a constant state of fear of rapists.)

Chief Justice Roger Tawney, a Catholic and a Democrat from the border state of Maryland (best remembered for writing the Dred Scott decision declaring that blacks were property and should not be granted equal protection because of their inferiority to whites), was an advocate of states' rights who sought to limit the president in his exercise of the war power to "military" matters. A generation earlier, John Quincy Adams, when he became a member of Congress, goaded the South with the claim that the executive could use the war power to rid the nation of slavery. A generation later, in Lincoln's time, it was the abolitionists who sought the use and extension of the war power. One can imagine the shock Southern legislators must have felt listening to this abolitionist talk.

Americans did not actually become citizens of the United States until after the Civil War. Until then, they were citizens of their own states. John Quincy Adams and the abolitionists claimed that the time had already passed for the nation to be more than individual states. The Industrial Revolution was around the corner. Adams had called for a national program to improve the nation's transportation arteries, and within the generation after his presidency, continental trading, manufacturing, and transportation did occur. This could not have happened if the states had remained balkanized, "half slave and half free," as Lincoln put it. With this language, Lincoln recognized the oneness of the nation and the integral nature of the states to the union, that is, the *United* States. The words of description in this case were very important. If, as the South said, it was a war *between* the states, sovereignty rested with the individual states; if the war was a rebellion against legitimate authority—the federal government—then sovereignty would rest with the people as mediated *through* the national state. Furthermore, the war power could be introduced as a constitutional matter applicable to all states. The president becomes the commander in chief responsible for repelling invasions as well as rebellions.

This was heady stuff. Thus, once the Civil War began, Lincoln fortified Fort Sumter when Congress was out of session and told its members that if they did not like what he had done, they should impeach him. It was not a time for impeachment for a Congress that confronted war against the Southern states. The Constitution allowed for the use of the president's war power to protect the union. Moreover, it became a moral and political stratagem (over the objection of many) for Lincoln to introduce the Emancipation Proclamation, which was intended to free the slaves in the South and in the border states.

The Emancipation Proclamation was presented by Lincoln as a "military necessity." It had the immediate effect of causing some two hundred thousand former slaves to escape their bondage, and many of them joined Union forces. Their lives seemed to move from oppression and fear to personal risk as they were newly emancipated. Of course, freedom meant being cut from one's moorings and becoming a refugee on roads that could lead nowhere unless there were real guarantees and possibilities that would come from citizenship. And despite black Americans' legal status as full citizens, lynching continued to be a common practice through the 1930s and even into the 1950s. Other means of oppression were used in the 1960s, as civil rights workers learned. It would be foolish to believe that American blacks in the twenty-first century live without some fear of oppression.

Once the Civil War ended, forces emerged that resulted in a new type of militarism. It came in the form of imperialism, and it was predicated on the compromise between white Southerners and Northern capitalists. The Union's military retained the status of "occupier" in the South on the grounds that it was there to protect the former slaves. The force was ineffective compared to what the United States has meant by military presence in the twentieth and twenty-first centuries. For the entire South after the Civil War, there were fewer than six thousand Union troops at the time when all were withdrawn in 1877.

236 The Four Freedoms Under Siege

For freed slaves in the South, the war did not end in 1865. Organized gangs of returned Confederate army veterans who had lost their place in the social pecking order of the South sought to reclaim it by guerrilla attacks (what today we might call attacks by terrorists, insurgents, or freedom fighters) against Negroes whether they described themselves free or otherwise. The Ku Klux Klan and the night riders of DeForrest had little to fear from the Union army; in fact, they were soon legitimated as a result of the compromise of Northern business imperialism with Southern cotton growers who needed markets and Southern racism engineered by the Samuel Tilden's and Rutherford B. Hayes' forces for resolution of the 1876 presidential election in Hayes' favor.

The compromise added to the war against Native Americans, which by 1890 effectively ended with the massacre of the Sioux tribe at Wounded Knee in South Dakota. Native Americans who had a separate status as sovereign had learned throughout their history that the meaning of sovereignty for them was the reservation, a form of Bantuism applied in the twentieth century by white Afrikaners in South Africa to black tribes. The boundary lines of areas that were "reserved" for Native Americans changed as the needs of the United States changed economically and politically. The attitude of American officers was to kill as many Native Americans as possible, however it was to be done, whenever Indians acted as more than a passive mass or were not in a permanent state of fear.[11]

BATTLESHIP DIPLOMACY MAKES THE UNITED STATES A WORLD POWER

In 1890, after what was called the "closing of the frontier," American elites looked to compete with the imperial powers in areas far from American shores. It was one thing to threaten the Barbary pirates, to serve notice on the British that the United States would invade Canada if the British supported the South, or to take tentative steps in Asia with Commodore Matthew Perry. It was quite another to develop a doctrine for the emergence of the United States as a world power to reconfigure the American military so that it would be closer to the British imperial defense system, which was thought to be successful in the operations of an empire.[12]

Many held to this purpose but none with more determination than Theodore Roosevelt, who argued for a two-ocean navy second to none to guard our frontiers and sea lanes. Such a navy, led by battleships, would roam the seas, showing the new power of the United States against an old, tired Europe. It was thought that large navies were necessary in and of themselves, for with them necessarily came new bases and coaling stations, ostensibly for the protection of American trade but more for the navy to protect its warrior capabilities.[13]

By the Spanish-American War in 1898, it was the navy that made the United States a world power. Ironically, Czarist Russia knew that it could not keep up in the armaments game, especially in battleships, and proposed a general disarmament conference in 1899. Unfortunately for the Czar, this was exactly the period in which Theodore Roosevelt saw America's world role greatly enhanced as a result of its naval power. (TR acted as a peacemaker between Russia and Japan, winning the Nobel Prize for his efforts. It was somewhat similar to, but more palpable than, Henry Kissinger winning the Nobel Prize for ending the war in Indochina. For the first time, a nonwhite power won a war from the whites, and TR legitimated it.)

The Spanish-American War was clothed in the language of freedom and concern for Cubans and Philippine natives, but it had far different purposes. Marxists might have thought that the war itself emerged from the growth of the American industrial system, which needed more markets that would reach to China and the Philippines. But as president, William McKinley, the proud representative of the business class, was a reluctant warrior until pressure from the Hearst and Pulitzer newspapers demanded that the United States declare war on Spain for the ostensible reason of stopping Spanish atrocities in Cuba and the Philippines and to retaliate for the destruction of the American warship Maine in Havana harbor. This event, similar in truth-value to the claims that the North Vietnamese attacked the U.S. Navy in 1964 with its gunboats thereby necessitating war, proved to be false, but it did not affect the cries for war or the legitimacy of "yellow journalism." McKinley asked for and received a declaration of war from Congress. As is usually the case, the war itself was popular, at least for the first few months, as the Spanish proved inept warriors on sea and land, both in the Philippines and Cuba. It was a "splendid little war," as American Secretary of State John Hay so aptly put it. It had the effect of destroying Spanish ambitions in the Caribbean and allowed the United States to establish bases in the Pacific. The American war project also meant further territorial expansion as it added the Hawaiian Islands and Puerto Rico as prizes of war.

But the wars of 1898–1912 were not without problems. Although Philippine insurgents, like the Indians on the new American continent, realized that they were not going to be independent, they fought on. The result was a bloody war of attrition in which the United States lost five thousand troops while sixteen thousand Filipinos were killed. U.S. troops burned villages and tortured insurgents through scorched earth campaigns.[14] In hindsight, the offense has been counted as a great success. (Without a tinge of irony or self-doubt, the war hawks in the American press who supported the Iraq War used the Philippines as an example of a great success to be emulated!)

Some Americans were against the Spanish American War, but their strong feelings and opposition were based less on moral grounds than on the fear of polluting the white race.[15] However, the more popular position was one of Christian triumphalism and territorial expansion to bring the benefits of Caucasian leadership to the Philippines, while giving the

United States a staging area for trade with China. Some in the Senate spoke approvingly of this sentiment, as did Theodore Roosevelt. Roosevelt's "big stick" stratagem was not a metaphor. When President Taft cut back the number of battleships during his term, Roosevelt thought it a "despicable state of affairs." As the consummate imperialist and warrior, TR was eager to get the United States into the First World War, believing that the country would gain immeasurably from it. Indeed, as the former president, Roosevelt sought to command a division in France and offered to raise funds for it. Wilson did not take kindly to TR's showboating and politely refused the offer. But Roosevelt was a strong advocate of the National Security League, which reached one million members during the war. Its less than noble task was to root out unpatriotic speech and subversives among the civilian population.[16]

The First World War was an interesting case in which several features of presidential governing came together. Wilson seemed to have no interest in warring in Europe although the United States sent troops into unstable countries in South America. The United States had already stationed marines in China, but these wars and conflicts did not rise to the level of the American Civil War, a war that had a profound effect on Southerners such as Wilson. For him, the question of race was never far behind and if there was a war, it was one that had distinct racist overtones. Roosevelt's uncle, James Bulloch, was an admiral in the Confederate navy. (A Virginian by birth, Wilson resegregated the federal government even as he changed its organizational structure by setting up the Federal Reserve System and the Federal Trade Commission and championing the eight-hour day for railroad workers.) The Wilson administration also engaged in a small border war with Mexico. While some saw it as a training ground for larger actions, it is not likely that Wilson did, for he feared that his domestic policy would have to change in order to secure the support of those capitalists and businesses he had sworn to regulate.[17]

The *casus belli* (Latin term meaning an event that provokes, leads to, or is used to justify a war) for the war was the sinking of the British ocean liner Lusitania, which carried 128 Americans who drowned. Wilson did not react immediately, for he knew that the British also had attacked American vessels. There was a claim, promoted by the Germans, that the Lusitania doubled as a warship carrying war materials from the United States to the British. Wilson endeavored to keep a neutral position between Germany and Great Britain.[18]

In Milwaukee and Texas, there were a number of German enclaves, but they did not have the political strength of the British in the American public or among journals of opinion and newspapers. While the Americans fought for their independence against the British, there was a residual affinity between the former confederacy and British business and aristocracy. By 1917, there were important linkages between the British and American upper business classes. This relationship took material form on

Wall Street, where investors feared the collapse of the American economy if the government did not side with the British. The entire American bond market was in danger of collapse because it was so heavily invested in British bonds. J. P. Morgan himself and other bankers made their arguments in forceful ways with Wilson.

Wilson understood. He also saw the war as a likely good if the United States entered to save England and France. At the very least, a balance of power would be preserved in Europe with the United States playing the leading role of arbiter directly and through a League of Nations. Just as the American people believed—through many American presidents, from Adams to Buchanan, from Theodore Roosevelt to the American cold war presidents—that the Cuban people had to be *saved*, Wilson also believed that it was time for a world ideology of democracy, which had the additional saving grace of being a variant of his secular Presbyterianism. Thus the popular justification for America's entry into the war was to make the world "safe for democracy." (Ever since, it has not mattered which nation or people the United States believed it had to "save" or fight against or how large or small the war was; this innocuous slogan became the mantra of American intervention, though some policy makers worried about the costs of triumphalism and overreach in material terms.)[19]

For the United States, the First World War lasted approximately a year and a half; for other nations the horror lasted four years with changes that proved cataclysmic. In that postwar world of revolution, wartime devastation, and broken empires, the United States expanded its international role as first among equals and presented itself as having little interest in international affairs and faraway quarrels or riches. It saw itself as the representative of small states and a doctrine of national self-determination.

Many views have been offered as to why the United States, after proposing the League of Nations, refused to join. Senator Robert La Follette, an opponent of the League, thought the League was a cover story for the continued exploitation of the poor by well-off Europeans and Americans. The League, according to La Follette's Progressive Party platform, was the latest clever stratagem to legitimate imperial war and plunder the resources of other nations. Others thought the League collapsed because of something as petty as a personal grudge between Wilson, Theodore Roosevelt, and Senator Henry Cabot Lodge, the latter two having reservations about the treaty, which Wilson then refused to grant out of his own personal pique. In his failure to persuade recalcitrant senators, Wilson, who had written extensively on congressional government as a university professor and president, was unable to change course. And the 1920 elections repudiated Wilson's ideas.[20] He suffered a stroke as president that left him an invalid unable to battle the anti-league forces that linked anti-imperialist groups with those committed to the idea that the United States should never involve itself in European conflicts.

REST IN PEACE?

As much as the League of Nations has been maligned, it is useful to spend a moment lingering over its grave.

The League's preamble stated that "the maintenance of peace requires the reduction of national armaments to the lowest point consistent with national safety and the enforcement of common action of international obligation (Article 8, League of Nations Charter). The League's Charter recognized the horrifying nature of war. However, questions remained about how to persuade and enforce a conclusion that a particular war—once it was examined by the League—was not defensive and a threat to the peace. What steps could be taken to enforce Article 8? Shunning was to be a major tactic, which meant cutting off relations with the offending party. But under Article 16, much more was possible, as it made clear:

> Should any Member of the League resort to war in disregard of its covenants...it shall ipso facto be deemed to have committed an act of war against all other Members of the League, which hereby undertake immediately to subject it to the severance of all trade or financial relations, the prohibition of all intercourse between their nationals and the nationals of the covenant-breaking State, and the prevention of all financial, commercial or personal intercourse between the nationals of the covenant-breaking State and the nationals of any other State, whether a Member of the League or not. It shall be the duty of the Council in such case to recommend to the several Governments concerned what effective military, naval or air force the Members of the League shall severally contribute to the armed forces to be used to protect the covenants of the League.[21]

Article 16 also stated that nations would support each other financially if they were harmed by supporting the League's punishments. This was a far-reaching article, for it meant that war itself was to be *outlawed*, and the authority to make war as a sovereign nation was limited by international obligation.

For people of Europe and the United States, this was understood as a way to escape the fear of war. It emboldened Franklin Roosevelt in 1920 with James Cox when FDR ran for vice president as a strong advocate of the League of Nations. But the limits of the thought and language at the time did not touch racism and imperialism toward the third world countries. Nor did it touch the colonies of the "advanced states." Nor did it affect the Monroe Doctrine, which is specifically mentioned in the Charter as being an area off limits to League intervention because it is one of "regional understandings like the Monroe Doctrine for securing the maintenance of peace." So the United States retained the sovereign right to protect or intervene without fear of confronting the League militarily. This article, number 21, was followed up with Article 22, which organized the mandate system as a means of regulating imperialism.

The mandate system was intended to help the "backward" peoples of the world secure a position among the "civilized" nations. In fact, territories held by the Germans and Turks before the First World War were "distributed" among the war's winners: the British were awarded land with an enormous potential for oil which ultimately was named Iraq, Palestine (which included Jordan), and Tanganyika in Africa; the French were given Syria; resource-rich Congo went to Belgium.

The League of Nations was predicated on collective security, but nations, having been through the First World War, had no stomach to undertake action against Japan when it invaded Manchuria in 1931, or even Germany for its moves on the Sudetenland and Austria, or Italy for conquering of Ethiopia. (It was the Soviet Union in the dying days of the League that generated wrath sufficient to be condemned for its invasion of Finland.)

The American position on the League showed its ambivalence between being bound to the decision of other nations and being an independent operator. The ideal of the United States—certainly reflected in the statements of Woodrow Wilson, William Jennings Bryan, one of Wilson's Secretaries of State, and Newton Baker, his pacifist secretary of war—was to find a means of ending war. But the reality of American statecraft was that it was unable to be part of an international system or alliance that it did not control or guide, or in which it was not first among nonequals. When an alliance seemed to be a profitless errand, the United States had no compunction in leaving it and in making the argument that war was the way to defeat revolution.

The United States had joined Great Britain, France, and thirteen other nations in attempting ostensibly to keep the Soviets in the war against Germany. In fact, Wilson's maneuver was an attempt to destroy the Soviet state and carve up Russia and its holdings. The United States withdrew from this enterprise once it was clear that being engaged in another country's civil war was not a particularly fruitful effort.

It would be a mistake not to recognize the yearning for peaceful mediation to disputes internationally. That Wilson sought the initiation of such a system, which was intended to bring along other nations, was surely meant in good faith (just as the intention of Clinton's Department of State to foster an International Criminal Court had good-faith aspects at its inception). But America's good intentions came with so many reservations that its purpose as an exercise in symmetrical justice was lost, as were official American good intentions about international law. Yet for the public, this idealistic strain remains an important element of democracy. Indeed, it has always been taken for granted that the people are more prone to calls for peace than are the realists of power.

After the defeat of the League, the question hung over the Department of State as to how the United States was going to live in the world. American

isolationists made a good deal of headway through the 1920s and 1930s—
isolationism being defined as the United States staying out of war in
Europe or being involved in entangling alliances that committed us to
war through collective security arrangements such as the League of
Nations specified. (It cannot be emphasized too strongly that isolationism
is not an accurate term to describe American foreign policy in the 1920s
and 1930s. In fact, the United States protected gains from the Spanish
American War by stationing troops in the Philippines, changed its policy
toward South America so that economic imperialism was more important
than military presence, and assigned units of marines to China at various
times to protect American business interests and our missionaries.)

President Warren Harding, an underrated president because of his dislike of war, pressed for and was successful in achieving a naval disarmament among the heavily armed nations, notably the United States, Great
Britain, France, and Japan, with the understanding that Germany would
follow suit.[22]

Unlike the Democrats, the Republican Party limited its views of military force to the claims that the United States pressed under the Monroe
Doctrine. Under Presidents Coolidge and Hoover, a treaty to outlaw war
was championed successfully by the Republicans.[23] But beneath this
treaty, which accepted the principle of sovereignty over conquered people by the Western powers (and sometimes Japan), racism remained integral in people's thoughts, no less so than in the thoughts of American
presidents.[24]

The Second World War was one in which ideals and balance of power
were mixed together in a brew that killed some fifty-five million people.
But FDR's freedom from fear was more than a slogan by the end of the
war. Looking at the dead and wounded, the broken bodies and fractured
people, and the eruption from the human soul of every kind of misery
and sadism, people—even statesmen—realized that radical change was
necessary; war had become too traumatic.

Just how traumatic it was depended on the nation. The third world
found itself decolonizing itself from Europe, a process that it viewed as
exercises in liberation and independence. Military technology reigned
supreme. Several hundred thousand Americans were dead or wounded,
but the United States came out of the war an undisputed winner. It greatly
increased its industrial base, greatly increased the number of its military
bases around the world, and to some extent strengthened its welfare state
to include the highly successful G.I. Bill, which made home ownership
and university and skills education available to millions of mostly white
Americans, transforming Depression youths into middle-class white-collar workers and suburbanites in many cases. Again, it seemed to be proof
that war could be used for purposes of expansion and the establishment
of American ideology in other nations. In the bargain, it changed the desperate economic situation of the Depression that had not been solved

through the domestic New Deal. On the other hand, claims for freedom by the black-American minority within one generation after the Second World War and during the Korean and Indochina (principally Vietnam) Wars made clear that the American black population was not going to be consigned to lives of greater fear than that which gripped white America. Even Japanese American citizens, once they were released from the internment camps in the United States, believed that fear did not have to be part of their lives in the American setting, and they intended to have reparations for their time in internment camps.

AS IF CHINA WAS OURS TO "LOSE"

The irony of the Second World War in the Asian theater was the Japanese interest in seeking to share with the United States a co-Asia prosperity sphere. (In the twenty-first century, the United States seems to want Japan as a junior partner.) In 1941, the Japanese military and imperialist group intended that Japan not wait for the European colonizers to leave Asia. Japanese leaders believed that by securing a deal with the United States, European interests in Asia would wither, especially if the United States would legitimate Japanese claims in China. The United States was not prepared to do so, nor did FDR intend to legitimate Japanese claims to Indochina. After the Japanese attack on Pearl Harbor and its military moves on the Hawaiian Islands, the U.S. Congress formally declared war in recognition that a state of war existed as a result of the Japanese attacks. But the American war in Asia was not intended as a defensive war. Its purpose, reenforced through arms, was to show in no uncertain terms that, for the United States, the Pacific Ocean strategically was its ocean.

The Republican Party viewed China not only as its concern but also as an American possession. Thus, four years after the Second World War ended, the Right in the United States claimed that "subversives" in the State Department had "lost" China, a confession of arrogance that stemmed from the idea that China's role since the beginning of the twentieth century was to be a major market for American goods and religious missionaries.

The Chinese had their own modern history. After seeking to end Western domination in the 1911 revolution, the Chinese found themselves embroiled in a civil war in the late 1920s between several factions of the Kuomintang—the National People's Party that included Chiang Kai Shek. In the Second World War, the United States favored Chiang's group, which was more interested in fighting the communists than the Japanese, according to General Joseph Stilwell, the American advisor to Chiang. But the United States sided with the corrupt Chiang government over the communists for ideological reasons even though they had carried the war against Japan, knowing full well that much of the hundreds of millions of dollars of material given to Chiang was sold on the black market. The U.S. policy failed as Mao Tse-tung's Chinese communists defeated Chiang Kai

Shek and his forces, who then fled to Formosa (Taiwan). (Recent evidence suggests that Mao also spent much of his forces fighting Chiang over confronting the Japanese invaders.)[25]

Before the Koumintang unraveled, Secretary of State Dean Acheson decided to cut the losses of the United States after a failed mission led by General George C. Marshall, initiator of the Marshall Plan, to aid war-torn Europe. Marshall's purpose was to establish a coalition government of nationalists and communists. Perhaps this mission was doomed from the start, for it began from the position that the United States was the honest broker between the two sides. How the United States could act in that capacity was not clear. In Europe, the communists had joined postwar France's Gaullist government, but the United States insisted that there not be any such coalition. (Historically, the United States has sought to be an honest broker, as was the case in the Japanese-Russian War, but recently has had little success in the Middle East between the Palestinians and the Israelis. Few nations believe anymore that the United States is such a broker, at least at this point, since it had become the most imperialist of nations with its own purpose and interests.)

The Second World War was conducted with stunning brutality and racist hysteria. On the American side, the destruction of Tokyo and other major cities by conventional bombing—if continuous bombings that led to terrible firestorms can be defined as "conventional"—followed by the use of nuclear weapons on Hiroshima and Nagasaki, made clear that the boundaries regarding the international law of war were erased. (On February 14 and 15, 1945, Dresden, Germany, which had no war manufacturing targets of consequence but was swollen with refugees fleeing the Soviet advance from the East, was severely firebombed by British and U.S. air raids. Hundreds of thousands of explosives were dropped.[26] As many as half a million may have perished.) The United States was not alone in this regard. Japanese brutality toward China was unspeakable; for example, in the mid-1930s more than a hundred thousand noncombatants were killed in Nanking. Such events fueled within the United States the insistence of New Deal liberals to campaign for the removal of Emperor Hirohito and the Japanese imperial court as war criminals. That they were war criminals—either ordering or being complicit in an aggressive war—hardly seemed to be in dispute. In the case of Hirohito, General MacArthur and members of the Truman administration concluded that for the smooth occupation of Japan it was necessary to keep the emperor and his immediate group in place as a defense against popular revolt.[27]

A question has hung over the United States and American historical scholarship since the dropping of the atomic bombs on Japan. Several months before the destruction, the Japanese, through various sources including the Soviets and our OSS (Office of Strategic Services, the precursor to the CIA), had received word that the Japanese would surrender if they could keep in place the emperor and the imperial court.[28] Under the allied dictum of unconditional surrender, this offer was not accepted until after the United States used nuclear weapons, thus ushering in a new period of history—the age of nuclearism—and informing the world that through nuclear weapons America would retain its position as the world's supreme power.

Nuclearism for the United States has cost taxpayers an estimated $5.5 trillion up to just 1998,[29] while opening the floodgates of nuclear proliferation around the world in large states, small states, and nonstates, leaving behind highly toxic radioactive nuclear waste. Plutonium, the most dangerous radioactive element, has a half-life of twenty-five thousand years.[30]

The war in Europe against the Nazi regime and Germany brought together several elements. In domestic politics, the isolationist wing in America was discredited since some were less neutral and more pro-Nazi. For example, Charles Lindbergh was thought to be pro-Nazi, as was Henry Ford, who was an anti-Semite as well. In fact, American business prior to the Second World War, especially in electrical power and automobiles, was friendly to German aims both on business and ideological terms.[31]

These sentiments changed and isolationists, including a motley and disparate group of liberals and conservatives in Congress, were forced by circumstance to shift their outlook about the world. Four days after the Japanese bombed Pearl Harbor, Germany declared war on the United States on the grounds that the United States was not a neutral party but strongly supported the British. More important than the legalities of the matter, which the Nazis had no interest in except as propaganda, was the realization that Hitler and his group had adopted a course that inexorably led to war.

Franklin Roosevelt concluded, as Wilson had in 1917, that the United States had to forestall the hegemonic position in Europe, which it seemed was in Hitler's grasp. From the American side, war was a foregone conclusion after the Nazi invasion of the Soviet Union on June 22, 1941. The control of the entire European landmass by those who claimed that they were the authentic spokesmen of Western civilization was too much to endure.

By 1942, it became clear what the Nazi project was: destruction of the Jews; destruction of communism and the Soviet Union and control of all Soviet resources; use of slave labor from the East; and establishment of concentration camps for the purpose of exterminating those deemed "unworthy" (including gypsies, homosexuals, socialists, communists, Poles, Russians, the sick and retarded, and other "useless breeders"). Anyone who got in the way of the "new order" or did not fit into the arbitrary system of Aryanism was to be exterminated. It should not be concluded, however, that these political ideas were foreign to Western civilization. In the modern post-French revolutionary period, they were espoused by marginal groups and individuals who kept such notions to themselves, or in academic journals, or on the streets and in the cafes. The Nazis took these ideas and packaged them into mainstream practice.[32] It was frightening, intimidating, and nightmarish. Furthermore, the Nazis packaged the ideas across class lines. The historian A. J. P. Taylor has noted that Hitler wanted a settlement with the West and had little interest in war if his goals could be achieved by intimidation without war and if his complaints, for example, about German mistreatment as a result of a punitive peace treaty, could be considered.[33] But this view does not take into account Hitler's long-term goal of destruction of all those he hated and could not use.

After the Nazis attacked the Soviet Union, a distinguished U.S. senator, who later went on to become president, was hopeful that the world situation would result in the mutual destruction of Soviet communism and Nazi Germany. But this was not the weight of American opinion under Roosevelt who, in fact, had pressed for the diplomatic recognition of the Soviet Union in 1934. His reasons had nothing to do with being pro-Soviet; his reasons were primarily strategic, having to do with the Soviets, who Roosevelt thought of as a counterweight to increased Japanese influence in Asia.[34]

Once the United States was directly involved in the war in Europe, American military diplomacy concerned itself with what the contours of Europe would be after the war. The conventional wisdom is that the United States was naïve during the war and committed itself only to winning the war. But American leadership reflected long-term goals of military presence around the world. Churchill, whose politics were extremely conservative, sought the rehabilitation of the class structure in Europe as it existed before the war. And to no little extent, the United States supported this conservative thrust. Thus, once the Italian government switched to the allied side in 1943, it was the government of the royalist Right that was put in place. This was a government acceptable to the United States and preferable to the Italian resistance movement, which included socialists, communists, and the independent Left. Given the choice between supporting Leftist movements, whether in Italy, Greece, or France, the United States by the end of the war had no hesitance in supporting a Rightist and Christian Democratic leadership to reassert the status quo in Europe, without Nazism. But the American definition of the status quo was one that would be open to change.

In the mid-1940s, the United States had no interest in protecting the fallen or failing European empires in Indonesia, India, or Africa.[35] During this turbulent period, American foreign policy was administered at the assistant secretary of state level. Until the early 1950s, the assistant secretaries were either active duty generals or colonels in the armed forces. George C. Marshall, chief of staff during the Second World War, became secretary of state in 1947.[36] This was the period in which the American government was reorganized so that the distinction between civilian and military leadership on the operational level was no longer compartmentalized.

In part, this change occurred because the military performed occupation functions, albeit with civilian advisors. Adding to the militarism was the downgrading of the fledgling United Nations because of the U.S.-Soviet collision, fears of communism, and independent nationalist movements that resulted in the United States organizing world military alliance systems of status quo states, from NATO to SEATO (Southeast Asian Treaty Organization), ANZUS (Australia-New Zealand-United States), and the Baghdad Pact, a defense agreement with Middle East countries.

Key to this strategy was General and then President Dwight D. Eisenhower. (It is useful to make a distinction between bellicosity and militarism. For example, Eisenhower was a militarist, but he was not bellicose in the way that other military leaders such as Air Force General Curtis LeMay were (or the way that Bush II's civilian advisors were). LeMay, whose planes had destroyed most of Tokyo using "only" conventional weapons, argued that *he* could destroy all of Japan without resorting to nuclear weapons.[37]

FROM THE ASHES OF THE LEAGUE OF NATIONS, A PHOENIX STRUGGLES TO RISE

With some American leaders and diplomats who followed FDR's lead, the world's security was to be mediated through the five permanent members of the United Nations Security Council. They were to act unanimously with each having a veto over actions requiring the use of troops or other warlike actions. The permanent five had to act in concert because they had the collective responsibility for ensuring the peace after carrying most of the burden of the Second World War. In reality, of course, the burden was carried by Great Britain, the Soviet Union, the United States, and China. But this idea of collective action by the permanent five was aborted with the death of Roosevelt and the beginning of the cold war.

There were many reasons for the failure. The Soviet Union had emerged in the minds of America's policy makers as a competing world power with global ambitions. The results of decolonization and brutal civil wars throughout the third world created a reordering and instability in international politics. Chiang Kai Shek's Nationalists, despite losing the civil war to Mao and the Communist Party, were "allowed" by the West to hold onto the Chinese seat on the Security Council. Great Britain could barely recover from two world wars and losing India as its prize possession—and only with U.S. aid. France was made a permanent member of the Security Council at the insistence of the United States even though Vichy France—which occupied approximately one-third of France—retained its independence by being a puppet of Nazi Germany.

Thus, just as the UN grew out of the horror of the Second World War, it foundered because the nature of the war had given rise to the reconfiguration of power in the world.

If the United States had recognized the Chinese communists early on, it would have been able to normalize relations with China decades before Nixon broke the ice by encouraging trade with them. That critical error led to another one: the United States took away the basis of discussions about the disposition of North Korea and allowed the Soviets the latitude to be far more amenable to working out a Korean settlement.

U.S. foreign policy might have changed enough so that the United States would have had a very different attitude toward the cold war. To be sure, such a change would have been hard but far from impossible. Saddest of all, the United States very likely would have avoided what turned into the first of our post-Second World War quagmires in distant lands whose people and terrain we knew little about. Generations of Americans have little or no idea how horrible the Korean War was or even when it was fought.

The Korean War began on June 25, 1950, just five years after the end of the Second World War. When it ended in a stalemate three years later, more than one hundred and seventy thousand American and United Nations troops had been killed and wounded. The South and North Koreans and the Chinese communists had some two million casualties between them. One million civilians were killed in South Korea. The United States spent about $67 billion on the war.[38] Hundreds of billions more have been spent maintaining the tens of thousands of U.S. troops stationed in South Korea ever since. U.S. taxpayers, as usual, have footed most of the bill. And are still paying.

American involvement in Korea came after border struggles between South and North Korea because each intended to unify the country under its respective banner. At first, President Truman found himself in a political quandary. The Democrats, already open to the charge of losing China to Mao's communists in 1949, thought that they would be open to the charge of losing South Korea.[39]

The Republicans were quick to say that Dean Acheson, a hated symbol for them, who exuded personal disdain and arrogance coated in witticism toward adversaries, had implied that South Korea was outside the U.S. defense perimeter and thus was the cause for the attack by the forces of Kim il Sung (father of North Korea's current dictator Kim Jong-il). So it was not likely that for domestic political reasons President Truman would fail to respond when North Korea invaded the South. Using the "Uniting for Peace Resolution" of the UN for cover, the United States had already sent in American troops to intervene, believing that American primacy was being challenged.[40]

The Korean War proved several brutal facts that the American political leadership did not take into account sufficiently. They presented the war to the American public and the American military as a "limited war." The argument was that the war would not be expanded to include China (which sat ominously on North Korea's northern border) and the United States would not use nuclear weapons.

The war was inconclusive, although it made clear that a predominantly white nation with superior technological force could not overcome the efforts of the indigenous North Koreans supplemented by the Chinese army. The Chinese communists had no intention of having their revolution undone by the United States and made this clear through the Indian ambassador when the United States seemed to occupy North Korea and thereby threaten Chinese hydroelectric power stations.

Two and a half years into the war, Eisenhower, then the Republican presidential candidate, said he would go to Korea to end the stalemate. But as president, he threatened the Chinese and North Koreans with the use of nuclear weapons. Whether this was a military trick is not known. The war had also been for Americans an exercise in expansive war plans with General MacArthur seeking permission to unleash Chiang Kai Shek's troops in Formosa as a means of destroying the communist-led revolution in China. The American generals who commanded the Second World War in Europe did not favor this. They and Democratic Party leaders saw war in Asia as a peripheral war; America's real interests were in Europe. Indeed, the Korean War was used as the occasion to justify NATO and a buildup of American forces in Europe on the grounds that the Soviets would overrun west Europe.[41]

The Korean War period had all the elements that guarantee fear and anxiety in a populace, whether as a result of mounting casualties, labor strikes, increased unemployment, tripling the defense budget, or doubts about who was a security risk and who was a real American. It was the opposite condition that Roosevelt in his freedom from fear had intended American society to experience.

But America's leaders plowed on, thinking they could neutralize fear—or use it when necessary—in American life through huge defense budgets, more thermonuclear weapons, charging former New Dealers and Leftists as security risks, assuming that war by the United States was essentially without cost except to families whose children had been killed or wounded, and by pursuing the historic strategy of fighting on the territory of other nations or guiding them as members of the Free World.

After the Korean War, the United States sought CIA bases in Southeast Asia, an expansion of covert actions, and the organizing of military alliances that committed the United States to military advice and ultimately to a new war, this one in Vietnam. That war, however, started inauspiciously with the United States stationing less than a thousand troops in South Vietnam under Eisenhower. The American component grew to 16,000 under Kennedy, then expanded at one time to 550,000 men and women at arms in 1968. Ultimately 2.5 million Americans served in Indochina.[42]

The withdrawal from Vietnam during the Nixon term was necessary because the United States had lost on the ground, could not equalize in intensity the fierce nationalism of the North Vietnamese, did not use nuclear weapons on the North (but bombed ferociously nevertheless), and lost the support of a substantial number of the American people and even the elites. Presidents Johnson and Nixon were also faced with a domestic cultural revolution. On the political side, blacks were chanting "We are not afraid," meaning that they were going to challenge their situation in the United States even as Johnson tried to get ahead of the black revolution with his Great Society poverty package. The *Leave It to Beaver* television picture of American society had nothing in common with the traditional family. Instead, it was a time that promoted drugs (some of the drugs, such as LSD or "acid," a potent mood-changing drug, were introduced through CIA contracts)[43] and free love as the antidote to war and conventional religion. Fearlessness came in the form of self-gratification, caring for others, and cynicism about any official explanation.

In April 1975, the lost war did not stop President Gerald Ford (no doubt with the prodding of Henry Kissinger, whom he inherited after Nixon resigned) from ordering the American springtime bombing of Cambodia after the war, just as President Truman had done in 1949 to China. The United States was sending a message that they could be back on Mainland China if they chose to do so. The purpose of this strategy was to instill fear among the victors.

Like the Second World War, the Indochina War had complex effects on American society. The armed forces were demoralized—American military leadership was no match for Vietnam's General Giap and his military planners—and the war served as a rallying point for the American citizenry in ways that shook the United States, not dissimilar to what had happened in the North during our Civil War. But the most crucial point was the conclusion that the war itself made no sense. The ideological claims that the United States had to stop the domino effect in Indochina because of the communist menace had little if any validity because the leaders of the communist nations had little in common with one another. They had different national purposes, cultures, and long-standing rivalries among themselves.

One might have thought that the large number of American and Indochinese dead and wounded and the destruction of the land would have acted as an inhibitor of American purpose. But even during the worst of the war, it was business as usual for President Nixon and Secretary of State Henry Kissinger. They acted as supporters and allies of coups in Chile, Angola, and wherever it appeared that the United States might be ideologically threatened, and where the Four Freedoms might take root in their Rooseveltian meaning and give third world nations their independence from imperial control.

Through most of the cold war, the American government's security intention was to reenforce the political claims of white South Africa and support militarily those governments that were economic and military clients of the United States. Nixon threatened the total destruction of North Vietnam and Kissinger passed this on to the North Vietnamese, who advised Nixon that they were unconcerned and told him to go ahead with the devastating Christmas bombings. Presidents see such actions as reflecting the American will when, of course, they are showing their own will, which means sacrificing the lives of others, as would be the case with Bush II, Cheney, and Rumsfeld thirty years later.

American policy makers claimed that the communists, or the insurgents, or the nationalists, or whoever was outside the Free World orbit of the United States, were making trouble. As Secretary Rusk put it, "While we are sleeping, two thirds of the world is plotting to do us in."[44] The American military was the instrument to ensure stability by hunting down and catching the "others" before they harmed us. The result was often the reverse as insurgents saw the United States as the enemy to be confronted, which then required, or so it was thought, a greater U.S. military response. This response could be aimed at those like Marcos in the Philippines or Noriega in Panama who forgot that the United States was paying for them to act as leaders. And when they forgot, they were overthrown. In Noriega's case, it was through direct intervention and then a war in Panama, just as President Reagan encouraged a limited military and CIA intervention in Nicaragua and Grenada. Reagan also called on the policy of nuclear preemption against the Soviets and insisted on sending long-range missiles to West Germany, which resulted in the protests of millions of people in the United States and elsewhere.

It is fair to say, however, that while Reagan greatly increased the defense budget when he became president, he also sought a radical nuclear disarmament program, abolishing nuclear weapons with the Soviet Union as the means of lifting the sword of Damocles over humanity and nature. But advisers to both Gorbachev and Reagan stopped the possibility of such disarmament. Reagan's advisers insisted on keeping the antimissile system program, the price Gorbachev would charge for implementing comprehensive nuclear disarmament.[45]

THE MORE WE CHANGE PRESIDENTS, THE MORE OUR WAR OBJECTIVES STAY THE SAME

One of the ironies of power in this period is how presidents who have the least sensitivity for others favor disarmament, and radical disarmament if possible, but are pulled back from this instinct by advisors who are fearful of changing the status quo. And so freedom from fear remains an ideal.

Some thought Jimmy Carter, a Naval Academy graduate who was a nuclear submarine expert, was a pacifist because of his stand on human rights. The concept of human rights was pressed in the 1970s by liberal members of Congress[46] and was adopted by Carter as a means of staking out a claim that the United States could continue its foreign policies and interventions on moral principles. Indeed, he had asked the Joint Chiefs of Staff for a memorandum excluding nuclear weapons from the American arsenal, but they thought it impossible to do and in effect refused to present such a plan.

A first strike plan was prepared during the Kennedy administration for attacking the Soviet Union and was rejected. In fact, the language of victory in war seemed to change, and it was more than a linguistic shift. America was to "prevail" in nuclear war, although in 1961 plans were made by the Department of the Army to occupy the Soviet Union after such a war. (How U.S. forces could survive the lethal radioactivity was not clear.) By the beginning of the 1990s, General Lee Butler, the leader of the Strategic Air Command, upon his retirement called for abolition of nuclear weapons.[47] However, his views did not change American reliance on military force and nuclear weapons, as the world's defense ministries learned with the presidency of George W. Bush.

Bush II's father, George H. W. Bush, presented himself as an internationalist when in fact he was a prudent imperialist—not unlike many Democrats then and now.[48] This meant finding a way to use the UN and the alliance system to support the U.S. picture of the world. While there is evidence that the Bush family historically was involved in war profiteering, the issue remains whether Bush I had other purposes than war for its own sake. Here, the answer is yes. No doubt Prime Minister Thatcher, acting as Bush I's tutor ("Remember, George," she famously lectured him, "this is no time to go wobbly."),[49] insisted on a belligerent stance toward Iraq, for Great Britain feared the power of a recovering Iraq in terms of oil prices. Similarly, the Israelis complained about Saddam because of his belligerent anti-Zionist pronouncements. Other Arab nations feared Saddam Hussein's bold moves. Part of that fear was generated by then Secretary of Defense Cheney, who apparently misrepresented CIA documents, saying to King Fahd of Saudi Arabia that the Iraqis were about to invade his country.[50] Fahd then agreed to base U.S. troops in Saudi Arabia, which gave Osama and the Wahabbists an argument that the "infidels" were defiling holy territory.[51] This decision would come back to haunt the Saudis and Cheney when he became vice president. (Of course, that is hindsight—unless it can be proved that American leaders do not read even the history of their own country.)

For the prudent imperialists in Bush I's administration, there was the need to protect the Middle Eastern oil supply, teach leaders of client states that they were limited by American interests, test out the Powell strategy of destroying the Iraqi army in war, and give meaning to the Bush presidency at a time when the United States sought a world purpose unhindered by the imploding Soviet Union.

In the first Persian Gulf War, Bush I stopped American troops from entering and fighting Baghdad with the result that "only" one hundred thousand Iraqis died in the war. (U.S. casualties: 148 battle deaths, 145 nonbattle deaths, 467 wounded in action,[52] but thousands suffered debilitating ailments.) The United States concluded that it was more important as a matter of strategy to keep Iraq unified than face a situation in which the Kurds sought a separate state, one that happened to have a great deal of oil in its territory. The result was that the United States stood aside as Saddam's forces caused the exodus of tens of thousands of Kurds to Turkey, which was leery of having them. Saddam, who is a Sunni, arranged for the killing of some thirty thousand Shiites. The Kurds themselves were split among different factions and became pawns in international politics, as Kissinger demonstrated when he led the Kurds to believe that they had the support of the United States and Iran in their struggle against Iraq for independence. (Kissinger and the Iranians soon ended this fantasy.)

After the war, Bush I was hailed as a great wartime leader. He had impressive favorable poll ratings around 90 percent. Americans felt safe. Gasoline prices did not climb inordinately. Finally, commentators were saying that the United States had restored its prestige and wiped out the "Vietnam syndrome." Which meant that the United States was no longer consigned to a noninterventionist status.

Poll numbers like Bush I's are found in authoritarian nations for maximum leaders. But the bloom soon faded. For a short time, his victories in Panama and Iraq created a politically invincible shield around him. His concern in Panama was finding a government that the United States could control once the Americans gave up ownership of the Panama Canal. After unrelenting harassment by the Bush administration, Noriega gave them a gift by declaring war on his former protector. Using war planes and troops to destroy civilian areas, especially in poor sections of Panama City where indigenous peoples lived, it was calculated that U.S. forces killed and wounded between two thousand and three thousand Panamanians, while suffering twenty-six losses.[53] The United States arrested Noriega and installed a new president, who took his oath of office at an American Naval base.

This new "legitimacy" that Bush I imposed at the point of a bayonet was enough for those who doubted the purpose of the American intervention. The administration found that if it could present Noriega as a Hitler-type, and a drug dealer to boot, American liberals would not raise the fundamental question of American imperialism.

THE COST OF FALSE SECURITY

The pattern of American intervention in the third world, which was first organized by the United States in the nineteenth century, continued with barely a complaint—except for a little pesky opposition from the Left. As long as the United States did well at the imperial game, what was the harm? It assured markets and cheap labor, and it kept American military leaders performing tasks that showed their value, especially to the business classes.

During the cold war, the military-business relationship became so close that in his last days as president, Eisenhower famously warned of the dangers of the American military-industrial complex. It has not been a concern of many other retired military and Defense Department officials who take advantage of contracts, stock options, and high-salaried employment with defense contractors. This connection ensured (with congressional support) automatically high and continuous defense and national security budgets and supplemental budgets, which by 2004 were more than half a trillion dollars a year—nearly half of what the rest of the world spent on its military.[54] (The cost of U.S. military presence in Iraq and Afghanistan alone, if the United States remains in the region until 2010, is projected at more than $1.3 trillion—or $11,300 per U.S. household.)[55]

The United States spends over half of its budget on building up the National Security State and, in that process, building up a national militarized and police-type state apparatus that Americans now take for granted, though it did not exist prior to the Second World War.

The excessive cost of defense is a fundamental error, whether viewed as the product of fear (of the Russians, the Chinese, the terrorists, or our own citizens), or triumphalism, or military-industrial waste and fraud, or ignorance of what a realistic defense means. It has spawned four more errors, each one fateful in its own way.

1. It goes without saying that the United States needs a common defense as part of an international legal system that defends rather than threatens. Instead, it developed a military imperialist model of defense.

2. We now know as of September 11, 2001, that this crushing defense expense did not defend anything. On the contrary, it hardened our thought processes and assumed that all human needs, actions, and feelings can be reduced to self-deception or subsumed under the banner of imperial wars abroad or sophisticated military technology.

3. As a result of having the biggest arsenal of weapons in history, we as a nation are taxed to give us a false sense of security and a false sense that our wealth and good intentions give us special global responsibilities irrespective of the wishes of others.

4. The government decided that taxpayers should have a panoply of violence, from spies to acceptance of torture as an instrument of state

terror to the capacity to fight thermonuclear war at the strategic level. So we deceived ourselves that we were secure without understanding that, in fact, each one of these war doctrines in theory or practice represented a terrible error in terms of American thinking. Why? If state-of-the-art weapons were used, they would necessarily have to be used to kill and injure great numbers of innocent populations, especially if nuclear weapons and weapons of mass destruction are used

No one should underestimate what amounts to another—though often subliminal—military imperative, namely, training under battlefield conditions: soldiers must learn to use and be part of the newest hi-tech military apparatus; the sophisticated weapons and communications systems that are coordinated among the armed services need testing in small wars on a continuous basis. Military forces require training and money. Often that money is a military Keynesian employment project that has no redeeming value unless it is used. Otherwise, arming counts as conspicuous military consumption and waste but is presented as a positive good. There is no better example than the Star Wars missile shield program, which would seem like an old B-movie complete with the leading actors if it were not an accurate portrayal of the present state of the National Security State.

Edward Teller, cofather of the hydrogen bomb with mathematician Stan Ulam, put the missile shield bug in the ear of President Ronald Reagan. Teller had pushed for an antimissile weapons system since the 1960s, beginning with his notion of an X-ray laser beam powered by a hydrogen bomb that he claimed would wipe out swarms of incoming Soviet missiles. It never got out of his laboratory, but it did inspire the "modern" missile shield that came to be called Star Wars. The mad scientist in Stanley Kubrick's 1964 movie *Dr. Strangelove* supposedly was modeled after Teller and partly after Kissinger, Herman Kahn, and Thomas Schelling, who would win the 2005 Nobel Prize for Economics. (The movie's complete title was prescient: *Dr. Strangelove or: How I Learned to Stop Worrying and Love the Bomb*) The connection gets more bizarre. In the 1940 movie *Murder in the Air*, Ronald Reagan played a government agent who protects a Hollywood fantasy-machine that can destroy incoming bombs before they hit the United States.

Reagan made a number of war movies during the Second World War. When he became a politician, he continued to play the role of combat veteran. Maybe he believed his own mythology because he was such easy prey for Teller.

Taxpayers have poured some one hundred billion dollars into Star Wars since 1983. Bush II, who attached himself to the project using the war on terrorism as a shield, proposed to spend $250 billion more on an antimissile plan over the next two decades. These numbing figures notwithstanding, the military *still* has not come up with a missile defense system that works regardless of the propaganda put out for congressional and public consumption. Every missile shield test, even though tightly scripted to be a public relations victory of military science over nature, has failed as of 2006.[56]

Many Pentagon projects such as Star Wars are ineffective and some are outright worthless, yet they are supported because war planners and politicians believe that by raising the cost of attacking the United States, no nation or group would try. This idea is based on sophisticated weaponry as the necessary component to defense and aggression. Military defenses are the search for invulnerability. Their intention is to make people feel *vulnerable*. The objective of an invulnerable strategy is "enough is never enough," and our propaganda is fashioned to make this strategic delusion into reality. The art of fear, practiced by many administrations since the formation of the nation, is an important tool in the hands of the authoritarian whose task is to assuage one's fears as he or she lines up mass support for further traumas similar to wars in Afghanistan and Iraq—or worse.

But to be equally clear, this self-deception is not without material benefits to a great many Americans. Communities fight to keep military bases open, even when the Department of Defense deems them unnecessary.[57] Scientists and engineers are kept employed. Defense and aerospace contractors are subsidized to forestall reconsideration of American social and economic purposes. And because there are no alternatives and very few serious planning attempts at conversion from military to civilian uses, areas throughout the nation fear closing military bases. The young, particularly in rural America, who volunteer to serve in the armed forces do so out of patriotism for sure but also out of necessity because so many of the communities they come from are struggling economically. Local businesses have been forced to close, so there is often no other choice for work but to serve in the armed forces and "see the world." How many come back with life and limb physically intact—and to what kind of life—is another question. What does it mean, after all, to serve your country?

REPRISE: WHAT DID WE GET FROM OUR WAR POLICIES?

The Vietnam War experience seemed to sap the will of the American people for war and war imperialism. Its leaders had counted on sophisticated technology to hold down the number of casualties but to no avail. The war itself brought trauma to the over 2.5 million soldiers who served in a land not their own and for a purpose that was reduced to saving yourself and your buddies.[58] In the process, the United States destroyed the land (an action that came to be known as ecocide), killed millions, and turned millions into refugees. Parts of the war were televised (the "living room war," it came to be called), and the millions who took their cues from the civil rights movement were not about to support an imperialist war abroad even though the civil rights movement was split on the war because of their loyalty to President Johnson and their hopes that the war would either be won or a settlement negotiated. Roy Wilkins of the NAACP accepted the idea that the United States was a warrior state and the most that could be done was hope that it would fight idealistic battles as it had done in the Civil War and the Second World War. But the Vietnam War was only a distant cousin to these other wars.

So after the United States dropped more bombs on Vietnam than it dropped in Europe during the Second World War; after facing a demoralized, critical, rebellious armed force that had lost their will to fight; after the Pentagon sent word to Congress that it should not waste more money on the war or the South Vietnamese, the United States left Vietnam and the rest of Indochina.

What is extraordinary about the U.S. defeat is that from an economic and political position in Asia the United States *gained*. In fact, it resolved its differences with the communist Vietnamese, who welcomed multinational corporations and banks into Ho Chi Minh City (formerly Saigon) and Hanoi. There are no permanent friends and enemies in international politics, only interests, as George Washington noted.

Nevertheless, the war frightened American leaders into taking stock of what they could do militarily, even in the third world. But this brief respite from war making and sublimated war activity did not last long.[59] The CIA carried on operations in Africa and Latin America. In the United States, the "chicken hawks" (as their opponents in the military called them) in the Bush II administration, few of whom had served a day in the military and had no desire to do so, called for getting over the Vietnam syndrome in favor of a "muscular foreign and national security policy." (Here, there was a grudging respect for Israel, which is self-consciously a warrior state, expanding its boundaries, building nuclear weapons, and constantly increasing its defense budget with assurances that the United States will remain its steadfast ally and bankroll whatever the charges are.)

Contrary to popular belief, American imperial policy did not end with the Indochina policy or begin only under Bush II. Ford bombed Cambodia although the CIA was brought under control. During Carter's watch, the CIA encouraged the development of Muslim fundamentalists in Afghanistan as the means of stopping the Soviet intervention. That would result in a "blowback" effect when the same CIA-supported fundamentalist groups came back to attack the United States.

Reagan fought a covert war in Latin America, barely managed to sidestep the Iran-Contra scandal in Nicaragua, and was fortunate to see the collapse of the Soviet empire, which he wrongly claimed (and which has been claimed for him by conservatives ever since) was as a result of a buildup of nuclear missiles in Europe and a greatly increased defense budget. It is true that the Soviets could not afford the arms, a point made in the Kennedy administration. Its demise came because the depressed everyday life in the Soviet Union could no longer be masked or sugar-coated. The disparity between what was advertised and what existed in goods and services was too great.

Bush I settled scores with Panama while leading a coalition of forces against Iraq as it sought to punish Kuwait for demanding repayment of loans. Although Saddam Hussein had been an ally of the United States, the Bush I administration held that his invasion of Kuwait was an attempt to restore Kuwait to its former position as a province of Iraq and therefore was a breach of boundaries and a violation of international law. Clinton held himself to bombing Iraq and the Balkans and interventions in Latin America (notably Haiti, to correct a prior intervention and covert operation of a previous administration). He ordered continuous bombing of Serbia without a declaration of war, which again subverted the Constitution. In all cases, the United States did not give up its first-use policy regarding nuclear weapons.

Nevertheless, the differences between the post-Indochina war presidents, the "prudent imperialists," and Bush II were substantial in terms of style and of the assumptions that gripped the policy elites.[60] For Bush, it was "our way or the highway."

There is an irony here, perhaps the irony of imperial engagement. The more the United States spreads its military around the world, the more it involves itself in elective wars, the more isolated the United States becomes in the world, the more it exposes American society and its military to danger and demoralization, the more it creates fear.

While stupidity, arrogance, rigidity, and policy deafness are part of politics and the presidency, amazingly, it was only in Bush II's presidency that all of these features came together to make the perfect storm in which tens of thousands needlessly suffer and die or live lives of fear and pain. Bush II turned freedom from fear into a mockery, and the hopes of so many were turned into ashes, their own and others.

As the U.S. government continues its project of worldwide "freedom" for its own self-protection, it will have to narrow dissent and decrease effective freedom within the United States. This will all be done in the name of protecting and extending freedom to Americans and supplying security, which increasingly will be understood as a commodity that can be sold. The commodity is national security This situational fear would no longer be reserved for blacks and Latinos, Native Americans and Muslims, and middle- and upper-class white men and women.

This does not have to be the human condition in the twenty-first century. Democracy allows for dialogue, consensus, and the employment of wisdom and scientific knowledge to locate that humane spirit in reality that engages people, helping them to see others beyond the social role.

Whether it is a person manning a nuclear weapon, a worker in a factory who must act to stop toxic chemicals from destroying the water table, or someone creating and defending social spaces, fear is now another obstacle to overcome. These fears are made mostly by men, and overcoming them requires ingenuity and empathy toward humankind. For such ideas and ideals to work, the project of humankind must be more than the individual; it must be collective and social, seeing in each of us our needs and fears. It is a sentiment found among us that can redirect the powerful and the state from destroying what cries out to flourish. As has been noted here, for Americans this requires a different public philosophy and practice.

It will not be easy. In their heads, even Americans with good jobs are tuning out, abandoning the public space, and just trying to get on with their own lives.

Chapter 20

Can You Sign a Separate Peace?

WILL YOU BE ALLOWED TO TRY?

According to numerous polls,[1] Americans have serious doubts about, if not contempt for, leaders who do not know how to govern, leaders they no longer trust, arrogant leaders who keep their dangerous policies and actions from the public that pays their salaries, leaders who lie about those policies, leaders who ignore the health and welfare of the wretched even in their own country, leaders who encourage rather than rein in greedy corporations (beginning with the profiteers of war and natural disaster). These leaders are often active participants in organized religious bigotry; of course, they can't see the degradation of the environment for the trees. These days, one can describe the leader in America with any of these deformed attributes. Or all of them.

In the meantime, citizens still play the American dream game, but in their hearts they know the game is rigged. Even those doing well enough just want to get through it in one piece. "Sleep till noon and screw 'em all [society]," author Max Shulman observed in 1950, a time when citizens were labeled "the Silent Generation," which easily could be the mantra of some of the exhausted in this generation. That is fine, but people should understand that just trying to negotiate a separate peace is more complicated than they thought, and there are a great many contradictions along the way.

We first have to keep in mind that if there is a natural, organic way that people can live in the world, then we have to define what it so we can move toward it with others. People may drop out, or think about doing so, but they also believe strongly that there is within us a nonhierarchical and associative capacity to live in the world. And it is democracy, properly construed and practiced, that allows that human tendency to emerge. That is a signal purpose of democracy.

Democracy is not meant to be an instrument of repression.[2] It gets complicated because on top of that natural way, a variety of social structures have been built up during this period of the National Security State that would have to be moved aside to get us out of the box we have allowed the leaders of the most powerful country in the world to put us in.

This disconnect between our political institutions, our governmental agencies, and what is obviously necessary to function acceptably is not a condition handed to us just by the Bush II administration; the institutions established through the Constitution were predicated on a dialectic between conflict and cooperation, with cooperation coming in second. The historical result has been that people come to believe that the way in which institutions function is the only way they can function.

But there is another trope. The major democratic movements of our time have been attempts at changing social institutions so that they will be more in line with the human capacity for empathy and cooperation. The jury is still out on whether technology is able to help these human capacities. Certainly, there is nothing to suggest that it can, judging from the development and use of military technology, no matter how surgically precise we are told we can be when using it. Science and technology, even with the best of human intentions, can end with dreadful, unforeseen consequences. But how horrifying is it for humanity when the consequences are intended to be terrible for particular groups and nations?

Of course, there has always been surgically precise bombing corresponding to the technology at the time (for example, dumping scalding oil on the barbarians at the gates), but now this idea is positively Orwellian. This kind of language has become a sop to the masses for leaders who feel that without such language people's critical sense would overtake the top-down political process and the people would see through it and act against leaders who are trying to sell them on the idea that war is always just.

We now have in America an "official" state propaganda system that uses this language as a softening and obfuscating language that allows policy makers and bureaucrats to avoid facing up to to what they are doing. Take the phrase "collateral damage," the term for innocent civilians killed by those "surgically precise" air strikes from planes attacking in safety from thirty-five thousand feet. Of course, this kind of language helps bureaucrats and defense officials mask from themselves what they are doing. Such language results in a moral hardening of a nation, certainly its elites.

This moral hardening is reflected in the new American dropouts—whether they live deep in the heart of big cities or in the remote countryside—who watch the daily horrors played out on television like everyone else and are just as concerned as the families who have suffered the casualties of war but still think, "I've got my piece and my peace; besides, there's nothing I can do to fix the hopeless mess that this country has become." But that leads to the question of whether or not the individual can even sign a separate peace and whether or not people have signed a separate peace to take care of themselves by keeping quiet.

Indeed, keeping quiet plays into the hands of the political elites who do not count critical participation as an important feature of democracy. In fact, they see it as an impediment to what they think of as good government.[3] After all, our electoral system is predicated on *restricting* the right to vote, even though we tell ourselves otherwise. Perhaps more important for people is that their daily lives simply do not allow them to sign a separate peace as citizens.

So if you get sick, you are right back in the general system again in terms of being part of the medical system. If something goes wrong with your car or you can't pay your mortgage, you find out very quickly that you are still part of a system. If you find out that your child is not doing well at school because the education system where you live is failing and you have aspirations for your child, you find out very quickly that you are not alone. You are not able to sign a separate peace because the system will not allow you to keep to that separate peace since the system keeps changing the rules and it is difficult if not impossible to keep up.

This was the horror of authoritarian and totalitarian states we read about. The rules kept changing without public accountability and the person could never sign a separate peace. It was very difficult to be a collaborator because what you are supposed to believe and act on today is not what you are supposed to believe and act on tomorrow. Take the German Jews who fought for their Kaiser in the First World War. When Hitler came to power, at first they were exempt from being arrested and thrown into the concentration camps and believed themselves safe from prosecution. But by the mid-1930s, this exemption was worthless, and off went the Jewish war veterans in the same cattle cars with the less pure, all to terrible fates. (There's a lesson here for Americans who often say that they have nothing to fear from surveillance and wiretaps, as if they will be the ones who decide whether they have done something wrong.)

Some hold that we should simply let competing elites fight it out and the rest of us should be content with our own lives. But the sobering fact is that we simply can't sign a separate peace because we are caught willy-nilly in the battles of the time. So if, at a moment's notice, one human being, say, the president of the United States, decides that he or she speaks for the world (or is trying to outdo his father's legacy through conquest or his notion of liberation) and decides to launch a preemptive war, that single human being has preempted my private space and my social space. So I had better realize that I must work with others to help establish systems of politics in which such world sovereignty vested in one person is not possible. And if I am governed by men and women whose purpose is to remake my country and the world only as they see fit, then I had better figure out what is going on and reject my passive inclination to just go along.

IS CONTENTMENT THE ANTIDOTE TO ANXIETY?

Americans are nothing if not complicated since we are prepared to do two contradictory things: One, we're prepared to say that contentment is an aspiration that may not be necessary in our lives. Two, as a society we believe in struggle and competition in every aspect of our society and we don't mind it. On the contrary, we think competition is something that breeds excellence. But at the same time, we have doubts about that competition because we know that our country's great technological achievements have come much more from cooperation and teamwork than from competition. So we are confused as to whether competition breeds excellence or just more anxiety, especially given what comes out of the progress that we've achieved. We believe in love, but we are unclear about how to express it in our institutional structures or in in our politics, which, we always say, have more base purposes expressed through conflict and animosity.

Some social commentators will say that cooperation is all well and good, but there will always be people ferociously competing for power, money, and status. And if that is what they want, then they are probably giving up contentment. Perhaps they are forgoing love as well, because it is hard not to under those conditions. And the system will favor them whether in business, education, or defense.

However, other commentators will say that maybe competing is their idea of contentment and pleasure. It may work for a while, but even in the context of contentment, they may have doubts about society as a whole and where they fit into it. They may feel guilty for being contented, or for having withdrawn, or for living the private lives that they have arranged only for themselves.

Clearly, for the upper-middle class there is an attempt to find such personal contentment outside of the narrowly political. Acquisition of things is the organizing principle, and many modern conveniences are organized to this end. Soon, a person may never have to touch money—either to receive or spend it. The world will be checkless and cashless. Does this create happiness and contentment? Does the attitude that our "big technological daddy" will take care of it create contentment? Not likely. Just as it is unlikely that having access to hundreds of television channels creates contentment. Just as it is unlikely that the sweatshop worker making sneakers in Thailand can stay contented for long, however lucky she or he feels to have a job.

The best measure of our discontent is in what we waste. We are like children always in need of a new thing. We focus on it for a moment, then throw it away, then look for a new gratification. Here, freedom is turned into gluttony, which becomes insatiable. But the gluttonous are hardly free of fear. In fact, they become less free even as this insatiability is trumpeted by the government as the means to an increase in gross national product. In other words, our measures, at least for some, fly in the face of contentment and happiness. We are in danger of fulfilling the prophecy of the bumper-sticker wisecrack: "He Who Dies with the Most Toys Wins!" And so it is not surprising that the young in universities wonder how they can escape the choices that lead to lack of freedom and to passivity.

TURNING YOUR BACK ON THE WORLD IS NOT SO EASY

Questions of anxiety, which might occur naturally, have been blown apart by living in the continually expanding National Security State. Does this sense of anxiety for an increasingly conscious middle class breed cynicism? Does it breed new knowledge about what, in fact, is going on? Does that allow for action, or does that allow for a people indeed saying: "The hell with this, we're signing a separate peace, we're out of this"?

What is so interesting about this formulation is that it turns out that one must have meaningful, dignified, nonexploitive work, get a few more dollars in one's pocket, have one's vote count, gain access to like-minded people through the Internet, which builds new communities of relationships, and be free of oppression. Therefore, very big changes are required in order to have these conditions predominate. And they should occur, but what is interesting is that while these goals and aspirations are recognized as achievable, they require the most profound political action and political activities. So the kind of peace and quiet people think they have found in the "beautiful places" they live in or crave is not so peaceful and quiet after all; they must work for them with others.[4]

There are times in history when some people, reluctant to risk becoming engaged in the social and economic world as it exists, have turned their back on it. People set up monasteries in an attempt to start all over again. There were obviously indications of that at the time after Christ and in the decaying periods of the Roman Empire. In the 1960s, the dropout movement and the development of separate communities, communes, and the hippy movement were also an attempt to say, "Look, we can start all over again." But, in the end, you really can't start all over again unless it's within the system. The reason is both simple and complex: all people bring with them all the baggage of the society in which they live; it is internalized in the person. There is just no way to escape that. It is the dead hand of the past on your shoulder that Marx talks about. Even more perplexing, we now have a series of more and more ill-defined public objectives, and they are evaporating or disappearing to the point that there seems to be no real means to get to those objectives or to gain meaning from them.

Our personal objectives may indeed be achievable, but they are very limited; you can try for the brass ring of money, or try for power, or whatever, but that merely goes to reinforce the system as it is and puts others at risk as a result of your success. One of the things that we always love about America is that there are supposedly social spaces to do things. The theory of the open society, in part, is that groups of people are able to get together to push their point of view or innovation in some sort of pastiche of pluralism that allows for both letting off steam and obtaining a certain amount of happiness and contentment. What is involved in the democratic idea is a sense that if different groups are heard from, we can work out a system of accommodation between the groups that allows for the defining and resolution of a problem, indeed, a way to transcend that problem.[5] And it involves not only transcending of the problem but also laying the basis of a common morality in the society from which a new value system develops, then intersects with the formation of the common good that takes account of individual happiness. This value system builds on people's moral impulses, which are then reinforced through shared social ethics.

A way to understand this is through the term "empathic invariance," which means "putting yourself in the other person's shoes" because you have the innate capacity to do so. Empathic invariance is a natural, dominant feature we are born with but that ends up being degraded and destroyed by social systems predicated only on conflict and domination. Empathic invariance is not imprinted within us in the way that language is; it is a moral impulse that requires nurturing. Our language, as we use it, can either strengthen or weaken this moral impulse. When we say we are going to "take out" a neighborhood in Iraq by block-busting bombs, we are masking from ourselves what we are really doing: destroying a piece of this moral capacity. Perhaps this is what is meant by the phrase "hardening our hearts." (It is puzzling why the Right has so much trouble with empathy.)

Empathic invariance can be fostered within the family or a house of worship, but it is through real democracy that it has the best chance of developing and reconstructing our society in a rational way. So empathic invariance is not meant to overthrow anything; it is a means to help us to escape the lies, myths, and forced choices of institutions that diminish us as humane beings. It begins with seeing ourselves beyond the alienating social roles that not only make us unnecessarily fearful of ourselves and others but also deny critical thought and empathy for others.

When we talk of the need for reconstructing our society, it includes a moral dimension that can only be comprehended through persistent dialogue and cross-examination of our values and methods lest we end up the way the eminent sociologist Pitirim Sorokin did. Sorokin headed the Center for the Study of Altruism at Harvard in the 1940s. Then, during the cold war, Harvard closed the center in favor of an institute that assumed conflict rather than cooperation as its leading idea. Society today should be fearful that the same result will occur as university science and social science departments seek government funding from the Department of Defense and the Department of Homeland Security. Peace studies and conflict resolution studies will be further marginalized in favor of fear in the form of security studies.

YOU AND THE NEXT WAVE OF DEMOCRATIC RECONSTRUCTION

With an emphasis on security and its technological, military, and command aspects, democracy is transformed into a Spartan state. And when it is linked to the idea that it is serving democracy—and does so through permanent war—it becomes obvious, as Noam Chomsky has noted, that this is the description of a *failed imperial state*.

Since Bush II, a failing state has several unmistakable features: (1) debilitating wars, (2) self-deception of the people, which is reinforced through ritual and propaganda but has less and less to do with people's everyday reality, (3) claims of democracy as information are forged for the public or covered by secrecy laws, (4) the hollowing out of the productive capability of the nation, which makes American society increasingly dependent on other nations, (5) reclassifying documents, categorizing citizens as enemies and using technology as the instrument (for example, through biometrics and the identification and control of individuals), (6) production of fear as security, (7) starving the public social sector in favor of a state given over to kleptocracy and endless war. Thus ideas of peaceful negotiation are lost and popular movements that were successful in bringing back greater individual freedom find themselves under attack as the authoritarian-minded trumpet the importance of maintaining stability and tradition.

Many democratic ideals put into practice as a result of the changing value system that emerged from the 1960s and 1970s in the United States are burlesqued as political correctness—when they are not scoffed at as old hat. Nevertheless, they laid the groundwork for social equality and fairness. They also defined freedom as something more than a slogan. The United States, as a result of these popular domestic movements, is a far different and better place than it was before the movements of liberation in civil rights, women's rights, environmental rights, and gay rights. These movements opened and extended definitions of freedom. They touched the empathetic sense of caring, and they saw justice as linked to fairness, even truth. Scientific progress, for example, in the case of DNA used for the establishment of innocence in criminal cases, gives real meaning to the idea that a defendant is innocent until proved guilty. The process of proof becomes more rigorous—and less political. And yet the struggle in the criminal law is also the story of control over minorities and the dispossessed. Again, one need look no further than who occupies our prisons and jails or the social, educational, and economic inequities in the society as a whole (and in the world) to comprehend how far society is from what it needs to become.

When we look at what needs to be done but is left undone—deliberately or through bungling—it is understandable that we feel a wave a futility coming over us, if not swamping us. Yet, there is the other side. Not many will believe that the era of public lynching, or fractured people living in psychological and social closets, or imperial wars, defined either freedom or security. And not many believe that those who lived with blinders about the suffering of others reflected the American promise.

The struggles that continue in American life, including church and educational institutions, center around what the shape of reconstruction is to be. Whatever its contours, it will not be utopia, nor is it likely that the "traditionalists" will be able to move the clock back to a preindustrial age—except through nuclear war.

Here is the question a society seeking new freedoms while protecting old freedoms needs to ask: what will the individual face politically and socially in a National Security State that is set up to limit the actual participation of the citizens and too often their elected representatives as well? For example, the state is structured to ensure that the education system does not get to reinforce democratic values. (This is the negative side of education.) But universities and schools are also optimistic places where critical and reconstructive thought should not be totally dismissed. They can be the instruments for framing, securing, and perpetuating a social ethics that reflects progressive change. Educators, students, benefactors, and taxpayers need to recognize that education is not divorced from politics and that one of the things that is most complex about American politics is the way that it is set up in terms of groups and issues. One way to think about it is that people get caught up in a particular issue and they work hard on that particular issue. And often they are able to succeed in effecting change. Take a very small example on the most basic level: persuading local officials to install a traffic light at a dangerous intersection takes a lot of time and energy, even when dealing with friendly officials.

The next question becomes: As a matter of organization, how do we go from getting the traffic light—or organizing the election of one person—to a more general understanding of what is going on in the world? How do we not only understand it but also translate it into a more comprehensive set of activities that people naturally come to, then accept, then work toward?

Besides secular changes through a social ethic, the values of the religious Left and liberation theologians can be an effective searchlight. When the religious modernists began talk about a general direction to be taken for liberation and emancipation, it had an effect. They claimed that religion and belief in God demanded creative freedom and social responsibility. This direction is tried in every nonfundamentalist doctrine. Many of the progressive changes of the twentieth century were linked to theologians and Protestant leaders who claimed that reform was necessary, including the regulation of capital.

Churches have been natural organizing places throughout American history because they carried three cultures: the culture and stories of the past, which you either are for or want to liberate yourself from; a vision of what must be done in the present; and a plan for where you need to go and how to get there. For some, the church is even the place that invites one to everlasting life through good works and monetary success, although this must be discounted as an exercise in false advertising.

There is no road map alone that will get you where you need to go, nor is there a road map in the usual sense where you can delineate paths and see possibilities. You have to be able to take the chance that things will backfire on you. That means that you also must be committed to a kind of risk in the most profound way. You may be wrong about the choices you make, but you also know that you may be right with regard to the stand you take, who you stand up to, and who you stand up with in your attempt to set up the frame of reference for an emancipation or reconstruction. To paraphrase Dewey's point, we must be in the right frame of reference, then mistakes—and many of them—can be tolerated. Indeed, mistakes may be necessary.

Obviously, taking a risk is an existential choice of consequence. For most people, it is a melding of political stance and economic status, which means they might take a risk as long as they don't lose their job (even though they may be trapped in a job in the "free" economy that dictates their fate on a daily basis). People are understandably concerned about stability for themselves and their families. Most fear they could lose not only their jobs but also their benefits and pensions (if they still have benefits and pensions) and possibly risk not finding a comparable job—or any job—thereby losing their human worth. They may be inclined to accept these dislocations calmly. But that doesn't necessarily mean that people who attempt to protect their financial or economic interests are reactionary. Remember, "self-interest" and "selfish interest" are not the same.

Here, again, each situation has to be weighed on its merits. One would think that the massive losses of pension and 401(k) money people have experienced in recent years because of corporate greed and ineptitude would spur them on to take risks they would not otherwise have attempted. But under duress, risk produces surprising effects in people. During the Weimar Republic in Germany (1919–1933), the middle classes feared inflation and loss of class position, and workers feared unemployment.[6] The middle classes were very frightened, as they used to say, of losing their inherited silver tea services and lace napkins. Once it looked as though they would have to pawn them for food, they turned to the extreme Right and to Nazism, surrendering their social public space to Hitler in the process even though, in fact, Hitler found himself running poorly in some national elections. What Americans have learned, or should have learned, from the Weimar-Nazi era is that no part of the public can ever surrender the social public space and certainly not the progressive elements that hold to principles of emancipation, freedom, and human rights. The freedom to say and act on "no" and "yes" continuously is a constituent element of a modern democracy—as long as it functions well enough to allow it.

But people cannot depend upon there always being a social public space available if and when they want to seek it out. The point is that they have to have the psychological attitude to be prepared to develop that space. The meaning of psychological attitude in this context is the development of an idea and the sense of legitimacy for the idea. Inherent in a social idea is the ability to present that idea to or with others, whether or not it can be presented to authority.

Even if you are not developing the idea but are just receptive to it, any project is then linked to a chain of creativity: I start something, you talk to me, I make a change for that, and we move forward in that way so that the project itself becomes a means of collegial linking. And that then opens up more and more space. The projects and our links to one another are catalytic.

Now, at a certain level, authorities will attempt to shut down those spaces. Bush II's Patriot Act is really a series of attempts to shut down those spaces. And there will also be attempts to shut down various organizations outside the mainstream.

This means shutting down freedom of movement but mostly freedom of speech, which, of course, necessitates the right to think freely. This shuts down hope of freedom from fear, which in turn shuts down the capacity to build something real in the world, defend it, and then expand its projects. In turn, this creates fear or more fear.

More than ever before, we need a new kind of awareness, a new consciousness that accepts the idea that you are able to bring about change in the real world by undertaking actions that will lead to acceptable risk. Those actions can be writing, blogging, organizing, or whatever suits you or the group. But you need to understand that we must to defend our right to bring about democratic change in the real world because in times of repression the authorities will—perhaps relentlessly—seek to repress those projects, even books, Internet access, and other forms of expression, even art, all in the name of security.

IT'S YOUR FREEDOM—IF YOU CAN KEEP IT

The question now is: where are we going as a country and as citizens?

Unlike a democratic leader such as FDR was with all his flaws, in the neoconservative manifestation, the strong leader is found, not in democracies but in authoritarian and totalitarian regimes. Thus the strong leader must be unyielding, not subject to reality as shared by mere mortals. He—because it is almost always a he—must get others to believe that he has the only way for the nation to be preeminent and to fulfill its true destiny, which he embodies. He needs to argue to his supporters that war is a necessary concomitant of their power and the power of the nation he leads. He must claim that he speaks for the democratic will, and he must assert preeminence in this claim. He is like the wolf who claims legitimacy over others, getting people to believe that they are simply sheep who are told what to believe, how to act, and what is the truth. So if people opt to be sheep—and it is their option—they must understand that they are agreeing to follow the leader's recipe—and they must be prepared to have the leader devour their rights.

The flawed leader thrives on war and chaos and the suffering attendant to it. He turns other people's sacrifice into his view of patriotism, which he expects others to share and enforce. By seeking to occupy all the social and economic spaces and democratically unaccountable corporate institutions of the nation as his support, he favors the rich and the powerful in tax giveaways, justifying crony capitalism and kleptocracy. The leader claims the rule of law as a conservative mantra but, in fact, champions the thinking of Nazi philosophers that there are no norms in chaos.

It is the leader who decides the norms whether by whim or by fear. The political habit of mind is always present in politics whether in authoritarian regimes or emergency laws in our own nation. If they become dominant and institutionalized, democracy becomes a cliché. It means inhibiting critical thinking, closing down public spaces for dissent, and shutting down creative alternatives that are necessary for a democracy that is something other than a feel-good phrase. The new patriotism of the Bush II democracy is little more than the phrase "shut up and salute," little more than wearing an American flag on your lapel and slapping "Support the Troops" stickers on your SUV as if that relieved you of any guilt for allowing aggressive wars to be fought. We are *expected* to trust the leader and those laws that reinforce the power of the executive branch to make war. The nation is expected to proclaim a cultural war that must be won domestically against the weak, the defenseless, the artists, the intellectuals, the teachers, labor unions, and churches that hold to progressive doctrines.

As the government and its repressive institutions grow, the leader and his cohorts in the American context cynically claim that the government must be small. Instead, the leader expands government into every aspect of life (except the global corporations) as an instrument of repression. There is no trust for the rule of law or rationality, except insofar as they are defined by the leader and his group. They dare to claim that they speak for the faithful and for God even as they sell off the air and the water to their friends and supporters at bargain-basement prices.

It is incontestable that the "Leader Principle" has now found its way into American politics through the engine of the Republican Party, no matter how some Republicans try to distance themselves from their neoconservative colleagues. In its present manifestation, the "Leader Principle" destroys the possibilities of democracy. But the danger of the "Leader Principle" does not have to come with the Republican Party label. It could emanate from the Democratic Party, just as slavery once did.

Throughout the bloody history of states, leadership has meant unchecked hierarchy, command, and coercion. But America invented a different kind of democracy, a different kind of leadership as a challenge to itself and other nations. In a democracy, it is catalytic leadership that is most needed for the twenty-first century to wrest control from tyrants and mass manipulators and others who strive to pervert our good sense and conscience and shut us out of the public and political space. Such leadership can come from great teachers, books, and dialogue that help people regain their zest for life, leading to new thoughts, and creating projects that are intended to ennoble others as well.

Who are the teachers? Sometimes it is the victim or the sick and despondent who open a new path for others that deepens the humanity among people. Other times it may be the legislator or scientist who opens new vistas that expand humanity's moral purpose. Sometimes it is as a result of an epiphany which is then turned into a sustained moral, political, and intellectual purpose: the search for the underlying covenants that will help humanity and Americans overcome the downward spiral that has gripped much of the American leadership class.

The fundamental covenants—freedom, love, law, reason, responsibility, dignity, social and economic justice—that will define American society and its role rest on values that increasingly must be understood as linked conceptions. The authors have attempted to spell out these conceptions, for they can overcome the stupid (and ultimately futile) martial spirit that has distorted political philosophy and political practice since the Greeks, finally cresting ominously in our time. We have sought to connect the dots between the disparate, complex, often incongruous causes that have led to these failures. And we have offered solutions, some practical, others more complex. All come with a certain amount of risk, if they are to succeed.

But when all is said and done, you must confront yourself with a stark choice: it's your freedom—if you can keep it.

Afterword

Lifting the Siege
of the Four Freedoms

WHAT NEEDS TO BE UNDONE

As this paperback edition went to press, George W. Bush had compounded every problem we addressed in the hardcover edition of *The Four Freedoms Under Siege*. He has deeply wounded America's future, which will not be easily healed by Barack Obama despite his profound victory in the 2008 presidential elections. Together with the accumulating effects of permanent war and the fear and mistrust it causes—and the Bush administration's illegal, unethical, secretive, irresponsible, toxic policies—who has not felt the coarsening of American life?

Unsurprisingly, the United States finds itself squarely in the eye of a perfect storm of disasters brought on by an administration more corrupt than Harding's, and more uncaring of people's daily lives and tribulations than any other in American history. Though an Obama administration may prove to be enlightened and forward thinking, at this point our freedoms still remain under siege, harkening back to Franklin Delano Roosevelt who was faced with the task of reconfiguring capitalism in order to save it.

DISASTER: THE TRUE COSTS OF BUSH'S WARS

By November 2008, Bush's Iraq War and occupation was well into its fifth year. But the real shock and awe he once proudly hailed was that more than 4,100 U.S. troops had been killed, more than 30,000 wounded (according to the Pentagon's Operation Iraqi Freedom U.S. Casualty Status), and the minds of many broken, perhaps forever, by combat and post-traumatic stress disorder. More than 300 coalition forces had been killed. Some 32,000 troops with non-hostile injuries, diseases, and other medical problems required medical air transport, according to the Defense Manpower Data Center.

Reliable estimates of Iraqi civilian casualties as a result of American bombing and the consequences of U.S. strategy reached well over one million. Further, four and a half million Iraqi men, women, and children were displaced by the civil war between the Sunnis and Shias (and armed conflict within the groups) unleashed by an American aggressive war of choice.

Around the war's fourth year, American television executives began losing interest in waving the flag. While there were, of course, dutiful clips of the maiming and killing of U.S. troops and Iraqi civilians from roadside bombs and suicide bombers, it was more entertaining (and much less expensive) to air "reality" shows and the latest sagas of the Spears family and Paris Hilton. (Afghanistan, where "only" about 2,700 U.S. troops had been killed and wounded since that war's inception in 2001, was all but canceled from prime time when it became clear that Bush's boast to capture Osama bin Laden "dead or alive" was hollow.)

Yet, then Senator Obama and Senator John McCain, during the 2008 presidential race, scampered to the ledge of continuous war in Afghanistan, apparently believing that with enough troops and funding the United States could become the first world power since Genghis Khan's Mongol Empire to control Afghanistan against indigenous Afghanis. (They also agreed that U.S. armed forces should be expanded by 97,000 troops.) As of August 2008, roughly 60,000 foreign troops were operating in Afghanistan, including 33,000 Americans, and the new commander of the U.S. Central Command, Gen. David Petraeus, wanted more. Never mind that a large increase in U.S. troops had not stabilized the situation in the eastern part of the country, nor had the United States halted bumper crops of opium poppies or the profits that sustained Afghan farmers even as it provided funds for the Taliban.

Bush's secretary of defense, Robert M. Gates, made clear that the war on terrorism was unending and America's first priority. Shrugging off their war follies, Bush and his conservative national patriotic armchair warriors continued to use permanent war as the definition of the American state in practice. In moments of self-induced fear, the United States could threaten "adversaries" such as North Korea, Syria, and Iran to protect and extend the increasingly shaky global dominion of the United States. (The United States bombed what was believed to be a Syrian nuclear site in October 2008, even as the Syrian government handed over information about al-Qaeda to the U.S. government. In fact, a confidential 2004 Pentagon order approved by Bush allowed the United States to raid al-Qaeda cells in some twenty nations outside U.S. war zones.)

Putting out the story that it wanted to capture or kill al-Qaeda terrorists, the United States sought protective occupation over part of nuclear-armed Pakistan after September 11 as a way to control as much as it could of the rugged Pakistan-Afghan border. This strategy has been turning what was simply anger in Pakistan at the United States into hatred. Since August 2008, the United States has launched scores of missiles at targets in Pakistan. A few mid-level al-Qaeda operatives reportedly were killed; hundreds of innocent Pakistanis certainly were. (Apparently sovereignty is a concept for the powerful. Smaller states know that they are constantly vulnerable to the loss of their territory for any set of reasons the aggressive larger state may introduce.)

In January 2008, Bush and Iraqi Prime Minister Nouri al-Maliki signed a "status of forces" agreement intended to continue the United States' involvement in Iraq long after the expiration on December 31, 2008, of the UN Security Council Resolution that had been the core legal authority—and cover—for the war. The Bush administration claimed the agreement was similar to some eighty military relationships the United States had with other countries and thus did not require congressional approval. Opponents argued it would tie a future president's hands. Nevertheless, it is what McCain and other leading Republicans would have championed. Obama, faced with the claims of the Departments of Defense and State and the CIA, will probably not strenuously object because such an agreement is really a back-door way to ensure U.S. control over Iraq's oil (the world's third largest proven reserves), the cost of oil, and internal Iraqi relations with Iran, while protecting our contractors.

George W. Bush was often accused of fighting his wars on the cheap. Yet, by 2008 the Iraq War had cost U.S. taxpayers more than half a trillion dollars, although some economists believe the war's true cost will exceed \$3 trillion, making it the most costly war for the United States since World War II. These staggering figures do not include the expanding national security budget, which is running at over \$950 billion annually, or take into account the stubborn fact that Americans are paying interest on the Iraq War debt to those who "lent" monies to the United States.

Even though the poorer classes—lifeblood of our armies—indeed do come "cheap," they believed that by volunteering to fight in Iraq and Afghanistan—many serving two, three, or four tours—the government would provide them with reasonable veterans' benefits. However, the government cut their health care and counseling benefits, although for the first time in history it did provide them with daily doses of antidepressants to calm nerves strained by repeated and lengthy tours. Moreover, veterans' services were depleted by permanent war. In February 2007, the *Washington Post* reported that hundreds of seriously injured Iraq War veterans faced squalid living conditions and bureaucratic hell at Walter Reed Army Medical Center, the Army's top medical facility, five miles from the White House. A 2008 RAND Corporation study calculated that some 300,000 current and former service members were suffering from post-traumatic stress disorder and depression (one in five returning from Iraq and Afghanistan reported symptoms) and roughly 320,000 may have experienced possible traumatic brain injury while in the war zone. Numerous cases surfaced throughout the country of the Army and the Veterans Administration unable or unwilling to treat such injuries. In March 2008, the *New York Times* reported that veterans had to "battle the V.A. over treatment, tests, prescriptions, and plans for therapy and assistance at home."

As was the case with Vietnam War veterans, there has been an epidemic of suicides among Iraq War veterans. A few of the "luckier" veterans hired civilian lawyers to sue the army for promised disability benefits, because military lawyers had worked against them. (Contrast the government's veterans' policies with the recent combined pay of the CEOs of the top thirty-four defense contractors: $984 million. Source: Institute for Policy Studies/United for a Fair Economy report, "Executive Excess 2007.")

In 2007, Michael B. Mukasey replaced the hapless Alberto Gonzales as attorney general. Although Mukasey was presented in the media, Congress, and the White House as having a better legal mind than Gonzales, both shared a similar belief that waterboarding was not necessarily illegal and refused to rule out the use of that torture. (With this legal opinion, both men sought to immunize themselves and the CIA from possible future lawsuits. In any case, this interrogation technique used during the Spanish Inquisition may not gather any more useful intelligence for its CIA torturers than it did for torturers in the service of King Ferdinand and Queen Isabella in 1478, or for the Catholic Church that employed the method to root out Jews who were Conversos attempting to mask their Jewish heritage. Note: the United States first practiced waterboarding in the Philippines when it became an American territory at the beginning of the twentieth century.)

Continuing to invoke the fear of September 11 into his last year in office, Bush frightened the Democratically controlled Congress (including then Senator Obama) into granting the ultra-secretive National Security Agency (NSA) expanded license to spy on Americans without a court warrant. In 1975, the late Frank Church warned his fellow senators of the dangers of an unregulated NSA. Even Church could not have envisioned a political climate in which a president such as Bush would succeed in strong-arming Congress into giving telephone companies immunity to secretly intercept calls and e-mails of U.S. citizens for the NSA (See chapter 7, note 3). Both political parties tried to shield AT&T from civil suits on the grounds that it and other telephone companies were protecting the security of the country when, in fact, they had become an arm of the National Security State.

DISASTER: THE IRAQ WAR COMES TO THE U.S. ECONOMY

Imagine how much better off the state of the union would have been if the costs of Bush's wars and the national security paranoia he successfully perpetrated and perpetuated had been spent on improving the lives of Americans.

- Public schools continue to be shortchanged for educational and construction money as well as teacher training in districts throughout the country despite Bush's No Child Left Behind Act of 2001. Especially starved for funds were children from inner cities and rural communities. Yet according to the Bill and Melinda Gates Foundation, one third of *all* U.S. high school students drop out—one of the highest dropout rates of all industrialized nations—and another third who graduate are incapable of mastering some form of college-level work. (A pittance of the money spent each day on the Iraq War could have provided child development services to an additional 58,000 economically disadvantaged children in Head Start for one year.) Presidents and lawmakers would do well to remember FDR's dictum that "the school is the last expenditure upon which America should be willing to economize."

- The number of adults without medical insurance climbed to 47 million. According to a 2007 U.S. census report, this was an increase of more than 2 million from 2005. The number of uninsured children rose to 8.7 million. Those with medical insurance saw their premiums increase while their claims were being reduced and often denied. Bush twice vetoed a children's health bill that would have cost $12 billion over five years on the grounds that it was too expensive and would protect too large a category of children. Universal health coverage at a decent level for all citizens seemed an obtainable benefit for other industrialized nations, but not for the United States. The U.S. system had become wasteful and pathological, creating angry doctors, fearful patients, overworked medical personnel, and an estimated $350 billion spent annually on a medical bureaucracy that produces forms and mounds of red tape without visible value.

- The nation's infrastructure—highways, bridges, tunnels, dams, levees, drinking water, and sewer systems—had so

deteriorated that the American Society of Civil Engineers
reported that it will cost $1.6 trillion to repair. State and lo-
cal governments received a triple-whammy: less federal
funds and real estate tax revenue to make vital repairs
coupled with skyrocketing rebuilding costs. Little was done
to rebuild New Orleans after Bush's Katrina fiasco in 2005.
The city continues to suffer from gargantuan mistakes of
the Federal Emergency Management Agency (FEMA), dis-
ease-ridden trailers ordered by FEMA, white speculators,
and a broken school system. New Orleans has become the
poster child for racism and poverty. Indeed, remedying the
decay of U.S. cities virtually vanished from the agendas of
both political parties.

- The majority of scientists have believed for years that global
warming (or "climate change") was often caused by humans,
from the carbon emissions of global corporations (including
those in the United States) to the failure of governments (including ours) to institute and enforce rigorous pollution standards. Not until 2007 did Bush reluctantly admit that human
activity might contribute to the carbon emissions that trap
heat in the atmosphere that leads to global warming. As tem-
peratures kept rising, the north polar ice cap and mountain
glaciers melted abnormally, and the seas began rising almost
imperceptibly but enough to threaten to swamp whole countries such as the island republic of Maldives, Bush's solution
was to "talk" about long-term goals to reduce the problem.
Meanwhile, his Environmental Protection Agency (EPA), like
so much of Bush's big business-oriented government, did not
comply with the Supreme Court's surprising decision in 2007
that called for the EPA to begin regulating carbon emissions
from automobiles. Once again, action through government
failed in the face of natural disasters to which human beings
mightily contributed.

    Another deep, underlying problem: the U.S. military
acted as a vested interest by attempting to exclude itself from
any need to live within EPA standards with its waste, and
Bush found no reason to challenge them.

DISASTER: THE SPOILS OF WAR

Why should the last years of the Bush administration have surprised Wall
Street or Main Street? For much of 2008, the stock market practically

advertised it was due for a fall, yet the wild roller-coaster ride it began to go on September 15, 2008, scared even seasoned investors. The market routinely plunged seven, eight, nine hundred points one day, sometimes soared by as many points the next day, then plunged again—and again. Even those with little or no money in the market but burdened by heavy debt feared that the country was in a financial meltdown not seen since the Great Depression in the 1930s. (According to author Kevin Phillips, from 2001 to 2007, domestic financial debt nearly doubled to $14.5 trillion from $8.5 trillion.) Notwithstanding federal safeguards, retirees—from the 1950s Silent Generation, to the baby boomers of the 1960s, to the 51 million Gen Xers, whether uninformed or indifferent to American history—suddenly feared that the economy of the country (which many were surprised to discover was closely tied to the world's economy) and *their* family's hard-won nest egg and economic security may have been built on a house of cards. Would the government rescue them?

Frantic, the Bush administration and Congress chose instead to bail out major banks for an unprecedented $700 *trillion* (plus Congressional pork projects), in effect nationalizing the banks. No one knew if it would work.

To a large degree the turmoil was caused by the excessive demands of a war that never should have been fought (and the dread of war with Iran—possibly a nuclear war), combined with a culture of corporate greed and personal greed encouraged by Bush. In his defense, Bush opened widely the policy door espoused by President Bill Clinton. Both embraced much of Ronald Reagan's trickle-down economics, rejecting FDR's ideas of an Economic Bill of Rights for all Americans (See chapter 15).

If the United States was not officially in a recession by the autumn of 2008, as prominent economists believed, most Americans sensed that they were in one, such was the pervasive fear, anxiety, and crisis in every corner of the country:

- The housing bubble, which drove so much of the Bush economy, burst. New home sales decreased by 26 percent, the steepest decline since records began in 1963. More than 2 million homeowners lost their homes or faced foreclosure, many because they signed dubious adjustable rate mortgages from predatory lending companies and could not afford new higher payments. Growing numbers of homeowners with good credit fell behind on their mortgage payments. Many owed more on their homes than the homes were worth.

- The unregulated subprime mortgage market collapsed, panicking Wall Street, which then unnerved stock markets around the world, which further panicked Wall Street and Main Street. A severe liquidity crisis ensued. Bear Stearns, the country's fifth largest investment bank, failed. Lehman Brothers failed. Citigroup, Morgan Stanley, and Merrill Lynch lost an estimated $265 billion in subprime investments, some so complex as to be incomprehensible even to veteran analysts. (Merrill Lynch was forced to merge with Bank of America.) IndyMac, one of the nation's largest mortgage lenders, failed when its risky loans could not weather the housing downturn. It was the second biggest federally insured financial company in history to fail. Smaller banks across the country failed. (Bankers and politicians like to assure depositors that their money is protected by the Federal Deposit Insurance Corporation, but few mention—if they know—that the FDIC was created in 1933 by FDR's New Deal.) When the stocks of Fannie Mae (the Federal National Mortgage Association) and its sister enterprise Freddie Mac fell 77 percent, the government-backed, shareholder-owned giants that guarantee or own *$5 trillion* in U.S. home mortgages, the government (i.e., U.S. taxpayers) had to rescue them from insolvency to save the U.S. financial system. Fearing A.I.G., one of the world's largest insurers, would collapse, the government bailed *it* out for $150 billion. To stay afloat, a number of U.S. financial institutions sold off parts of their firms to foreign banks and such nations as Abu Dhabi, Kuwait, China, and South Korea.

- The U.S. auto industry, after years of unrealistic management, crashed. Would the U.S. government save the millions of workers, suppliers, and dealerships dependent on Detroit?

- To the dismay of the middle class, who twice were responsible for electing Bush, their median family income was lower than when he assumed office in 2001.

- More predictable was the continued hardship of the economically poorer class despite the much-ballyhooed increase in the minimum wage in 2007. Overcoming nearly a decade of Republican opposition, Democrats finally succeeded in raising the minimum wage to a measly $5.85 an hour, scheduled to reach $7.25 an hour by 2009. The latter figure adds up to a grand total of $13,195 a year, assuming a person could work thirty-five hours a week for fifty-two straight weeks. The government's stated poverty threshold for a family of four with two children under eighteen in 2007 was $20,614. Is it any wonder that 37 million Americans are classified as poor and 60 million others as near poor? Or that more Americans suffer from hunger today—over 38 million, including 14 million children—than they did in 1999? Or that a record number of Americans—a projected 28 million—received food stamps in 2008? (Lack of food and poor diet have obvious health risks. A further irony in our land of plenty: 127 million Americans of all economic classes are classified as overweight and 60 million more as obese. Among diseases caused by overeating and poor diet: coronary heart disease, high blood pressure, and type 2 diabetes.)

- Food prices kept rising, stimulated by a combination of personal market judgments that seemed rational on the surface yet have turned out to be disastrous. One main reason, as *Time* magazine pointed out on March 27, 2008, is the quintupling of U.S. production of corn not for human consumption, but to produce ethanol as a biofuel alternative to oil. Despite expert opinion that converting food crops into fuel is misguided—perhaps a scam—famous individual speculators and multinational corporations invested billions in biofuels. Not surprisingly, U.S. farmers sold one-fifth of their corn for ethanol production and many soybean farmers switched to corn. Between the land rush for farm-grown fuels, the increased cost of oil to run farms, and the Midwest floods in the spring of 2008 that damaged millions of acres of cropland, corn doubled in price, which raised the price of cattle feed, which in turn raised the price of meat as well as milk, eggs, and cheese. Paradoxically, massive clearing of tropical forests to plant biofuel crops creates much of the carbon emissions biofuels are supposed to reduce. (Forces unrelated to corn sent wheat and rice prices sky-high, provoking a food crisis for the poor in many countries and food riots. In April 2008, the World Bank said that rising food prices would likely push more than 100 million people worldwide into deep poverty.)

- The gyrating oil markets surged to a record high of more than $147 a barrel on July 11, 2008, only to drop later in the year to around $60 a barrel, a price barely conceivable by oil traders a generation earlier when oil was $12 a barrel. Even before that, the poor and the elderly, many scraping by on Social Security—and many in the working middle class—worried that hard times would force them to choose between paying the mortgage (or rent), food, prescription drugs, heating bills, or medical appointments. (Oil companies made huge profits. In 2007, Exxon Mobil set a record for the highest annual profit ever by a U.S. corporation: $40.6 billion. In 2008, Exxon Mobil set a record for quarterly profits: $11.68 billion.)

- The national debt, much of it caused by payments for past, present, and future wars and increased oil prices, ballooned to more than $11.5 trillion from $5.6 trillion when Bush was elected in 2001. Yet, the United States remains tethered to trillions in armament spending, which will deepen crises throughout the world for millions of people and ignite regional arms races. American governments will learn the hard lesson that military Keynesianism no longer is the elixir to ensure relatively full employment. In fact, more than 1.2 million jobs were lost in the first ten months of 2008. Overall, the Department of Labor reported that 10 million persons were unemployed. The number of persons working part time for economic reasons rose to 6.1 million. With the unemployment rate rising to 6.5 percent, the gainfully employed had a sense of foreboding that they could be next to be terminated. It did not seem to matter whether you wore a white collar, a blue collar, or an open collar, the pie was shrinking.

- The U.S. trade deficit—importing more goods and services than the United States exports—more than doubled during the Bush years to a high of $856 billion in 2006 from $400 billion in 2002. So far, the United States has been able to finance its alarming debt through the heavy investment in Treasury Bonds from foreign sources including Japan, China, South Korea, Saudi Arabia, and Kuwait, in effect a savings bond for them but a subsidy for the United States to continue its profligate ways. (During this period, the manufacturing crisis for the United States, fostered by bipartisan globalization policies, which aided global corporations and financial services, resulted in U.S. investments in Chinese and Asian factories manufacturing products for the American import market.) As Joel Geier, associate editor of the *International Socialist Review*, has pointed out, however, the trade deficit becomes unsustainable as it comes up against the credit/debt crisis and the declining value of the dollar. The United States, now the world's largest debtor nation, has borrowed $3.5 trillion from foreigners and then refused to defend its currency, allowing the dollar to be devalued by 30 percent. The result: foreign investors in American bonds and other debt instruments have lost roughly $1 trillion. This has not added either to the creditworthiness or the interest of foreign investors to continue their indirect sponsorship of costly American wars and foolish economic policies that have led to trade and federal budget deficits.

The Bush administration forecasts a federal budget deficit of nearly a half trillion dollars in 2009, galloping towards $1.3 trillion by the end of 2010. The record deficit did not reflect the full cost of the Iraq and Afghanistan wars, massive economic stimuli that will continue under Obama, necessary infrastructure expenditures as an instrument of employment, and the rebuilding of mass transportation. For individual homeowners, a further erosion of the housing market finds groups arguing for equity at least on a par with the banks and insurance companies.

For the Obama administration, another question presents itself: the shadow of U.S. foreign creditors dumping their U.S. Treasury holdings. In fact, it has already happened. In April 2008, China sold more U.S. Treasury Bonds than at any time in the previous seven years, a signal that it may be diversifying the world's largest foreign-exchange reserves, according to *Shanghai Securities News* (Note especially *International Socialist Review*, March–April 2008, vol. 55. Geier also notes that the bulk of $1.5 trillion in foreign currency debt that the Chinese hold is in American government debt.)

TAKING A HARD LOOK AT THE METAPHORIC GLASS

You know you are in a perilous period in American history when the optimist and pessimist no longer vie with each other but eerily agree that the glass is neither half full nor half empty—it is instead shattered.

The question is: should the country revert to business as usual and recover whatever fragments it can? Or, must Americans out of necessity walk carefully through the shattered pieces in order to make a fresh start with a totally "new glass"?

The year 1776 was one of those rare revolutionary moments. It was a time in which the populace believed, as did their leaders and writers, that if a people were committed to practical hope and collective futures and the idea of America was greater than the struggles over class, race, and gender that were sure to come, then the American people and its government would give definition and meaning to the pursuit of happiness. It would become an idea that would be found individually and collectively through the common good, which would reflect an economic bill of rights for all the people and constitutional legal rights such as habeas corpus for all who live under the flag of the United States.

Bloody as our history has been when we fight preventive and preemptive wars abroad and within, the United States can still be the place where falsity and oppression do not have to define our way of life and our government to ourselves or others. The pursuit of just laws and actions can be our twenty-first-century covenant if only we will admit that:

- Every day people from other nations wonder why we destroy the hopes that others continue to place in American society when we support corrupt, oppressive dictators for reasons of realpolitik. (Will President Obama continue this dubious—and immoral—policy?)

- They wonder why the U.S. Constitution is treated like so much butcher paper to cover over the putrefying smell of an aggressive war foisted on the American people by a president (aided and abetted by many Democrats in Congress) addicted to lies around weapons of mass destruction and increased surveillance of American citizens. (How will Obama, a former Constitutional law professor, treat and interpret the Constitution?)

- They wonder how it is that the United States, when it fights wars, convinces itself that it is not a warrior nation when its political problem is to recognize and overcome that very fact. (Obama certainly has the knowledge and intellect to do this.)

- They wonder how Bush and his Svengalian vice president could escape impeachment and accountability before the Congress for subverting settled constitutional law and flouting international law for which there was no basis for the American attacks. Indeed, the Nuremberg judgment and American domestic law, had they been applied strictly, would have seen a number of the Bush armchair warriors in the dock. Yet, it appeared that the laws were not self-executing; political will was necessary and after the Clinton impeachment fiasco such will was not present in Congress. Thus it was easier for a compliant media to accept Bush's argument that the United States was under attack from Iraq and Afghanistan and therefore had the U.N. Security Council's blessing to make war when the Council's resolution plainly did not give the United States that authority on its own say so. Thus lies became truth in ways that would have astounded even Orwell.

If Bush II had qualms about any of these questions, he never let on in public. Quite the contrary: his arrogant policies would become his great vision, the definition of national security and imperial democracy, the proof that he was a great man and a servant of God beyond anything Bush I attempted. Bush II's political task was to create a public relations illusion. The United States would remain number one in the world, unchallenged and unchangeable because of our might and credibility. Iraqis and others would feel awe and fear while we as a people pretended to build something called democracy even as our government went on a destructive rampage.

Throughout American history, from seventeenth-century puritanical claims of building a Shining City on the Hill, to nineteenth-century claims of Manifest Destiny, to twentieth-century "wars that would end all wars" and "make the world safe for democracy" (and American exports), Americans have accepted this special view of themselves and their nation. And to protect us and guide our ways, there was always God, who like a forgiving father or Dutch uncle, would light the way when leaders swathed themselves in the blankets and shrouds of Jesus or the tallis for those paying homage to the Old Testament. Nothing has changed in the first decade of the twenty-first century; America (as shown in chapter 19) is still a warrior nation sending bellicose messages that others had better shape up.

As we have said: Such activities are not the province of one political party or as a result of a leader born into a high socio-economic class. A long line of presidents before Bush tailored the U.S. Constitution to suit their ideologies. At the top of the income wealth pyramid we find that Bill Clinton as president was the willing instrument of the rich, whether it was tax breaks for them or announcing to the welfare poor with a Reaganesque flair, "Welfare as we know it" was over. As commander in chief, Clinton presided over a bombing war in the Balkans without a declaration of war from Congress, reaffirming the docility of Congress and abandoning the Constitution. No wonder that some argue that the

Constitution is irrelevant in modern circumstances. Bombing Hiroshima and Nagasaki with nuclear weapons and the creation of H-bombs thousands of times more deadly than "ordinary" nuclear weapons have not been inhibited by our Constitution and Bill of Rights. Are there any clues for future generations?

Or suppose there is widespread starvation, pogroms and fratricide, rape, murder, and civil war in parts of Africa, Asia, or Latin America? How does our Constitution advise us to act? Are there any clues regarding linkages between individual crises and their multiple effects worldwide, like the interconnections of global warming and access to food and water—both of which are in extreme crisis—that result in hunger and malnutrition? Are there any clues regarding the distribution of energy and strategies for peace and disarmament that guide Americans in how they will have to live, and in what ways *before* there is an accumulated collapse in every arena? (Is America finally open to a new but better New Deal?) And are scholars, journalists, universities, and think tanks able to readjust to what and how they think about this series of interrelated disasters or sequential disasters that seem to lend themselves to quick fixes, but are only temporarily fixed at best when wrong judgments are made?

In Plato's *Statesman*, a guardian is successful if he leaves office with the same set of problems that he had going in—no better, no worse. The horror story of our time is that by any measure the nation and the world is worse off in significant ways than it was at the end of World War II. Yet, Nazism was defeated and Fascism tamed, with oppressive empires such as the Dutch, French, and Belgian destroyed through the active engagement of the United States in the process. But imperialism comes in new forms.

While Bush and an approving Congress were spending blood and treasure for our adventures in Iraq and Afghanistan, other powers were filling the invariable power vacuum. China, India, Europe, and Brazil are not as dependent on us as they once were and no longer asking for our permission. Those we failed to defeat in war, like Vietnam, and those some politicians and neocons foolishly thought we had overwhelmed in the Cold War, like Russia, no longer fear serious consequences from the United States. Thus, when Russia sent troops into Georgia in August 2008 to protect its sphere of influence in South Ossetia and Akhbasia—and to pressure Georgia not to join NATO—Bush blustered, then pressured Poland to accept American antimissile missiles, further infuriating Russia. These episodes demonstrate that American foreign and national security policy needs retooling for what the reality is in the world and how the United States will live in that changing reality for the well-being of Americans and billions of other people. Reality need not begin by assuming the Russians are our enemies or that Russia is there for the taking by the United States and the West through organizing new strategies of encirclement.

This set of new conditions makes it all the more puzzling why Americans have yet to commit themselves to a planning and implementation process that will change our expenditures so that large-scale political, environmental, and nuclear disasters (nuclear proliferation, smuggling nuclear material to terrorist groups, radioactive nuclear wastelands) do not have to occur as a result of our actions—or inaction.

War, starvation, disease, inflation, environmental spoliation, and severe recession domestically and around the world possibly leading to a full-blown depression—these problems can only be ameliorated and resolved with popular citizen involvement and new citizen movements. Roosevelt understood that in a democracy a publicly elected servant was not a commander but instead a catalyst that moves people into action by giving them the public space to take action within new and democratically agreed on frameworks. However, FDR also urged us never to forget that "the ultimate rulers of our democracy are not a president and senators and congressmen and government officials, but the voters of this country."

Approximately 133 million people voted in the 2008 elections, a record high. But if citizens only vote and then walk away until the next election cycle, little will be accomplished and the nation will continue to travel down the slippery slope of disaster. We must realize that like a person, a nation needs head, heart, hand, and soul not only to survive but to endure.

The surprising excitement around the elections suggests that people were "sick and tired and not going to take it anymore." With the rise of Barack Obama, there was a quality of democratic hope in which Americans announced that they were no longer passive. It seemed that they were saying that their intention was not only to judge the government, but also to participate in it.

If Barack Obama was the first presidential candidate to truly harness the power of the Internet to win office, a new generation of Americans should be able to use the Internet continuously as watchdogs, not only to guard against future incursions on their freedoms by the Executive and Congress, but to rollback unjust and illegal laws that have steadily chipped away at our freedoms—and, in the case of Bush, even stolen them outright. Obama announced that he wishes for his presidency to be transparent. Using the Internet in all of its permutations can be an instantaneous way of holding his feet to the democratic fire.

AFTER THE GLASS SHATTERS

Given the anxious state of the union, this is no time to settle for mere fragments of the shattered glass. We face, as Martin Luther King Jr. put it, "the fierce urgency of now," by which he and we mean the unresolved American democratic problems of permanent war, economic hardship and unfairness, the fragility of the environment, class disparity, gender equality and identity, and, yes, race. Which poses questions unique in American history: Will our first African-American president, who did not run on the issue of race, initiate a national discussion to heal our racial wounds? Will the image and actions of this intelligent, charismatic leader continue to lift up African Americans and bridge the 400-year divide with white Americans when his election euphoria wears off from media overexposure and impatience with not quickly "fixing" the economy and ending the wars? Will Obama prove in his actions and words that the United States is in fact a human blending—that we are all one people? Or will a black man in the White House bring old wounds to a new and even uglier surface than the covert racism of the 2008 campaigns of Hillary Clinton (with an assist by her husband) and McCain's running mate, Gov. Sarah Palin, who seemed to feed off slurs and threats against Obama and blacks from her white audiences?

The authors—children of the Depression, war, the Cold War, surveillance, and McCarthyism—no less worried about the future than our fellow citizens, choose to raise a brand new glass, brimming with fresh ideas—even ones mistakenly discarded—and new infusions of energy and hope for a changing and beleaguered world, and we offer a toast to this and future generations.

Last Words

Ahead of History: Marcus Raskin and the Institute for Policy Studies

THE PIANO PRODIGY CLASHES WITH THE POLITICAL THINKER

I first met Marcus Raskin at a high school party on a sweltering summer night in Milwaukee in 1949. Someone called out: "Marc, play something!" Unaccountably wearing woolen pants and a long-sleeved oxford shirt, the fifteen-year-old sat down at the piano where, I assumed, he would bang out "Tea For Two" or a little boogie-woogie. He played Beethoven's "Appassionata" sonata. For most of us, it was our introduction to classical music.

When Marcus Raskin was a child, it was discovered that he had absolute pitch and could pick out notes without looking at them on the piano the family managed to keep in their modest flat above his father's plumbing business. He learned the first year John Thompson instruction book in a week, played the Grieg piano concerto at twelve. At sixteen he was accepted by New York's Juilliard School as a special student where he became a student of Leland Thompson and Rosina Lhevinne, who would become Van Cliburn's teacher.

A year later, he abruptly changed course to study at the University of Chicago college and law school with such preeminent scholars as Rexford Guy Tugwell of FDR's Brain Trust, and Quincy Wright, one of America's leading international lawyers, for whom he served as assistant while in the law school. (The student would become a lifelong friend of the two mentors.)

Why throw away a promising career as a concert pianist? "Too many fine players of my generation ended up giving piano lessons to children who had neither interest nor talent," Marc once explained. "I cared deeply about other things beyond playing the piano and had always loved thinking and reading about political theory and politics." (But he never really gave up the piano. Fifty years later, he was selected to play in the Van Cliburn Foundation's first International Piano Competition for Outstanding Amateurs in Fort Worth. "I wasn't too bad," Marc mused.)

Indeed, even in high school, Marc Raskin *knew* about the people and events that made 1949 arguably the pivotal year of the twentieth century, reshaping our country, the world, and our lives as much or more than the Second World War, which we had eagerly followed on newspaper maps as our brave troops beat back the hated Nazis and "Japs" (as they were then called by the press) to protect our freedoms. We never considered what those freedoms meant, but intuitively we believed that we had them.

One day I asked Marc some questions about China and the Korean War, which was then in its early stages. He promptly gave me a hefty volume titled "The State Department White Paper on China"—"a good overview of the issues," my friend solemnly advised. On another occasion, when we were discussing the Army-McCarthy congressional hearings, Marc growled: "My God, we desperately need a new freedom in this country!" then quoted Justice Louis Brandeis (not a name Marc's friends were familiar with) on "the right to be left alone."

On long walks in the working-class neighborhood of Milwaukee where the Raskin family had once lived, Marc's junior high classmate, Jerry Silberman (who would change his name to Gene Wilder when he became an actor), remembers: "It wasn't music or art (or girls) that drove Marcus, but rather how, if he were ever in a position of power, he wanted to change the world so that people, like these poor families around us, would have decent homes to come home to."[1]

To repair the world—*tikkun olam*, the great Hebrew concept of right-eousness, justice, or fairness—by Marc's own design has been his task ever since.

MR. RASKIN GOES TO WASHINGTON

In 1958, Marcus Raskin arrived in Washington DC with his new wife, Barbara Bellman Raskin, who was still years away from becoming a best-selling novelist. Marc has three children from his marriage to Barbara Raskin, who died in 1999: Erika, a novelist; Jamin, a law professor at American University, author, Maryland state senator, and one of the country's leading experts in repairing election and campaign finance law; and Noah, former assistant dean of American University Law School and businessman. He is also the father of Eden, his twenty-year-old daughter with his second wife, Lynn Randels. "Lynn has the analytic capacities of a Scottish philosopher," Marc says proudly, yet adds wistfully, "This omnicompetent woman with charm and inner and outward beauty has decided, like the most interesting in her generation, to eschew interest in government for business."

Marc and I were born during the first years of FDR's presidency and came of age imbued with the New Deal's idea that government could help to resolve public problems through the application of intelligence and passion. In 1959, Marc found work as a legislative counsel—to a number of congressmen *simultaneously*. A few days into the job, he sent a memo to every liberal House Democrat that sounds as if it were written about the twenty-first century:

One may make certain generalizations about Americans and American life in the past six years. Americans are bored. They are apathetic about politics. They are afraid. They see no way to exercise control over their own destinies. They see insurmountable problems. They are alienated from the vast commitments their government has undertaken in defense of certain vague abstractions. They do not understand the technology of science, which seems more and more to control their very lives, and their very existence on earth. They have withdrawn from the awesome complexity and almost hopeless dread, which is the general social and political scene. The American people have hoped that their leaders playing the role of "Big Daddy" would take care of the many problems which presently grip the world, so that they themselves might withdraw from the necessity of social and political action.[2]

One of the Congressmen Marc worked for, Robert Kastenmeier of Wisconsin, eager to organize House liberals into an effective voting bloc, formed the Liberal Project. Marc was appointed group secretary and told to contact any scholar and creative thinker he felt could establish common ground with liberals and prepare suitable policy papers. He quickly lined up philosopher Hannah Arendt, psychoanalyst Erich Fromm, sociologist David Riesman, and cybernetics pioneer Norbert Wiener. Kastenmeier, assuming his young aide knew everybody under the sun, said, "I wouldn't have had the nerve to do it."[3] Marc Raskin knew none of these celebrated intellectuals. "I simply called up anyone I thought would be useful. I saw no reason not to have discussions with people who I viewed as people I wanted to know." One of the people he sought out was a visitor to the Kastenmeier office, scientist Leo Szilard. A few years later, Szilard's influence would change Raskin's life—and liberalism.

On election night, 1960, Marc was giving a lecture at Harvard in Riesman's freshmen seminar. The Kennedy-Nixon race was in doubt, but it was clear that the election would be a disaster for the Congressmen Marc worked for. Half of them lost—half his base in Congress and half his wages.

"So the question is: what am I going to do?" he says. "I'm twenty-six, I have a wife and child. Dave Riesman thought that I should work in the White House and recommended me to McGeorge Bundy as his assistant on national security affairs and disarmament. My own views were not those of Kennedy's New Frontier, but I believed that I would be able to press my ideas much better within the White House."

An enthusiastic Bundy wrote to Riesman: "Marc Raskin has a remarkably powerful and lively mind. We shall probably have some disagreements, but I shall feel a lot better for knowing that certain problems have passed by his critical eye on their way to resolution."[4]

On the day of Marc's first National Security Council (NSC) meeting, President Kennedy had privately admitted to his closest aides that

Fidel Castro's army had routed the administration-backed Cuban exiles attempting to invade the country at the Bay of Pigs. Putting on a game face, Bundy told his NSC staff: "I guess Che [Guevara, Castro's number two] learned more from Guatemala than we did." Everyone except Marc laughed.

"We were meeting in the office of Bundy's deputy, Walt Rostow," Marc remembers. "On the table is a huge bowl of fruit. Everybody's devouring the fruit—Mac, Walt, Arthur Schlesinger, Dick Goodwin, others. It was like a scene from the Roman Empire. The talk was bullshit laced with the juices of overripe fruit. The problem was that those Cuban exiles who weren't lying dead on the damn beaches were about to be captured. And the United States had a *policy* issue: are we going to give the exiles air cover? And the United States said no. That was the issue in Guatemala in 1954, when the United States overthrew Jacobo Arbenz, the Guatemalan president who tried to redistribute holdings of United Fruit to landless peasants. Guevara held a minor post in that government. So I bluntly asked Bundy, 'It's interesting that Che learned from Guatemala, but what have *we* learned?'"

Bundy, a New England patrician, believed in debate up to the point where it challenged the existing values of the system. He took Marc's question for what it was: a dissenting statement. Marc got a terse call from Bundy's administrative assistant: "Mr. Bundy would prefer if you didn't come to the staff meetings. He would prefer that you just come in at the end of the day and meet with him alone to talk."

"My first day!" Marc says, reflecting on the putdown. "It was a very, very clear statement: they are *here*, and you are *there*." It was also very clear to him at that moment that the New Frontier was not the New Deal.

But if he had been appointed to be a minority of one, it still seemed perfectly reasonable to him to argue policy positions with Bundy and the others even though that was not something a young staff person was supposed to do, especially one who had differing positions on such Kennedy notions as a program of civilian defense shelters. In fact, Marc wrote so many policy papers that ran counter to the administration's policies that Bundy once heatedly asked him, "Are you working for me or am I working for you?" Marc continued churning out his early-warning papers.

In a memorandum to Bundy written a year and a half before the United States detected the presence of Soviet missiles in Cuba, Marc suggested that

the United States should not withdraw from Guantanamo [U.S. naval base in Cuba] since such a move would appear as an indication of weakness both at home and to the Communist world. However, fundamental changes in our relations to that base could still occur. We might endeavor to turn it into a series of hospitals and technical institutions for the Cuban people, staffed by U.S. personnel. This will change the nature of the threat toward Cuba and make our presence there more palatable.[5]

On the arms race, he philosophized:

Given the explosive nature of the twentieth century, and the fact that man is both good and evil, rational and irrational, we should not expect the arms race to go on at the present level or as it is being projected into the future without something going wrong. Proliferation of nuclear weapons will occur, population increases will occur, the revolutions of the twentieth century will continue (one which we started, not the Communists), and intense pressures of an economic sort will cause political unrest. Any and all of these are enough to cause U.S. involvement in a military conflict of gigantic proportions—without having resolved the problems after involvement.[6]

Anticipating the problems of globalization, a nonexistent economic concept in 1961, Marc urged the Kennedy administration to

begin a study of the relationship of international corporations to U.S. foreign policy with specific recommendations for ways of changing those relationships where the national interest of the United States is adversely effected.[7]

As the months passed, tensions between Bundy and his young assistant went well beyond disagreements over policy. Bundy had valued Marc as "a brave and independent thinker." Now Marc had become a little too independent and determined in his own ways of thinking to suit Bundy.

As if that were not enough, Marc became an administration liability after the publication of *The Liberal Papers*, an outgrowth of the Liberal Project. "I was the staff advisor—FDR's son, James Roosevelt, was the editor—and the Republicans were out for blood," he recalls. "After all, sixty thousand copies had been sold, not an inconsequential number in those days or now."

Few Republicans had read the book, but they knew a hot issue when they saw it. Republican Senate Minority Leader Everett Dirksen railed that this "Democratic-sponsored book could well be renamed 'Our American Munich.'" A Republican National Committee press release urged "All Republicans To Make A Major 1962 Issue Of Democratic Book Which Goes Beyond The Communist Line." That was enough for Bundy. He moved Marc over to the Bureau of the Budget to advise on education, not realizing that education was one of Marc's passions.

Marc plunged into his new work, writing pioneering papers anticipating critical problems in education that are only now beginning to be dealt with, like the consequences of technology:

The interest of a free democratic society in education is roughly consonant with enabling the citizen to control his fate and together with his fellow citizens theirs. Operatively, this means that democratic societies or republican/democratic governments function on the ability of the citizen to know...to make rational political, social, and moral choices for himself and his society. The sad but true state of affairs is that technology and change have resulted in people of all ages not knowing what the few know nor understanding how what is known by the few affects and changes the many. Continuing education becomes the only way to bridge the gap.[8]

THE WISE MAN INSTITUTE

Always in the back of Marc's mind was the dream of his new mentor, Leo Szilard, collaborator with Einstein and an important theoretical physicist for the Manhattan Project, which built America's first atomic bomb. But after Hiroshima, Szilard became so concerned about the dangers of nuclear war that he envisioned an institute *in* Washington, but not *of* Washington, where wise men would come to work on the great issues of the day but not be part of government.

Late in 1961, Marc asked another young intellectual, Richard J. Barnet, to help him develop what would become the Institute for Policy Studies. Dick Barnet, a summa cum laude from Harvard, had joined the new Arms Control and Disarmament Agency after the publication of his first book, *Who Wants Disarmament?* But he grew frustrated when he was required to hand out large grants of money to people like Herman Kahn, the controversial thermonuclear war strategist, for research projects for new, more destructive weapons systems.

Marc and Dick knew from their government experience that there were two distinct official Washingtons. In the first Washington were consultants to the government who knew enough about what the government was doing to have an influential voice in its criticism but were on the government payroll and therefore were unlikely to criticize it. In the second Washington were those who were not consultants to the government because they had the wrong politics and therefore did not know what was going on and could not even give good criticism because they were too ill-informed about the whole thing to be taken seriously.

The Institute for Policy Studies—or IPS as it would alternately come to be called by friends and by those Marc and Dick never imagined would become their enemies—would be a place where creative thinkers (called "fellows") would examine the great and often controversial issues of American policy, conduct exhaustive research, offer alternatives to what government should and should not do, and show how society could be organized to overcome America's chronic problems of war and intervention in the affairs of other nations, economic and social disparity, racial injustice, and ignorance. The IPS project would not be to educate servants of the state, but to help the servants and the citizenry *question* the state.

In the spring of 1963, Marc and Dick, wearing long faces, stood on the steps of the Supreme Court, holding a draft of their vision for the Institute. They had just shown it to Justice William O. Douglas, one of the Court's great liberals, hoping for his blessing, but there was a sadness in the man.

"It's a good idea," Douglas lamented, "but reason and truth are out of fashion in American life. If I were your age, I would not start an institute in Washington. I would start it in the Himalayas," the noted mountain climber told them. "But you won't pay any attention to me and probably shouldn't. So you'll go around this country trying to raise money and you will probably succeed, but you will find that you will be witnesses at an inquest of a dead society."[9]

Six months later, the Institute for Policy Studies opened its doors.

Douglas was right about money; Marc and Dick would spend a great deal of their time raising it because they insisted IPS had to be wholly independent. The institute would refuse government contracts and would not be answerable to political parties, corporations, single-issue causes, or donors with pet projects.

Relieved of having to use their brains to justify fashionable policies, the fellows were free to challenge conventional wisdom and orthodoxy from the Right and center—and from the Left when they thought fellow liberals had it coming. Their blueprint was to put into practice philosopher John Dewey's theory that ideas were agendas for action. In this way, Marc, Dick, and their new colleagues hoped to break through barriers that had traditionally separated thinkers from doers. Not only was this unheard of in Washington at the time, it was *revolutionary*.

The notion of setting up a think tank of intellectuals outside of government that would come up with both imaginative and pragmatic policy ideas is common today, but "there was nothing like the Institute for Policy Studies in the early 1960s," says Christopher Jencks, an original IPS fellow, now professor of social policy at Harvard.[10] There was nothing like IPS in Washington, America, or the rest of the world.

U.S. V. COFFIN, FERBER, GOODMAN, RASKIN, AND SPOCK

While planning IPS, Marc had said, "It is not enough to analyze problems and propose neat theoretical solutions. The fellows themselves must be actively engaged in creating change. Taking personal risk is the way of maintaining relevance to one's intellectual work."

Risk became dangerously personal for him in January 1968. President Lyndon B. Johnson was escalating the war in Vietnam while trying to suppress dissent at home. Marc—an early organizer of the antiwar movement, which he took into the halls of the Justice Department—was the principal writer with Arthur Waskow of "A Call to Resist Illegitimate Authority," an influential antidraft manifesto signed by prominent intellectuals and ministers who publicly refused to support what they termed "an immoral and illegal war." Along with four other men, including Dr. Benjamin Spock, "the baby doctor," Marc was charged with conspiracy (though the men barely knew each other) to "counsel, aid, abet, and hinder the operations of the draft."

Dubbed by the media "the Boston Five" because of the trial's site, they faced five-year sentences in federal prison and ten-thousand-dollar fines. Marc—represented by former Nuremberg prosecutor Telford Taylor and distinguished Boston lawyer Cal Bartlett—was acquitted, but the others were found guilty. Eventually, Dr. Spock and graduate student Michael Ferber were also acquitted. The appeals of Reverend William Sloan Coffin and Mitchell Goodman were reversed and remanded, but they went free when the government dropped the case.

Unchastened, Marc, with Barnet and colleague Ralph Stavins, organized a study to explain to the American public for the first time how the Vietnam quagmire had happened. "I felt that the United States had had its good name dragged through the mud by its leaders who I viewed as war criminals," Marc reflects. "They put into harm's way young Americans to commit these crimes and allowed for the destruction of literally millions of people in South and North Vietnam for no obvious apparent reason in the context of that time in terms of U.S. interests and certainly not in terms of the Vietnamese people."

But Marc's friend Hannah Arendt argued, "In order to make this stick you have to have proper names of people; you have to find out what X and Y did, that X ordered this and Y signed this order."

For several years, Stavins, Barnet, and Marc, aided by a team of students, conducted some three hundred interviews with top advisors to presidents Kennedy and Johnson, generals, admirals, and middle-level officials who occupied strategic positions in the national security bureaucracy. Most talked openly. Some informants backed up their oral statements with documents they possessed. The finishing touches came from some Department of Defense materials that gave background information supplied by Vietnam analyst Daniel Ellsberg.

At the time, Barnet prophetically said that our "military's delusions" in Vietnam would twist America's foreign policy for years to come. Indeed, since the Institute's founding more than four decades ago, Raskin, Barnet, and their IPS colleagues have been ahead of history. Garry Wills wrote in *Esquire* that the institute has "a feel for what is coming up next"; its fellows work to "their own odd and independent rhythm, proleptically, one step or two ahead of everyone else."[11]

HIGHLIGHTS OF THE WORK OF IPS FELLOWS

Ten years before President Ronald Reagan was credited with ending the cold war, Raskin and Barnet met in Moscow with Mikhail Gorbachev's senior advisors and learned, contrary to CIA estimates, that the Soviet Union was an overgrown third world country, its military threat was wildly exaggerated, and communist solidarity was a myth. Raskin passed their insights to the State Department, which paid no heed.

Several fellows have made huge innovations. Among Richard J. Barnet's many prescient books on globalization and foreign affairs are *The Roots of War* and *Intervention and Revolution*. Barbara Ehrenreich has been writing pathbreaking books on women, families, work, and poverty, including *Nickel and Dimed* and *Bait and Switch*, for more than twenty years. Three decades before the acolytes of Speaker of the House Newt Gingrich peddled their idea of decentralization (mostly to benefit the well-off), Paul Goodman showed in theory and Milton Kotler demonstrated in practice how decentralization could help the poor and defenseless. Christopher Jencks's warnings in the 1960s presaged today's crisis in education.

In the sanctuary of IPS, Ariel Dorfman, forced into exile by Chilean dictator Augusto Pinochet, wrote books and plays exposing the nature of dictators. The anti-imperialist critiques of Saul Landau and Peter Kornbluh proved to be tragically true in El Salvador, Nicaragua, and Chile. Landau has made more than three dozen films and documentaries, including *Paul Jacobs and the Nuclear Gang*, which received the George F. Polk Award for investigative journalism and an Emmy. He has also written several important books on Latin America. Kornbluh edited *The Pinochet File*.

In 1963, IPS predicted that a digital divide would be created if computers were denied to the poor and lower class. Current IPS Director John Cavanagh has coauthored books with Barnet and Robin Broad on global issues and fair trade, and with Sarah Anderson in 1999 he revealed the extent of the emergence of two nations in America: one prospering, the other slipping further and further behind in pay and opportunity. Phyllis Bennis's research before the U.S. invasion of Iraq showed how the war would ultimately harm both countries. Marc Raskin's prescient warnings throughout the Iraq War showed how illegitimate Bush II's authority was.

IPS remains a crossroads where the skeptical and the worried still come to write and teach, shape their humanistic agendas, and form coalitions with the great citizen movements. They help to make them click, always as scholars and grassroots organizers and frequently as leaders because they were first on the scene: antiwar and civil rights movements in the 1960s; disarmament, environmental, anti–nuclear power, and women's movements in the 1970s; anti–U.S. intervention in Latin America and anti-apartheid in South Africa in the 1980s; global fair trade (as opposed to so-called "free" trade), self-reliant communities, and environmental and economic justice in the 1990s; and, in the twenty-first century, fighting the out-of-control problems carried over from the last century by ignorance or design, including for the first time in history the all-too-real prospect of a world nuclear war in which there will be no winners.

Now the third generation guides IPS as it continues to build and sustain a political and philosophical culture that has produced thousands of books, articles, films, papers, pamphlets, lectures, seminars, and public discussions. None of this would have come about if not for Marcus Raskin's vision of what the Institute of Policy Studies would be.

THE TEACHER

Marcus Raskin in his early seventies is no stranger to cancer and heart bypass, "plus a little valve work, if you please," he is wry enough about it to add. Yet he outworks men and women half his age. He divides his day between IPS, where he is the distinguished fellow, and George Washington University, where he is a distinguished and controversial professor of public policy. He is rumpled and usually in need of a haircut; it is very much how he looked when we were boys. (My dear mother thought Marc was faintly subversive, not because of his political views, of which she knew little, but because of his appearance.)

Marc would look tired even on the off chance that he actually decided to try for a good night's sleep. This is not an option, however, since he reads and writes far into the night. (Including this one, he has authored twenty books on international affairs, government, national defense, and political philosophy.) In between this schedule, he still waltzes and badgers potential donors to the IPS with the same vigor he had in his thirties, makes time for his eight grandchildren, and is a mentor to all kinds of people, even to those who have long since "made it," like composer Philip Glass. "Marc really got me started," Glass remembers. "I heard him playing the Berg Piano Sonata in a dorm lounge when we were students at the University of Chicago, and I got the idea that I wanted to study piano and music. For the next two years, Marc gave me lessons and technical exercises."[12]

Marc's longtime friend Gore Vidal, not uniquely, relies on him: "He knows where everything is, in and out of Washington, who everyone is, he's a good guide."[13]

Marc is a most *unconventional* guide, Christopher Jencks realized when he first met him in 1962. Jencks recalls, "One couldn't fail both to be charmed by the number of ideas he had and a little shaken by the number of them that seemed outside the range of things that anyone else I knew took very seriously, or that I did. He was just thinking about the world in very different ways."[14]

Yet, as Pulitzer Prize–winning investigative reporter Seymour M. Hersh, who has known Marc since the 1950s, observed: "Marc is as American as apple pie. He's profoundly a believer in humanity, the goodness of souls, the redemption—he could have been a good Catholic. He has a faith that's a very powerful faith when it comes to human character. So you can never get discouraged with Marc. He's like a rock. Tenacious. And a great, profound believer in the democratic values of this country."[15]

Indeed, Marc Raskin has always been there for me, no more so than when I was writing my first book, *The Duping of the American Voter*[16] at a time when the stench of Nixon's corrupt presidency was still in the air. Marc urged me to probe past conventional wisdom and show how the dishonesty and deception of political advertising not only infects Republicans and Democrats alike but also mocks freedom of speech and, with it, the other freedoms Americans like to believe they are entitled to.

—*Robert Spero*

Notes

THE CLEAR AND PRESENT DANGER TO OUR FREEDOMS FROM OUR NATIONAL SECURITY STATE

1. Annual Message to Congress, January 6, 1941, the Franklin D. Roosevelt Presidential Library and Museum, http://www.fdrlibrary.marist.edu/4free.html.

2. Samuel I. Rosenman, *Working with Roosevelt* (New York: Harper & Brothers, 1952), 262–63.

3. Inspired by FDR, Norman Rockwell put a face on the Four Freedoms in 1942 with his legendary paintings. Critics have dismissed Rockwell for idealizing small-town America, but his paintings dramatized the issues at stake for the whole country: *Freedom of Speech* (a young man speaking his mind at a New England town meeting), *Freedom to Worship* (people of various creeds and colors praying together), *Freedom from Want* (three joyous generations gathered at the Thanksgiving table), *Freedom from Fear* (parents tucking their children into bed, the father holding a newspaper with the headline: "BOMBING-ATTACKED").

   More than sixty years later, millions of Americans who have never heard of Norman Rockwell can describe his *Four Freedoms* series. Why do the paintings continue to make this indelible impression? Apparently, they represent the freedoms people fear they may lose. How else to explain that on September 12, the day after the al-Qaeda attack on New York City and Washington DC, the most visited Web site of the Curtis Publishing Company was Rockwell's *Four Freedoms* series.

4. Marcus G. Raskin, *The Common Good* (New York and London: Routledge and Kegan Paul, 1986), 272.

5. Seymour M. Hersh, "Torture at Abu Ghraib," *The New Yorker*, May 10, 2004, 44.

6. William Safire, "Threat of National ID," *New York Times*, A15, December 24, 2001.

   It could be argued that Safire is being consistent with a traditional conservative position, because conservatives in the 1930s were against the Social Security card on the grounds that while it was said that you were only supposed to use the card for Social Security purposes, it would begin being used as an identity card. Alf Landon, the Republican presidential candidate in 1936, predicted that your Social Security Number would follow you from cradle to grave.

7. Associated Press, "FBI Apologizes to Oregon Lawyer Detained in Madrid Bombings," May 25, 2004, http://www.refuseandresist.org/detentions/art .php?aid=1385.

8. Richard Waters, "U.S. Group Implants Electronic Tags in Workers," *Financial Times*, A1, February 12, 2006.

9. At the end of the Second World War, one of the issues in international law was incendiary speech of the kind that Hitler used against the Jews. This is speech that fires up people to hate another group of people or another nation. At the time, it was thought that incendiary speech was out of bounds and had to be controlled, and many international lawyers support such an idea; this does, however, contradict the right of free speech. Some have argued that the question is a matter of context. In *Brandenburg v. Ohio* (395 U.S. 444, Docket No. 492 [1969]), the Supreme Court made clear a powerful standard that protects free speech: a state cannot stop an individual or group from advocacy of violence except when violence is imminent and a lawless action is likely to occur.

    The dilemma is that we are able to deal with an individual who wants to spew hate or worse, but the state—the government—must be held to a much higher standard than the individual because we give the state the power, and thus the means, of violence and punishment. The question is, how are the citizens to keep a check on the state when the state shares its secrets with very few in positions of power and more often than not excludes the elected representatives of the people? Giving a selected few in Congress access to some executive secrets can never constitute a dialogue with Congress and other important agencies.

10. Marcus. G. Raskin, *Being and Doing* (New York: Random House, 1971), 61.

CHAPTER 1

1. Attorney General John Ashcroft, "Prepared Remarks of before the National Religious Broadcasters Convention," Nashville, February 19, 2002, http:// ali-www.cs.umass.edu/~burrill/ashcroft.html.

2. Mitchell Palmer suffered an assassination attempt on his life, which in his mind justified rounding up the unwanted and marginalized. See Paul Jacobs and Saul Landau, *To Serve the Devil: Natives and Slaves* (New York: Vintage Press, 1971).

3. The operations of internal security and national security/foreign policy during and after the Second World War were organized separately in the administrative apparatus. The cumulative effect, however, was a spider's net of increasing state power engulfing individuals. See Marcus Raskin, *The Politics of National Security* (Transaction Books, New Jersey, 1977); Marcus Raskin, *Essays of a Citizen, From National Security State to Democracy* (See "The National Security State versus Democracy") (Armonk: M.E. Sharpe, 1991); Marcus Raskin, *Notes on the Old System* (New York: David McKay, 1973), especially chapter 6, "National Security State to Democracy"; Fred Cook, *The Nightmare Decade: The Life and Times of Senator Joe McCarthy* (New York: Random House, 1971).

4. "Ashcroft: Critics of New Terror Measures Undermine Effort," CNN, December 7, 2001, http://archives.cnn.com/2001/US/12/06/inv.ashcroft .hearing.

5. David Greenberg, "Fathers and Sons," *New Yorker*, July 12 and 19, 2004, 97, discussing Peter Schweizer and Rochelle Schweizer, *The Bushes: Portrait of a Dynasty* (New York: Doubleday, 2004).

6. Roland Watson, "El Salvador Style 'Death Squads' to be Deployed by U.S. Against Iraq Militants," *Times Online*, January 10, 2005, http://www.timesonline .co.uk/article/0,,11069-1433353,00.html.

7. "Belief that Iraq Had Weapons of Mass Destruction Has Increased Substantially," the Harris Poll® #57, July 21, 2006, http://harrisinteractive .com/harris_poll/index.asp?PID=684.

8. Patriot Act provisions from Federal Bar Association, "Highlights of New Antiterrorism Law."

9. According to a November 3, 1993, Justice Department memorandum on "The Legal Significance of Presidential Signing Statements," "Presidential signing statements that purported to create legislative history for the use of the courts was uncommon—if indeed it existed at all—before the Reagan and [George H. W.] Bush Presidencies. However, earlier presidents did use signing statements to raise and address the legal or constitutional questions they believed were presented by the legislation they were signing. Examples of signing statements of this kind can be found as early as the Jackson and Tyler administrations, and later presidents, including Lincoln, Andrew Johnson, Theodore Roosevelt, Wilson, Franklin Roosevelt, Truman, Eisenhower, Lyndon Johnson, Nixon, Ford and Carter, also engaged in the practice" (http://www.usdoj.gov/olc/signing.htm). But George W. Bush is the champion statement signer, with over eight hundred in just five and a half years in office. The forty-two presidents before Bush II issued a total of six hundred signing statements.

10. Neil A. Lewis and Eric Schmitt, "Lawyers Decided Bans on Torture Didn't Bind Bush," *New York Times*, June 8, 2004, http://www.nytimes.com/2004/ 06/08/politics/08ABUS.html?ex=1402027200&en=31f4ba9107488f17&ei=500 7&partner=USERLAND.

11. *Salim Ahmed Hamdan, Petitioner v. Donald H. Rumsfeld, Secretary of Defense, et al.*, 05-184 (June 29, 2006). Salim Ahmed Hamdan, once a driver for Osama bin Laden, was captured in Afghanistan in the fall of 2001 by Afghan forces allied with the United States, sent to Guantanamo during 2002, and later designated as one of six prisoners eligible for trial by special military tribunal—a military commission—created by the Bush II administration.

12. The minority [Democratic] staff of the House Judiciary Committee generated a four-hundred-page report with well over a thousand footnotes that "identifies substantial evidence that the president, the vice president and other high-ranking members of the Bush administration misled Congress and the American people regarding the decision to go to war in Iraq; misstated and manipulated intelligence information regarding the justification for such a war; countenanced torture and cruel inhuman and degrading treatment; permitted inappropriate retaliation against critics of the administration and approved unlawful domestic surveillance." This report, "The Constitution in Crisis" (unpublished), generated by Congressman Conyers

shows a systematic intention and even a willful attempt to flaunt the laws of the United States in areas such as civil rights, military law, laws concerning conflict of interest, misuse of intelligence, and privacy laws. This arrogation of power, when it goes unchecked, becomes part of the custom creating laws that damage—even destroy—constitutional democracy.

13. Franklin D. Roosevelt, speech, Philadelphia, June 27, 1936.
14. Patriot Act provisions from Federal Bar Association, "Highlights of New Antiterrorism Law."
15. The Homeland Security Council, "Homeland Security Planning Scenarios, Executive Summaries," July 2004, http://www.globalsecurity.org/security/library/report/2004/hsc-planning-scenarios-jul04_02.htm.
16. Patriot Act provisions from Federal Bar Association, "Highlights of New Antiterrorism Law."
17. Interview with David Cole, *Now With Bill Moyers*, Public Affairs Television, August 22, 2003, http://www.pbs.org/now/transcript/transcript231_full.html. The figures Cole cites apply through August 22, 2003, the date of the program.
18. Jane Mayer, "Outsourcing Torture," *The New Yorker*, February 17, 2005.
19. *Gideon v. Wainwright*, 372 US 335, Docket No. 155 (1963). This landmark Supreme Court decision established the right of defendants in felony trials to have legal counsel. Clarence Earl Gideon was charged with breaking into a poolroom intending to commit a misdemeanor—a felony at that time under Florida law. Being indigent, Gideon asked the trial judge to appoint an attorney to defend him but was denied such counsel. Florida law required the appointment of lawyers only in capital cases. The U.S. Supreme Court disagreed. Justice Hugo Black wrote the majority finding: "every defendant stands equal before the law. This noble ideal cannot be realized if the poor man charged with crime has to face his accusers without a lawyer to assist him."
20. Anthony Lewis, "The Silencing of Gideon's Trumpet," *New York Times Magazine*, April 20, 2003.
21. *Hamdi v. Rumsfeld*, 124 S. Ct. 2633, plurality opinion, decided June 28, 2004.
22. *Susette Kelo, et al. v. City of New London, Connecticut, et al.*, 125 S.Ct. 2655 (2005).
23. AP, "Gay Army Linguists Say They Were Ousted," *New York Times*, November 15, 2002.
24. Eric Lichtblau, "F.B.I.'s Translation Backlog Grows," *New York Times*, July 28, 2005. http://www.nytimes.com/2005/07/28/politics/28fbi.html?ex=1280203200&en=ebddb809c1628fc0&ei=5088&partner=rssnyt&emc=rss.
25. Patriot Act provisions from Federal Bar Association, "Highlights of New Antiterrorism Law."
26. Ibid.
27. American Civil Liberties Union, 2005 Work Plan.
28. "More than 60,000 people are on watch lists, meaning OSI (Office of Special Investigations) officials are alerted when they try to enter the country." http://www.newhousenews.com/archive/story1b062000.html. Another source states that "the watch list of over 100,000 names will be widely acceptable to law enforcement agents, border police, airport workers as well as some private industries. It will contain the names of both international and domestic "suspects." Democracy Now! "Gov't Sets Up Massive Watchlist of 'Known and Suspected Terrorists,'" September 18, 2003, http://www.democracynow.org/article.pl?sid=03/09/18/183235.

29. Project Minaret was an operation coordinated by the NSA, CIA, and FBI in which watch lists were made to counter "subversive domestic activities." Between 1967 and 1973, "over 5,925 foreigners and 1,690 organizations and U.S. citizens were included on Project Minaret watch lists.... Additionally, the NSA Office of Security Services maintained reports on at least 75,000 Americans between 1952 and 1974. This list included the names of anyone that was mentioned in a NSA message intercept." Attorney General Elliot Richardson ended the operation. (These are very conservative estimates.) http://en.wikipedia.org/wiki/Project_MINARET.

30. Patriot Act provisions from Federal Bar Association, "Highlights of New Antiterrorism Law."

31. Leigh Estabrook, *Public Libraries and Civil Liberties: A Profession Divided*, (Urbana, IL: U. of Illinois Library Research Center, January 2003); http://www.lis.uiuc.edu/gslis/research/civil_liberties.html (narrative); http://www.lis.uiuc.edu/gslis/research/finalresults.pdf (questionnaire with summary of responses); "Public Libraries' Response to the Events of 9/11," cited in Nancy Kranich, "The Impact of the USA PATRIOT Act on Free Expression," the Free Expression Policy Project, Brennan Center for Justice at NYU School of Law, December 5, 2005, http://www.fepproject.org/commentaries/patriotact.html.

32. Kay Murray, "The USA Patriot Act: What Writers Should Know," *Authors Guild Bulletin*, Winter 2005.

33. John Mutte, "Patriot Act Amendment Comes Close to Winning," *Publishers Weekly*, December 12, 2005, http://www.publishersweekly.com/article/CA435300.html?pubdate=7%2F12%2F2004&display=archive.

34. George W. Bush, "President Bush Discusses Homeland Security at the FBI Academy" (speech, Quantico, Virginia, September 10, 2003).

35. In late 2005, many Americans became increasingly disillusioned when it was revealed that George W. Bush called for the wiretapping of possibly thousands of Americans in violation of the Foreign Intelligence Surveillance Act (FISA) of 1978. James Risen and Eric Lichtblau, "Bush Lets U.S. Spy on Callers Without Courts," *New York Times*, December 16, 2005.

36. David Martin, "With a Whisper, Not a Bang—Bush signs parts of Patriot Act II into law—stealthily," *San Antonio Current*, December 24, 2003, http://www.sacurrent.com/site/news.cfm?newsid=10705756&BRD=2318&PAG=461&dept_id=482778&rfi=6.

37. Civil liberties groups and moderates and progressives in Congress had sought to rid the Patriot Act of its most egregious provisions. For months, intense negotiations were carried on in Congress. But in the end, as David Cole wrote in *The Nation* on April 3, 2006, "Congress voted to extend all sixteen provisions originally set to expire on December 31, 2005, making only minor modifications to a handful." (The reauthorization bill easily passed both houses with thirty-four Democrats voting with all fifty-five Republicans in the Senate and forty-three Democrats voting with two hundred and fifty-seven Republicans in the House.) Cole maintained that "the principal problem with the reauthorization debate was that most of the act's worst provisions were not even on the table. These include sections making it a crime to offer 'expert advice' to a proscribed political group, regardless of content; allowing the government to freeze the assets of suspected charities

without any showing of wrongdoing, and based on secret evidence; and permitting foreign nationals to be locked up without charges, deported for innocent political associations and kept out of the country for endorsing any group the government labels as 'terrorist'—under a definition so capacious that it could include the African National Congress and the Israeli military."

38. Patriot Act provisions from Federal Bar Association, "Highlights of New Antiterrorism Law."

39. Scott Shane, "Official Reveals Budget for U.S. Intelligence," *New York Times*, A18, November 8, 2005. The official, the Deputy Director of National Intelligence for Collection, revealed the figure in an apparent slip during a talk.

40. David E. Sanger, "An Old Hand in New Terrain of Top Intelligence Job," *New York Times*, February 18, 2005, http://www.nytimes.com/2005/02/18/politics/18negroponte.html?ei=5090&en=14e56f0f186c593b&ex=1266382800&partner=rssuserland&pagewanted=all&position=. Negroponte's career as ambassador, low-density warrior, and covert operative took him from Honduras to Iraq as viceroy before becoming director of national intelligence during the Bush II administration.

41. In June 1970, President Richard Nixon approved the Huston Plan, which "called for various agencies of government, including the CIA, FBI, and military intelligence agencies, to conduct wide-ranging intelligence-gathering activities targeted toward dissident groups and individuals." The plan was revoked soon after as it violated basic civil liberties but some of its recommendations remained. http://www.aarclibrary.org/publib/church/reports/vol2/contents.htm.

42. William Finnegan, "Homeland Insecurity," *New Yorker*, February 7, 2005, http://www.newyorker.com/talk/content/?050207ta_talk_finnegan.

43. Patriot Act provisions from Federal Bar Association, "Highlights of New Antiterrorism Law."

44. Morris Ernst, head of the ACLU, became a strong supporter of J. Edgar Hoover during FDR's presidency. In 1940, Ernst and Hoover made a deal in which the ACLU would remove communists from the organization and the FBI would keep the House Un-American Activities Committee away from the ACLU. "Hoover cultivated Ernst shamelessly and then dropped him when he had no further need for him." http://www.crimelibrary.com/gangsters_outlaws/cops_others/hoover/8.html

The ACLU challenged McCarthy and the House Un-American Activities Committee "on the tenet that only peoples' acts, not their beliefs, should be penalized." The ACLU also dealt with censorship of communist literature during this time, saying that this was an attack on free speech. http://www.princeton.edu.

45. Maureen Dowd, "A Defense That's Offensively Weak," *Falls Church News-Press* (*New York Times* News Service), March 10, 2005, http://www.fcnp.com/501/dowd.htm.

46. Patriot Act provisions from Federal Bar Association, "Highlights of New Antiterrorism Law."

47. Ibid.

48. In twentieth-century thought, John Dewey presented the argument that freedom for the person is an exercise in growth; he wrote that it is not a static conception, as if a person were no more than a rock. John Dewey, *John Dewey: The*

Later Works, 1925–1953," Volume 7, 1932 (Carbondale: Southern University Press, 1932), 305–6.

The problem is different, however, than Dewey thought. Suppose growth had become malignant and the system, in fact, was not growing for the development of human potential through social acts but instead generating social aggression. Consider the example of expanded wars and technologies for destruction—ostensibly for security but in reality resulting in the reverse— with the social systems locked into a pathological frame of reference.

CHAPTER 2

1. Donald Lazere, "Money and Motives," *Inside Higher Education,* July 20, 2005, http://www.utexas.edu/conferences/africa/ads/907.html.
2. "The War Behind Closed Doors," "Excerpts from 1992 Draft," "Defense Planning Guidance,"*Frontline*, PBS, February 20, 2003.
3. George W. Bush, "President Increases Funding for Bioterrorism by 319 Percent" (speech, University of Pittsburgh, February 5, 2002).
4. "Buying Guns? No Big Deal,"*60 Minutes*, CBS News, March 20, 2005, http://www.cbsnews.com/stories/2005/03/18/60minutes/main681526 .shtml.
5. Sources for U.S. arms sales to foreign nations: Frida Berrigan and William D. Hartung, with Leslie Heffel, "U.S. Weapons at War 2005: Promoting Freedom or Fueling Conflict?" http://www.worldpolicy.org/projects/arms/reports/ wawjune2005.html; "Foreign Military Sales Deliveries and Commercial Exports Licensed Under AEAC," *Foreign Military Sales, Foreign Military Construction Sales and Military Assistance Facts as of September 2003*, Published by Deputy for Operations and Administration, Business Operations/ Comptroller, DSCA, Department of Defense; Project Ploughshares, "Armed Conflicts Report 2004," 2004; http://www.worldpolicy.org/projects/arms/ reports.html.
6. "White House Tries to Trim Military Cost," *New York Times*, C1, December 6, 2005. The *Times'* sources include the Department of Defense and the Government Accountability Office.
7. "Former Military Leaders Challenge Gonzales Nomination," *Bloomberg.com*, January 3, 2005, http://www.bloomberg.com/apps/news?pid=10000087& sid=a7nN9G6jWI0M&refer=top_world_news.
8. *Roper v. Simmons*, 03-633 (2005).
9. *Nuclear Nonproliferation Treaty.* George W. Bush reiterated his lack of concern for the Nuclear Nonproliferation Treaty in July 2005 when he announced his wish to give India sensitive nuclear technology and advanced nuclear-capable weapons systems that would violate the U.S. Nonproliferation Act of 2000 and the 1968 Nuclear Nonproliferation Treaty. Steven Zunes, "Bush Administration Stokes Dangerous Arms Race on Indian Subcontinent," http://www.fpif.org/fpiftxt/170.

    Comprehensive Nuclear Test Ban Treaty, http://www.ctbto.org/treaty/ treaty_text.pdf. In December 2000, Bush was quoted in a publication of *Foreign Policy in Focus* as saying, "We can fight the spread of nuclear weapons, but we cannot wish them away with unwise treaties." He went on to say that the CTBT was "unverifiable, unenforceable, and ineffective." http://www .fpif.org/pdf/gac/0012pentagon.pdf.

Anti-Ballistic Missile Treaty. In December 2001, Bush announced that the United States would withdraw from the ABM because it "hinders our government's ability to develop new ways to protect our people from future terrorist or rogue-state missile attacks." http://news.bbc.co.uk/1/hi/world/americas/1707812.stm.

Biological Weapons Convention. In July 2001, the Bush administration announced that it would not support a protocol to the BWC because it would do little "to deter countries from seeking biological weapons" and would not increase the ability of the United States to assure compliance to the BWC. http://www.armscontrol.org/act/2001_09bwcsept01.asp.

Chemical Weapons Convention. In the summer of 2001, Bush halted the power of the CWC significantly by denying CWC inspectors' access to American chemical manufacturers citing "national security issues and corporate espionage." http://michaeldigioia.com/published_nonlethal.html.

International Criminal Court. Bush was adamantly opposed to the ICC, a stance he has held since before the court's inception in 2002. He stated that he feels it "is fundamentally flawed because it puts American servicemen and women at fundamental risk of being tried by an entity that is beyond America's reach, beyond America's laws, and can subject American civilian and military to arbitrary standards of justice." The Bush administration made many bilateral agreements with countries in which it offers aid if they will not hold Americans accountable to the ICC. Apparently Bush II understood what he was doing with this objection given the way the United States fought the Iraq War. In August 2006, he asked Congress to rescind the third section of the Geneva Treaty on War Crimes so that American soldiers would not be held personally liable. http://www.useu.be/Categories/Justice%20and%20Home%20Affairs/July0202ICCCourtUSBush.html.

Fissile Material Cutoff Treaty. The Bush administration's Special Representative for Nuclear Nonproliferation, Jackie Sanders, stated in October 2004 that "the nature of an FMCT imposes significant practical limits on its verification" and that while the ban would halt production of fissile material used in nuclear weapons and explosives, other activities using fissile material not banned by the FMCT would not be affected. 164.109.48.86/is/Archive/2004/Nov/01-441408.html.

10. Peter Slevin, "Report Urges Tighter Nuclear Controls—White House Not Doing Enough to Secure Weapons Materials, Analysts Say," *Washington Post*, A02, May 24, 2004.

11. Science & Technology in Congress, "United States Signs Kyoto Protocol," September 1998, http://www.aaas.org/spp/cstc/pne/pubs/stc/bulletin/articles/12-98/kyoto.htm.

12. Professor Martin Parry, Jackson Environment Institute, School of Environmental Sciences, University of East Anglia, "Climate Change and Millions at Risk," memorandum to the United Kingdom Parliament, Select Committee on International Development Minutes of Evidence, July 23, 2002, http://www.publications.parliament.uk/pa/cm200102/cmselect/cmintdev/519/2012902.htm.

13. Associated Press, "Bush: Kyoto Would Have 'Wrecked' Economy," On the Net: Danish Broadcasting Corporation, July 1, 2005, http://asia.news.yahoo.com/050630/ap/d8b27s700.html.

14. Nicholas D. Kristof, "A Livable Shade of Green," *New York Times*, op-ed column, July 3, 2005.
15. "Climate Change Research Distorted and Suppressed," Union of Concern Scientists, excerpt from the 2004 UCS report Scientific Integrity in Policymaking, June 2005 update, EPA internal memo, April 29, 2003, http://www.ucsusa.org/scientific_integrity/interference/climate-change.html.
16. Andrew C. Revkin, "Top-level Editing on Climate Issues," *New York Times*, A1, June 8, 2005; Andrew C. Revkin, "Former Bush Aide Who Edited Reports Is Hired by Exxon," *New York Times*, A1, June 15, 2005.
17. Helena Cobban, "Unintended Consequences: A Forum on Iraq and the Mideast," *The Nation*, August 15, 2005.
18. "The Rise of the Religious Right in the Republican Party," *Theocracy Watch*, October 2005, http://www.theocracywatch.org/; Adam Nagourney, "G.O.P. Right Is Splintered on Schiavo Intervention," *New York Times*, March 23, 2005, http://freerepublic.com/focus/f-news/1368571/posts.
19. Kirkpatrick, David D., "Battle Splits Conservative Magazine," *New York Times*, http://www.nytimes.com/2005/03/13/weekinreview/13kirk.html?ei=5090&en=6e75395c6aaa1811&ex=1268456400&adxnnl=1&partner=rssuserland&adxnnlx=1155819840-RsNDEihQaItNlcBg9LaFzQ.

CHAPTER 3

1. "World Trade Center Explosion and Fire NY, NY February 26, 1993," *9-11 Research*, http://911research.wtc7.net/cache/wtc/bombing93/npfa_bombing93.htm.
2. "Terrorist Attacks (within the United States or against Americans Abroad)," *Infoplease*, http://www.infoplease.com/ipa/A0001454.html.
3. Bush Administration's First Memo on al-Qaeda Declassified, Document Central to Clarke-Rice Dispute on Bush Terrorism Policy Pre-9/11, National Security Archive Electronic Briefing Book No. 147, Edited by Barbara Elias, February 10, 2005 http://www2.gwu.edu/~nsarchiv/NSAEBB/NSAEBB147/.
4. "Events Related To bin Laden, Osama," *Harper's*, April 21, 2005, http://harpers.org/OsamaBinLaden.html.
5. Bush Administration's First Memo on al-Qaeda Declassified, Document Central to Clarke-Rice Dispute on Bush Terrorism Policy Pre-9/11, National Security Archive Electronic Briefing Book No. 147, Edited by Barbara Elias, February 10, 2005 http://www2.gwu.edu/~nsarchiv/NSAEBB/NSAEBB147/.
6. "Press Briefing by National Security Advisor Dr. Condoleezza Rice," May 16, 2002, http://www.whitehouse.gov/news/releases/2002/05/20020516-13.html.
7. Chalmers Johnson, "America's Empire of Bases," January 15, 2000. *Tom Dispatch.com*, Common Dreams NewsCenter, http://www.commondreams.org/.
8. Dave Moniz, "Army Misses Recruiting Goal," *USA Today*, March 3, 2005, http://www.usatoday.com/news/washington/2005-03-02-army-goal_x.htm.
9. The Church Committee presented the Interim Report "Alleged Assassination Plots Involving Foreign Leaders" during the 94th Congress, November 20,

1975. The committee's findings were presented to Congress in April 1976. http://www.aarclibrary.org/publib/church/reports/contents.htm.
10. The 9/11 Commission framework was limited to what the Bush II administration negotiated with them. Note that President George W. Bush consented to spending only one hour with the commission on policy. The meeting was held simultaneously with Vice President Cheney.
11. A personal note on the political nature of the word "terrorism": Orlando Letelier and Ronni Moffitt, two of Marcus Raskin's colleagues at the Institute for Policy Studies, were assassinated near the White House in 1976 by agents of Chilean dictator Augusto Pinochet. This was a clear case of state terrorism. Pinochet, with Washington's blessing—if not its collusion—had overthrown Chile's elected president, Salvador Allende, a Marxist, in 1973—on September 11! In January 2005, the eighty-nine-year-old Pinochet was placed under house arrest by the Chilean Supreme Court in connection with accusations of murder and kidnapping that had occurred under his seventeen-year dictatorship.
12. International Criminal Court, Article 4, "Legal Status and Powers of the Court," http://www.icc-cpi.int/library/about/officialjournal/Rome_Statute_120704-EN.pdf. The document reads: "The Court may exercise its functions and powers, as provided in this Statute, on the territory of any State Party and, by special agreement, on the territory of any other State." The court is a last resort and the United States refuses to accept this stance.
13. In a speech given to the American Society of International Law in April 2003, Supreme Court Justice Stephen Breyer stated, "We face an increasing number of domestic legal questions that directly implicate foreign or international law." http://www.humanrightsfirst.org/us_law/inthecourts/Supreme_Court_New_Interl_Law_Just_Breyer%20.pdf.

In a debate with Supreme Court Justice Antonin Scalia in April 2005, Breyer stated that in terms of international law, "It's appropriate in some instances to look at other places. It's not binding by any means. But if they have a way of working out a problem that's relevant to us, it's worth reading." http://www.law.com/jsp/article.jsp?id=1114160707182.
14. J. William Fulbright, *The Arrogance of Power* (New York: Random House, 1967).
15. Bernard Schwartz, *Super Chief: Earl Warren and His Supreme Court—A Judicial Biography* (New York: New York University Press, 1983); Lucas Powe Jr., *The Warren Court and American Politics* (Cambridge, MA: Belknap Press, 2000); Roger Newman, *Hugo Black: A Biography* (New York: Fordham University Press, 1997); Bruce Murphy, *Wild Bill: The Legend and Life of William O. Douglas* (New York: Random House, 2003); David Marion, *The Jurisprudence of Justice William J. Brennan, Jr.* (Lanham, MD: Rowman and Littlefield, 1997).

CHAPTER 4

1. *Schenck v. United States*, 249 U.S. 47 (1919).
2. Administration's Draft Anti-Terrorism Act of 2001, Testimony of John Ashcroft, United States Attorney General, to the U.S. House Committee of the Judiciary, September 24, 2001, http://www.house.gov/judiciary.
3. George W. Bush, "With My Signature, This Law Will Give Intelligence and Law Enforcement Officials Important New Tools..." (remarks, Washington

DC, October 26, 2001), http://www.whitehouse.gov/news/releases/2001/10/images/20011026-5.html.

4. Matthew Rycroft, "The Secret Downing Street Memo," *Sunday Times*, May 01, 2005, http://www.timesonline.co.uk/article/0,,2087-1593607_3,00.html. Rycroft was a Downing Street foreign policy aide.

5. Elisabeth Bumiller, "Bush and Blair Deny 'Fixed' Iraq Reports," *New York Times*, A7, June 8, 2005.

6. "Top Bush Officials Push Case Against Saddam," *CNN Inside Politics*, September 8, 2002, http://archives.cnn.com/2002/ALLPOLITICS/09/08/iraq.debate/.

7. George W. Bush, "Address to the United Nations" (address, New York, NY, September 12, 2002), *CNN.com*, http://archives.cnn.com/2002/US/09/12/bush/transcript/.

8. George W. Bush, "President Bush On Iraq," October 7, 2002, OnlineNewsHour, Transcript. http://www.pbs.org/newshour/bb/middle_east/july-dec02/bushspeech_10-7.html

9. Ambassador J. Richard Blankenship's remarks to the American Men's & Women's Club, Nassau, Bahamas, October 8, 2002, http://usembassy.state.gov/nassau/wwwhiraq.html.

10. George W. Bush, "State of the Union" (speech, Washington DC, February 5, 2002).

11. Colin Powell, "The Good Soldier Powell," *International Herald Tribune*, February 5, 2003, http://www.iht.com/articles/2004/11/15/opinion/edpowell.htm.

12. Bradley Graham, "Prewar Memo Warned of Gaps in Iraq Plans," *Washington Post*, A13, August 18, 2005.

13. "Tracking Intelligence Failures," *New York Times*, A11, April 1, 2005.

14. George W. Bush, "President Says Saddam Hussein Must Leave Iraq Within 48 Hours" (address, Washington DC, March 17, 2003), http://www.whitehouse.gov/news/releases/2003/03/20030317-7.html.

15. George Allen, statement made on March 19, 2003, http://allen.senate.gov/PressOffice/3172003.htm.

16. George W. Bush, "President Bush Addresses the Nation" (address, Washington DC, March 19, 2003), http://www.whitehouse.gov/news/releases/2003/03/print/20030319-17.html.

17. "Tracking Intelligence Failures," *New York Times*, A11, April 1, 2005.

18. John Ashcroft, "Al Qaeda Intends to Attack U.S.," March 26, 2004, *CNN.com*, http://archives.cnn.com/2004/US/05/26/terror.threat/.

19. Peter Johnson, "Amanpour: CNN Practiced Self-censorship," *USA Today*, September 17, 2003, USATODAY.com-Amanpour: CNN practiced self-censorship.

20. "Tailings Must Be Moved, 2 States Tell Congressmen," *Westerner*, March 19, 2005, http://www.thewesterner.blogspot.com.

21. Janet Burton Seegmiller, "Nuclear Testing and the Downwinders," The History of Iron County, http://historytogo.utah.gov/utah_chapters/utah_today/nucleartestingandthedownwinders.html.

22. *Paul Jacobs and the Nuclear Gang,* directed by Jack Willis, Saul Landau, and Penny Bernstein, 1980. The film won the 1980 Emmy Award for best TV program and the George F. Polk Award for investigative journalism on TV. http://saullandau.com/movies.html.

23. Anthony H. Cordesman, "Outside View: Pentagon Cost Overruns," United Press International, April 29, 2005, http://www.washtimes.com/upi-breaking/20050429-070103-4105r.htm.

24. Seymour M. Hersh, *The Price of Power*, (New York: Summit Books, 1984).

25. Richard C. Holbrooke, *Counsel to the President*, (New York: Anchor Doubleday, 1992).

26. Scott Peterson, "Remains of Toxic Bullets Little Iraq," *Christian Science Monitor*, May 15, 2003.

27. George W. Bush, "President Welcomes President Chirac to White House" (remarks, November 6, 2001), http://www.whitehouse.gov/news/releases/2001/11/20011106-4.html.

28. Dick Cheney, "Cheney Takes Aim At War Critics" (address, American Enterprise Institute, Washington, November 21, 2005), *CBS/AP*, http://www.cbsnews.com/stories/2005/11/21/politics/main1062120.shtml.

CHAPTER 5

1. George W. Bush, "Gov. Ridge Sworn-In to Lead Homeland Security" (remarks, Washington DC, October 8, 2001), http://www.whitehouse.gov/news/releases/2001/10/20011008-3.html.

2. Ibid.

3. Press Briefing by Ari Fleischer, Washington, March 19, 2002, http://www.whitehouse.gov/news/releases/2002/03/20020319-7.html.

4. Greg Barrett, "Homeland Security Runs Gamut of Pork," *Baltimore Sun*, March 25, 2005, http://www.fortwayne.com/mld/journalgazette/news/nation/politics/11228556.htm?template=contentModules/printstory.jsp.

5. Ibid.

6. Kate O'Beirne, "Introducing Pork-Barrel Homeland Security," *National Review*, September 8, 2003. Posted on Web site of U.S. Representative Christopher Cox, http//cox.house.gov/html/coverage.cfm?id=691.

7. Ibid.

8. U.S. Department of Transportation, "DOT Releases Preliminary Estimates Of 2001 Highway Fatalities,"April 22, 2002, http://www.dot.gov/affairs/nhtsa3102.htm.

9. "In Hospital Deaths from Medical Errors at 195,000 per Year USA," *Medical News Today*, August 9, 2004, http://www.medicalnewstoday.com/medicalnews.php?newsid=11856.

10. U.S. House Committee on Transportation and Infrastructure, "Six Million Loaded Containers Enter U.S. Ports Each Year," Security Of Shipping Containers Entering & Departing The United States To Be The Focus Of Congressional Hearing, March 11, 2002, http://www.house.gov/transportation/press/press2002/release206.html.

11. Eric Lipton, "Homeland Security Chief to Shift From 'Sky is Falling' Approach," *New York Times*, A21, March 17, 2005.

12. Michael Chertoff remarks presented at the Homeland Security Policy Institute, George Washington University, Washington DC, March 16, 2005, U.S. Department of Homeland Security, Press Room, http://www.dhs.gov/dhspublic/display?content=4391.

13. Elisabeth Bumiller, "Fingerprint System Bogged Down, Report Finds," *New York Times*, December 30, 2004, http://www.nytimes.com/2004/12/30/politics/30fingerprint.html?ex=1142485200&en=955845976b02ed3b&ei=5070.

14. Michael Chertoff, remarks, presented at George Washington University, the Homeland Security Policy Institute, George Washington University, Washington DC, March 16, 2005, U.S. Department of Homeland Security, Press Room, http://www.dhs.gov/dhspublic/display?content=4391.

15. Jeff Bailey, "For Delta, Another Obstacle to Normalcy," *New York Times*, August 8, 2006.

16. Michael Chertoff, remarks, presented at the Homeland Security Institute, George Washington University, Washington DC, March 16, 2005. U.S. Department of Homeland Security Press Room, http://www.dhs.gov/dhspublic/display?content=4391.

17. *New York Times Co. v. United States*, 403 U.S. 713 (1971).

18. Ian Seiderman, "FDR's Bill of Rights," Letter to the Editor, *New York Times*, April 21, 2005.

CHAPTER 6

1. Richard Posner, *Law, Pragmatism, and Democracy* (Cambridge, MA: Harvard University Press, 2003).

2. David Margolick, Evgenia Peretz, and Michael Shnayerson, "The Path to Florida," *Vanity Fair*, October 2004, http://www.makethemaccountable.com/articles/The_Path_To_Florida.htm.

3. Greg Palast, "1 Million Black Votes Didn't Count in the 2000 Presidential Election," *San Francisco Chronicle*, June, 20, 2004, http://sfgate.com/cgi-bin/article.cgi?file=/chronicle/archive/2004/06/20/ING2976LG61.DTL.

4. David Margolick, Evgenia Peretz, and Michael Shnayerson, "The Path to Florida," *Vanity Fair*, October 2004.

5. Ibid.

6. Robyn E. Blumner, "When Five Voted for Millions," *St. Petersburg Times*, September 26, 2004, citing David Margolick, *Vanity Fair*, October 2004, http://www.sptimes.com/2004/09/26/Columns/When_five_voted_for_m.shtml.

7. Antonin Scalia, concurring, *George W. Bush et al. v. Albert Gore, Jr. et al.*, No. 00-949 (00A504), 531 U.S. 98 (2000), "On Application for Stay," http://www.daveross.com/scotus1209.html.

8. Jamin Raskin, *Overruling Democracy: The Supreme Court vs. The American People* (New York: Routledge Press, 2003); Bruce Ackerman, *Bush v. Gore: The Question of Legitimacy* (New Haven: Yale University Press, 2002).

9. Scott Shane, "Never Shy, Bolton Brings a Zeal to the Table," *New York Times*, May 1, 2005, 1.

10. John Paul Stevens, dissenting, *George W. Bush et al. v. Albert Gore, Jr. et al.*, No. 00-949, 531 U.S. 98 (2000), "On Writ of Certiorari to the Florida Supreme Court," http://www.romingerlegal.com/floridacourts/supreme_opinions/USStevensDissent.html.

11. Blumner, "When Five Voted for Millions."

12. "Carter, Baker to Work on Election Reform," Associated Press/ABC News, March 25, 2005,http://abcnews.go.com/Politics/print?id=613372.

13. "Caltech-MIT Team Finds 4-6 Million Votes Lost in 2000 Election," analysis, California Institute of Technology and Massachusetts Institute of Technology, July 16, 2001, http://web.mit.edu/newsoffice/nr/2001/voting2.html.

14. Responding to some fifty thousand complaints from Ohioans about irregularities found in the state in the 2004, Congressman John Conyers and the minority [Democratic] staff of the House Judiciary Committee began an investigation in January 2005 and prepared a status report. The committee noted "numerous, serious election irregularities in the Ohio presidential election, which resulted in a significant disenfranchisement of voters. The final staff report of close to four hundred pages was as complete as possible without subpoena power." http://www.truthout.org/docs_05/010605Y.shtml.

Sometimes, petty regulations discourage voting. A June 7, 2006, editorial in the *New York Times* observed that Ohio's secretary of state, J. Kenneth Blackwell, a Republican, "instructed county boards of elections to reject any registrations on paper of less than 80-pound stock—about the thickness of a postcard. His order was almost certainly illegal, and he retracted it after he came under intense criticism. It was, however, in place long enough to get some registrations tossed out." For the 2008 election, it appears that Republicans in Ohio—and Florida—have a variety of strategies to make voter registration more difficult. Republicans would never say it, of course, but they worry they will lose if too many poor and minority voters register—they will vote against them. That seems to have been the intention of Georgia's Republican legislators, who passed a law requiring voters to show a government-issued photo ID at the polls before they could vote—in effect an unconstitutional poll tax. U.S. District Judge Harold Murphy barred the state from imposing the law, stating that it would "most likely prevent Georgia's elderly, poor and African-American voters from voting." Bill Rankin, "Judge Halts Voter ID Law," *Atlanta Journal-Constitution*, October 19, 2005, http://www.ajc.com/search/content/auto/epaper/editions/today/news_34551f78820e80e50027.html.

15. Madison's view of how the federal government should operate excluded the idea of bonds of affection so important in eighteenth-century thought and the reason for the American revolution.

16. The Federalist No. 15, "Insufficiency of the Present Confederation to Preserve the Union," *Independent Journal*, December 1, 1787. http://www.constitution.org/fed/federa15.htm.

17. In 1971, Marcus Raskin wrote, "During the cold war it would have seemed shockingly impertinent to think of America as a colony. When I suggested that the Vietnam War and the civil rights struggle were related because white 'citizens' were powerless in such public matters as foreign policy, and black 'citizens' were also powerless, thus showing evidence of Americans as colonized, the notion was put down as a metaphor. Now it appears that the idea of America as a colonized society is neither impertinent nor metaphorical. It is closer to a realistic description of what the American body politic is than can otherwise be imagined." (*Being and Doing*, xii; see note 3 of chapter 1.)

18. See note 8.

19. Kevin Krajick, "Why Can't Ex-Felons Vote?" *Washington Post*, A19, August 18, 2004. http://www.washingtonpost.com/wp-dyn/articles/A9785-2004Aug17.html.

CHAPTER 7

1. Eric Lichtblau, "F.B.I. Goes Knocking for Political Troublemakers," *New York Times*, A1, August 15, 2004.

2. Lisa Myers, Douglas Pasternak, Rich Gardella and the NBC Investigative Unit, "Secret database obtained by NBC News tracks 'suspicious' domestic groups," MSNBC, December 14, 2005, http://www.msnbc.msn.com/id/10454316/.

3. James Risen and Eric Lichtblau, "Bush Lets U.S. Spy on Callers Without Courts," *New York Times*, December 16, 2005, 1. (The *Times* admitted that it sat on the story for a year, bowing to the White House request not to publish the article before the election because it "could jeopardize continuing investigations and alert would-be terrorists that they might be under scrutiny.")

    This is not the first time the secret National Security Agency has come under fire. Investigating the NSA in 1975, Senator Frank Church (D-Idaho) was shocked by the extent of its reach in a much less sophisticated technological age. A fearful Church warned "that capability at any time could be turned around on the American people, and no American would have any privacy left, such is the capability to monitor everything: telephone conversations, telegrams, it doesn't matter. There would be no place to hide.... There would be no way to fight back because the most careful effort to combine together in resistance to the government, no matter how privately it was done, is within the reach of the government to know.... I don't want to see this country ever go across the bridge. I know the capacity that is there to make tyranny total in America, and we must see to it that this agency [the National Security Agency] and all agencies that possess this technology operate within the law and under proper supervision, so that we never cross over that abyss. That is the abyss from which there is no return."

4. George W. Bush, "President's Radio Address," Washington, December 17, 2005, http://www.whitehouse.gov/news/releases/2005/12/20051217.html.

5. Eric Lichtblau, "F.B.I. Watched Activist Groups, New Files Show," *New York Times*, A1, December, 20, 2005.

6. Leslie Cauley, "NSA Has Massive Database of Americans' Phone Calls," *USA Today*, 1A, May 10, 2006.

7. Eric Lichtblau and James Risen, "Bank Data Is Sifted by U.S. in Secret to Block Terror," *New York Times*, A1, June 23, 2006; Sheryl Gay Stolberg and Eric Lichtblau, "Cheney Assails Press on Report on Bank Data," *New York Times*, A1, June 24, 2006.

8. Douglass K. Daniel, "U.S. Classifies Documents at Record-setting Pace," Associated Press, April 5, 2005, http://www.unknownnews.org/0504120405classifiedinfo.html.

9. Tony Snow, "Clinton Will Forever Be Measured Against What He Could Have Been," *Jewish World Review*, January 18, 2001, http://www.jewishworldreview.com/cols/snow1.asp

10. "The Effects of the Bush Tax Cuts on State Tax Revenues," Citizens for Tax Justice, May 2001, http://www.ctj.org/html/statefx.htm.

11. Office of Management and Budget, Executive Office of the President, Department of Defense, December 21, 2005, http://www.whitehouse.gov/omb/budget/fy2005/defense.html.

12. Bryan Bender, "Oversight of War Spending is Faulted," *Boston Globe*, December 4, 2005, http:www.boston.com/news/world/articles/2005/12/04/oversight_of_war_spending_is_faulted.

13. William D. Nordhaus "The Economic Consequences of the War with Iraq (study of the cost of the war in Iraq in late 2002)," http://www.econ.yale.edu/~nordhaus/homepage/homepage.htm.

14. Congressional Budget Office's Economic Projections for 2003 Through 2013, http://www.cbo.gov/showdoc.cfm?index=4493&sequence=6, cited by David Firestone, "Dizzying Dive to Red Ink Poses Stark Choices for Washington," *New York Times*, September 14, 2003.

    As shocking and fiscally damaging as the deficit numbers cited in "The Authoritarianism of Premeditated Budget Deficits" section are, some believe that they are actually *low*! CNN's Lou Dobbs, decried, "Our federal government keeps two sets of books: one that shows our budget deficit shrank to $319 billion last year [2005] and the Treasury Department set that shows $760 billion.... It turns out that our national debts and commitments actually stand at an incredible $49 trillion.... The federal government uses a quaint accounting system that would be illegal for any large enterprise in America." Lou Dobbs, "It's Good to Be a Superpower," *CNN*, August 17, 2006, http://www.cnn.com/2006/US/08/15/dobbs.august16/index.html. However, there is no law that mandates that the federal government should have the same accounting system as a profitmaking corporation.

15. "Quotations From & About Casey Stengel," *Baseball Almanac*, http://www.baseball-almanac.com/quotes/quosteng.shtml.

16. *Fresh Air*, WHYY, National Public Radio, October 2, 2003, http://www.npr.org/templates/story/story.php?storyId=1452983.

17. Ed Kilgore, "Starving the Beast," *Blueprint Magazine*, Democratic Leadership Council, June 30, 2003.

18. Paul C. Light (Director, Governance Studies,) Center for Public Service, Fact Sheet on the New True Size of Government, September 5, 2003, http://www.brookings.edu/gs/cps/light20030905.pdf.

19. National Coalition for Homeless Veterans, "Most Often Asked Questions Concerning Homeless Veterans," http://www.nchv.org/background.cfm.

20. President George W. Bush, Post-Election Press Conference, Washington, November 4, 2004

21. Amy Klamper, "Pentagon Report Criticizes New Version of C-130J Transport Plane," *CongressDaily*, January 24, 2005, http://www.govexec.com/dailyfed/0105/012405cdpm3.htm.

22. Byron Dorgan, "Global Shell Games" *Washington Monthly*, July/August, 2000, http://www.washingtonmonthly.com/features/2000/0007.dorgan.html.

23. Jack Rasmus, "Crash Landing," *In These Times*, June 6, 2005, http://www.inthesetimes.com/site/main/article/2137/.

24. REAP...Review of U.S. Union Membership, October 1, 2004, http://www.reapinc.org/Profile%20Trade%20Union.html.

25. Wagner Act, *Encyclopædia Britannica*, 2005. Encyclopædia Britannica Premium Service. 21 Dec. 2005, http://www.britannica.com/eb/article?tocId=9075846.

26. The Pullman company manufactured railroad sleeping cars. Its workers lived in a town owned by the company, and as a result of depressed conditions in

the 1890s the company cut wages substantially but kept prices in the town at their former high level, destroying workers' capacity to survive financially. The strike was broken by federal troops, but it was pivotal in labor history because of the issues it raised.

27. Industrial Fires, http://www.emergency-management.net/indl_fire.htm.
28. Steven Greenhouse, "Workers Assail Night Lock-Ins by Wal-Mart," *New York Times*, January 18, 2004, http://www.nytimes.com.
29. Conrad F. Meier, *Health Care News*, June 1, 2001, The Heartland Institute, http://www.heartland.org/Article.cfm?artId=672.
30. "Bush Administration Record on Public Lands: Irresponsible Management of the People's Land," the Wilderness Society, February 2005, http://www.wilderness.org/Library/Documents/BushRecord.cfm.
31. "U.S. Law & Policy: In Depth: Report Gale Ann Norton, An Environmental Profile," Natural Resources Defense Council, http://www.nrdc.org/media/pressreleases/010112.asp.
32. Kate Zernike and Annie E. Kornblut, "Link to Lobbyist Brings Scrutiny to G.O.P. Figure," *New York Times*, A1, May 23, 2005.
33. Center for Media & Democracy, SourceWatch, http://www.sourcewatch.org/index.php?title=J._Steven_Griles.
34. People For the American Way, Report on William G. Myers III, http://www.pfaw.org/pfaw/general/default.aspx?oid=13640.
35. "SFI= Same Old Forest Industry," advertisement, *New York Times*, May 20, 2005, Signers included Natural Resources Defense Council, Sierra Club, and Greenpeace.
36. Alan C. Miller and Tom Hamburger, "Whitman Denies Knowing Mercury Study Was Stalled," *Los Angeles Times*, March 19, 2004 (originally posted at http://www.latimes.com/news/science/environment/lanmercury19mar19,1,1889402.story?coll=la-news-environment).

CHAPTER 8

1. The legislation would limit participation to a low, specific-dollar amount for individual taxpayers. Those who received an earned income tax credit of, for example, $50, would receive the same vote credit as would those on welfare and other taxpayers.
2. United States Constitution, Article 3, Section 2 (3).
3. Jeffrey H. Birnbaum, "The Road to Riches Is Called K Street," *Washington Post*, A01, June 22, 2005.

In a front-page article in the June 18, 2006, *New York Times*, Eric Lipton reported that "at least 90 officials at the Department of Homeland Security or the White House Office of Homeland Security—including the department's former secretary, Tom Ridge; the former deputy secretary, Adm. James M. Loy; and the former undersecretary, Asa Hutchinson—are executives, consultants or lobbyists for companies that collectively do billions of dollars' worth of domestic security business.... More than two-thirds of the department's most senior executives in its first years have moved through the revolving door." For instance, "Carol A. DiBattiste, who made $155,000 in 2004 as deputy administrator at the Transportation Security Administration, earned more than $934,000 last year from ChoicePoint, a Homeland Security Department contractor she joined in April 2005, the same month she left the agency."

What is ChoicePoint? Adm. Loy explained in his June 3, 2003, statement before the House Appropriations Committee Subcommittee on Homeland Security: "ChoicePoint is the leading provider of identification data to all federal law enforcement agencies, as well as 7,500 state and local agencies and major corporations across the country. More than half of the nation's largest 1000 corporations use ChoicePoint to review the backgrounds of prospective employees. Nonprofit organizations also use ChoicePoint to screen volunteers who work with children and the elderly. ChoicePoint's database of more than 17 billion public records includes in excess of 63 million criminal convictions and other identity verification data." http://www.tsa.gov/public/display?theme=81&content=090005198002d4e5.

According to the online encyclopedia Wikipedia, "ChoicePoint maintains a database of names, addresses, *Social Security numbers* [italics added], credit reports, and other sensitive information. Its DNA laboratory aided in the identification of victims of the WTC attacks, and data supplied by ChoicePoint was used in the Beltway Snipers investigation." http://en.wikipedia.org/wiki/ChoicePoint.

4. Leslie Wayne, "Same Washington, Different Office—John Ashcroft Sets Up Shop As Well-Connected Lobbyist," *New York Times*, March 17, 2006, C1. Ashcroft, Bush II's first attorney general, explained: "Clients would call in an individual who has a reputation for the highest level of integrity. Those who have been in government should not be forbidden from helping people deal with government, which is what I see myself doing." Wayne reported that Ashcroft used the word "integrity" scores of times during the hour-long interview.

5. "New Technology Can Help Prevent Civilian Casualties, Bush Says," commencement remarks, U.S. Naval Academy, Annapolis, May 27, 2005, http://usinfo.state.gov/usinfo/Archive/2005/May/27-168520.html.

6. "News & Highlights From the Boycotts Final Year," May, 2005, *Coalition of Immokalee Workers*, http://www.ciw-online.org/2004-05news.html.

7. Gabriel Kolko, *Another Century of War?* (New York: New Press, 2002).

8. The Pentagon Papers became the colloquial term for "United States-Vietnam Relations, 1945-1967: A Study Prepared by The Department of Defense," a 47-volume, 7,000-page, top-secret United States Department of Defense history of the United States' political and military involvement in the Vietnam War from 1945 to 1971, with a focus on the internal planning and policy decisions within the U.S. Government. The study was commissioned in 1967 by Secretary of Defense Robert McNamara. The Pentagon Papers included 4,000 pages of actual documents from the 1945–1967 period, and 3,000 pages of analysis. (http://en.wikipedia.org/wiki/Pentagon_Papers)

9. "The Defense Budget Time Bomb," Transcript, America's Defense Monitor, Produced May 5, 1996, by the Center for Defense Information, http://www.cdi.org/adm/934/transcript.html.

10. David Von Drehle, "FBI's No. 2 Was 'Deep Throat,'" *Washington Post*, A01, June 1, 2005.

11. "Nuclear Oversight," Government Accountability Project, November 2005, http://www.whistleblower.org/template/page.cfm?page_id=10.

12. Paul Douglas Ethics Institute of Ethics and Public Affairs, University of Illinois, December 25, 2005, http://www.igpa.uiuc.edu/ethics/fitzgerald-bio.htm.

13. Christopher Lee, "Whistle-Blower Case at Issue," *Washington Post*, A27, October 25, 2002.

14. "AFGE Protests Mandatory Pledge for Homeland Security Employees," American Federation of Government Employees AFL-CIO News, November 29, 2004, http://www.afge.org/Index.cfm?Page=PressReleases&PressRelease ID=401.

15. Andrew C. Revkin, "Climate Expert Says NASA Tried to Silence Him," *New York Times*, 1, January 29, 2006.

16. Juliet Eilperin, "Debate on Climate Shifts to Issue of Irreparable Change," *Washington Post*, A01, January 29, 2006, , http://www.washingtonpost.com/wp-dyn/content/article/2006/01/28/AR2006012801021.html.

17. Andrew C. Revkin, "NASA Chief Backs Openness," *New York Times*, A1, February 4, 2006. A particularly revealing example (reported by Revkin in the February 4 *New York Times*) was an order issued by George Deutsch, a Bush II presidential appointee in NASA's headquarters instructing the agency's Web designer to add "theory" after every mention of the Big Bang. "The Big Bang is 'not a proven fact; it is opinion,'" wrote Deutsch. "It is not NASA's place, nor should it be to make a declaration such as this about the existence of the universe that discounts intelligent design by a creator," the 24-year-old Deutsch added. His resume said he had graduated from Texas A&M University and had been an intern in the "war room" of the 2004 Bush-Cheney reelection campaign. (On February 8, *The Times* reported that Deutsch had resigned from NASA when Texas A&M "confirmed that he did not graduate from there, as his résumé on file at the agency asserted.")

On February 16, 2006, Revkin reported that "Top political appointees in the NASA press office exerted strong pressure during the 2004 presidential campaign to cut the flow of news releases on *glaciers, climate, pollution and other earth sciences* [ital. added], public affairs officers at the agency say."

On August 8, 2006, Revkin reported that federal scientists at the National Climatic Data Center said that the first seven months of 2006 "were the warmest such stretch in the continental United States for any year since climate record-keeping began in 1895.... The long-term trend we're seeing cannot be explained without the influence of greenhouse gases," said a spokesman for the Center.

18. "About False Claims Act (FCA) Lawsuits," Project on Government Oversight, January 2, 2002, http://www.pogo.org/p/environment/ea-001028-oil.html.

PART TWO: FREEDOM TO WORSHIP

CHAPTER 9

1. Horace Greeley Foundation, quote from Harold Laski, *The American Democracy* (New York: Viking, 1948).

2. Fawn M. Brodie, *Jefferson: An Intimate History* (New York: W. W. Norton, 1974).

3. Jane I. Smith, "Patterns of Muslim Immigration," U.S.Info.State.Gov Publications. (Based on information from the Hartford Institute for Religious Research), http://usinfo.state.gov/products/pubs/muslimlife/immigrat .htmu. Note as well that in its inception as a religion, Protestantism did not

command the support of those who came to the New World who were not believers. See Franklin Hamlin Littell, *From State Church to Pluralism: A Protestant Interpretation of Religion in American History* (New York: Anchor Books, 1962), 32.

4. Pope Leo XIII, in his 1891 encyclical "Rerum Novarum," observed the disparity between the plight of exploited workers and the vast prosperity of wealthy industrialists. The blatant injustice called for strong intervention on the part of the church. The encyclical was a call for social justice and for the dignity of workers, http://www.cst-phl.com/051027/main.html. In 1981, Pope John Paul II released "Laborem Exercens," an encyclical concerning decent wages and working conditions. In 1986, Rembert Weakland, Archbishop of Milwaukee, was the chair of a bishops' letter called "Economic Justice for All: Pastoral Letter on Catholic Social Teaching and the U.S. Economy." In 1997, Weakland followed up the letter in an address: "Economic Justice for All, 10 Years Later," (Race Superiority Studies), http://woodstock.georgetown.edu/wbc/wbc-r42.htm. See also: Garry Wills, "Under God: Religion and American Politics" (New York: Simon and Schuster, 1990).

5. Note the treatment of Anne Hutchinson who challenged the ministers of Puritanism and who was banished for this effrontery. The Puritans persecuted the Quakers. A supporter of Hutchinson, Mary Dyer, was hanged as a Quaker. See Franklin Hamlin Littell, *From State Church to Pluralism: A Protestant Interpretation of Religion in American History* (New York: Anchor Books, 1962). The Hutchinson River Parkway, an old but essential automobile route from New York City through Westchester County, is named after Anne Hutchinson who lived in the area. A commemorative sign can be seen while driving. The Commonwealth of Massachusetts placed a statue of Anne Hutchinson in front of the state house in 1915 and added a statue of Mary Dyer in 1959, the only seventeenth-century Massachusetts colonists so honored, according to the Massachusetts Historical Society, http://www.historycooperative.org/journals/mhr/6/bremer.html.

6. "Father Charles E. Coughlin, The Radio Priest," *Detroit News*, Rearview Mirror, http://info.detnews.com/history/story/index.cfm?id=43&category=people.

7. John Cornwall, *Hitler's Pope: The Secret History of Pius XII* (London: Penguin, 2000).

8. Ibid. Hitler defended his action in a talk with Bishop Berning and Monsignor Steinmann. After reminding the priests that the church had banished Jews into ghettos and forbidden Christians to work with them, Hitler explained that he regarded the Jews as "nothing but pernicious enemies of the State and Church, and therefore he wanted to drive the Jews out more and more, especially from academic life and public professions." He was only going to do more effectively what the Church of Rome had been attempting to do for so many centuries. Quote from John Toland, *Adolf Hitler* (New York: Ballantine Books, 1976), 311.

9. John Cornwall, *Hitler's Pope: The Secret History of Pius XII* (London: Penguin, 2000). Note especially the work of John Dewey. Throughout his life, Dewey pitted science (verification open to corrections) and religion holding to fixed principles, a feature of absolutism. Joseph Ratner, *Intelligence in the Modern World: Philosophy of John Dewey* (New York: Modern Library, 1939).

10. Marcia A. Hamilton, *God vs. the Gavel: Religion and the Rule of Law* (New York: Cambridge University Press, 2005).

11. "U.S. Presidents and the Bible." http://www.bebaptized.org/u.htm.

12. Ibid

13. Ibid.

14. Peter Meyer, *James Earl Carter: The Man and the Myth* (Kansas City: Sheed Andrews and McMeel, Inc., 1978), 61, 66.

15. Sidney Blumenthal, "The Religious Warrior of Abu Ghraib," *Guardian*/UK, May 20, 2004, http://www.guardian.co.uk/Iraq/Story/0,2763,1220781,00 .html.

16. Mike Mount, "Air Force Probes Religious Bias Charges at Academy," CNN Washington Bureau, Thursday, May 5, 2005, citing report from Americans United for Separation of Church and State, http://www.cnn.com/2005/US/ 05/03/airforce.religion/.

17. David Vest, "Billy Graham, Tangled Up in Tape," CounterPunch's Booktalk, March 5, 2002, http://www.counterpunch.org/vestgraham.htm.

18. Katherine van Wormer, "'Dry Drunk' Syndrome and George W. Bush," *CounterPunch*, October 11, 2002, http://www.counterpunch.org/wormer1011 .html.

19. Ibid.

20. Alan Bisbort, "Dry Drunk," *American Politics Journal*, September 24, 2002, http://www.americanpolitics.com/20020924Bisbort.html.

21. "A Library of Quotations on Religion and Politics by George W. Bush," citation from *New Orleans Times-Picayune*, December 25, 1999, http://www .beliefnet.com/story/33/story_3345_1.html.

22. George W. Bush, "President Delivers 'State of the Union,'" Washington, January 28, 2003, http://www.whitehouse.gov/news/releases/2003/01/ 20030128-19.html.

23. Ibid.

24. George W. Bush, "President Bush Addresses the 51st Annual Prayer Breakfast," Washington, February 6, 2003, http://www.whitehouse.gov/ news/releases/2003/02/20030206-1.html

25. George W. Bush, "Address to a Joint Session of Congress and the American People," Washington, September 20, 2001, http://www.whitehouse.gov/ news/releases/2001/09/20010920-8.html.

26. Erna Paris, "The New World Disorder," *The Globe and Mail*, March 3, 2003, http://www.ernaparis.com/news/globe_disorder.htm.

27. David Greenberg, "Fathers and Sons," *New Yorker*, July 12 and 19, 2004.

28. Robert MacFee Brown, "The Need for a Moral Minority," http://www .harvardsquarelibrary.org/speakout/brown.html.

29. George W. Bush, "President Bush Delivers Graduation Speech at West Point," West Point, New York, June 1, 2002, http://www.whitehouse.gov/news/ releases/2002/06/20020601-3.html.

30. George W. Bush, "President Bush Addresses the 51st Annual Prayer Breakfast," Washington, February 6, 2003.

31. *The Scofield Reference Bible* (New York: Oxford University Press, 1909, 1917, copyright renewed 1937, 1945), 625.

32. Ibid., 631.

33. Ibid., 714.

34. "Onward, Christian Soldiers," words by Sabine Baring-Gould (1865), music by Arthur S. Sullivan: "St. Gertrude," 1871, http://www.cyberhymnal.org/htm/o/n/onwardcs.htm.

CHAPTER 10

1. Christian Coalition, Wikipedia, http://en.wikipedia.org/wiki/Christian_Coalition.
2. Focus on the Family, http://family.org/.
3. Tony Perkins Biography, Family Research Council, July 11, 2005, http://www.frc.org/get.cfm?i=BY03H27.
4. Tony Perkins, "Justice Sunday," Family Research Council: April 24, 2005, http://www.frc.org/get.cfm?i=PR05D09.
5. The KKK could not sustain that number during the Depression because of corrupt leadership in Indiana and a murder conviction against a Klan leader, David Stephenson.
6. Frances Fitzgerald, "Holy Toledo," *New Yorker*, July 31, 2006.
7. William V. D'Antonio, "Walking the Walk on Family Values, *Boston Globe*, Boston Globe.Com News, October 31, 2004, http://www.boston.com/news/globe/editorial_opinion/oped/articles/2004/10/31/walking_the_walk_on_family_values/.
8. Bill Keller, "God and George W. Bush," *New York Times*, op-ed, A17, May 16, 2003.

CHAPTER 11

1. Jason DeParle, "In Battle to Pick Next Justice, Right Says Avoid a Kennedy," *New York Times*, A1, June 27, 2005.
2. Robert H. Bork, *Slouching Towards Gomorrah: Modern Liberalism and American Decline* (New York: Regan Books, 1996).
3. Paul Krugman, "What's Going On?" column, op-ed page, *New York Times*, March 29, 2005.
4. "DeLay Statement on Terri Schiavo," released by then House Majority Leader Tom DeLay (R-Texas) "Mourning the Passing of Terri Schiavo," March 31, 2005, http://releases.usnewswire.com/GetRelease.asp?id=45102.
5. In late 2005, the House of Representatives approved a budget reconciliation bill that made reductions in many areas that would hit poor people hard. In terms of Medicaid, users will be made to pay more of their own money for health care as cuts of almost thirty billion dollars—given Bush II assumptions and Rightist administrations—that will occur over the next ten years to 2015. In terms of childcare, "some 330,000 children in low-income families in which the parents are working and are not on welfare would lose their child care subsidies" by 2010, http://www.cbpp.org/10-21-05bud.htm.
6. George W. Bush, "Remarks by the President in Announcement of the Faith-Based Initiative," Washington, January 29, 2001, http://www.whitehouse.gov/news/releases/20010129-5.html8.
7. George W. Bush, "Rallying the Armies of Compassion," Overview of the Faith-Based and Community Initiative Report, Washington, http://www.whitehouse.gov/news/reports/faithbased.html.

8. George W. Bush, "President Promotes Faith-Based Initiative," Washington, April 11, 2002, http://www.whitehouse.gov/news/releases/2002/04/20020411-5.html.

9. Don Lattin, "Moonies Knee-deep in Faith-based Funding Pushing Celibacy, Marriage Counseling Under Bush Plan," *San Francisco Chronicle*, October 3, 2004, http://www.sfgate.com/cgi-bin/article.cgi?f=/c/a/2004/10/03/MOON.TMP.

10. Robert Longley, "Bush-friendly Church Gets $1 Million 'Faith-based' Grant," *About News and Issues*, http://usgovinfo.about.com/od/rightsandfreedoms/a/bushchurch.htm.

11. Laura Meckler, "$1 Billion of Your Money Was Given to Religious Groups in 2003," Associated Press, January 2, 2005, http://groups.yahoo.com/group/deathtoreligion/message/8901.

12. Ron Suskind, "Why Are These Men Laughing?" *Esquire*, January 1, 2003, http://www.ronsuskind.com/newsite/articles/archives/000032.html.

13. Ibid.

14. Ibid

15. Introduction to Suskind's *Esquire* article, http://www.ronsuskind.com/newsite/articles/archives/000032.html.

16. Executive Orders Disposition Tables Administration of George W. Bush (2001–Present), The National Archives, *Federal Register*, http://www.archives.gov/federal-register/executive-orders/wbush.html.

17. David Kuo, "Shooting from the Heart," Beliefnet, 2005, http://www.beliefnet.com/story/160/story_16092_2.html.

18. *Elk Grove Unified School Dist. v. Newdow*, No. 02-1624. Decided June 14, 2004, http://caselaw.lp.findlaw.com/scripts/getcase.pl?court=US&vol=000&invol=02-1624.

19. "Muslim Chaplin Captain James Yee's Muzzle," *Washington Post*, Comment, April 18, 2004, cited in *American Muslim Perspective*, http://www.archives2004.ghazali.net/html/yee_muzzle.html.

20. Marcia A. Hamilton, *God vs. the Gavel: Religion and the Rule of Law* (New York: Cambridge University Press, 2005), 143–72.

21. Garry Wills, "The Bishops vs. the Bible," op-ed, *New York Times*, June 27, 2004.

CHAPTER 12

1. Zelman, Superintendent of Public Instruction of Ohio, et al. v. Simmons-Harris et al. No. 00-1751. Decided June 27, 2002. But in 2006, the Florida Supreme Court struck down a Florida law that created the first statewide education voucher program in the United States (Florida Supreme Court, Case Number: SC04-2323, John Ellis "Jeb" Bush, Etc., Et Al. vs. Ruth D. Holmes, Et Al., decision released January 5, 2006). Reported Sam Dillon in *New York Times*, January 6, 2006, "In a ruling expected to reverberate through battles over school choice in many states, the Florida Supreme Court struck down a voucher program yesterday for students attending failing schools, saying the state Constitution bars Florida from using taxpayer money to finance a private alternative to the public system."

See Simone Weil's *Gateway to God* (Glasgow: Collins, Fontana Books, 1974); *The Notebooks of Simone Weil* (New York: Routledge, 2004); and the biography by Simone Pétrement, *Simone Weil: A Life* (New York: Pantheon Books, 1976).

CHAPTER 13

1. It is a great mystery that people are prepared to accept a hierarchic structure, often brutal in nature, because it purports to represent that which is not understood or that which is not there. The power of this predominately patriarchal system is that it took upon itself the cloak of morality as it also complemented status quo power and worse. As the philosopher of religion Ernst Bloch put it, the poor and the exploited saw that the "shepherds of his soul" stood in complacency as it supported the most ruthless elements in political and economic life. Ernst Bloch, *Atheism in Christianity* (New York: Herder and Herder, 1972), 58.

2. There are numerous reasons for the failure of Soviet communism, which are detailed in Marcus Raskin, "Death in the Soviet Union," *Visions and Revisions* (Amherst, MA: Interlink, 1995). Russia had some of the greatest theoreticians in the world, but they were unable to turn their capacities into concrete projects of technological innovation for the society; this was a task that Nicholai Bukharin, the leading Soviet theoretician—before he was executed in the Moscow trials orchestrated by Stalin—had thought critical.

    The official Russian Orthodox Church lived very comfortably in the Soviet Union with its priests living at peace by the end of the 1930s with Stalinism. Authoritarian systems have a way of adjusting to one another. In fairness, after the Second World War, the struggles went forward between the West's view of Christianity against Sovietism, especially as it related to competition over the control of lands in eastern Europe and the propensity of both sides to cross over into the ideological and political territory of the other regarding the ideological and practical issue of property.

3. For an incisive account of the politics and science of survival, see Mario Biagoli, *Galileo Courtier* (Chicago: University of Chicago Press, 1993), 312–52. Biagoli discusses what Galileo had agreed to; namely, that he would not hold or defend that the "sun is the center of the world and the earth moves." Biagoli argues that the patron system was fundamental in understanding the rise of particular scientific views; when the patron died, the scientist had to find a new protector. Pope Urban VIII had been a close friend of Galileo but, according to Biagoli, set Galileo for his fall from favor in order to protecting the church and himself against doctrines that might undercut the church's power and indeed their entire belief system. One can understand the importance of the scientist when he is legitimated socially, plays the role of the courtier, and then turns against (or is turned against) the system he served. The interesting modern case is that of J. Robert Oppenheimer, the scientific head of the Manhattan Project. Note Kai Bird and Martin Sherwin, *American Prometheus* (New York: Knopf, 2005).

4. David F. Noble, "The Ascent of the Saints—Space Explorations," chap. 9 in *The Religion of Technology* (New York: Knopf, 1997), 115 et seq. It was not only earthlings finding God in genes and the Armageddon of war. Noble, the

gifted historian of technology, points out the religious sentiments (those that were more than public relations) that gripped astronauts in space.

5.   The question of the belief in documents such as the Bible, which simultaneously use myth as reality and a teaching device to the young, is given a powerful gloss as scientific endeavor in its most profound sense resolves some questions and then opens doors to even more complex ones. The result is that humankind still seeks a form of belief, many in absolutism. That sentiment is found throughout the United States, Russia, the Middle East in different religions, and in Asia. The expropriation of certain words such as "democracy" by absolutist and Rightist movements in the United States betrays the idea of openness and discovery so important to freedom, scientific inquiry, and democracy. John Dewey, "Experience as Problematic: Ethical, Religious, Political, and Social Dimensions," sect. 8 in *The Philosophy of John Dewey*, vol. 2, *The Lived Experience*, ed. John McDermott (Chicago: University of Chicago Press, 1981).

6.   Marcus Raskin and Herbert Bernstein, et al., *New Ways of Knowing* (Totowa, NJ: Rowman and Littlefield, 1987). This book of essays questions the basis of how knowledge is made, opening the further question of whether there can or should be a moral component to scientific inquiry beyond the proscription that scientists should not lie about their process or results. This, of course, does not deal with the more profound questions of the implications of certain scientific discoveries. It should be noted that scientists early on pointed out the danger of *E. coli* getting into the food chain and that experiments with *E. coli* could become very harmful.

In the popular mind, scientists have gone through different stages: first as the creators of Frankensteins, then as providers of life-saving miracle drugs, and now as deniers and pretenders to God. But do scientists have special responsibilities inherent in their manipulation of nature? The obvious answer is yes; the question is how these responsibilities are to be recognized and fulfilled.

7.   When religions teach peaceful solutions of disputes while analyzing their own traditions for that instrumental purpose, humanity has a chance of survival. If religious institutions act and use up people's lives worrying about Heaven, Hell, and the Devil, people will think of the world as a prison without any possibility of improvement in ways that matter to themselves. The chance of a civilization accepting of conflict but not of the war system will not be aided by religion nor, one might say, will God be any happier because Her name is constantly invoked whether as light or sitting on a throne or even nowhere except in our hearts.

8.   After the Second World War, religious philosophers and theologians sought this understanding and pressed these arguments in their work. Perhaps most important were Gandhi, Martin Buber, Paul Tillich, Jacques Maritain, Dorothy Day, Ernst Bloch, and A. J. Muste. One of the most significant social and religious inventions over the last two decades are reconciliation commissions based on the ideas of truth, justice, and then reconciliation and forgiveness. They have proved important and successful, especially in South Africa, where Bishop Tutu plays a leading role in the formation and execution of the process.

PART THREE: FREEDOM FROM WANT

CHAPTER 14

1. United States Department of Agriculture, Census of Agriculture, cited in *New York Times*, June 4, 2004.
2. Richard J. Barnet and Ronald E. Muller, *Global Reach: The Power of the Multinational Corporations* (New York: Simon & Schuster, 1975).
3. Victor Davis Hanson, "A Secretary for Farmland Security," op-ed, *New York Times*, December 9, 2004.
4. Sherwood vs. Walker, http://islandia.law.yale.edu/ayers/mutual.htm.
5. "Even Bush Administration, Meat Producers Back Away From Organic Standards Bill Change While USDA Remains 'Neutral,'" *Agribusiness Examiner*, February 21, 2003, Issue #223, citing an Associated Press story.
6. Elaine Zelmanov, "High Priestess of Slow," *Mother Jones*, May 5, 2003, http://www.motherjones.com/news/featurex/2003/05/we_405_01.html.
7. Amir Attaran, Donald R. Roberts, Chris F. Curtis, and Wenceslaus L. Kilama, "Balancing Risks on the Backs of the Poor," *Nature Medicine*, July 2000, Vol. 6, Number 7, 29-731.
8. National Center for Infectious Diseases, Centers for Disease Control and Prevention, December 5, 2003, http://www.cdc.gov/ncidod/diseases/food/index.htm.
9. "Mad Cows and Democratic Governance: BSE and the Construction of a 'Free Market' in the UK," David M. C. Bartlett, Department of Politics, University of Leeds, UK, Abstract, *Crime, Law and Social Change*, Volume 30, Number 3, 237–57, September, 1998, Springer Science+Business Media B.V., Formerly Kluwer Academic Publishers B.V., http://www.springerlink.com/(25s4tnysxrnot0ezgxpuytmu)/app/home/contribution.asp?referrer=parent&backto=issue,2,8;journal,49,60;linkingpublicationresults,1:102868,1.
10. Donald G. McNeil Jr., "U.S. Reduces Testing for Mad Cow Disease, Citing Few Infections," *New York Times*, A13, July 21, 2006.
11. Gardiner Harris, "At F.D.A., Strong Drug Ties and Less Monitoring," *New York Times*, A1, December 6, 2004.
12. Marian Burros, "Eating Well; A Vulnerable Food Supply, A Call for More Safety," *New York Times*, October 31, 2001, http://query.nytimes.com/gst/fullpage.html?sec=health&res=9C07E5DA1530F932A05753C1A9679C8B63. In the July 10, 2002 *New York Times*, Burros reported that Carol Tucker Foreman, director of the Food Policy Institute at the Consumer Federation of America, underscored the problem of the Agriculture Department wearing two hats: "The tradition at U.S.D.A. is you do everything possible to avoid closing a [meat and poultry] plant because the U.S.D.A.'s mandate from Congress is to promote consumption and production of agricultural projects. But there is a conflict of interest between that and public health, and protection of public health always comes in second." (http://query.nytimes.com/gst/fullpage.html?sec=health&res=9800E3DA1430F933A25754C0A9649C8B63)
13. General Accounting Office, cited by Tom Bearden, in "Bad Beef," Online NewsHour, September 20, 2002, http://www.pbs.org/newshour/bb/health/july-dec02/beef_9-20.html.
14. Anita Manning, "Listeria Fear Prompts Largest U.S. Meat Recall," *USA Today*, October 13, 2002. (Sources: USA TODAY research, The American Meat

Institute), http://www.usatoday.com/news/nation/2002-10-13-wampler-recall_x.htm.

15. "Clouds of Injustice: Bhopal Disaster Report," Amnesty International, November 29, 2004, http://web.amnesty.org/pages/ec-bhopal-eng.

16. Wikipedia, "Berkshire County, Massachusetts, 2000," http://en.wikipedia.org/wiki/Berkshire_County,_Massachusetts.

17. "Progress Towards the Millennium Development Goals, 1990–2005," The United Nations Statistics Division, June 13, 2005, http://unstats.un.org/unsd/mi/mi_coverfinal.htm.

18. John Cavanagh and Jerry Mander, eds., *Alternatives to Economic Globalization: A Better World is Possible* (San Francisco: Berrett Koehler Press, 2004).

CHAPTER 15

1. Franklin. D. Roosevelt, Message to Congress on the State of the Union, January 11, 1944, http://www.worldpolicy.org/globalrights/econrights/fdr-econbill.html.

2. Bill Clinton, *My Life* (New York: Knopf, 2004); John F Harris, *The Survivor: Bill Clinton in the White House* (New York: Random House, 2005); Lani Guinier, *Lift Every Voice: Turning a Civil Rights Setback Into a New Vision of Social Justice* (New York: Simon & Schuster, 1998).

CHAPTER 16

1. "Transcript Al Smith Dinner Speeches by Bush and Gore," October 19, 2000, Published: Free Republic.com a conservative forum, Source: Fox News, http://www.freerepublic.com/forum/a39f13cb7182c.htm.

2. "Poverty: 2004 Highlights," Current Population Survey (CPS), 2005 Annual Social and Economic Supplement (ASEC), the source of official poverty estimates, U.S. Census Bureau, Housing and Household Economic Statistics Division, Last Revised: August 30, 2005, http://www.census.gov/hhes/www/poverty/poverty04/pov04hi.html.

3. David Brooks, "Reacquaint Republicans With Republican Tradition," *New York Times Magazine*, August 29, 2004.

4. "Child Poverty," Analysis of Census Bureau Data, Children's Defense Fund, October 2004, http://www.childrensdefense.org/familyincome/childpoverty/default.aspx.

5. Paul Krugman, "For Richer," *New York Times Magazine*, October 20, 2002.

6. "Food Security in the United States: Conditions and Trends," Economic Research Service, United States Department of Agriculture, Household Food Security in the United States, 2004, http://www.ers.usda.gov/Briefing/FoodSecurity/trends/.

7. "Executive Excess 2005 Report," Institute for Policy Studies and United for a Fair Economy.

8. However, it appears that Germany *did* aid the United States with military intelligence data before the U.S. invasion. Note February 27–March 3, 2006 newspaper reports, including the *New York Times* and the *Washington Post*.

9. De Gaulle speech referenced in Marcus G. Raskin, *The Common Good* (New York and London: Routledge and Kegan Paul, 1986); Mahbub Ul Haq, Inge Kaul, Isabelle Grunberg, *The Tobin Tax: Coping with Financial Volatility* (New

York: Oxford University Press, 1996); Brian Urquhart and Erskine Childers, "Renewing The United Nations System," *The New York Review of Books*, http://www.dhf.uu.se/pdffiler/Urquhart.pdf. President Jacques Chirac, speech, International conference on "Solidarity and Globalization: innovative financing for development and against pandemics," February 28, 2006, http://www.diplomatie.gouv.fr/en/francep-priorities_1/ development_2108/innovative-ways-to-fund-development_2109/ international-conference-on-solidarity-and-globalization-innovative-financing-for-development-and-against-pandemics-february-28-march-1-2006_3964.html.

10. Attempts have been made in this direction by the U.S. Catholic Conferences statements on economic justice versus capitalism.

11. James Surowiecki, "A Farewell to Alms," *New Yorker*, July 25, 2005, 40.

12. *The American Treasury 1455–1955*, Selected, Arranged, and Edited by Clifton Fadiman, (New York: Harper & Brothers, 1955), 45.

13. Elsa Walsh, "Minority Report," *New Yorker*, August 8 & 15, 2005, 44.

14. "Incarceration and Race," Human Rights Watch, http://www.hrw.org/ reports/2000/usa/Rcedrg00-01.htm.

15. Ewing v. California, U.S. Supreme Court, Certiorari to the Court of Appeal of California, Second Appellate District, No. 01—6978, Decided March 5, 2003, http://www.law.cornell.edu/supct/html/01-6978.ZS.html.

16. *The World Book Encyclopedia*, 1974, s.v. "John R. Alden."

17. Robert Pear, "Welfare Spending Shows Huge Shift," *New York Times*, A1, October 13, 2003.

18. Pamela J. Loprest, a senior research associate in the Income and Benefits Policy Center of the Urban Institute, "Fewer Welfare Leavers Employed in Weak Economy," No. 5 in Series, "Snapshots of America's Families III." Posted: August 21, 2003, http://www.urban.org/url.cfm?ID=310837.

CHAPTER 17

1. Barbara Starfield, MD, MPH, "Is U.S. Health Really the Best in the World?" *Journal of the American Medical Association* 284 (July 26, 2000), http://www .nutritionreallyworks.com/JAMA.html. Note, however, that the United States is the largest of the nations by population.

2. Ibid.

3. Center on Budget and Policy Priorities, "The Number of Uninsured Americans is at an All-time High," analysis of data released by the Census Bureau, August 29, 2006, http://www.cbpp.org/8-29-06health.htm.

4. Ibid.

5. "The State of America's Children 2004: A Continuing Portrait of Inequality Fifty Years After *Brown v. Board of Education*," Children's Defense Fund, Posted July 13, 2004, http://www.childrensdefense.org/pressreleases/ 040713.aspx.

6. "The Number of Uninsured Americans Continued to Rise in 2004," Center on Budget and Policy Priorities, analysis of data released by the Census Bureau, August 30, 2005, http://www.cbpp.org/8-30-05health.htm.

7. Ibid.

8. Cathy Schoen, MS, Michelle M. Doty, PhD, Sara R. Collins, PhD, and Alyssa L. Holmgren, "Insured But Not Protected: How Many Adults Are

Underinsured?" The Commonwealth Fund, Journal/Source: Health Affairs Web Exclusive, June 14, 2005, http://www.cmwf.org/publications/publications_show.htm?doc_id=280812.

9. Center on Budget and Policy Priorities, "The Number of Uninsured Americans Continued to Rise in 2004," analysis of data released by the Census Bureau, August 30, 2005, http://www.cbpp.org/8-30-05health.htm , citing Ha Tu, "Rising Health Costs, Medical Debt and Chronic Conditions," Issue Brief No. 88, Center for Studying Health Systems Change, September, 2004.

10. Institute of Medicine of the National Academies, "Insuring America's Health: Principles and Recommendations," January 14, 2004, http://www.iom.edu/CMS/3809/4660/17632.aspx.

11. Address of the Chairman of the Association of American Medical Colleges, November 10, 2002, commenting on the Flexner Report, which linked American medicine to science as a means of building on scientific discoveries and data. Ralph Synderman calls for a new next stage "prospective medical care" that one might charitably describe as developing new delivery models, which build on managed care but are highly personalized.

12. There is an expanding market in the United States for alternative theories of medicine including greater attention to diet and willingness on the part of patients to identify "new" categories of healers such as ancient Chinese (or Oriental) medicine. The National Institutes of Health recognizes alternative cures as important and beyond pharmaceutical drugs. National Center for Complimentary and Alternative Medicine, http://nccam.nih.gov/.

13. PRNewswire-FirstCall, "NDCHealth Reviews 2004 Pharmaceutical Market Information," May 2, 2004, http://www.prnewswire.com/cgibin/micro_stories.pl?ACCT=603950&TICK=NDC&STORY=/www/story/05-02-2005/0003537082&EDATE=May+2,+2005.

14. Stephanie Saul and Jenny Anderson, "Doctors' Links With Investor Matchmakers Raise Concerns," New York Times, A1, August 16, 2005.

15. PRNewswire-FirstCall, "NDCHealth Reviews 2004 Pharmaceutical Market Information," May 2, 2004, http://www.prnewswire.com/cgibin/micro_stories.pl?ACCT=603950&TICK=NDC&STORY=/www/story/05-02-2005/0003537082&EDATE=May+2,+2005.

16. Steffie Woolhandler, MD, MPH, Terry Campbell, MHA, and David U. Himmelstein, MD, "Costs of Health Care Administration in the United States and Canada," New England Journal of Medicine 349 (August 21, 2003): 768–75, http://content.nejm.org/cgi/content/abstract/349/8/768 (abstract).

17. Katherine Eban, "Waiting for Bioterror," The Nation, December 9, 2002, http://www.thenation.com/doc/20021209/eban/2 (posted November 21, 2002).

18. Michele Keller and Bushra Khan, "'Good Doctor' Frist Doesn't Care About Women's Health," National NOW Times, Spring 2003, http://www.now.org/nnt/spring-2003/frist.html.

19. U.S. Department of Justice, June 26, 2003, http://www.usdoj.gov/opa/pr/2003/June/03_civ_386.htm.

20. Dr. Wolfe and the Public Citizen Health Research Group have monitored all aspects of the health industry since its inception in 1972–1973.

21. Lee B. Reichman, MD, Executive Director, New Jersey Medical School National Tuberculosis Center, "Why AIDS in Asia Should Worry Us," Letter to the Editor, New York Times, July 11, 2004, http://www.nytimes.com/

2004/07/11/opinion/L11AIDS.html?ex=1137214800&en=e97c6cbf068d8e4a
&ei=5070.

22. "Deficiencies in US Medical Care," Letters, *Journal of the American Medical Association*, 284, no. 17 (November 1, 2000), http://jama.ama-assn.org/cgi/content/extract/284/17/2184-a. Since the 1970s, members of Congress have offered legislation for a comprehensive national health plan. For an in-depth view of the Kennedy/Long/Ribicoff plans, see Marcus Raskin, "The Federal Budget and Social Reconstruction" (Washington DC: IPS, 1978). Note especially essays by Louise Lauder, Marilyn Elrod, James Gordon, Janet Sledge, and Sandra Kelman. The bureaucratic quagmire of the Nixon bill was extended in the Clinton legislation, which included protections for private insurance companies, with the government serving as protector and sometimes regulator. In 2006, there were two comprehensive pieces of legislation, which were based on the assumption that the health system needs fundamental change. One bill, HR676, the "United States Insurance Act," was sponsored by several dozen members of Congress. The Chief Sponsor was Congressman John Conyers (D-Mich.). A second bill, HR3000, was named the "Josephine Butler United States Health Service Act." It was sponsored by Congresswoman Barbara Lee (D-Calif.). Both bills reject a market-based solution to the health crisis on the grounds that while not explicitly stated, the conservative method of sticking with a private system will continue to result in spiraling insurance and high technology costs for new medical machinery, which increasingly only the rich will be able to afford.

23. Gloria Borger, "A tale of two titans," *U.S. News & World Report*, June 6, 2004, http://www.usnews.com/usnews/opinion/articles/040621/21glo.htm.

24. The National Coalition on Health Care, "Facts on Health Insurance Coverage," http://www.nchc.org/facts/coverage.shtml, citing Institute of Medicine, "Hidden Costs, Values Lost: Uninsurance in America," The National Academies Press, June 17, 2003.

25. National Health Information Center, "Health Highlights: June 1, 2006," http://www.healthfinder.gov/news/newsstory.asp?docID=533044.

CHAPTER 18

1. Fawn M. Brodie, *Jefferson: An Intimate History* (New York: W. W. Norton, 1974). There is no reason to romanticize the moral character of the founding fathers. The scurrilous attacks and counter-attacks concerning race between Jefferson, Hamilton, and other supporters should disabuse us of the notion of the "gentlemanly" standards of eighteenth and early nineteenth century political debate.

2. Marcus Raskin, position paper, Bureau of Budget, 1961, records of the Institute for Policy Studies, 1961–1992, 186.3 c.f., Wisconsin Historical Society Archives, Madison, Wisconsin 53706.

3. "The State of America's Children 2004: A Continuing Portrait of Inequality Fifty Years After Brown v. Board of Education," Children's Defense Fund, Posted, July 13, 2004, http://www.childrensdefense.org/pressreleases/040713.aspx.

4. "Education Secretary Says He Understands, Endorses Church-state Separation," http://religion.com/, April 10 2003 archives, http://www.onreligion.com/article.php?story=20030913222120586.

5. Felicia R. Lee, "Survey of the Blogosphere Finds 12 Million Voices," *New York Times*, B3, July 20, 2006.
6. John Cavanagh, Director, Institute for Policy Studies, interview with Robert Spero, Washington DC, April 2, 1998.
7. Ibid.
8. For an extended discussion of citizenship and its obligations in the modern world, see Marcus Raskin, *Essays of a Citizen, From National Security State to Democracy* (Armonk: M.E. Sharpe, 1991); *Visions and Revisions* (New York: Interlink Publishing Group, 1998), final chapter; Marcus G. Raskin, *The Common Good* (New York and London: Routledge and Kegan Paul, 1986).
9. This was Herbert Hoover's view, which drew sharp distinctions between political democracy and the operations of a corporation for the purpose of creating production.

PART FOUR: FREEDOM FROM FEAR

CHAPTER 19

1. Exchange of open letters between Albert Einstein and Sigmund Freud concerning questions presented to them by the League of Nations, published as a pamphlet "Why War?" in Paris in 1933.
2. Dan Baum "This Gun for Hire," *Wired*, February 2003, http://www.wired.com/wired/archive/11.02/gunhire_pr.html.
3. Matt Fellowes, Bruce Katz, Amy Liu, and Nigel Holmes, figures based on "The State of New Orleans: An Update," Op-Ed, *New York Times*, July 5, 2006.
4. Tom Roberts, *National Catholic Reporter*, December 27, 2002, ncronline.org/NCR_Online/archives/122702/122702b.htm
5. Fawn M. Brodie, *Jefferson: An Intimate History* (New York: W. W. Norton, 1974).
6. Jill Zuckman, "Kerry Zeroes In On Cheney Draft Record," *Chicago Tribune*, April 28, 2004, http://www.chicagotribune.com/news/nationworld/chi0404280272apr28,1,6443180.story?coll=chi-newsnationworld-hed.
7. David R. Mets, *Master of Airpower: General Carl A. Spaatz* (Novato: Presidio Press, 1988), 302–5.
8. Judith Nies, *Native American History* (New York: Ballantine Books, 1996). The long-term project on the part of the more liberal-minded white leaders who sought land for white settlers while seeking to limit genocide was Indian removal—or what in current parlance would be called "ethnic cleansing."
9. It should be noted that Jefferson was by no means an advocate and suffered the obloquy of the Federalists who claimed that he was weak and unpatriotic because he did not jump to making war with European powers. He believed that economic expansion was the primary means of increasing American standing. Such policies included, besides the Louisiana Purchase, applying means to "guide" Indians into the money economy, which resulted in the indebtedness to stores operated by the United States. The result was continued loss of Indian lands reserved for them through "treaties."
10. Historians consider Polk as a "near great" president. Interestingly, Lincoln opposed the Mexican War as an aggressive war although the Supreme Court under Chief Justice Tawney ruled that the United States does not fight

aggressive wars, only defensive wars (*Fleming v. Page*, 9 Howard 615, http://www.radford.edu/~mfranck/images/490%20seminar/Bates%20opinion.pdf). For a very sympathetic account of American expansion and the powers of the president, see Rexford Guy Tugwell, *Enlargement of the Presidency* (Garden City, NY: Doubleday Publishers, 1960).

11. Judith Nies, *Native American History* (New York: Ballantine Books, 1996).

12. William Appleman Williams, *Tragedy of American Foreign Policy* (New York: W. W. Norton, 1988); *The Roots of the Modern American Empire* (New York: Oxford University Press, 1984); *Empire as a Way of Life: An Essay on the Causes and Character of America's Present Predicament Along With a Few Thoughts About an Alternative* (New York: Oxford University Press, 1982).

13. Admiral Alfred T. Mahan, *The Interest of American Sea Power: Present and Future* (http://indypublish.com/, 2005).

14. http://en.wikipedia.org/wiki/PhilippineAmerican_War#American_torture_and_scorched-earth_campaigns.

15. Robert Beisner, *Twelve Against Empire: The Anti-Imperialists 1898–1900* (New York: McGraw Hill, 1968).

16. In December 1914, S. Stanwood Menken founded the National Security League. The NSL "was a private initiative that sought to advocate for the conservative political and economic policies held by many of the most influential capitalists, industrialist (sic) in the country." The League was against the "various disturbing elements generally masquerading under the guise of socialism." The NSL found little sympathy with Wilson and his partisans "who were clearly for peaceful solutions to world conflict." The idea for the NSL began during the Theodore Roosevelt years (http://toto.lib.unca.edu/findingaids/mss/Biltmore_industries/seely_women/cocroft/). The NSL was funded by U.S. Steel, the Rockefeller oil companies, "and others concerned with national defense" (www.fff.org/freedom/0595c.asp). "Prominent in the organization of the National Security League were Frederic R. Coudert, Wall Street attorney for the British, French, and Russian governments; Simon and Daniel Guggenheim; T. Coleman DuPont, of the munitions family; and a host of prominent Morgan-oriented financiers; including former Morgan partner Robert Bacon; Henry Clay Frick of Carnegie Steel; Judge Gary of U.S. Steel; George W. Perkins, a Morgan partner who has been termed "the secretary of state" for the Morgan interests; former President Theodore Roosevelt; and J. P. Morgan himself" (http://www.lewrockwell.com/rothbard/rothbard66.html). "He [TR] supported the National Security League" (http://tigger.uic.edu/~rjensen/tr.htm). He was not an official member but he was a staunch supporter.

17. Arthur Link, *Wilson: The Struggle for Neutrality, 1914–1915*, Vol. 3 (Princeton: Princeton University Press, 1963); Arthur Link, *Woodrow Wilson and the Progressive Era, 1910–1917* (New American Nation Series), (New York: Harper Collins, 1954).

18. Harry V. Jaffa, "The Sinking of the Lusitania: Brutality, Bungling, or Betrayal?" http://www.winstonchurchill.org/i4a/pages/index.cfm?pageid=49.

19. By 2005, others believed democracy was an empty slogan—one that no self-respecting leader had to take seriously in cases in which popular elections did not favor the American government's candidate.

20. The LaFollette Progressive Party platform reaffirmed the position of LaFollette progressives against entanglement with Europe. It became the basis for LaFollette's campaign for president in 1924, which garnered more than five million votes—17 percent of the votes. It should also be noted that in the run up to the 1932 Democratic nomination, Franklin Roosevelt did not campaign for the League of Nations and America's entrance after seeing James Cox defeated on the issue (with himself as vice presidential candidate) in 1920.

21. http://www.geocities.com/Heartland/Valley/8920/European/leachart .html.

22. President Harding stated at the Washington Conference (1921–1922) that there should be no more war. The Republicans rejected collective security and instead favored disarmament. The treaty, an arms control measure, called for a 10-year ban on new warships as well as outlawing poison gases. It should be noted, however, that the United States did not approve a treaty in 1925, which outlawed the use of poisonous gases. The American political purpose in world politics sought a military, that is, naval balance, which would retain for the United States freedom of the seas that, in turn, would establish and protect open markets.

23. Hoover believed that the Kellogg-Briand Pact in 1928 would lead to a new period of international relations that stated war was obsolete. As he said on July 24, 1929, "I dare predict...that the influence of the 'Treaty for the Renunciation of War' will be felt in a large proportion of all future international acts." One must not forget that Hoover chaired a relief effort to Russia after the First World War. He concluded that militarism was wasteful and anticapitalist. This view lost any credibility among Republicans by 1960. See Alexander de Conde, *A History of American Foreign Policy*, (New York: Scribners & Sons, 1963), 512.

24. For example, in Hoover's book on mining and engineering, he refers to nonwhites as the minor "race." At the London Disarmament Conference of 1935, the Japanese objected to the way they were treated and walked out of the conference when they were not given parity with the United States and other Western powers on shipbuilding. The Japanese sought a substantial enough force to give them a strong hand in negotiations with Pacific powers, including the United States, on matters of commerce and spheres of influence in the Pacific. Under FDR, the United States had no intention of signing onto such an arrangement. See "Isolated Japan; Anglo-American Diplomatic Cooperation 1927–1936," *Pacific Historical Review*, xxx (May) 1961, 169. Noted by Alexander de Conde, *A History of American Foreign Policy*, (New York: Scribners & Sons, 1963), 514.

25. Three volumes edited by Franz Schurmann and Orville Schell (New York: Random House, 1967) concerning *Imperial China* (vol. 1), *Republican China* (vol. 2), and *Communist China* (vol. 3) give a clear picture of China's internal struggles from the beginning of the twentieth century to the beginning of the 1960s.

26. "1945: Thousands of bombs shower Dresden," BBC News, bbc.co.uk, http:// news.bbc.co.uk/onthisday/hi/dates/stories/february/14/newsid_3549000/ 3549905.stm.

27. Liberal New Dealers and columnists were especially exercised over the fact that Hirohito was not tried as a war criminal. See Timothy P., Maga *Judgment at Tokyo: The Japanese War Crimes Trials* (Lexington: University Press of Kentucky, 2001).

28. The head of OSS operations in Switzerland, Allen Dulles, went to the Potsdam Conference in Germany in 1945 (when Truman, Stalin, and Churchill—who was succeeded by Clement Atlee when Atlee's Labor Party defeated Churchill's Conservative Party in 1945—to confer on post–Second World War arrangements in Europe and Japan and, one may speculate, for the purpose of laying out Japanese peace terms. Switzerland was a listening post for Axis and Allied agents.
29. Steve Schwartz, "The Real Cost of Nuclear Weapons," The Brookings Institution, cited in *In Democracy's Shadow*, Marcus Raskin and Carl LeVan, Editors (New York: Nation Books, 2005), 133.
30. Daniel B. Bullen and James M. McCormick, "Disposing of the World's Excess Plutonium." *Policy Studies Journal*. 26.4 (1998): 682–703, cited in "Nuclear Waste: Storage and Disposal Methods," http://www.etsu.edu/writing/3120f99/zctb3/nuclear2.htm#nw6.
31. Henry Ford, a bizarre mixture of pacifist and anti-Semite, published the anti-Semitic Czarist-era forgery, "The Protocols of the Learned Elders of Zion," in his newspaper, the *Dearborn* (Michigan) *Independent*, in the 1920s as proof of a Jewish plan for world domination. The notorious myths are still cited by anti-Semites, especially in the Middle East.
32. The Nazis were also eager to control the Middle East for the purpose of controlling oil, which it needed for domestic use but mostly for feeding its war machine. World conquest seemed to Hitler to be in Germany's grasp if it could be sure that Japan would "stay the course" militarily after Pearl Harbor. What the Nazis feared was that the attack on Pearl Harbor was merely a brilliant strategy to attain a quick, favorable, negotiated settlement with the United States. This would have exposed the Nazis to fight both the United States and the Soviets without Japan.
33. A. J. P. Taylor, *The Origins of the Second World War* (New York: Simon & Schuster, 1961).
34. Gordon A. Craig and Gilbert Felix, eds., *The Diplomats: 1919–1939* (Princeton: Princeton University Press, 1953).
35. The stance of Roosevelt before and during the Second World War favored an end to European empires and the third world. His view was a cause of great concern for the British, especially Winston Churchill.
36. With the emergence of the National Security State, citizen warriors were specifically trained through the war and industrial colleges. They had the effect of "civilianizing the military and militarizing the civilians" for world responsibilities and expanding missions.
37. This was consistent with studies and recommendations to General H. H. "Hap" Arnold after the Second World War (Arnold directed the Army Air Forces throughout the war) that the Air Force should not rely solely on the atomic bomb. The American answer to the Air Force was overseas bases and heavy bombers as the major delivery vehicles for the United States.
38. *The World Book Encyclopedia*, 1974, s.v. "Walter G. Hermes."
39. For a brief but incisive account, see Fred Cook, *The Nightmare Decade: The Life and Times of Senator Joe McCarthy* (New York: Random House, 1971), 209–38.
40. Under the terms of the United Nations Charter, in very special circumstances, the UN General Assembly may authorize sending troops to answer a threat to the peace.

41. Bruce Cumings, *Origins of the Korean War, Vol. 1: Liberation and the Emergence of Separate Regimes, 1945–1947* (Princeton: Princeton University Press, 1981); Bruce Cumings, Ervand Abrahamian, and Moshe Ma'Oz, *Inventing the Axis of Evil: the Truth about North Korea, Syria and Iran* (New York: New Press, 2006). The Defense budgets favored the buildup of U.S. military forces in Europe, with very little increase in budgets for the American war in Korea.

42. There was another aspect to the war in Indochina: demoralization of troops as a result of no coherent and workable military strategy, no moral base for the American enterprise, and dreadful combat conditions that led to the practice of "fragging" in which enlisted men killed and maimed their own officers and sergeants. Such events were common occurrences and became, for the general staff, one important reason to withdraw from the war in Vietnam. See David Cortright, *Soldiers in Revolt* (New York: Haymarket Books, 2005). See also: Bruce Cumings, *"Origins of the Korean War," Vol. 1: Liberation and the Emergence of Separate Regimes, 1945–1947* (Princeton: Princeton University Press, 1981); Bruce Cumings, Ervand Abrahamian, and Moshe Ma'Oz, *Inventing the Axis of Evil: the Truth about North Korea, Syria and Iran* (New York: New Press, 2006); I. F. Stone, *The Hidden History of the Korean War, 1950–1951* (New York: Little Brown, 1988); *After 20 Years*, (New York: Random House, 1966); Richard J. Barnet and Marcus Raskin, *After 20 Years: Alternatives to the Cold War in Europe* (New York: Random House, 1965).

43. The Olson case concerning a CIA agent who was unknowingly fed LSD and who committed suicide became a minor cause célèbre in the late 1970s when his family sued the CIA.

44. http://en.thinkexist.com/quotes/dean_rusk/.

45. Francis Fitzgerald, *Way Out There in the Blue: Reagan, Star Wars and the End of the Cold War* (New York: Simon & Schuster, 2000).

46. The leading advocate of the time in the House of Representatives was Congressman Don Fraser of Minnesota, who sought an "objective" standard for denying assistance to particular nations that had egregious human rights records. It was hoped that with a scorecard kept on them, their improvement with regard to human rights would allow the offending nation to then receive economic assistance from the United States.

47. General Lee Butler, "Abolition of Nuclear Weapons" (speech at National Press Club, Washington DC, December 4, 1996), Nuclear Age Peace Foundation 1998–2006, http://www.wagingpeace.org/articles/1996/12/04 _butler_abolition-speech.htm.

48. Bush I came from Skull & Bones, the secret, elite Yale society, to war hero, a fine resume for a prudent imperialist. He served a term in Congress where he voted against the Voting Rights Act of 1964, lost his bid for Senate, became envoy to China, ambassador to the UN, director of the CIA, and then vice president. Kitty Kelley, *The Family: The Real Story of the Bush Dynasty* (New York: Anchor, 2005); Kevin Phillips, *The American Dynasty: Aristocracy, Fortune, and the Politics of Deceit in the House of Bush* (New York: Viking Press, 2004).

49. One may speculate that Thatcher feared Bush I's "wobbly" response because his administration backed the Iraqis in their war with Iran, giving commercial licenses to Saddam for the manufacture of chemical materials used in the war with Iran. Bush I's senior advisors, Richard Cheney and Donald Rumsfeld, actively favored Saddam Hussein against the Shiite fundamentalist revolution inspired by Ayatollah Khomeini in Iran.

50. "Oral History: Richard Cheney [Dick Cheney]," *Frontline*,PBS Online, http://www.pbs.org/wgbh/pages/frontline/gulf/oral/cheney/1.html.
51. Robert Fisk, *The Great War for Civilisation: The Conquest of the Middle East* (New York: Knopf, 2005); Noam Chomsky, *Hegemony or Survival: America's Quest for Survival* (New York: Metropolitan Books, 2003); Phyllis Bennis, *Beyond the Storm: A Gulf Crisis Reader* (New York: Olive Branch Press, 1991).
52. "Fast Facts About Operations Desert Shield and Desert Storm," U.S. Department of Defense, January 16, 2006 (From the 1991 *Defense Almanac*), http://www.defenselink.mil/news/Aug2000/n08082000_20008088.html.
53. After the 1983 truck bombing of the Marine Corps barracks in Beirut, Lebanon killed 241 American servicemen and injured 60 (the bloodiest day in the Marine's history since fighting to secure Iwo Jima in the Second World War), President Reagan, who had stated that America would never leave Lebanon, abruptly pulled out. Reagan then found a new target: the tiny Caribbean island nation of Grenada, which the United States invaded ostensibly to save some American students. (The students later denied they were in any danger.) The American public forgot about the loss of American lives in the Middle East, as Reagan's forces "defeated" Grenada. (http://www .asu.edu/clas/polisci/cqrm/APSA2004/Cramer.pdf)
54. "Highlights from SIPRI Yearbook, 2005," Stockholm International Peace Research Institute, http://yearbook2005.sipri.org/highl/highlights.
55. Linda Bilmes (Kennedy School of Government, Harvard University), "The Trillion-Dollar War," op-ed, *New York Times*, August 20, 2005, http://www .nytimes.com/2005/08/20/opinion/20bilmes.html?ex=1282190400&en=e68 42bf28ce308c3&ei=5090&partner=rssuserland&emc=rss.
56. William S. Broad, "Accountability Office Finds Iself Accursed," *New York Times*, 18, April 2, 2006. Reagan, of course, was an accomplished film and political illusionist. He may have known that the Star Wars program was an elaborate ploy that forced the Russians into a missile arms race. His domestic political task was to fool Congress into thinking that the Defense Department test program was a success. In fact, the program was a multi-billion-dollar lie, which Congress accepted. It then applauded Reagan for his cleverness in lying to them and increasing the high tech budget as a means of ensuring the continuation of the cold war strategy in which the United States and the Soviet Union would arm themselves in agreed-upon steps.
57. 2005 Defense Base Closure and Realignment Commission Report, http://www.brac.gov/.
58. http://www.archives.gov/research/vietnam-war/casualty-statistics.html. See also William M. Hammond, *Reporting Vietnam: Media and the Military at War* (Lawrence: University Press of Kansas, 1998).
59. Various doctrines were put forward by Secretary of Defense Caspar Weinberger and General Colin Powell. The doctrine rested on the idea that the United States not intervene militarily unless it had the overwhelming support of the American people.
60. The neoconservatives in policymaking positions in the Bush II White House and the Department of Defense saw the world as an empty space, which it could fill where necessary and remake its contents through force, visions of a better future, bribes, and free markets dominated by American corporations. They did not believe that the United States should even be in a position of

responding to others. Its talk was to be sure that other nations accepted American will; otherwise, they were classified as enemies. Ideologically, the neocons brought with them a mishmash of beliefs stemming from Lenin, Stalin, Wilson, and Trotsky. Albert Wohlsetter and Irving Kristol were the intellectual godfathers to former Deputy Secretary of Defense Paul Wolfowitz. Kristol had a greater reach through his magazine *Public Interest* and as an advisor to conservative foundations. Other neocons found their intellectual roots through the political philosopher Leo Strauss. Whatever his faults, there is always a danger in a philosopher being known by those who claim to be his disciples. See Anne Norton, *Leo Strauss and the Politics of American Empire* (New Haven: Yale University Press, 2004).

CHAPTER 20

1. President George W. Bush's Approval Ratings: Washington Post-ABC News, http://www.washingtonpost.com/wpdyn/content/custom/2006/02/02/C U2006020201345.html; New York Times-CBS News, http://www.nytimes .com/packages/pdf/politics/december-poll.pdf; Zogby Poll, http://www .zogby.com/news/ReadNews.dbm?ID=1077.
2. Even Socrates saw his doomed fate in Athenian democracy as a result of repression. Modern democracies as well have included many examples of legally constituted repression of persons, like in France, for example. However, the social and political space is there within the process of government to transcend repression and correct defects. The tragedy is that the changes can also result in regression, as we see in America at the beginning of the twenty-first century.
3. Note the analysis of the Civil Rights Commission Report: "Voting Irregularities in Florida during the 2000 Presidential Election," http://www .usccr.gov; Jamie Raskin, *Overruling Democracy: The Supreme Court vs. The American People* (New York: Routledge Press, 2003).
4. Even if a person finds some peace, under the terms of the Patriot Act, the use of National Security Letters gives the government carte blanche to engage in a fishing expedition investigating all aspects of a person's life in the past, the present, and continuously.
5. This seems to be the overarching message of John Rawls in his "Political Liberalism." Underneath his views lurk relativism.
6. Peter Gay, *Weimar Culture* (New York: W. W. Norton, 2001); Franz Neumann, *Behemoth: The Structure and Practice of National Socialism, 1933–1944* (New York: Oxford University Press, 1944).

LAST WORDS

1. Gene Wilder, letter to Robert Spero, October 30, 1994.
2. Marcus Raskin, papers, records of the Institute for Policy Studies, 1961–1992, 186.3 c.f., Wisconsin Historical Society Archives, Madison, Wisconsin 53706.
3. Robert Kastenmeier, telephone interview with Robert Spero, Washington DC, February 6, 1995.
4. Marcus Raskin, papers, records of the Institute for Policy Studies, 1961–1992, 186.3 c.f., Wisconsin Historical Society Archives, Madison, Wisconsin 53706.

5. Ibid.
6. Ibid.
7. Ibid.
8. Ibid.
9. Richard J. Barnet, interview with Robert Spero, Washington DC, September 8, 1994.
10. Christopher Jencks, interview with Robert Spero, Evanston, Illinois, October 29, 1994.
11. Garry Wills, "The Thinking of Positive Power," *Esquire*, March 1971.
12. Philip Glass, telephone interview with Robert Spero, New York, July 1, 2003.
13. Gore Vidal, telephone interview with Robert Spero, New York, March 20, 1998.
14. Christopher Jencks, interview with Robert Spero, Evanston, Illinois, October 29, 1994.
15. Seymour M. Hersh, telephone interview with Robert Spero, Washington DC, March 24, 1998.
16. Robert Spero, *The Duping of the American Voter: Dishonesty & Deception in Presidential Television Advertising* (New York: Lippincott & Crowell, 1980).

Index

abortion, 151
  pressure on Catholic politicians (2004
    presidential campaign), 157–58
Abrahamic tradition, 129
Abramoff, Jack, 27, 103
Abu Ghraib, 10, 36
access, as a determinant of power in
  National Security State, 27
Acheson, Dean
  China policy, 244
  and "glory days," 15
  and Korean War, 248
ACLU (American Civil Liberties Union)
  and J. Edgar Hoover, 304
  opposition to Section 215 of the Patriot
    Act, 22–24
Adams, John, 5–6
Adams, John Quincy, 232, 234–35
Afghanistan War, and international rules of
  war, 8
"age of anxiety," 226
agricultural surplus export program,
  176
  and changes in agriculture and eating
    habits of Americans, 176–77
  and growth of "agribusiness," 177
al-Qaeda
  attacks prior to September 11, 43
  and campaign in Afghanistan, 7
  fictional link with Iraq, 47
Albright, Madeline, 229
Alien and Sedition Acts (1798), 5–6
  objections to and modern resonances, 6
Allen, George, 58
Allende, Salvador, 308

Amanpour, Christiane, 59–60
American Center for Law and Justice, 143
American citizens
  belief in triumphalism/"prudent imperi-
    alism," 44–45
  "bonds of affection" heritage, 42
  changes in eating habits, 176–78
  colonization of, 83, 312
  cost of the Patriot Act, 30–31
  and economic insecurity of budget
    deficit, 94–96
  expectations of consumerism, 118
  freedom challenges since September 11,
    xxi
  freedom vs. security polling, xxiii
  historic belief in invulnerability, 44
  and "ideas with social legs," 220–21
  and "politainment," 118
  pride in technology, 55
  and public opinion shift in, 2005, 9
  on razor's edge with suspension of
    checks and balances, 26
  and security index, 21
  "self-made" myth, 199–200
  self-perception stages, 129
  and sense of social mobility, xxv–xxvi
  support for our use of weapons of mass
    destruction, 64
  See also poverty in America
American imperial law, 14–15, 74
Americans for Peace Now, 140
Americans United for Separation of Church
  and State, 140
Angola, 251
Anti-Ballistic Missile Treaty, 306

antienvironmentalism, 102–5
anti-Semitism
    as organizational feature of Christian
        churches, 133
    See also Catholic Church
Arbenz, Jacobo, 276
Arendt, Hannah, 291, 296
Arnold, General H. H. "Hap," 332
Ashcroft, John
    advice on torture policy, 10
    "clear and present danger" doctrine
        (support for), 56
    detention provision of Patriot Act, 17–18
    and imposition of sanctions, 4
    legacy, 36
    as lobbyist, 316
    strategy for Patriot Act, II, 24
    support for Patriot Act, 3, 7
    vision of "enemy-other," 129
    warnings of al-Qaeda attack, 59
Atlee, Clement, 332
Auden, W. H., 226
authoritarianism
    and Catholic Church, 105
    and challenge of active citizenry, 105–6
    internalization of, 105–6
    recipe for, 11–12
    See also antienvironmentalism; corporate
        power (unbridled); economic insecu-
        rity; propaganda; right to vote, and
        false majority; secrecy

Bacon, Robert, and National Security
    League, 330
Baker, James A. III, 76, 77–78
    and election reform, 79–80
Baker, Newton, 241
Banking, and the Patriot Act, 29–30
Barnet, Richard J., 294
    books on globalization and foreign
        affairs, 296
Bartlett, Cal, 296
Bartlett, David M. C., 180
Bechtel, 97
Begin, Menachem, 47
Bellarmine, Cardinal Roberto, 166
Bennett, Robert F., 66
Bennis, Phyllis, 297
Berger, Victor, 5
Berlin, Isaiah, 139
Berning, Bishop, 318
Bernstein, Leonard, 226
Berrigan, Daniel, 140

Berrigan, Philip, 140
Beveridge, Albert, 230
Bhopal chemical disaster, 182
Biagoli, Mario, 322
Bil Mar Foods, product recall, 182
Bin Laden, Osama, 7
    and American Middle East policies,
        170–71, 252
    capture (feelings about), 226
    motivation of, 48
biochemical threats, 60
Biological Weapons Convention, 306
bioterrorism
    mixed messages of Bush II administra-
        tion, 16–17
    no plans or no public information about
        safety plans since September 11, 17
Black, Justice Hugo L., 72–73
Blackwell, J. Kenneth, 312
Blair, Tony, 57
Blankenship, J. Richard, 57
Blix, Hans, 58
Bloch, Ernst, 322, 323
Boas, Franz, 144
Boeing, 97
Bolsheviks, and religious institutions, 165
Bolton, John R.
    appointment as UN ambassador, 51
    and Florida election results, 78
Bonhoeffer, Dietrich, 159
Bork, Robert H., 149
Boston Five, 295–96
boycotts, 115
Boykin, William, 135
Bradley, Harry, 33
Bradley, Lynde, 33
Brandeis, Justice Louis, 290
Brandenburg v. Ohio, xxiv, 300
Breyer, Justice Stephen, 12, 308
Brinton, Crane, 187
Broad, Robin, 297
Brookfield, Wisconsin, church shootings, 70
Brown, H. Rap, 89
Brown, John, 139
Bryan, William Jennings, 241
Buber, Martin, 128, 171, 323
Bukharin, Nicolai, 322
Bulloch, Admiral James, 238
Bundy, McGeorge, 291, 292
Burros, Marian, 181, 324
Bush, George H. W., 333
    defense doctrine, 50

first Iraq War, 8
oratory abilities, xix
and Panama, 258
as a prudent imperialist, 252–53
understanding of challenges to executive power, 33
Bush, George W.
alcoholism, 136–37
anti-labor positions, 99–100
antienvironmentalism, 38–39, 102–5
background, 136
changes in U.S. stated military doctrine, 62–64
"clarifying" tactic with Patriot Act, 4
definition of "civilization," 51
distinction between civil liberties and security, xxiii
executive orders, 154
exploitation of September 11 trauma for political agenda, 34
"family-made," 200
ideas about "inherent" powers, 25
and Kyoto Protocol, 38
and National Security State, xx
No Child Left Behind, 217–18
oratory abilities, xix
and Patriot Act, II, 24–25
policy on torture, 10
pressure for restrictive reading of the Constitution, 3–4
prior to September 11, 33, 137–38, 152
public disdain for Geneva Conventions, 10
religion/public religiosity, 135
and the Religious Right, 138
and secrecy, 7–9, 88, 91
signing statements, 10, 301
Social Security "reform" as part of undoing New Deal agenda, 79, 96
"staying the course" as permanent war, 14
temperament/"dry drunk," 136–37
view of America's role, 14–15, 137–38
war on terrorism as a "religious war," 8
See also Florida, electoral machinations in; neocons in Bush II White House; Right, the
Bush, George W. and the Iraq War
and change to "first-strike" policy, 62
chronology, 56–59
"clear and present danger" shout, 53–54
familial matter, 8

fictional link between Iraq and al-Qaeda, 47
"Mission Accomplished" boast (2003), 60
as modern "Crusade," 141–42
secret Iraq agenda, 7–9, 137
Bush I. See Bush, George H. W.
Bush II agenda post-September 11
assault on international law, 35
balance of power issues, 35
capitalizing on fear and "terrorist threat," 39–40, 112
change away from environmental focus, 38–39
control of oil resources, 36
critics as part of "threat," 39
exploitation of trauma to implement Rightist agenda, 33
and "para-law," 36
permanent war project, 70–72
reelection strategy using war on terrorism, 34
suspension of civil liberties, 35
tax cut bill within 48 hours of attack, 34
unilateralism and multilateralism shifts, 35
See also civil liberties abuses of Bush administration; Republican foreign policies; Republican social policies
Bush II. See Bush, George W.
Bush, Jeb, 76, 77
Butler, General Lee, 252
Byrd, Robert, 3

"Call to Resist Illegitimate Authority," 295
Carnegie, Andrew, 156
Carter, Jimmy, 252
and CIA support of Muslim fundamentalists in Afghanistan, 257
and election reform, 79
oratory abilities, xix
religion, 134, 135
signing statements, 301
use of nuclear threat, 62
work for peace and humanity, 55
Castro, Fidel, 46
Catholic Church
and anti-Semitism, 132
attempts to shield pedophile priests, 151
and authoritarianism, 105
and Democratic Party, 130, 133
and help for people fleeing Nazis, 159
political organization, 128

political positions, 158–59
and pressure on Catholic politicians
    (2004 campaign), 157–58
and Roberts Court, 133
social purposes aligned with FDR, 132
Catholic League for Religious and Civil
    Liberties, 143
Cato Institute, 40
Cavanagh, John, 219, 297
"Ceremonial deism," 155
Change
    and catalysts, 116–17
    in churches, 151
    finding the spirit to, 171
    and fundamentalism, 146–47
    and nonviolent methods, 170
Chemical Weapons Convention, 306
Cheney, Dick
    critics as part of "threat," 39, 64
    and defense doctrine of Bush I adminis-
        tration, 50
    draft deferments, 230
    early pressure to restrict Freedom of
        Information Act, 3–4
    favored Saddam Hussein against Iran,
        333
    Halliburton, 110
    lobbying for Iraq wars, 55, 252
    and military "modernization," 34–35
    and National Security State, xx
    view of America's role, 14–15
Chertoff, Michael, 28–29, 67, 152
    admission of limited capabilities against
        terror attacks, 71
    recommendation for national identity
        card, 71–72
Chez Panisse, 179
Chiang Kai Shek, 243–44
Chile, 251
China
    errors in U.S. policy toward, 248
    modern history and U.S. goals, 243–44
ChoicePoint, 315–16
Chomsky, Noam, 267
Christian Coalition, 139, 143
Church Senate Committee hearings (1975),
    46
church and state separation
    historical examples of, 162
    military chaplain issues, 155–56
    military and religious mixing, 156
    opening prayer in Congress tradition, 155

and pluralist communities, 149, 163
religious conflicts and resource competi-
    tions (Marxist view), 156
and tax exemption, 157
See also faith-based initiatives; Liberation
    Theology movement; prayer
Churchill, Winston, 246
    concerns about FDR position on ending
        empires, 332
CIA, intelligence on Iraq, 56
Cities for Peace project, 116–17
Citizen Budget Juries, 109–12
    jury system and democracy, 111
    and Ninth Amendment, 109
civil liberties abuses of Bush administra-
    tion, 89–91
civil liberties vs. security debate, xxiii, 6
Clark, Wesley, 56
Clarke, Richard, memo to Condoleezza
    Rice, 43
"clear and present danger" doctrine, 53–54
    alternative to focus on terrorism, 112
    manifestations of prior to Iraq War, 56
    See also nuclear weapons (danger of);
        outsourcing and globalization (danger
        of); worldwide pandemic (danger of)
clerical fascism, debate about, 147
Clinton, Hillary Rodham, and economic
    rights for the middle class, 191
Clinton, William, 28
    budget surplus, 94
    and detention, 18
    and economic rights for the middle
        class, 191
    as "Gingrich lite" rather than liberal, 191
    and Iraq, 47
    Kyoto Protocol (1998), 38
    legacy of diminished purpose for
        Democratic Party, 33
    management of FEMA, 66
    military actions, 258
    trade legislation opposed by the Left, 219
Cobban, Helena, 39
Coffin, William Sloan, 140, 296
Cole, David, 18, 303
"collateral damage," as a form of terrorism,
    48
Columbine High School shootings, 70
competition, and American culture, 98, 264
Comprehensive Test Ban Treaty, 305
    and "bunker-busting" nuclear weapons,
        63

computer monitoring, 29
ConAgra Food, 182
conservatives
    agreements over voting restrictions, 40
    and challenges of Katrina and corrup-
        tion, 42
    and Christian fundamentalists, 41
    and concerns about secular humanism,
        130–31
    differences/factions, 40–42
    irony of "big government" rant, 66, 95
    opposition to Liberation Theology,
        159–60
    pessimism of, 108
    "preserving life" and lowering environ-
        mental standards, 104–5
    "social" vs. "process," 40
    vs. Rightists, 34
    and xenophobia, 40–41
Constitution, 83–86
    "Constitution in Crisis" report
        (Conyers), 302
    reasons to reexamine, 84–86
    technology and patents, 113
    and voting, 83–84
    See also Four Freedoms; freedom of
        speech; Ninth Amendment
Conyers, John, 80, 214
    "Constitution in Crisis," 301–2
    health care bill, 328
Coolidge, Calvin, 242
Cooney, Philip, 38–39
Cooper, Cynthia, 120
Coors, Joseph, 34
Cordesman, Anthony H., 61
Cornwell, John, 132
Cornyn, John, 151
corporate power (unbridled), 96–102, 201
    defense baronies, 96–97
    job terminations/moves, 97
    pension terminations, 97
    See also unions
corruption, as challenge to conservative
    movement, 42
Coudert, Frederic R., and National Security
    League, 330
Coughlin, Father Charles, 132, 133, 140
"Cow Case," 178
Cox, James, 240
    defeated on League of Nations issue,
        331
creationism, 151

Cuba
    and expanded definition of universal
        preventive medicine, 209
    U.S. policy toward, 46
Cuomo, Mario, 158

d'Amato, Alphonse, 67
Darrow, Clarence, 99
Darwin, Charles, and revolution in science,
    168
Day, Dorothy, 159, 323
de Gaulle, Charles, 197
    ideas on international poverty, 197–98
de Tocqueville, Alexis, observations about
    postrevolution leadership, 39
Deal, Nathan, 179
Debs, Eugene V., 99
decentralization concept/practice, 297
Decter, Midge, 40
defense
    errors spawned by, 254–55
    excessive spending, 254
    and security, 93–94
    spending and budget deficit, 94
Defense Appropriations Bill, and "signing
    statement," 10
DeLay, Tom, 147, 150
democracy
    in America, 81–82
    founding fathers' views of, 84, 216
    gap, 217
    and ideas with "social legs," 220
    issues for liberals and moderates, 221–22
    Jacobin concept, 215
    and the jury system, 111
    and lack of/inadequate education, 218
    and legitimacy of elections, 75–76
    link to freedom, 215
    and repression of persons, 335
    and transparency of government, 86
    See also United States as a formalist
        republic
Department of Homeland Security, 66–68
    fanning flames of anxiety, 70
    pork-barrel projects, 66–67
    size of, 66
detention, 17–20
    and rendition, 18
    and right to a lawyer, 18–19
Deutsch, George, 303
Dewey, John, 228, 269, 295, 304–5, 318, 323

Dewey, Thomas E., acceptance of New Deal ideas, 201
DiBattiste, Carol A., 315
Dilulio, John, 153–54
director of National Intelligence, 27–28
Dirksen, Everett, 293
Dissent magazine, 51
Dlott, Susan, 80
Dobbs, Lou, 314
Dobson, James C., 143
Donohue, William, 143
Dorfman, Ariel, 297
Douglas, Justice William O., 294–95
Dowd, Maureen, 29
Downing Street Memo (2002), 57
Dr. Strangelove, 255
Dred Scott decision, 234
Dulles, Allen, 332
DuPont, T. Coleman, and National Security League, 330
Dyer, Mary, 318

Eagle Forum, 145
Economic Bill of Rights, 189–90
    and concept of "redistribution," 191–93
    limitations of, 191
    and "Second" Bill of Rights, 190
    and security of the better off, 192
    See also national health (U.S.)
economic insecurity, budget deficit, 94–96
"economic royalists," 16, 122
Egypt, and rendition, 18
Ehrenreich, Barbara, books, 296
Einstein, Albert, 167, 168, 294
Eisenhower, Dwight D.
    acceptance of New Deal ideas, 201
    and alliances after Second World War, 247
    and Bonus Marchers, 190
    continuation of export of agricultural surplus, 176
    "Crusade" characterization of anti-Nazi struggle, 134
    "God" insertion into Pledge of Allegiance, 162
    oratory abilities and deliberate ambiguity, xix
    signing statements, 301
    warnings of dangers of military-industrial complex, 254
elections
    legitimacy and democracy, 75–76
    media manipulation of, 80–81
    reverse polling in, 2004, 80
    See also Florida, electoral machinations in; Ohio elections 2004
Electoral College, and redistribution, 192
electronic tagging, xxiii
Eliot, T. S., 226
Elk Grove Unified School Dist. v. Newdow (2002), 162
Ellsberg, Daniel, 120, 296
e-mail, government surveillance of, 21, 29
Emancipation Proclamation, 235
"empathic invariance," 266
Emperor Hirohito, 244, 331
"enemy combatants," imprisonment of, 10
Enron, 105–6, 120, 201
Environmental Protection Agency (EPA), changes under Bush, II, 38–39
Ergonomics Program (OSHA), changes to, 99
Ernst, Morris, and J. Edgar Hoover, 304
evacuation plans
    and bioterrorist attacks, 17
    and Gulf Coast hurricanes (2005), 17
executive, role of, 11–12

failed imperial state, characteristics of, 267
faith-based initiatives, 135, 152–54
Faith Force Multiplier, 135
Falwell, Jerry, 50, 139
    support for Israel, 147
Family Research Council, 143
"family values," (code for "patriarchy"), 146
federal antidanger measures in conflict with liberties prior to Patriot Act. *See also* Alien and Sedition Acts; McCarthy, Joseph R.; Roosevelt, Franklin Delano/internment of Japanese Americans; Wilson, Woodrow/"deposit" of immigrants
Federalist Party, 5
    concerns about the French Revolution, 5
Feeney, Father, 132
Feingold, Russ, 9
Feith, Douglas, 152
Fellowship of Reconciliation, 140
Felt, W. Mark, 120
FEMA, 66
Ferber, Michael, 296
FISA court (Foreign Intelligence Surveillance Court of Review), 20

dangers of secrecy, 21
  as "fig leaf of legality," 25–26
FISA (Foreign Intelligence Surveillance Act)
  1978, violation of, 303
Fissile Material Cutoff Treaty, 306
Fitzgerald, A. Ernest, 120
Fitzgerald, F. Scott, xxvi
Fleischer, Ari, 66, 152, 154
Flexner report, 327
Florida, electoral machinations in, 76–79
  and legitimating the illegitimate, 79–80
  as a metaphor, 81
Florida Supreme Court, 78
Focus on the Family, 143
Food for Peace program, 176
food safety issues
  "back to nature" movement, 179
  contaminated food risks, 179–83
  food inspection in the U.S., 181–83
  and risk assessment, 182
  unstandardized labeling of "organic"
    foods, 178
  See also Mad Cow disease
Ford, Gerald, 4, 13, 250
  signing statements, 301
Ford, Henry, 156, 245
Foreign Intelligence Surveillance Act (FISA)
  1978, violation of, 303
Foreign Intelligence Surveillance Court of
  Review (FISA court). See FISA court
Foreman, Carol Tucker, 324
Four Freedoms
  guidance for Liberal Project, 108
  not defined by authoritarian cabals in
    Washington, 15–16
  paintings of, 299
  See also freedom from fear; freedom
    from want; freedom of speech; free-
    dom to worship
Four Freedoms speech
  background, xvii–xviii
  bipartisanship of the times, xix
  modern addition of "freedom of the
    mind," xxvi
  relevance to the present, xx
  as rhetoric to frame future war effort, xix
  use to expand National Security State,
    xx
Fourth Amendment, and government
  requests for Web-surfing data, 29
Fox News, 59
"Fragging," 333

Franco, Francisco, 138
Franklin, Benjamin
  ideas to tax religious property, 157
  observations on Iroquois democracy, 231
Fraser, Don, 333
free press, 73
  and issues to be considered, 73–74
freedom from fear, 223
  fears and contradictions, 225
  fears prior to September 11, 226–27
  and status quo as "safe" policy of presi-
    dents, 251–53
  See also wars and National Security
    State, alternatives to
freedom from want, 173
  agricultural export strategy, 176
  and basic necessities, 183–84
  and change in role of federal govern-
    ment, 175–76
  child mortality, 186–87
  and contributions from those who
    have/cultural strategy, 183
  and export trade strategy, 176
  goal of the New Deal, 175
  "have-nots," 184, 199–200
  historical movements supporting,
    175–76
  and international taxation system, 198
  and role U.N. could play, 197–98
  world conditions, 184–86
  See also agricultural surplus export pro-
    gram; food safety issues; globaliza-
    tion; poverty in America
Freedom of Information Act, early pressure
  on, 3–4
freedom of speech
  exercise of, 72–74, 123
  as foundation for other freedoms,
    xxiii–xxiv
  and imagination, 116
  and "Information Age," xxiv–xxv
  and National Security State, xxi
  and "reasoned instability," 108
  and Section 215 of the Patriot Act, 22–24
  and struggles between capital and labor,
    99
  in the workplace, 101–2
  See also free press
freedom of thought, and "reasoned instability," 108
freedom to worship, 128–29
  for Muslims, 129–30

religion as a disestablishment idea,
127–28
vs. "freedom of religion," 127
See also church and state separation;
irreconcilable differences between religious groups
Frick, Henry Clay, and National Security
League, 330
Frist, Dr. Bill, 208
Fromm, Erich, 291
Fukuyama, Francis, 40, 51
Fulbright, J. William, 49
fundamentalists, 146–47
and belief in documents, 323
and opposition to abortion, 151
question of religion or power, 147

Galileo, Galilei, 166, 308
Gandhi, Mahatma, 170, 171, 323
Gary, Judge, and National Security League,
330
Gavanagh, John, 297
gay rights, 151
General Electric, 97
Geneva Conventions, 11, 15
and Bush II agenda, 36
See also Hamdan v. Rumsfeld (2006)
George, Stefan, 112–13
Gergen, David R., 138
Giap, Vo Nguyen, 250
Gideon v. Wainwright (1962), 18, 302
Gingrich, Newt, 40, 112, 199
Giuliani, Rudolph, 67
Glass, Philip, 298
globalization
and need for a socially shared epiphany,
170
and Patriot Act banking policies, 30
and sweatshops, 186
Goebbels, Joseph, 59, 117
Goering, Hermann, 118
Gonzalez, Alberto
advice on torture policy, 10
on Geneva Conventions, 36
requests for Web-surfing data (2006),
29
Goodman, Mitchell, 296
Goodman, Paul, 96, 117, 297
Goodwin, Dick, 292
Gorbachev, Mikhail, 251
Gore, Al
debate with Bush and religion issue
(2000), 137

and Florida election results, 77
Graham, Billy, 41
and anti-Semitism, 136
and Bush II alcoholism recovery, 136
"Zelig" character, 136
Grant, Ulysses S., 231
Greeley, Horace, 127
Green, John, 147
Griles, J. Steven, 104
Groppi, Father James, 145
Gross, Terry, 95
Groton, influence on FDR, 131
Guantanamo
chaplain spying case, 155
policies toward prisoners, 10, 36
recommendations about prior to Soviet
Missile Crisis, 292
Guevara, Che, 292
Guggenheim, Simon and Daniel, and
National Security League, 330
Gumbleton, Bishop Thomas, 145

habeas corpus, 13
Hale, Nathan, 46
Halliburton, 97, 110
Hamdan v. Rumsfeld (2006), 11, 12, 15, 301
Hamdi, Yaser Esam, 19
Hamilton, Alexander, 82
Hamilton, Marcia, 133
Hansen, James E., 121
Harding, Warren, 104, 242
rejection of war, 331
Harris, Katherine, 77–78
Hay, John, 237
Hayes, Rutherford B., 236
Head Start, 152
health right, 212. *See also* national health
(U.S.)
"Hedgehog and the Fox, The" 139
Hersh, Seymour M., 216
Hitler, Adolf, xviii
and the Catholic Church, 318
changing rules of exemptions as lessons
about surveillance, 263
short- and long-term goals, 246
Japan as key to German world conquest,
332
Hobbes, Thomas, 231
Holmes, Justice Oliver Wendell, 53, 230
Hoover, Herbert
antiwar treaty, 242
belief in Kellogg-Briand Pact (1928), 331

belief in role of religion in governing, 134
and Bonus Marchers, 190
fear of war, 228
Hoover, J. Edgar, 28
and ACLU, 304
Hospital Corporation of America (HCA), 208
"hot facts," 117–19
Hughes, 97
Hume, David, 231
hunger (elimination of)
eating as "political act," 179
as goal of New Deal, 175
growth of agribusiness, 176–78
organic food issues, 178–79
Huntington, Samuel P., 40, 51
Hussein, Saddam
biological and chemical weapons use with no U.S. complaints, 17
capture (feelings about), 226
fear of (Arab nations), 252
and Sunni dominance, 130
and U.S. support for his war with Iran, 72
Huston Plan, 28, 304
Hutchinson, Anne, 318
Hutchinson, Asa, and domestic security company consulting, 315

imagination, and expanding social spaces, 116
inclusiveness, 41
information, as a determinant of power in National Security State, 27
"Information Age," and freedom of speech, xxiv–xxv
Institute for American Values, 51
Institute for Policy Studies (IPS)
ahead of history, 296
development of, 294
goal, 294
independence of, 295
realizing Dewey's theory of ideas and action, 295
work of IPS fellows, 296–297
Intelligence Reform and Terrorist Prevention Act of 2004, 25
and sharing intelligence and criminal information, 26–29
intelligent design, as political attack on evolution, 168–69

International Criminal Court, 48–50, 74, 241, 306, 307
international law as viewed by Bush II, 15. See also American imperial law
Internet
and blogs, 219
and discourse, 49
and new communities, 265
and "secrets," 118–19
and work for change, 30–31
Iran-Contra scandal, 257
Iraq War
and Bush II agenda, 7–9, 55–59
and CIA intelligence on, 56
as an "elective war," 56
and "embedded" reporters, 59
and "first-strike" policy, 62
and international rules of war, 8
and Vietnam Syndrome, 8
withdrawal, 227
WMD (weapons of mass destruction) myth, 8–9, 58–59
Iraq War (Bush I), 252–53
consequences in Iraq, 253
irreconcilable differences between religious groups
belief in, 169
social conditions fueling, 169
Israel, as a warrior state, 257

Jackson, Andrew, 232, 233
signing statements, 301
Jackson, Justice Robert H., on executive authority, 11
Jacobs, Paul, 61
James, William, 228
Jaspers, Karl, 171
Jay Treaty, 5
Jefferson, Thomas, 5, 82
belief in economic expansion, 329
wars, 232
Jencks, Christopher, 295, 297, 298
Jews, in Bush II administration, 152
Johnson, Andrew, signing statements, 301
Johnson, Lyndon B.
considerations of nuclear weapons in Vietnam War, 62
domestic cultural revolution, 250
and impact of protest movements, 114
Poverty Program, 208
and right to vote, 140
and secrecy, 88
signing statements, 301

understanding of "preserve and protect," 229
"Josephine Butler United States Health
Service Act," 328
jury system, and democracy, 111

Kaczynski, Ted, 70
Kahn, Herman, 255
Kaiser, Henry J., 214
Kastenmeier, Robert, 291
Katrina
and FEMA, 66
human disaster and fat contracts, 228–29
and impact on conservative movement,
42
Kay, David, 58–59
Kellogg-Briand Pact (1928), 331
Kennedy, John F., 28
on Bay of Pigs, 291–92
continuation of export of agricultural
surplus, 176
Defense Department identification of
threats to U.S. during presidency of, 54
New Frontier and not New Deal, 292
oratory abilities, xix
Kennedy, Justice Anthony, 37
and criticism by Robert Bork, 149
Kennedy, Ted, 214
Kerik, Bernard, 67
Kerry, John, 80, 230
pressure from Catholic Church over
abortion issue, 157–58
Key Largo, 76
Khalizad, Zalmay, 47
Khrushchev, Nikita, visit to nuclear facility,
92–93
Kim il Sung, 248
Kim Jong-il, 63, 248
King Fahd, 252
King Ibn Saud, 169
King, Martin Luther, Jr., 140, 159, 170, 171
King, Rodney, 201
Kissinger, Henry, 74, 134, 237, 250, 255
and Kurds, 253
and secrecy, 92
kleptocracy, 229
Know-Nothings, 201–2
Koppel, Ted, 59
Kornbluh, Peter, 297
Kotler, Milton, 297
Kristol, Irving, 335
Kristol, William, letter on Iraq policy (1998),
47

Krugman, Paul, 195
Ku Klux Klan (KKK), 144, 236, 320
Kuo, David, 154
Kyoto Protocol, 38

Lafayette, Marquis de, 5
LaFollette Progressive Party Platform, 331
Landau, Saul, 297
Landon, Alf, 201
warnings about Social Security number,
300
lawyers, rights to, 18–19
leaders
acceptance of hierarchic structure,
322
American attitudes toward, 261
in authoritarian governments, 12
bellicosity and idealism, 231
democratic vs. strong, 270–71
"Leader Principle," 271–72
"national interest" vs. personal conflicts
and competitions, 8
rituals that reinforce power of, 70
Leadership
concerns about after change, 39
and personal responsibility for aggressive war, xviii
League of Nations, 239
idea of collective security, 241
preamble and charter, 240
Leave It to Beaver, contrast to reality, 250
Lee, Barbara, 328
legitimacy, politics of, 75–76
LeMay, Curtis, 247
Lerner, Rabbi Michael, 140
Letelier, Orlando, 308
Lewis, Anthony, 18
Lewis and Clark, 234
Libby, I. Lewis, 152
The Liberal Papers, 293
Liberal Project, 107, 293
guidance from Four Freedoms, 108
new directions for, 122–23
question of success with/without state
power, 107
risks, 122
and social movements, 114–22
and technology, 112–13
See also boycotts; change, and catalysts;
Citizen Budget Juries; "hot facts";
imagination; nonviolent confrontation;
protest movements; whistleblowers

liberal social polices, flaws of, 202
Liberation Theology movement, 159
Lieberman, Joseph, 44
    legislation to create Department of
        Homeland Security, 66
Likud Party (Israel), and support from
    Religious Right, 147
Lincoln, Abraham
    Emancipation Proclamation, 235
    militancy, 233
    opposition to Mexican War, 329
    recognizing the national unity, 235
    signing statements, 301
    on social contract, 176
Lindbergh, Charles, 245
Lippmann, Walter, 111
Lipton, Eric, 315
Locke, John, 231
Lockheed Martin, 97
Lodge, Henry Cabot, 239
Lombardi, Vince, 98
Loprest, Dr. Pamela, 202
Loy, Adm. James M., and domestic security
    company consulting, 315
Lusk, Herbert H., 153
Luther, Martin, 133
Lynn, Barry, 140
Lyon, Matthew, 5

MacArthur, Douglas, 230, 244
    and Bonus Marchers, 190
    plans to attack China, 249
Machiavelli, thoughts on takeover of
    power, 33
Mad Cow disease, 180–81
Madison, James
    exclusion of "bonds of affection" by fed-
        eral government, 312
    ideas to tax religious property, 157
    opposition to the Sedition Act, 6
    theoretical discussion about the repub-
        lic, 82
    war and expansion, 232
Mandela, Nelson, 117
"Manifest Destiny," 234
Mao Tse-tung, 243–44
Marcos, Ferdinand, 251
Marine Barracks Bombing (Beirut, 1983),
    334
Maritain, Jacques, 198, 323
Marshall, Chief Justice John, 133
Marshall, George C., 244, 246–47

Marx, Karl, 265
mass transit, concerns about
    terrorism/indifference to negligence, 16
"Mayberry Machiavellis," 154
McCain, John, 230
McCain Amendment, and Bush "signing
    statement," 10
McCarthy, Joseph R., excesses searching for
    communist infiltrators, 6–7, 14, 228
McDonnell Douglas, 97
McGovern, George, 176
McKeon, Richard, 106
McKinley, William, 237
McNamara, Robert, 120
    and the Pentagon Papers, 316
McVeigh, Timothy, 9–10, 70
media
    and election manipulation, 80–81
    and information, 119
    and propaganda, 59
    as purveyor of passivity and con-
        sumerism, 218–19
    See also television
Mennonites, 140
Merriam, Charles, 175
Millennium Challenge Account, 199
Milosevic, Slobodan, 74
Moffitt, Ronni, 308
Monroe, James, Monroe Doctrine,
    232–33
Moon, Sun Myung, 153
Moral Majority, 139
Morgan, J. P., 156
    and National Security League, 238, 330
Moussaoui, Zacharias, and FBI failure, 120
MoveOn.org, 219
Mueller, Robert, requests for Web-surfing
    data (2006), 29
Murder in the Air, 255
Murdoch, Rupert, 199
Murphy, Judge Harold, 312
Muste, A. J., 139, 323
Myers, William G., III, 104

national health (U.S.)
    community health clinics, 208
    Congressional comprehensive health
        care efforts, 328
    corporatization of, 208
    costs, 207
    growth of pharmaceutical companies,
        206

growth of technology in hospitals, 207
history of physician certification, 205–6
HMOs, 207, 208
ranking, 203–5
spending, 205
and vulnerability for contagious diseases, 208
national health (U.S.) transformation alternatives, 209
government-financed insurance, 212–13
implementation challenges, 213–14
more nurses, 213
national goals, 209
new social/environmental model, 209–11
new social responsibility, 211–12
national identity card, xxii–xxiii
national driver's license as first step, 25
recommendation for, 71–72
See also electronic tagging
National Interest, internal disagreement at, 40
National Labor Relations Act (1935), 98–99
National Security Agency
criticism of, 313
eavesdropping, 90
National Security League (NSL), 330
National Security Letters (NSL), 23, 335
National Security State, xx
and adaptation of parts of Four Freedoms speech, xx
and appearance of support of the people, 83
birth of, 66
and characteristics of a failed imperial state, 267
cost of, 254
defense baronies, 97
determinants of power in, 27
and freedom of speech, xxi
and free speech, xxv
internal role of, 51
and militarization, 87
and the military, 93–94
and permanent conflict, 45
and reasons to transform the Constitution, 86
social structures to be disassembled for democratic reform, 262
strangling effect on freedom, xxi
See also surveillance; wars and National Security State, alternatives to

National Security State since September 11, 2001
new expansions, xxi–xxii
See also national identity card
NATO, impact of September 11 on, 51–52
Nazi project in Europe, 245–46
Negroponte, John, 27
Nelson, Anna, 4
neocons in Bush II White House, 334–35
New Deal
agenda to undo (Bush II), 79, 96
conflict with Southern plantation owners, 176
and federal judiciary choices, 36
and labor unions, 98–99
objectives, 175
and working class, 41
See also hunger (elimination of)
Newdow, Michael, 162
Niebuhr, Reinhold, 134, 140
Ninth Amendment, and Citizen Budget Juries, 109
Nixon, Richard
domestic cultural revolution, 250
Huston plan, 28, 304
militancy, 233
religious background, 134
and secrecy, 88
signing statements, 301
strategy to override the CIA, 28
use of nuclear threat, 62
Vietnam policy, 114, 250–51
No Child Left Behind Act (NCLBA) 2002, 217–18
Noble, David, 166
nonviolence, as a tactic of change, 170
nonviolent confrontation, 115–16
Nordhaus, William D., 94
Noriega, Manuel, 251, 253
Norquist, Grover, 95, 103
Norton, Gale, 103
Norway, and expanded definition of universal preventive medicine, 209
Novak, Michael, 51
NSL (National Security League), 330
NSL (National Security Letters), 23
"nth country" and nuclear proliferation problem, 60
Nuclear Nonproliferation Treaty, 60, 63–64, 305
nuclear weapons (danger of), 60–61
and Armageddon, 166

and use of in Hiroshima and Nagasaki,
    166–67, 232, 244–45
NYPD Blue, 146

O'Connor, Justice Sandra Day
    on "ceremonial deism," 155
    and Florida election results, 78
Office of Homeland Security
    limitations of in Bush II second term,
        65–66
    limitations of at startup, 65
    reasons for, 66
    as step to consulting jobs, 315
    See also Department of Homeland
        Security; Lieberman, Joseph
Ohio elections 2004, 80, 312
    as a metaphor, 81
oil
    and Bush II agenda, 36
    and FDR, 169
    and first Iraq War, 252–53
    Nazi interest in, 332
Olin, John M., 33
O'Neill, Paul, reports of cabinet focus on
    war, 8
O'Neill, Tip, 211
Oppenheimer, Robert, 166
    parallels to Galileo, 322
OSI (Office of Special Investigation), 302
outsourcing and globalization (danger of),
    61

Pacelli, Eugenio, 132
Paige, Rod, 218
Palmer, Alexander Mitchell, 4, 6, 300
"para-law," 36
Patriot Act
    administrative implications of, 19–20
    and "clarifying tactic" of Bush II admin-
        istration, 4
    cost to Americans, 30–31
    and dream world of imperial power,
        xxvi
    as example of colonization of
        Americans, 83
    and free speech, xxv, 270
    historical antecedents in other crises, 4–7
    origin of, 3
    ostensible goals, 7
    and Patriot Act II, 24–25
    and privacy concerns, 22–24
    speed of passage, 3

stealing power, 9
    support for by Republicans and
        Democrats, 9
    See also Patriot Act provisions; travel
        and the Patriot Act
Patriot Act Improvement and
    Reauthorization Act 2006
    assistant attorney general for National
        Security (new position), 27
    creation of director of National
        Intelligence position, 26, 27–28
    downgrade of CIA, 26
Patriot Act provisions, 9–31
    bioterrorism, 16–17
    computer monitoring, 29
    detention, 17–20
    federalizing terrorism against mass tran-
        sit, 16
    increased penalties, 9–10
    money laundering, 29–30
    roving wiretaps, 20–21
    search warrants (nationwide), 22–25
    Section 215 (violation of First
        Amendment), 22–24
Patton, George S., 190
Paul Jacobs and the Nuclear Gang, 297, 309
Peabody, Endicott, 131
"Pentagon Papers," 120, 302
Perkins, Frances, 145
Perkins, George W., and National Security
    League, 330
Perkins, Tony, 143
Perle, Richard, 152
    letter on Iraq policy (1998), 47
perspectives on September 11
    as an opportunity to recast criminal and
        national security law (Bush II admin-
        istration), 7
    as payback for American social evils
        (fundamentalist Rightists), 7
Pinochet, Augusto, 74, 92, 297, 308
Plato, 113
Pledge of Allegiance, 161–62
pluralistic communities
    and church/state separation, 149, 163,
        164
    and school choice issues, 163–64
    teaching tolerance, 164
"politainment," 118
Polk, James, 233, 329
Pope Benedict XVI, 166
Pope Leo XIII, 318

Pope Paul XII, 132, 138
Pope Urban VIII, 322
port security, 69
Posner, Richard A., 76, 81
post-September 11 Bush II agenda. See Bush
    agenda post-September 11
Potsdam Conference (1945), 332
poverty in America, 195–96
    and gap with "haves," 196
    and imperialism, 197
    racial and ethnic imbalance in, 199–200
    and "self-made" dream to keep down
        have-nots, 201
    welfare policies (Clinton and Bush II),   202
Powell, Colin, 344
    address to Security Council (2003),
        57–58
prayer
    nonreligious benefits of, 161
    "winking," 163
    See also Pledge of Allegiance
presidential signing statement. See signing
    statement
prisons, as modern slavery, 200
Progressive Caucus (House of
    Representatives), 219
Project Minaret, 303
Propaganda
    and the media, 59
    primary purpose of, 88–89
    use of obfuscating language, 262
Protestant hegemonic, 130
protest movements, 114–15
"prudent imperialism," 44–45
Public Interest, 321

Raskin, Jamin, 290
Raskin, Marcus, xx
    anticipating globalization, 293
    conspiracy charges as one of the "Boston
        Five," 295–96
    early life, 289–90
    meeting with Gorbachev's advisors,
        296
    as mentor, 298
    pioneering papers on technology,
        293–94
    recommendations about the arms race,
        293
    recommendations about Guantanamo
        prior to Cuban Missile Crisis, 292
    and The Liberal Papers, 293

vision, 297
    work in Kennedy White House, 291–92
    work as a legislative counsel, 290–91
    See also Institute for Policy Studies
Raven-Hansen, Peter, 17–18
Reagan, Ronald
    and Cold War end, 296
    as "godfather" of Rightists, 34, 211
    and Iraq, 46
    nuclear preemption policy, 251
    pullout of Lebanon and "victory" in
        Grenada, 334
    and secrecy, 88
    "starving the beast" policy, 95
    Star Wars project, 255, 334
    and Vietnam Syndrome, 8
"reasoned instability," 108
redistribution concept, 191–93
    abandoning Electoral College, 192
    social and political examples of redistri-
        bution, 192
Red Lake, Minnesota, shootings, 70
Rehnquist Court
    on Congressional expansion of rights, 101
    on voting and the Constitution, 83
Reid, Harry, 200
religion
    and civil war, 150
    and conflict (Marxist perspective on), 156
    differences from worship, 128
    difficulties predicting politics of, 145–46
    as a disestablishment idea, 127–28
    and exclusion, 150
    persecution and bias in the United
        States, 131
    political practice of, 165
    and politicians, 133–34
    and radical change, 151
    and state to Bush, II, 135
    See also prayer
religion and science
    and belief they "speak for God," 166
    consultants to power, 167
    dialectical relationship, 165
    historical conflicts, 166
    See also intelligent design
Religious Left, 139–41
Religious Right, 138, 141–42
    absolutism, 144
    "good and evil" framing of messages,
        144
    and Israeli Right, 147

overview of leaders and groups, 143
patriarchal bias, 144–45
racist origins, 144
support for military establishment, 144
vs. Liberation Theology, 159–60
religious war, 8
rendition, 18
Republic, The, 113
Republican foreign policies, 37
"ex-treaties," 37–38
Republican Party
and big government, 95
change from isolationism in, 2000, 14
and Christian fundamentalists, 147
and environmental positions, 102
Republican social policies, 36–37, 95–96
reverse polling, 2004 election, 80
Rice, Condoleezza, 229
memo from Richard Clarke, 43
talk show appearances supporting Iraq
War, 57
Richardson, Sid, 156
Ridge, Tom, 28, 65
and domestic security company consulting, 315
"internal room" recommendation, 67
Riesman, David, 291
Right, the
conservative differences/factions, 40–42
fear of redistribution, 200
Libertarians, 40
modern day Know-Nothing Party, 201
and National Security State, xx
Rightists vs. conservatives, 34
and September 11 as organizing political
principle, 42
and slavery, 200
takeover of word "Christian," 133
view of civilization, 193
vs. social reforms of three generations,
41
world view, 39
See also neocons in Bush II White House
right to vote, 102
and the Constitution (Rehnquist Court),
83
and the Constitution (Warren Court), 83
and false majority, 102
Voting Rights Act (1965), 80
See also democracy; elections
risk, 68–70
daily, 68

invented, 68
public space, 69–70
unaccountable, 68–69
See also security
risk assessment strategy
and food and drug safety in U.S., 181–83
and safe planes, 72
Roberts, John, and "winking," 163
Roberts Court, religious composition of,
133
Robertson, Pat, 50, 139
call for assassination in Venezuela, 143
concerns about faith-based initiatives,
153
Rocco, Johnny (fictional character), and
prophetic insights, 76, 79
Rockefeller oil companies, funding for
National Security League, 330
Rockwell, Norman, paintings of Four
Freedoms, 299
Roosevelt, Eleanor, 145
Roosevelt, Franklin Delano
challenging vision for twenty-first century, xvii–xx
and change of federal government role,
175–76
common purposes with Catholic
Church, 132
declarations of war as recognition of
executive limits, 11
and "economic royalist," 16, 122
and export trade strategy, 176
freedom to worship vs. "freedom of religion," 127
and International Criminal Court concept, 74
internment of Japanese Americans, 6,
228
and League of Nations, 240, 331
public religious utterances, 134
roots of his sense of Christian responsibility, 131
and Saudi oil, 169
signing statements, 301
and the U.N. as New Deal of international politics, 171
understanding of challenges to executive power, 33
and women's issues, 145
See also Economic Bill of Rights; Four
Freedoms speech
Roosevelt, James, 293

Roosevelt, Theodore, 102–3, 233
    "big stick" stratagem, 238
    building the navy, 236–37
    and National Security League, 238, 330
    signing statements, 301
Rosenman, Samuel, xvii
Rostow, Walt, 292
Rousseau, Jean Jacques, 113, 215
Rove, Karl, 154
Rowley, Coleen, 120
Rudolf, Eric Robert, 70–71
Rumsfeld, Donald
    and C-130J Hercules plane, 97
    early pressure to restrict Freedom of
        Information Act, 3–4
    favoring Saddam Hussein over Iran, 46,
        333
    letter on Iraq policy (1998), 47
    lobbying for Iraq War, 55
    and "modernization," 34–35
    public disdain for Geneva Conventions,
        10
    shaking hands with Saddam Hussein, 46
Rusk, Dean, 230, 251
Ryan, George, 37

Sadat, Anwar, 49
Safire, William, fears of this government
    encroachment on individual liberties, xxii
Salazar, Antonio, 138
Salvation Army, military descriptions and
    religious work, 156
Sanders, Bernie, 109
Sanders, Jackie, 306
Sara Lee Corporation, product recall, 182
Scaife, Richard Mellon, 33
Scalia, Justice Antonin
    early pressure to restrict Freedom of
        Information Act, 3–4
    and Florida election results, 78
Scalia, Eugene, 121
Schelling, Thomas, 255
Schenck, Charles, 53
Schenck v. United States (1919), 16, 53–54
Schiavo, Terry, 36–37, 150
    and split between "social" and
        "process" conservatives, 40
Schlafly, Phyllis, 145
Schlesinger, Arthur, 292
Schools. *See* pluralistic communities
Schröeder, Gerhard, 137
Schwarz, Fred C., 133

Schwarzenegger, Arnold, 49
Scopes "monkey" trial, 99, 151
search warrants (nationwide), 22–25
    in terrorem effect, 22–25
    and Section 215, 22–24
second-strike policy, 62
    and danger of change to first-strike pol-
        icy, 62–64
secrecy
    and authoritarianism, 88
    executive, 91–92
    legislative, 92
    reasons for, 92–93
    See also Internet; transparency
Section 215 of the Patriot Act, 22–24
secular humanism, 130–31
    challenge to religious believers,
        133
security
    definitions of, 50–52
    index, 21
    vs. civil liberties debate, xxiii, 6
    See also risk
Seiderman, Ian, 73
Sekulow, Jay, 143
September 11
    attacks by al-Qaeda prior to, 43
    framework for hearings (9/11
        Commission), 308
    as an organizing political principle for
        the Right, 42
    warnings about, 43
    See also Bush II agenda post-September
        11; terrorist attack(s) on U.S. soil (next)
Shamir, Yitzhak, 47
Sharon, Ariel, and support from Religious
    Right, 147
Shays, Christopher, 40
Shays, Daniel, 232
Sherman, William T., 231
"shock and awe," 56
Shulman, Max, 261
signing statements, 10, 301
Silberman, Jerry, 290
slavery, as basis of American institutions,
    200
Smith, Gerald L. K., 133, 140
social responsibility, 211
Social Security
    "adequate," 190
    cards as de facto identity cards,
        xxii

reforms as part of New Deal undoing agenda (Bush II), 79, 96
Socrates, example of democracy and repression, 335
Sojourners, The, 140
Sorokin, Pitirim, 266
sovereignty, 94
Soviet system failure, reasons for, 322
Spanish-American War, 237
special interest groups, and free speech, xxiv
Spellman, Cardinal Francis, and armed forces ceremonial rank, 156
Spender, Stephen, 226
Spero, Robert, political advertising and government, 336
Spinoza, Baruch, 162
Spock, Dr. Benjamin, 295
Stalin, Josef, 92
Starfield, Dr. Barbara, 203
Star Wars, 255–56, 334
state sovereignty, as cover for aggressive war, xviii
state terrorism, 46
    American state terrorism, 46–47
    assassination of Letelier and Moffitt, 308
Stavins, Ralph, 296
"staying the course," 14
Steinmann, Monsignor, 318
Stengel, Casey, 95
Stephenson, David, 320
Stevens, Justice John Paul, 13, 15, 163
Stone, I. F., 216
Strauss, Leo, 335
Subversive Activities Control Board, 14
Summers, Lawrence, 186
Superman myth, 113
Supreme Court
    the Constitution and voting (Rehnquist Court), 83
    and constitutional boundaries to the executive, 10–13
    eminent domain decision (Connecticut), 19
    enemy combatant ruling (2004), 19
    "enemy of traditional culture" to conservatives, 149–50
    and government loopholes, 19
    selection of Bush, II, 13, 33, 76, 78, 79
    vouchers for private schools, 163
    See also Hamdan v. Rumsfeld (2006); Rehnquist Court; Roberts Court; Warren Court

surveillance, 87
Suskind, Ron, 153–54
Sweden, and expanded definition of universal preventive medicine, 209
Synderman, Ralph, 327
Szilard, Leo, 291, 294

Taco Bell boycott, 115
Taft, Robert, acceptance of New Deal ideas, 201
Taft, William Howard, 238
Taliban, 7
Tawney, Chief Justice Roger, 234, 329
Taylor, A. J. P., 246
Taylor, Telford, 295
technology
    and the Liberal Project, 112–14
    and the responsibilities of scientists, 323
television, concerns about from Right and Left, 146
Teller, Edward, 255
"terrorist"/"terrorism"
    and anger over U.S. economic-social-political policy, 49–50
    and anger over U.S. foreign policy, 47–48
    and "collateral damage," 48
    different meanings in different parts of the world, 46
    as a form of communication, 49
    and increased penalties in Patriot Act, 9–10
    negotiating with, 50
    targeting the "unchallenged superpower," 50
    terrorists as criminals, 48–50
    as vague legal terms, 9–10, 16
    vs. "zealot," 10, 45–46
    See also state terrorism
terrorist attack(s) on U.S. soil (next), 70–71
Terry, Randall, 143, 150
Thatcher, Margaret, 180, 252, 333
Thorpe, Kenneth E., 212
threats (national)
    identifying, 54
    other than terrorism, 112
    responses to, 54–55
Tikkun magazine, 140
Tikkun olam, 290
Tilden, Samuel, 236
Tillich, Paul, 323
Tobin, James, 198

torture, 10–11
    and Supreme Court, 11
transparency
    and democracy, 86
    See also secrecy
traumatic events in politics, historical uses
    for, 33
travel and the Patriot Act, 9
Triangle Shirtwaist factory fire, 99
triumphalism (nationalist), 44–45, 141
    bellicosity and idealism of American
        leaders, 231
    challenges to, 52
    as threat to our security, 55
Truman, Harry S.
    continuation of export of agricultural
        surplus, 176
    "glory days," 15
    and Korean War, 248
    oratory abilities and policies, xix–xx
    signing statements, 301
    use of nuclear weapons, 62
    Youngstown Steel Seizure case, 19
Tugwell, Rexford Guy, 289
turf protection, as a determinant of power
    in National Security State, 27
Turkmenistan oil pipeline, 47
Tutu, Bishop Desmond, 323
Tyler, John, and signing statements, 301

Ulam, Stan, 255
"Unabomber," 70
unions, from New Deal to present, 97–102
United Airlines, pension plan termination,
    97
United Fruit, 292
United Nations
    as international New Deal, 171
    marginalization of by American
        Rightists, 197
    mistrust at inception, 247–48
United States as a formalist republic, 82–83
    and oligarchy (system of degraded aris-
        tocracy), 216
    political nation members, 216
United States as warrior nation, 13, 137,
    142, 225, 227, 229, 230, 238, 257
United States Insurance Act, 328
Universal Declaration of Human Rights, 73,
    199
Unocal Corporation, 47
Urquhart, Brian, 198

U.S. Air Force Academy, proselytizing
    cadets, 135–36
U.S. Steel, funding for National Security
    League, 330

Vietnam Syndrome, 8, 253
Vidal, Gore, 298
Vietnam War, 249–51
    consequences of, 256–57, 333
    lessons about the media, 59
    protests, 114
Vioxx, and FDA deregulation, 181
Virchow, Rudolph, 210
Vivian, J. T., 140
Voting Rights Act (1965), 80. *See also* right
    to vote
vouchers for schools, court cases, 163, 321

Wagner Act (1935), 98
Wag the Dog, 93
Wallis, Jim, 140
Wal-Mart, 97
    and locked stores, 99
Walzer, Michael, 51
Wampler Foods, 182
War Powers Act (1973), 93–94
Warren Court
    and civil liberties, 50–51
    and federal judiciary choices, 36
    and voting, 83
wars
    alliances post-Second World War, 247
    and American isolationism in, 1920s and
        1930s, 242
    and American people, 230–31
    and domestic repression, 9
    first Iraq War, 252–53
    First World War, 238–39
    founding and buttressing United States,
        229–30
    and imperialist policies, 257–58
    importance of to Rightists, 34
    irony of goals of Japanese in Pearl
        Harbor attack, 243
    and irony of isolation, 258
    Korean, 248–49
    overview of wars in early America (pre-
        Civil War), 231–34
    and reconfiguring the military for naval
        dominance, 236–39
    requirement of National Security State,
        45

Second World War, 242–43, 244
See also Vietnam War
wars and National Security State, alternatives to, 228, 258–59
  conditions for contentment, 265–66
  implementations of democratic ideals, 267–68
  institutional support for peace studies, 266
  reconstruction (shape of), 268
  removal of social structures of National Security State, 262
  and risk-taking, 269–70
  use of technology to boost human capacities, 262
  values of religious left and Liberation Theology, 268–69
Washington, George
  belief in role of religion in governing, 134
  observations on interests and friends, 257
  and Shays' Rebellion, 232
  view of Indians as savages, 231
Waskow, Rabbi Arthur, 140, 295–96
"watch and index" lists, and internment concerns, xxiii
Waters, Alice, 179
Watkinson, Sherron, 120
Watt, James, 103
Waxman, Henry, 214
Weakland, Rembert, 318
Weekly Standard, 47
Weil, Simone, 161
Weinberger, Caspar, 334
Wesley, John, 145
whistleblowers, 119–22
  government preemption attempts, 120–22
Who Wants Disarmament?, 294
Wiener, Norbert, 291
Wilder, Gene, 290

Wilkins, Roy, 257
Willkie, Wendell, acceptance of New Deal ideas, 201
Wills, Garry, 158, 296
Wilson, Woodrow
  as advocate of export strategy, 176
  and concerns about "dangerous thoughts", 4
  "deposit" of immigrants, 6
  and First World War, 238–39
  his political vision as religious mission, 134
  and League of Nations, 239, 241
  signing statements, 301
  and war with Mexico, 238
  and women's right to vote, 145
Winfrey, Oprah, 136
wiretaps (roving), 20–21
  support for from both parties, 21
Witherspoon, John, 162
Wohlsetter, Albert, 335
Wolfe, Dr. Sidney, 208
Wolfowitz, Paul, 152, 335
  and defense doctrine of Bush I administration, 59
  letter on Iraq policy (1998), 47
  lobbying for Iraq War, 55
  selection as head of the World Bank, 51
Woodward, Bob, 120
Woolsey, R. James, Jr., 68
WorldCom, 105–6, 120
worldwide pandemic (danger of), 62
Wounded Knee massacre, 236
Wright, Quincy, 289

Yeats, William Butler, 226
Yee, James Joseph, 155
Youngstown Steel Seizure case, 11, 19
Yum Brands, 115

Zakheim, Dov, 152

About the Authors

Marcus Raskin is one of America's leading political thinkers and political activists. He is the Distinguished Fellow and cofounder of the Institute for Policy Studies in 1963 (the first think tank of its kind), professor of policy studies at George Washington University, and member of the editorial board of *The Nation*. He has been a Fulbright lecturer in Germany, taught at the Sorbonne, lectured at major U.S. universities, advised members of Congress and presidential candidates, and served as a member of the White House National Security Council staff during the Kennedy administration.

Marc Raskin's books on international affairs, government, national defense, and political philosophy have focused on the growing power over the citizen of the "National Security State" (a term he coined) that operates by its own rules and views and "by its nature is expansionist for it deals with the continuous creation of activities in all aspects of public life and has become the single most important function of millions of federal workers, unions, police agencies, defense corporations, universities, and scientists." Until *The Four Freedoms Under Siege*, however, Raskin had never devoted a book solely to the subject of freedom—and the impact of the National Security State on the loss of freedom of individual Americans.

Raskin is the author or editor of twenty books, including *In Democracy's Shadow* (2005), edited with Carl LeVan, and *Liberalism* (2004).

Robert Spero is an author, journalist, former advertising executive with Ogilvy & Mather, and was a Kennedy Administration official in the Agency for International Development and the President's Domestic Peace Corps Task Force under the direction of Attorney General Robert F. Kennedy.

Bob Spero's first book, *The Duping of the American Voter*, exposed the deceptive and dangerous ways presidential candidates (and now almost all political candidates) use virtually unregulated political television advertising—most of which would not pass the regulatory tests a simple soap commercial must pass—to conceal their true policy intentions and even their backgrounds from an unsuspecting—or passive—public. Not surprisingly, the book—the first one to raise such issues—raised the hackles of political consultants and aides to presidents and challengers. Subsequently, however, major newspapers and television networks began "grading" presidential campaign commercials for the truth, as Spero had.

Spero has always gone deep into the heart of the matter in his magazine articles. In "Showdown on Middle Neck Road," he stirred up a hornet's nest by showing that "a silent, undeclared war between American and Iranian Jews was festering in the wealthy suburb of Great Neck, New York"—but the article about the disparate cultures also was the beginning of a healing dialogue. "The Birth of Joshua" described for the first time the wonders of natural childbirth from pregnancy to birth from a *father's* point of view; until the article's publication, most obstetricians and hospitals viewed the husband's role in this natural, loving process as intrusive.